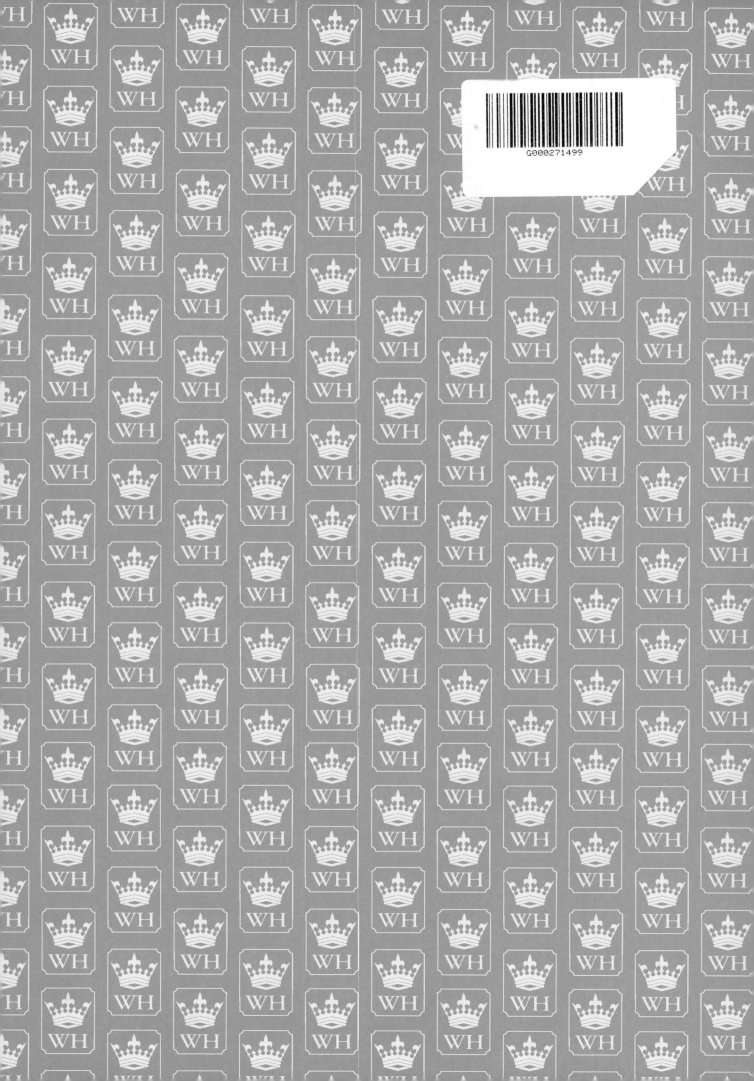

HEATHER
AND
HEAVEN

HEATHER
AND
HEAVEN

Walton Heath
Golf Club
1903–2003

Phil Pilley

with a Foreword by
Jack Nicklaus

Published by Walton Heath Golf Club, Tadworth, Surrey KT20 7TP

First published 2003
Reprinted 2004

© Phil Pilley 2003

ISBN: 0-9544498-0-0

British Library Cataloguing in Publication Data.
A catalogue record for this book is available from the British Library

Designed by Geoffrey Wadsley
Printed by Ian Allan Printing Ltd
Riverdene Business Park, Molesey Road, Hersham, Surrey, KT12 4RG

Acknowledgements

In his introduction and the various chapters the author mentions many of the people who have contributed to the work on this book. Here, he and the publishers would like to thank some of the many other people and organisations not specifically mentioned therein and apologise for any omissions. Thanks are due to:

The British Library Newspaper Library, Surrey History Centre, Public Records Office, Office for National Statistics.

The R&A, PGA, EGU, LGU and other golf organisations; the numerous British clubs approached for information; the Los Angeles Country Club; also the MCC Library and Somerset CCC.

The Walton-on-the-Hill and District Local History Society; Robin Marsh, David Metcalfe, Roger Packham, Ray Strank, the late Kenneth Clew.

Various commercial companies, including Costain, News International, Scottish Courage, Suttons Consumer Products.

Many individuals, including David Bonsor, Sir Nicholas Bonsor, Monty Court, Laura Davies, Bob Grant, John Hewett-Hicks, Mrs J. Jobson, Marjorie Mackie, Professor Barbara McEwen, John Moreton, Jack Nicklaus, Janice Owen, Peter Marsh, George Payne, John Pearson, Liz Pook, Roland Quinault,

The Editors and Sports Editors of numerous national and local newspapers; the publishers of *Golf Weekly*, who authorised reproduction of photographs and text from *Golf Illustrated*.

We would also wish to acknowledge the conscientious professional cooperation of Geoffrey Wadsley, designer, and Jonathan Bingham, of Ian Allan, Printing Ltd.

Finally, our thanks are due to the innumerable members, past and present, of Walton Heath Golf Club and Walton Heath Artisans Golf Club who have been interviewed and/or contributed information; also professional Ken Macpherson, club secretary Mike Bawden and the current office staff.

Bibliography

Credit to a large number of publications which the author has consulted or quoted from has been paid in relevant chapters and this applies particularly to *Golf Illustrated*, now absorbed by *Golf Weekly*, and *Golfing*. Permissions to reproduce pictures or passages of text have been much appreciated. Thanks are also due to the authors and publishers of the following works, whose contents have assisted in research. We apologise for any omissions.

Golfer's Handbooks (Macmillan); *Lady Golfer's Handbook* (LGU); *EGU Year Books* (EGU); *R&A Championship Records* (R&A); *Ladies' Golf in Surrey*, by Tim Cotton (SLCGA), 2001; Centenary, etc, histories of various clubs and associations.

The Amateur, by John Behrend (Grant Books), 1995; *The British Professional Golfers 1887-1930, A Register*, by Alan F. Jackson (Grant Books), 1994; *A Century of Opens*, by G. Cousins and T. Scott (Muller), 1971; *Colt and Co.*, by Fred Hawtree; *Edwardians at Play*, by Brian Dobbs (Pelham), 1973; *Encyclopedia of Sport*, by Webster Evans (St Martin's Press, NY), 1974; *Golf – A Way of Life*, ed. Peter Alliss (Cresset Press), 1989; *Golf in the Making*, by Ian Henderson and David Stirk (Henderson and Stirk), 1979; *Fifty-two Years of Sport* (Daily Mail); *Lawns for Sports*, by Reginald Beale (Simpkin, Marshall, Hamilton, Kent), 1924; *More Pages from My Diary*. (Country Life).

The Ryder Cup, The Illustrated History, by Michael Hobbs (Macdonald Queen Anne Press), 1989; *Shell Encyclopedia of Golf*; *Sport in Britain*, by H.A. Harris (Stanley Paul), 1975; *The Story of the R&A*, by J.B.Salmon; *The Tattenham Corner Branch*, by N. Owen (Lockwood Press); *The World of Professional Golf*, by Mark H. McCormack (IMG), various years; Sundry magazines and supplements, including *The British Century*, by John Keegan (*The Daily Telegraph*), 1999; *Railway Magazine*; *Through the Green* (British Golf Collectors' Society), various issues.

Chronicle of the 20th Century, ed Derrik Mercer (Chronicle Communications), 1988; *Encyclopedia of Britain*, ed. Bamber Gascoigne (Macmillan), 1994; *Illustrated Dictionary of British History*, ed Arthur Marwick (Thames and Hudson), 1980.

CONTENTS

JACK NICKLAUS in the 1981 Ryder Cup match at Walton Heath

Photo: Phil Sheldon

FOREWORD
by Jack Nicklaus

FOND MEMORIES have a way of bridging the gap between years and even decades. While it has been more than 20 years since my last playing appearance in a Ryder Cup, the experience of those matches in 1981 remains so fresh in my mind that it plays out in amazing detail each time the subject is raised.

There were Larry Nelson's four inspiring victories. There was my long-time friend Tom Watson, whom I partnered in three wins. There was a young German by the name of Bernhard Langer, who was introduced to the world in those matches and went on to a Hall-of-Fame playing career. There was an assemblage of talent on the United States' side like no other Ryder Cup team before or arguably since. Among the 12 of us there were 36 major championships, but, more important, a camaraderie and spirit that symbolize what the Ryder Cup stands for.

Of all these memories, none is more vivid and special than the backdrop on which these historic matches were played – Walton Heath Golf Club.

Of all the courses surrounding London, so many of them rich in storied tradition, there are few with as much history and honor as the wonderfully pure heathland layout of Walton Heath. Its windswept, fast conditions make Walton Heath a challenge for the world's finest players, and its enduring beauty helps keep it among the rankings of the world's finest courses. As a club, Walton Heath's history reads much like a storybook, with its characters bearing such names as James Braid, Sir Winston Churchill, The Prince of Wales (later Edward VIII), who became captain, and King George VI, who, like his brother, was first made an honorary member more than 80 years ago when Duke of York.

Walton Heath has played host to more than 80 significant amateur and professional championships, quite apart from historic challenge matches and other events. Perhaps there was no greater compliment paid to the club than when it was chosen to host those 1981 Ryder Cup matches. As important an event as that match was on a global level – being only the second Ryder Cup to incorporate all of Europe on one team – there were aspects that also had an endearing charm to them. Many of my teammates that year probably remember clubmaker Harry Busson, busily at work in his tiny shop. He was undoubtedly one of the last true craftsmen and several of our team members, including myself, brought home examples of his work.

Harry Busson holds another distinction that astounds me. He was one of only three men to occupy the position of club professional in the 100-year history of Walton Heath. Harry's predecessor was the great James Braid, the professional for over 46 years and who, in 1904, joined the legendary Harry Vardon and J.H. Taylor in the club's first exhibition match. This golf triumvirate combined to win 16 of the 21 Open Championships played in Britain immediately prior to World War I. After Harry Busson's tenure of nearly 30 years as professional Ken Macpherson took over and has already been there for more than 25. That the club has had only three professionals in a century of golf is a fact that stands as testament to the club's legacy and stability.

I heartily congratulate Walton Heath on its centenary. The club deserves – and now has – a centenary book to match the richness of its history. I have known author Phil Pilley for well over 30 years. He has produced and directed countless television programs. He has filmed everything from international golf championships to historical documentaries. It is an honor to say that I have been involved in many. Phil is widely respected in the golf and broadcast industries, and he has brought that same talent and passion to this piece of literary work. With as many illustrations as pages of text, this tribute to Walton Heath is an entertaining read that serves almost as a scrapbook to stir memories – some of the fondest belonging to me.

Good golfing,

FROM THE CAPTAINS

IT IS A GREAT privilege for us to be captains of Walton Heath in our centenary year and therefore to be associated with this publication.

Walton Heath is a very special golf club, as you will realise when you read this book, and its history has been brought alive by the way in which Phil Pilley has told its story.

We would also very much like to thank Philip Truett, our archivist, who has been a huge help during the last few years in helping this book to fruition.

PATRICK FRANKLIN-ADAMS
(Club Captain)
ALISON BARRATT
(Lady Captain)

Introduction

I SHUNNED GOLF for years. For this I had two reasons. First, I had become involved with the game professionally during a career in television and had no wish to mix business with pleasure. Second, I was carrying on a passionate, life-long affair with cricket – which, because I was better at it than I became at golf, I regard as an infinitely superior game.

Thus, like a fool, I did not succumb to the charms of golfing until late in life and invariably accept invitations to play with a profound sense of inferiority complex. When Philip Truett asked me to play with him at Walton Heath I made the severe tactical error, on the eve of our encounter, of looking for directions to the Club in the *AA Book of Golf Courses*. That cursed handbook's description of the Old course gave me a feverish, sleepless night. The carries were formidable, it said; the heather was desperate; the high-handicapper would be 'sorely tested.'

Heather and heaven indeed! What about hell? The title of this book, by the way, is shamelessly plagiarised – though with consent – from *The Daily Telegraph* of August 5, 2002. That day Bill Meredith, reporting the English Amateur Championship, wrote that

> a bewildering burst of back-to-back eagles followed by a birdie lifted Richard Finch into a field of dreams at Walton Heath, a wonderful mixture of heaven and heather.

I merely changed the order of billing to ingratiate myself with the heather.

When Mr Truett coerced me into writing his club's history as a labour of love I began it in a fragile frame of mind similar to the one in which I had teetered, terrified, on to the tee with him. It was, as Laurel and Hardy used to say, 'another fine mess' he had got me into. My disadvantage was that I wasn't a member; I was an outsider and had to swot up the subject from scratch – or rather from 24. Into the minute books I delved and into my local library I marched. Almost immediately I read that

> by tradition, *Country Life* was conceived on Walton Heath golf course in the Chilterns in about 1895.

It was a salutary warning that even sources generally regarded as impeccable could not be trusted – on geography and history, let alone golf.

Research into the earliest days of any subject, golf clubs included, is a fascinating, frustrating business. The original documents you want are never there, lost in the mists of time or, as in the case of Walton Heath, probably destroyed by the blitz. The minute books tell you everything but the detail for which you thirst; or they don't tell you anything – just imagine, a member kills a caddie and not a word appears in the club minutes. Trawls through local newspapers yield little or nothing about the elitist Edwardian game of golf and one has to compensate with enjoyment of the classified ads ('Wanted, second-hand false teeth') and tragicomic headlines ('Deliberate suicide').

Everywhere I have found errors – mistakes in print or through fading recollections. Among the more accurate sources is the late Cyril Hewertson, whose slim booklet in the 'seventies remains a factual précis of at least part of the club's history. I also inherited some of his notes and it was uncanny realising that I was incessantly following the same research paths and ending up in the same blind alleys.

Actually, now the job is done, I believe that being an outsider has helped me. I could be more objective. I did not feel I had to steer clear of controversies. I felt no need to deliver gratuitous pats on the back to contemporaries, though I have tried to give credit where it is due and to dispense justice to past heroes.

If you are looking forward to reading a succession of annual reports, lengthy accounts of general meetings and analyses of balance sheets I hope you will be disappointed – or that you will save your money. Above all I am interested in people, in this instance the cast of characters who, on or off the course, have acted out the dramas of the Walton Heath story. I am intrigued by their personalities, their merits and their faults. I have tried to bring them alive and I hope I shall interest you in them.

If indeed I am a historian, then I am one who likes neither dates, nor statistics, nor paragraphs that stagger on, one after the other, all starting with 'The following year' or 'The year after that.' In truth it is sometimes unavoidable, but to avoid the worst excesses I have not treated my story strictly chronologically from 1903 to

2003. I have, it is true, contained my chapters within four clear-cut time-spans (the dawn of golf on the heath, the Riddell years, the Carr era and the modern times of the Members' Club), but each explores a specific and interesting subject and all, in effect, have their own individual chronology. Woven within them are extracts from the writings and words of others, from the game's literary giants to Walton Heath club members.

In the following 248 pages you will find the admirable Braid, the brilliant but erratic Fowler, the contradictory Riddell, the champions, the visitors, the celebrities, the colourful crowds and their free shows on the heath, the head-to-head challenges and the match-play championships...

I am something of a romantic when digging up the past and a sucker for nostalgia, but I do not romance at the expense of factual history. In 150,000 words concerning a hundred years of a previously little-researched subject it will be a miracle if I have not, like those before me, made errors. What I can truthfully say is that I have dug deep in research, enquiry and cross-examination and whenever a fact has been checkable I have tried desperately to check it. Moreover every chapter possible has been scrutinised, not only by chairman Brian Meaby, who has assiduously read all the proofs, but by people with special knowledge of the subjects.

Elsewhere I have acknowledged various people and publications from whom I have gleaned information. Here I must pay tribute to those who have helped me personally at close hand: Robert Ruddell for his research and companionship on our dreary treks up the North Circular to the British Museum Newspaper Reference Library at Colindale; David Easby for work on results, records and competition details; among the ladies, Mary Coakes for her willing work and Libby Hagdrup for some stunning photographs. I should also mention Derek Stanton, who was bequeathed to me by the club as a researcher, did valuable work, then moved to another area entirely without permission.

Above all, there is Philip Truett. On the dust jacket he does himself less than justice by calling himself my research assistant. We occasionally look at things from different standpoints and he has submerged me with paper, but his enthusiasm and efficiency have known no bounds and our partnership, I hope he will agree, has been a happy and creatively satisfying one.

I hope you enjoy *Heather and Heaven*. It is a celebration of all aspects of a hundred years at wonderful Walton: champions and challengers, captains and caddies, peers and prime ministers, European Opens, the Ryder Cup, the heavenly heather...

There's night and day, brother, both sweet things;
sun, moon and stars, brother, all sweet things;
there's likewise a wind on the heath.[1]

PHIL PILLEY
Shepperton, 2003

---

[1] *Lavengro*, by George Borrow.

THE DAWNING

Chapter One

THE MAN WHO STARTED IT ALL
Cosmo Bonsor – first the railway, then the golf course

ROMANCE AND COLOUR overflow in the story of Walton Heath, so I shall afford myself an anti-romantic start.

Romance? Colour? There is the wild heath itself, 625 feet high[1] on the northern end of the North Downs, claiming neolithic man and Roman citizen among its alumni. There is a horseman riding by amid whins and heather, surveying his dream of changing a wilderness into a golf course and thereby perhaps saving his own soul. There is the James Braid connection, 46½ years of it... plus the peers and the poor who jostle in throngs to see the game's great gladiators. There are the *glitterati* who become members, rendering the club a refuge for the famous and a parliamentary annexe, where state secrets may filter through the cigar smoke or be carried by the wind on the heath...

The anti-romantic riposte? It concerns the Club's founding fathers and stepfathers. I have used the plural because, while the club was an infant, four men in particular came to play pioneer roles of profound influence. Do not think of them all as selfless do-gooders founding and nurturing a club exclusively through love for the game. Only one was an outstanding golfer and another, it would appear, did not play at all. Three had serious personal ambitions – career advancement, social progress or increased wealth. They had a feel and an affection for the game, but to a degree each saw Walton Heath Golf Club as a means to an end.

Two of these men had character faults as well as the seeds of genius and we shall encounter them in these pages. However, among those four there was only one founder in the true sense: he who envisaged the enterprise and put his money (and that of others) where his mouth was – the admirable Henry Cosmo Orme Bonsor.

So in act one of the Walton Heath drama Cosmo Bonsor is our leading actor – declaiming the prologue, kick-starting the plot and dictating the tune to and on which others will dance and capitalise. The action is set against the backdrop of the heath and will be a microcosm of the changing social order. Edward VII's breezy reign has begun. At the turn of the century Britain is still paramount, with the largest empire in history. Abroad, though, 22,000 of our soldiers and 6,000 Boers are dying in the South African wars, and at home the middle and upper classes flourish in comfort while masses strive to make do on £1 a week.

For centuries Walton, first granted by William the Conqueror to Richard of Tonbridge, had been governed feudally by Lords of the Manor – and by a few Ladies, including Catherine of Aragon until Henry VIII took the land away from her.

Towards the end of the 19th century Walton was still an almost isolated village. It had about 800 inhabitants, mostly agricultural workers and their families, dominated by a few wealthy landowners. In 1885 Cosmo Bonsor became one of the latter when he bought the 1,400-acre Kingswood Warren estate for £65,000 from its bankrupt owner.

He was seriously rich. At the turn of the century, says Sir Nicholas Bonsor, his great-grandson, Cosmo was worth £1¼ million, which today would equate to nearly £90 million.[2] He was born a few miles from Walton in Polesden Lacey, today a National Trust villa, which his grandfather had bought and largely re-built and which his father inherited. He was educated at Eton and had a Belgrave Square address in London.

A burly 6ft. 4in., he was a powerful figure in every sense. His business was beer. He had followed his father at Combe's brewery in the days when top hats for directors and staff were still *de rigeur*, with guinea fines threatened if you didn't wear one, and for 30 years became chairman of the Watney Combe Reid combine. But he was also Conservative MP for Wimbledon, a Lieutenant of the City

---

[1] Ordnance survey shows 190.3m as the highest point of the course.
[2] National Statistics estimate

SIR HENRY COSMO ORME BONSOR, Bt – after a portrait painted by Sir Arthur Stockdale Cope, RA, circa 1908.

Before the golf

The spikes of today's golfers follow in the footsteps of prehistoric man. On the course club workers have found a late Bronze Age axe and fragments of a Neolithic one – evidence that our ancient ancestors hunted the heath and may even have inhabited it. The trackway running north to south on the course's eastern boundary and adjacent to the outward holes on the Old Course is also believed to pre-date the Bronze Age.

Those celebrated hollows, so often claimed to be Roman camps, kitchens or whatever, apparently may be no such things, so caddie Curly's legendary information to an American visitor about greenside bunkers could have been wrong. 'Those bunkers were Roman stables,' he said. 'I've always wondered how they knew how to build them so near the greens.'

No? Jean Clew, local historian and archaeologist, assures me (although some members and others remain unconvinced) that the pits are 'solution hollows' – a geological phenomenon. The gently sloping heathland supports a unique geology, an undulating strata of chalk, flints, clay, sand and gravel. The hollows,

she says, are created when layers of clay and flint are pulled downward by the chalk beneath. Do not confuse them with the mysterious dips and dents running across the course, which are probably ancient field boundaries.

The Romans were certainly here, though. In 1772 a man named Hoar, having got permission to build a cottage near where the 14th tee of the New exists today, dug up fragments of tiles and a small brass figure and excavations revealed the remains of a Romano-

The mosaic pavement – a pen-and-water-colour impression (Sackler Library, Oxford)

British villa on Chussex Plain. In 1865 William Pocock and the Rev. Ambrose Hall discovered one of Surrey's proudest Roman treasures here – a mosaic pavement 21ft square, made from cubes of sun-dried clay, chalk and broken Samian ware.

Pocock noted its fragility and advised against removal, yet today, after soil movements and years of amateur excavations, no traces remain.

When the irrigation pipeline was replaced in 1967 more than 60 shards of pottery were recovered over a wide area.

Such artefacts indicate continuous occupation of the heath from about AD50 to AD400, during which time the Romans enlarged the trackway – which is now punctuated by Victorian coal-tax posts[3] and marks the boundary between the parishes of Banstead and Walton. Later, from medieval times, the only inhabitants were commoners and squatters scratching and digging for a meagre living. And finally came golf!

[3] The posts marked points where duty on coal, wine, etc, entering London was supposed to be payable – a right of the City since medieval times.

The heath in the days when Walton was an almost isolated village.

of London, a JP, chairman of the City's Income Tax Commission, an officer of the Legion of Honour, a Deputy Lieutenant of Surrey and a director of the Bank of England.

At the personal request of his friend the King, when Prince of Wales, he took over the finances of Guy's Hospital, where income was shrinking and wards were closing. Due to him, Guy's was restored and extended.

For more than 25 years at Kingswood Warren he played the role of benevolent squire. Bread, cheese and ale were

on tap for tradesmen, soup was served to passers-by for a week before Christmas and every year he gave shoes or clothing to every scholar at the Kingswood school. When one of his daughters married all Tadworth had a day's holiday, with tea and entertainment provided. When his employees' wives had babies hot meals were sent to them for a month via the master's carriage.

But behind Bonsor's genial demeanour and acts of kindness lurked the determination of the astute businessman. He had perceived the area's potential and, by now an MP, he determined to get a railway brought to Walton, Tadworth and Kingswood as well as to Epsom racecourse.

His motives went deeper than his wish to help the local populace and incidentally shorten his own daily carriage trips between home and Banstead station en route to the city. He had begun speculatively but shrewdly buying land. Bonsor wanted to attract well-off people to the area, push up the land values and increase the worth of his investments. He had two close associates: James Benson, a Bond Street jeweller, and Walter Brown, a retired baker and corn chandler.

Bonsor's campaigns, involving protracted struggles to overcome all opposition and get railway bills through Commons and Lords committees, illustrate what a formidable and tenacious figure he was. The first idea, in 1891, was an extension to the Epsom Downs line, which currently deposited racegoers at a point from where they faced a brisk two-and-a-half-furlong canter across fields to get near the horses and bookies. That bill having succeeded, he dropped the plan and, having persuaded his fellow brewer Vernon Watney to help back it, promoted a bill for a branch line from Purley through the Chipstead Valley. There was strong opposition to both schemes. Frederick Edward Colman, of the mustard firm, was offered £9,000 (£600,000 today) in exchange for some of his land but angrily refused: he did not at all fancy the idea of trains and houses spoiling his shooting and ruining the vistas from his Nork Park estate between Banstead village and the racecourse. Other landowners felt the same; some saw no need for a line; the rector of Walton grew emotional about threats to the beauties of his parish; the Epsom Grand Stand Association managers thought the trains would frighten the horses; the whole business was riddled with railway rivalries and politics.

Protagonists and antagonists pulled every stroke possible and Bonsor's side paraded a motley band of witnesses. Farmers spoke almost poetically about manure: this and other necessities would travel by train instead of being carted over hilly roads ('The wear and tear on horse-flesh is enormous,' said one, almost in tears). A colonel from the War Office envisaged the trains transporting troops and supplies to the North Downs, London's strategic line of defence; social workers dreamed of their whisking London's poor to the fresh air of the heaths; the racecourse people, seduced by the idea of an underground tunnel to safeguard their straight mile course, soon

Kingswood Warren – home of the Bonsors. It now houses a BBC department.

visualised the carriages carrying more punters to their front door; an earnest man from the City, faced with conservationists, claimed that game birds rather liked railway banks and that platelayers would deter poachers.

Cosmo and his colleagues had invested considerable sums and when he assured the committees that the balance would be raised they believed him. Eventually, in July 1900, the trains rumbled into Tadworth and Walton.

The final entrepreneurial touch came when those trains ran through to Tattenham Corner on June 4, 1901 – Derby Day. In its heyday the line had a certain style. The racing crowds brought a raffish colour, 'bookmakers' specials' ran and the elegant Kingswood and Burgh Heath station patronised by Bonsor boasted an elevated, open-air tea terrace whose unforeseen weakness was a propensity for steam and soot to envelope the customer and contaminate the tea.

By now Cosmo was into trains in a big way and had become chairman first of the South Eastern Railway and then, when the two rival lines agreed to work together, of the South Eastern and Chatham company. Thus did transport augment his business interests of brewing, banking, insurance and property.

Property? When news of his railway schemes leaked out land prices rose from £25 to £40 an acre, in some places even £80.

> The advantages claimed for the new line are that it will be a cheaper and more expeditious route to the Derby and bring a considerable influx of well-to-do residents into the area, *reported one local paper.*[4] One enterprising builder is reported already to have entered into a contract to build 250 homes at Walton-on-the-Hill, *stated another.*[5] The residents in this hitherto benighted part of Surrey are looking forward to a boom beside which that at Klondyke will pale into insignificance.

Tadworth and Walton station early in the 20th century.

[4] *Wallington and Carshalton Herald*, November 6, 1897.
[5] *Sutton and Epsom Advertiser*, July 31, 1897.

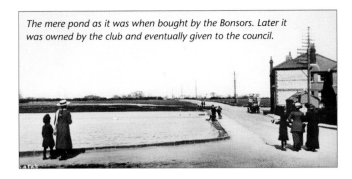
The mere pond as it was when bought by the Bonsors. Later it was owned by the club and eventually given to the council.

Such a bonanza did not happen immediately. One builder found it necessary to offer prospective buyers the inducement of a free season ticket to London. The change came with the start of golf.

Golf? The vision of a heathland course that would stand comparison with the classic seaside links of Scotland had found its way into Bonsor's shrewd mind before the first trains arrived, and now, with the railway in place, it had become an obvious next step. The game had come into fashion and clubs were being established in almost every quarter of the land. In 1890 Britain had fewer than 400 clubs and societies; by 1900 there were nearly 2,500. It was a game that successful chaps ought to play, and successful chaps could do so by moving house to these Surrey villages.

There was a snag to all this. There could not be a course on Walton Heath without agreement and a lease from the lord of the manor, who at that time was Henry Padwick from Horsham. He presided over a heath that until the middle of the 19th century had been used chiefly for pasturage and digging for turf, loam or gravel with one part used as a gallop for racehorses. Trainer William Nightingall still rented this gallop from Padwick, who derived other income from the sale of turf, loam and gravel as well as from shooting rights.

Deans Lane as it used to be. Photograph was taken near where the Riddell Hall is today, looking south towards the Club, with Chucks Lane on the immediate left. Photos: Walton-on-the-Hill and District Local History Society

First, Arthur Edenborough, a legal associate of Bonsor's, sounded out Padwick's manor steward, James Peat. It would appear from subsequent correspondence that annual rent of £100, at least for the first year, was then mentioned. Padwick's first reaction, in a letter to Peat dated August 4, 1901, was encouraging:

I thought the question of golf on the heath would turn up some day. I don't think a course would be prejudicial to the value of the manor and probably it would be popular with the better class of the commoners[6] – perhaps with all – for, judging from precedents, golf is a great attraction and always improves the value of the neighbourhood.

---
[6] Dwellers who had certain rights of common (eg, to graze animals or dig).

We ought to know what parts of the heath would be required, then communicate with Nightingall and Harry Crookenden *[who apparently held commoner's rights]*, asking what they have to say about it. Possibly we might lose so much that £100 per annum would not be adequate.

Encouraged, Edenborough got down to business with Peat:

I am now in a position to ask you to grant a 40-year lease of a sufficient acreage of Walton Heath to make an 18-hole golf course, the lease to be granted to Mr. H. Cosmo Bonsor of Kingswood Warren. I hope in a few days to send you a rough plan of the proposed links.

Two days later (September 13, 1901), Cosmo Bonsor himself emerged from behind curtains and wrote to Peat:

I am quite willing to undertake this responsibility on behalf of my neighbours provided that the rent and covenants are such as I consider fair, but as the cost of laying out the ground is estimated to exceed £3,500 I think it would be advisable for us to have some conversation before jumping to the conclusions in Mr. Edenborough's letter.

But Padwick had now had second thoughts. He expressed them to Edenborough on September 20:

In comparing the plan you sent with the map it seems that the course would practically occupy the whole of the heath. It would interfere with everything and everybody. Golf is a game played every day in the year, and Mr. Nightingall might very well object to what might be a constant nuisance to him. The loam-selling business might be almost lost. A sum of £50 pa for seven years after the first year would be a very inadequate return for what we would lose.

I cannot see my way to consider the proposal at all seriously. Mr. Bonsor is presumably a rich man, and so most likely are those associated with him. Let them *buy* the heath and do what they like.

Two days later Padwick reinforced his view to Peat:

The scheme won't bear examination and you may as well say so at once that I cannot see my way to let the heath for golf on any terms that the applicants are likely to propose. Twenty years ago the heath was valued at £9,000... If it comes to a question of selling we may talk it over. In the meantime I am well satisfied to leave matters as they are.

A new figure now entered the negotiations: Edwin H. Freshfield, one of Bonsor's friends and neighbours and partner in an eminent firm of solicitors. Bonsor, he told Padwick, had asked Freshfields to act for him. He now sought chapter and verse on what might be sold and for how much, plus details of income and expenditure and the names of those holding commoners' rights.

Others had become socially concerned and financially interested. On May 25, 1902, Harry Crookenden went to see Padwick, who reported their meeting to Peat:

> He knew Mr Bonsor was after the heath and he and others were not at all willing that he should have it. I told him we had an offer of £4,000 but I would not take it... He gave me to understand that he and others would go beyond that bid. *(There is evidence that Crookenden did so, to the tune of more than £5,000).*

Particulars of the manor were issued, replete with vintage estate-agency-speak: 'One of the most beautiful heaths for which Surrey is famous... Beautiful views... Fine building sites... Considerable revenue... Annual income £500... One of the best training grounds in the country... A very fine golf links could be formed.'

Eventually, on August 11, 1902, Cosmo bought out Padwick for £5,500 and Malcolm Bonsor became lord of the manor.

Malcolm Bonsor? He was Cosmo's 24-year-old eldest son who joined him on the brewery board. The truth surely is that Cosmo was the power behind the throne but that, at 54 and with so many public positions and responsibilities, he put his son into the lordship. They had bought:

> The manor of Walton-on-the-Hill with the manorial rights extending over the entire parish... and the waste lands of the manor over which the lord has exclusive right to sport, together with all the timber, underwood, furzes, turf, gravel, chalk and minerals in and under, within or upon the said waste lands.

The area was just under 500 acres, plus a further parcel of some 200 acres of common land which included 'the Six Mile Hill and part of the Derby racecourse to Tattenham Corner.' Included were the village green, mere pond and manor pound.

The holding of the heath was stated to be subject to 'rights of common of pasture' and in September 1902, Freshfield, whom Malcolm had appointed steward, wrote on his behalf telling the villagers and commoners why he had bought the manor and why he was seeking their

> "The heath is a delightful place, only sixteen miles from London and nearly 700ft high. It is covered with heather and gorse, and if there are no grouse and black game there ought to be. There are rabbits and partridges, and now there are also golfers."

Horace Hutchinson, *Country Life*, 1904

cooperation. Mr Bonsor, he said, had acquired the commons

> (1) To conserve them as open spaces and to preserve their natural attractions; *and*
> (2) To encourage golf, cricket and other games.

Not surprisingly there were local concerns, but any serious objections seem to have been overcome. No doubt the senior Bonsor's reputation as a conservator of Banstead Heath, where he had played a prominent role in establishing public access, helped mollify any militants.

The golf course, like the railway that made it possible, was a speculative business venture. That a club at Walton would attract more people and further raise land and property values there was no doubt.

Were the Bonsors interested in the game? Malcolm certainly was and played off 10 by Edwardian handicap standards, but his father's golf remains a mystery. Cosmo was on the committee of the Prince's Club at Mitcham where many members of parliament golfed. On the other hand, neither his grandson David nor great-grandson Sir Nicholas ever

The boy who grew up to be Lord of the Manor. The only known photograph of Malcolm Bonsor.

heard that he actually played and no handicap adorns his name in any Walton Heath members' list.

Before World War I Cosmo put Kingswood Warren up for sale and moved to The Red House nearby. In 1925 he was created a baronet.

Meantime it would appear that his participation in Walton Heath affairs in the early years of the century passed increasingly to Malcolm, although he remained a club member for many years. To continue the theatrical analogy initiated at the start of this chapter, Sir Henry Cosmo Orme Bonsor, Bt, had spoken his prologue clearly but briefly and would now gradually retire to the wings.

But not before he had commissioned the making of the course. Legally the way was now clear to proceed with one, but who should be paid to create it?

Bonsor's answer was to keep things in the family. Widowed, he had remarried and gained a new brother-in-law, a formidable all-round sportsman enthusiastically and ambitiously immersed in golf. This brother-in-law therefore would be the architect, the man challenged to create a top-class 18-hole layout from a wilderness.

It was a bit of a risk. William Herbert Fowler had never designed a golf course.

Chapter Two

THE ERRATIC GENIUS
Herbert Fowler transforms a wilderness

WILLIAM HERBERT FOWLER was a huntin', shootin' and cricketin' man. In the early 1880s, when Cosmo Bonsor was speculating about his speculating, Fowler, London-born son of a barrister, was in his mid-twenties, trained in law, partner in a private bank and a sportsman indulging himself in his fancies. He fitted comfortably into an age of cricket when Grace ruled and apparently affluent young men judged, wisely or unwisely, that they had time and money enough to play for their counties during time off from, er, work.

Yes, above all he was a cricketing man. Over 11 years he played for Essex, Somerset and MCC. He is quoted as saying that he toured Australia with Lord Harris's team in 1877 but the reference books do not corroborate this. At 6ft 3½in and approaching 15 stone he was a mighty hitter. Reputedly he once drove a ball 157 yards over Lord's pavilion, a yard or so further than one he struck off Grace at Gloucester.

In 49 innings he mustered 905 runs at an average of 18.46, while his fast bowling earned him 23 wickets at 22.65, so although *Wisden* once described him as Somerset's 'most valuable hand,' he was not one of the game's historic figures. In the context of this story the significance of cricket is that it kept him away from golf.

Fowler encountered our game in September 1879 when, at 23, he went to Bideford (Devon) on business and Captain Molesworth, RN, a great golfing character, offered to take him to the Royal North Devon and West of England club at Westward Ho!

> So off we went, the captain driving a tandem in a high dog cart, and as the road is of the switchback variety and the captain's driving rather nautical our voyage was of a somewhat exciting nature.[1]

He borrowed some clubs, soon cottoned on to the game

and became a member. In the club's autumn meeting he won the handicap prize and another day holed in one ('And I've given you a shot here!' protested his opponent). He continued to play a little in the early 1880's, but in summer he was cricketing for Somerset and in winter it was back to hunting and shooting – plus billiards, at which he excelled.

Nearly 10 years passed before he returned to golf and grew serious about it. After diligent practice nearer his home in Taunton he rejoined Westward Ho!, got down to scratch and won a gold medal. When he first visited St. Andrews at the age of 36 the conversion was complete and he became prominent in competitions there and elsewhere.

But why should the Bonsors choose him to survey the heath and create their course? After all, not only had he never designed a course, he hadn't had any formal training to do so.

Well, nobody had. Course architecture was an infant howling and wallowing in its own ignorance. In the eyes of Horace Hutchinson, pundit, author and twice Amateur champion, it was 'a wonderfully easy business, needing little training.'

Most courses were still being laid out as they had been for more than half-a-century – that is to say according to the ideas of professionals called in for advice. This did not always work: many of the pros thus summoned found that they were more adept at their trade of hitting balls than at the art of visualising holes or a biological science embracing everything from species of grass to loads of manure.

The most imaginative professional was almost certainly Willie Park Junior, twice Open champion, and when in 1900 and 1901 he produced Sunningdale and Huntercombe he exploded once and for all the theory that good golf was possible only on seaside links. Fowler

---

[1] *Great Golfers in the Making*, ed. Henry Leach (Methuen, 1907).

'No ordinary golfer and no ordinary man.' Fowler's action captured by George Beldam, pioneer sports photographer and Walton Heath member.
Great Golfers, Their Methods at a Glance, 1904 (by permission of Palgrave Macmillan).

thought that Woking, originally laid out by Tom Dunn but remodelled by Stuart Paton and John Low, was the first really good inland course, but now he personally had confirmed the glorious potential of the southern heathlands and exposed as dullards those men who had built so many poor inland courses on impervious clay soil. 'The London golfer played mainly on mud,' wrote Bernard Darwin, doyen of golf scribes.

Park would appear a serious candidate for the Bonsors to have considered, but one senses that Fowler anyway would have talked them out of using a professional. Besides, Park may not have been available: so busy did he become that he virtually worked himself to death.

So much for the professionals. As to amateurs with designs on designing there was scarcely even a short list to consider. The eminent Harry Colt, although credited with Rye (Sussex) back in 1894, was still secretary at Sunningdale – dabbling in design but several years away from full-time commitment to it. MacKenzie, Simpson, Campbell, Alison, Hutchison and Abercromby had not even begun.

All of which left Fowler – and in the circumstances our Herbert had a lot going for him. He was no ordinary amateur golfer. He understood the game; studied it, theorised about it, had grown obsessed with all branches of it – including architecture. He was also ambitious. On his own admission he was desperate to design a course and he

passionately pressed his case on the Bonsors from his advantageous position as Cosmo's brother-in-law.

Fowler was desperate for another reason. Forty-six years old, married, with a nine-year-old daughter to educate, a substantial house in Taunton to run, servants to pay, visits to London and jaunts to St. Andrews and elsewhere to finance, he had been living beyond his income and was seriously in debt. He was embarrassed at his bank and with the family, had not repaid £1,000 Cosmo had lent him and was having to sell up in Taunton. A letter to his uncle Joseph in March 1902 spelt out his despair:

> I have left Taunton only under stern necessity and with the intention of so regulating our expenditure as to fall in with your wishes, also with the hope that I may be able to get other work to bring in more income… at present the position seems rather too hopeless. In March 1897 the bank held no security for all my indebtedness. I was strongly advised by my brother-in-law to file my petition at once (and he promised to put me into some new business). I felt, however, that I could not do this.

Within months manna from heaven – or on earth, from the Bonsors – arrived. The promised 'new business' came in the form of the golf course job.

All previous reports have suggested that Fowler began his task in August 1902, but plans certainly existed in 1901, indicating an earlier survey, and Bonsor and he had discussed the project two years before that. We have Fowler's word for this in his letter to *The Times* in 1935:

> In 1899 my brother-in-law, the late Sir Cosmo Bonsor, consulted me as to the possibility of making a golf course on Walton Heath… In 1902 he bought the manorial rights and engaged me to lay out the course and form the club.

Fowler (left) takes time off from preparing the Old course to referee a 1903 match between Harry Vardon and J.H. Taylor at Burnham and Berrow.

Contributing a chapter to a book on golf architecture,[1] he recalled:

> When I first saw Walton Heath there was very little to make one suppose that a first-class course could be made upon it... it was all covered with heather of the most robust nature, some two to three feet high, and where there was no heather there were masses of giant whins.

Edwin Hanson Freshfield, appointed manor steward, explained to the commoners why this was so. The lifting and carting for sale of turf, loam and gravel had ruined the surface. Bracken, heather and gorse had taken the place of turf and threatened to destroy the grass altogether. Only a small part of the heath was fit for pasturage. These practices, he said, must cease.

Imagine the scene as Fowler – Norfolk-knickerbockered, tall on his horse, generously moustached – begins his survey and searches for hidden merits in the wilderness that may help him achieve his ambition and rescue him from the abyss of bankruptcy. One by one they emerge. First comes the dawning that the rough terrain on which he rides, walks and stumbles is, deep down, a 'glorious open space, with rolling ground and no trees or ditches;' next, realisation that the grass on the bridle-paths is 'of a very fine quality.' John Masefield would write of grass such as this:

> ...Short and sweet,
> And springy to a boxer's feet.[2]

...And to horses' hooves! Down the breeze has drifted the rhythmic drumming of the training gallops. Perhaps Herbert sees *Moiffaa*, who will be entered for the 1904 Grand National but with form so unimpressive that the villagers won't risk their money on him. He will win by eight lengths at 25 to one.

Fowler investigates further. The turf will improve when nurtured by men and fed by sheep. The ground is broken up by chasms and hollows which will help him make bunkers. More important, the drainage is good.

> No really good grass is grown where the drainage is bad, but the heath is on the chalk hills of Surrey and, though there is from six to 20 feet of varying soils over the chalk, it is always perfectly dry and even in the wettest weather never becomes really soft.

Yes, a fine course could be created here. That was Fowler's report and the Bonsors, probably in August, 1902, commissioned him to go ahead. Herbert enjoyed benefits the professionals elsewhere lacked. Often they were called in for brief visits, asked for instinctive decisions and paid off quickly, leaving the interpretation of their ideas to others. At Walton Heath, thanks to Cosmo and his fellow investors who put up something over £6,000 for the course, money was available for the time needed to do the job properly, while Fowler could remain a permanent

Fowler tackling his own course – in the bunker guarding the 18th hole. The bunker remains but the farm workers' cottages have given way to grander houses. Illustrated Sporting and Dramatic News, 1904

fixture able to dictate and oversee. Moreover, whereas most architects had only about 100 acres available for 18 holes, Fowler had far, far more.

> The next thing was to settle where to go... Eventually I concluded that in a certain spot I could make two extra good short holes and I worked backwards and forwards from the sixth[3] – happily named Port Arthur[4] by Mr. Justice Bucknill. To help ease upkeep I decided to keep the outgoing and incoming holes fairly near together; also to arrange them so that it would be easy to play a short round – and by playing the first and last six holes a capital 12-hole round was possible.

Fowler called in J.H. Taylor, already three times Open champion, for his opinion. The great man gave the plans his nod and paid further visits. Meantime Fowler ordered his horses, sharpened his scythes and marshalled his workers:

> Having settled roughly on the spots which I thought most likely to make interesting greens, we marked out the course and set to work to cut the heather and whins. This was a big job and cost a lot of money.
> Once having cleared the various growths, we employed a steam plough to break up the ground thoroughly to a depth of about 12 inches, then worked it with harrows until we had it quite clean and free from the numerous bracken roots. The top soil is a sandy loam and in it are small flints: it took a long time to get these removed by women and boys.

Some of the locals were unhappy. 'The gorse has been destroyed by hundreds of acres and the rides so cut up as to be almost impassable,' one of them wrote to the *Surrey Mirror* in May 1903, 'Has it been done for the benefit of the

[1] *Golf Greens and Greenkeeping*, ed. H.G. Hutchinson (Country Life), 1906.
[2] From *The Everlasting Mercy* (Macmillan, NY), 1911.
[3] The short sixth was abandoned in the 'thirties.
[4] Apparently impregnable Chinese port destined to be captured by the Japanese in the Russo-Japanese war.

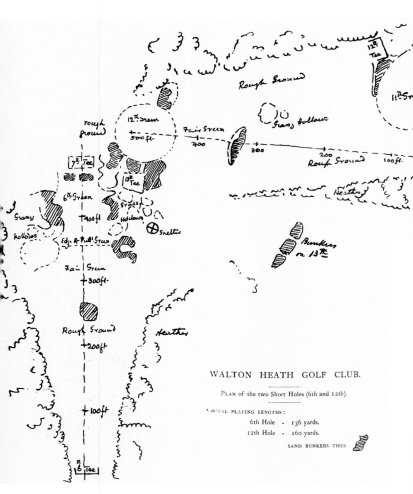

Fowler's plans for the two short holes that were the first he decided on for his layout. Neither hole exists in its original form today, but the greens are still there. The old sixth green is now the fifth on the Old and the former 12th is the green for the 14th on the New.

WALTON HEATH GOLF CLUB.

PLAN of the two Short Holes (6th and 12th).

NORMAL PLAYING LENGTHS :

6th Hole - 136 yards.
12th Hole - 160 yards.

SAND BUNKERS THUS

Horses for courses. Women and boys helped clear the ground.

speculative purchasers of the land adjoining the new railway? It is infamous that so beautiful a place should be so utterly spoiled.' Undaunted, Fowler pressed on:

The next step was to work in large quantities of manure. The ground was now ready for the seed, and in late August and early September 1903 we sowed 12 bushels to the acre of Dutch fescue. The greens were sown with a mixture of poas, fescues and agrostis. I had planned to clear the heather to a width of 70 yards, and of this we ploughed and sowed 50, leaving the rest rough.

We also left 100 yards in front of each tee rough. The ultimate result was that quite a good turf came at very little expense; I have found that at Walton it is only necessary to clear the heather and keep the ground well rolled and occasion-

ally harrowed for the natural grass of the country to come of itself. Having got in the seed, we had to keep out rabbits with miles of wire netting.

We now set to work to form some of the hazards. There are all kinds of hazards and most of them are bad. Trees, hedges and ditches are all unsatisfactory and the best are sand bunkers so long as they are properly placed and constructed. We are fortunate at Walton in being able to go down as deep as we like in making a bunker, and in any cases where the water does not go away of itself we sink a shaft about three feet square nearly to the chalk, then fill it with old pots, pans or large flints. They are then always dry and much the best type of bunker.

Fowler felt that only side hazards should be put in during construction and that any cross-bunkers should be left until he could see how the ball would run. In any case he believed that bunkers on the sides and especially near greens were the prime requisite, that players sliced and pulled more than they topped and that as a slice was the greater fault more bunkers should be placed on the right. So long as a green was well guarded and the approach shot difficult the hole would always be considered a good one, far more so than if its main difficulty lay in the tee shot.

Bunkers, he thought, should be shaped like an old hip bath, not with a steep bank and flat base as at many inland clubs but having a gradual curve from top to bottom so that balls did not lie hard against the face but ran down towards the centre. However they should be deeper than on most courses. Indeed, they became known as 'Fowler's graves.'

The seeds sown had come from James Carter and Company and were 'of the type supplied to His Majesty the King at Windsor.' Reginald Beale, Carter's golf and sports manager, proudly advertised the fact that the sowing on the rough heathland produced mature grass in eight months – four months less than had been managed at Sunningdale and, so he claimed, a record. Fowler was delighted:

We had laid on water to every green and tee. By March 1904 we were able to start rolling the turf, working daily on the greens; in April we began to play; in the second week of May we would be able to open the course.

It is said that Fowler designed his courses on the grand scale with big hitters like himself in mind, but he

The architect exhuming his ball from one of his own 'Fowler graves.'
Illustrated Sporting and Dramatic News, *1904*

frequently denied this and stressed that his aim was fairness to all, with a premium on straightness and accuracy as against length. This first course measured 6,424 yards, uncommonly long by the standards of the day, particularly inland. It was laid out, remember, as the new Haskell rubber-cored ball was beginning to threaten the 'gutty' and, with its extra length, causing people to argue whether courses should be altered to cope with it.

So, Fowler's first course is almost ready and awaits its first test. At this point let us leave the heath for a short while and further consider the man – because in the five years since he and Bonsor had first put their heads together much had happened to him.

Fowler the golfer

His skill and prestige had increased. 'A few years ago he was unknown and as he is now in his mid-forties his recent exploits appear particularly brilliant. He drives almost as far as James Braid, the Open champion' – so commented a 1901 newspaper.

He had finished equal 26th in the 1900 Open, made the first of three appearances for England against Scotland and reached the last 16 in an Amateur Championship. As befits a chap whose pockets now bulged with the membership cards of exclusive clubs, he entered the championships under different banners: R&A, Walton Heath and Honourable Company of Edinburgh Golfers. So recently almost on his uppers, he was playing and hobnobbing with the most distinguished figures in the amateur game.

As a rank outsider in the 1901 Amateur, held at St. Andrews, he suddenly found himself in the last 16 against Harold Hilton, the defending titleholder and twice winner of the Open. At this point Herbert's wheels came off. He was unwell and how much this influenced things we shall never know. Anyway, after six holes he was six down and at the next retired from the fray, leaving Hilton, as one reporter wrote, 'to enjoy the afternoon with his cigarettes,' Harold being a 40-a-day-at-least man.

'As others see us' – a magazine cartoon series. The World of Golf, *1906*

Perhaps the walk-off was an example of Fowler's Achilles' heel as a golfer, what one writer many years later called 'a temperament that was never over-anxious to oppose the adverse decisions of fate… If things were going his way he could be brilliant. If they were not he gave an impression that it was just not his day out and that was that.[5]

Herbert was no ordinary golfer and no ordinary man. He played in a cocoon of study, theory and experimentation. We may term him an eccentric. Perhaps Darwin's description, 'erratic genius,' is in all senses more accurate.

Fowler's early green staff.

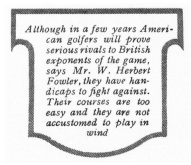

Although in a few years American golfers will prove serious rivals to British exponents of the game, says Mr. W. Herbert Fowler, they have handicaps to fight against. Their courses are too easy and they are not accustomed to play in wind

The Motor Owner, *1920*

[5] *Fry's magazine,* 1907

Fowler in the 1904 England team, 'playing and hobnobbing with the most distinguished figures in the amateur game.' From left, standing, S.Fry, H.Castle, Fowler, H.de Zoete, B.Darwin, J.Pease; sitting, H.Hilton, J.Ball Jr, H.Hutchinson.
Golf Illustrated, *1904*

At one time he believed in small, pellet-like balls and had a press made to produce them. He went in for short clubs, then long ones, then apparently dirty ones. John Low, the Scottish international, thought they looked 'as if they had been laid aside for some months in an unsuitable lodging house.' The steel heads were black and certainly not polished. Fowler's theory was twofold: first, the heads would retain their weight and shape if they were not constantly rubbed with sandpaper; second, the shining face of an iron attracted the eye away from the ball on the backswing. When Bobby Jones among others began forbidding his caddie to clean the centres of his irons people began to wonder if Herbert had been so eccentric after all!

Then there were his putters. The estimable Low had the most telling description: 'Mr. Fowler putts sometimes with a driving iron but often uses a mallet which looks like a sandwich box with a stick stuck through the middle. I can remember my disappointment when I discovered that the head was made of solid wood. The appearance and capacity of the thing warranted the hope that some very cunning engine or clockwork contrivance lay embowelled within the mahogany exterior.'

Fowler the pundit

'Mr W. Herbert Fowler is a true aristocrat if ever there was one,' wrote Arthur Croome, cricketer, athlete, golfer and course architect. 'Had he lived in Paris at the time of the revolution the mob would certainly have searched the city for a lanterne high and strong enough to finish him off. The marks of your true aristocrat are a firm belief that the best dog must come out on top eventually, an instinct for discovering the best of everything and an unshakeable conviction that what he selects as the best is the best... You will very soon find that his real contempt is reserved for what is second-rate, ignorant or ignoble. That is why he has so seldom been proved wrong about golf, though he has given utterance in the most unequivocal terms to more categorical statements than most people.'

Yes, Herbert was becoming a pontificating pundit. An R&A member since 1894, he was elected to that club's green committee in 1902 and poured a torrent of letters, articles and arguments into newspapers, magazines, books, clubhouse lounges and committee rooms. He was the game's 'Disgusted of Tunbridge Wells;' compulsively controversial; an opinionated nuisance in committee, perhaps, but listened to for the intelligence that lay behind the waffle.

The closed-shop roster for the Amateur, confined as it was to St Andrews, Prestwick, Muirfield, Hoylake and Sandwich, was anathema to him. Bogey contests reduced him to apoplexy. And that wasn't all. To *Golf Illustrated*:

MATCH-PLAY OR MEDAL: 'Match-play is the game of golf and medal play only a poor substitute.'

FOUR-BALL GOLF: 'Its influence is altogether bad and will do great harm to your game.'

ST. ANDREWS: 'The links are becoming less popular with R&A members owing to the hordes of women and children who are allowed equal facilities for play. The result is a horrible congestion and the hacking to pieces of the grand old course. If the town council do not soon wake up and get powers to regulate the play St. Andrews will become a kind of Margate, with golf thrown in.'

'This seems rather unkind to Margate,' replied the Editor of *Golf Illustrated*, 'especially as it has a golf course. We trust that by drawing attention to the superior attractions of Margate we may have done something towards relieving the "horrible congestion" of St. Andrews.'

Fowler at Walton Heath

The envelopes containing his letters and articles now bore Surrey postmarks. Fowler, his wife Ethel and their daughter Phyllis had left Somerset in 1902, but a comfortable life-style was still considered a necessity and eventually they moved into *Chussex*, an eight-bedroom villa in Nursery Road hard by the club, specially built for them, designed by the rising young architect Edwin Lutyens and named after the plain on the heath that was the site of the Roman villa.

The club company's certificate of incorporation, August 5, 1903.

Behind the scenes club affairs were swiftly gathering force. On August 5, 1903, the Walton Heath Golf Club Company Ltd, was incorporated with nominal capital of £3,000 divided into £1 shares and a first debenture issue of £8,000 at 5% interest was announced. Malcolm Bonsor would agree to lease the course to the company, of which he was to be a director, on a 21-year lease at £300 a year. He was awarded 2,993 shares plus £8,000 in cash.

For Fowler things were looking up. In November, happy with the progress of his course, he went to the Stag Brewery in London for the first meeting on record of the directors, whose chairman was The Hon. Alfred Gathorne-Hardy, third son of the first Earl of Cranbrook. Herbert was officially made managing director and club secretary and later Malcolm would transfer 1,000 of his shares to him.

An additional director was appointed – 40-year-old Harry Mallaby-Deeley, wealthy leading light of the Prince's Club on Mitcham Common. He was an expert on courses and their upkeep and would soon found another Prince's club at Sandwich on the Kent coast. Among his lesser claims to fame was his drive at Mitcham that bounced up into a horse's nostril – where it remained until the animal eventually sneezed.

Fowler's multi-talented, self-opinionated, industrious, faithful and faulted presence will lurk behind most of the 200-odd ensuing pages. So will another man about to join our cast of characters.

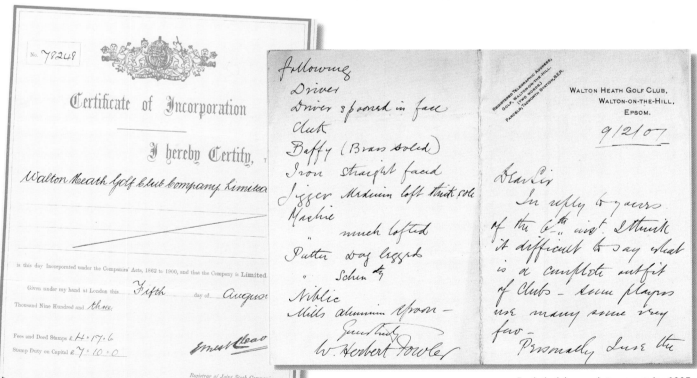

Fowler's clubs – reply to an enquiry, 1907.

A FIRST-CLASS GOLF LINKS NEAR LONDON.

The following is a short account of the various holes with their lengths :—

1st Hole, 291 yards.—A straight tee shot takes one over a small pond, about 120 yards from the tee. There is heather to the right and rough ground to the left. A mashie shot finds a beautiful green. An easy four hole.

2nd Hole, 420 yards.—A long and straight tee shot is necessary to " make " one, for a fine second which has to cross a deep gully with old gravel pits strewn about it. The green faces one on the opposite slope, and has two fine natural waves in it: A five hole, but a very fine four for the long division. Taylor and Braid both think this an extra fine hole.

3rd Hole, 300 yards.—Finely guarded green between the road on the left and the gallop on the right. There are three good bunkers, one on the left and two on the right. A four hole.

4th Hole, 450 yards. This is a fine hole with a splendid second shot. The green lies away to the right of the course, and is well guarded by bunkers. A five hole, but a possible four.

5th Hole, 222 yards. This is a splendid one-shot hole for the long driver. There is a bunker to catch a topped tee shot, and straightness is essential, as there is a deep bunker along the right side of the green and another on the left. All the slope of the ground is from right to left. The green is exceptionally good. A four hole, but three for the long driver.

6th Hole, 152 yards. This is a splendid short hole. The green is pear-shaped, with the narrow end nearest the tee. Both sides are built up from bunkers which run nearly to the back of the green. A shot played too strong would be caught by three pot bunkers. The green is all visible from the tee, and the slope faces the player, so that a shot can be pitched well up. There is no carry from the tee, and the half-running shot can be played if desired. There are a large number of natural pots on either side of the green. A fine three hole.

Within 20 yards of this green is the 12th hole, and the tee to the 13th, so that a capital 12 hole round can be played.

7th Hole, 489 yards.—The long hole going out. This hole is uphill nearly all the way, and is well bunkered. The green is a beauty of the basin type and has a fringe of whins on the far side. A very good five hole.

8th Hole, 444 yards.—There is a bunker 170 yards from the tee on the extreme right of the course, and two across the course at a distance of 320 yards. Two good drives should reach a fine large green. There are whins at the back of the green and two natural pots on the left. A fine hole. This is the farthest out hole and is the highest part of the course, and is marked on the ordnance survey as 720ft. above sea level. There is a lovely view of the two heaths from this point.

9th Hole, 410 yards.—This is slightly down-hill, with a bunker to carry 140 yards from the tee. Straightness is necessary, as the course runs between high whins. A pretty green with a small holly tree on the right side of it. A good four hole.

10th Hole, 240 yards.—Another long drivers' one-shot hole. Down-hill until the green is reached, but the green itself is on a slope against the ball. Bunkers are on the right and left of the green, and a post and rails in the far left corner to define a gallop, which passes close by. A four hole.

11th Hole, 344 yards. A fine drive and iron hole. Down a valley, with a slope from left to right. There is a road to cross with the second, which shot must be played well to the left to get near the hole. Two bunkers on the right, one in the green. The green is an extra good one. A four hole.

12th Hole, 175 yards. A fine cleek shot hole. There is a good bunker about 130 yards from the tee and two deep ones, one on each side of the green. A good three hole.

13th Hole, 329 yards.—A nice drive and iron hole. The green is well guarded by two bunkers, but there is ample room to play any kind of approach shot. Another very good green. A four hole.

14th Hole, 337 yards.—There is a fine large natural pot on the right to catch a sliced drive, and a bunker separates the green from the site of a Roman villa. A four hole.

15th Hole, 528 yards.—The longest hole on the course, but as it is all slightly downhill is not so severe as it would otherwise be. There are three natural pots, one on the right and two on the left, to catch a crooked tee shot. There will be other bunkers further down the course, and the large green slopes towards a deep natural hollow. A good five hole.

16th Hole, 386 yards. A fine two-shot hole. A chain of four bunkers of different design separate this course from the 17th, and straight play will be necessary to secure a four. The green is a fine one.

17th Hole, 474 yards.—This is probably the most difficult hole on the course for the long player. The tee shot must be straight, as there is a lot of bad ground to the left, and bunkers on the right. The green is placed on high ground to the left of the line taken in the tee shot, and is finely guarded by deep hazards on the right and heather on the left. The green slopes slightly to the right, and is one of the best on the course. A fine five hole.

18th Hole, 433 yards.—This is a hole of good length for the long drivers and has an excellent green. Two roads have to be crossed with the second or third shots, and there are other hazards, which make it a good hole to finish a match with. A five hole.

GOLF ILLUSTRATED, February 5, 1904

Approaching Fowler's old sixth green and looking up his seventh fairway. This 489-yard seventh, which continued up the hill in much the same direction as the previous holes, was lost during the many changes made during the 'thirties.

Fowler playing the second. The hollow still exists but its former rough ground is now fairway.
The World of Golf, *1906*

25

'JIMMY' – Spy's *cartoon of Braid in* Vanity Fair's *'Men of the day' series, published in 1907, three years after he came to Walton Heath.*

Chapter Three

ENTER THE CHAMPION
James Braid begins the first of 46 years

I N THE WINTER of 1903/4, as Fowler's 18 holes neared completion, the pro of the Romford club in Essex enquired with due humility as to whether his services might be useful to the fledgling enterprise, which currently had a course and clubhouse under construction, a board of directors, a secretary, 200 members waiting to play, but no professional. On the face of it there was nothing surprising in his approach because many pros were interested in the vacancy. After all, the membership promised to be affluent and the course something special, perhaps the best inland test in the country.

But the approach from the Romford man was singularly different. He was an Open champion, a man furthermore who had just enhanced his reputation by winning the *News of the World* Match-Play, a professional event which in terms of prestige ranked second only to the Open. His name was Braid – James Braid, a 33-year-old Scot. Next to Harry Vardon and J.H. Taylor he was the hottest property in golf – and getting hotter.

If, as we are told, Braid indeed approached Walton Heath and not vice-versa – for there is more than one version of the saga – perhaps he had been encouraged to do so by Taylor, who was deeply impressed by Fowler's plans. Anyway, Braid had visited the heath to see for himself in October 1903 and had deemed the embryo course nearer in character to a Scottish links than anything else he had seen away from the coast. The story goes that when he appeared he was actually put to work on it with a shovel!

Word got out. 'We understand that Braid has resigned his position at Romford and accepted a similar post at the new green laid out at Tadworth, about a mile-and-a-half south-east of the Epsom grandstand,' reported *Golfing* on January 7, 1904. The title 'Walton Heath Golf Club' had not yet entered the game's vernacular. The *Surrey Mirror* referred to 'the Walton-on-the-Hill club.'

This *Surrey Mirror* had previously ignored mention of the club, unable to find space for it amid its pages of parochial doings and advertisements for £5 bedroom suites, £1 overcoats and Doctor Davis's Famous Female Pills – 'a boon to womankind,' guaranteed to cure everything from giddiness and heart problems to hysteria and swelling after meals. Now, in a tiny, unheaded paragraph at the foot of its Walton column, it divulged that the club had secured the services of 'James Braid the well-known professional.'

The contract was for seven years from May 1, 1904, and he would get £100 per year. In addition he could charge and keep five shillings per hour for teaching and three shillings and sixpence for playing with members. He could be away 90 days a year, but not for more than a week at a time except for championships and only if he paid for a deputy.

Fowler, as managing director, signed the agreement for the golf club company and we should, for future reference, make a note of the solicitor who witnessed it: 'G. Riddell'.

Braid duly began his duties, travelling by train to Bonsor's new station and taking a 'growler' cab to the club. With him came his wife Minnie Alice and their sons, five-year-old James junior and three-year-old Harry. Soon they would settle happily in a house in Meadow Walk, which they named *Earlsferry*. It was on that town's border with Elie on the Fifeshire coast that Braid was born, the son of a ploughman. Soon after he arrived on the heath he recalled:

> At Earlsferry and Elie and around there it is all golf, and everybody must play unless he wishes to be taken for a crank or as somebody with whom there is something constitutionally or mentally wrong.[1]

---

[1] *Great Golfers in the Making*, ed. H. Leach, 1907. (Reproduced with permission of Palgrave Macmillan).

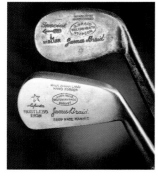

In that atmosphere he began his rough-hewn, self-taught apprenticeship to the game, hitting balls with primitive, improvised clubs when he was five or six, then caddying as a schoolboy and practising when there were no bags to carry.

> I never had any lessons. I simply watched the grown-ups and imitated them like a monkey.

At 13, when he left school, his parents ('dear old-fashioned people') refused to let him go into golf and he was apprenticed as a joiner a six-mile walk away. For a time his opportunities to play were limited, but when they occurred, in places like St. Andrews and ultimately Edinburgh, he competed with increasing skill. When he was 22 he beat a field of 140 in an event open to members of Edinburgh and Leith clubs, playing off scratch and breaking the record for the course – coincidentally the public Braid Hills (2d. a round), where he might queue for four hours to play on Saturdays.

The joinery was frustrating but eventually paid dividends. In 1893, soon after his triumph at the 'Braids', a friend working in London told him he could help get him a job as a club-

'Perennially capped, with a chunky moustache whose downward contours gave him a misleading look of melancholy'.
Golf, 1897

maker at the Army and Navy stores. He had never made a club in his life, but had the experience of working with wood and tools. He got the job. Young Braid was climbing the financial ladder. Sixpence an hour? Forget it, those bad old days were past. Now it was eightpence... and subsequently it would be a shilling.

He was now a professional and destined for a rapid rise. After an assistant's job at Hastings he went to Romford.

In Opens he did Romford proud: successively sixth, second, tenth, fifth and third. Then, in 1901, he broke through to win at Muirfield – despite striking his first drive over the boundary wall and at the last hole on the final day hitting down with such force at his gutty, stuck against a tufty mound, that the shaft of his cleek[2] cracked and the clubhead flew off. That same force, though, ensured that the ball reached the green and he won by

three shots from Vardon and four from Taylor.

He still did not quite have the stature of those two, both of whom had already won three Opens, but now he knew it was only a matter of time – a belief encouraged when he finished second and fifth in the next two years. Meanwhile he christened his newly-born son not just Harry but Harry *Muirfield* Braid.

This, then, was the man who became Walton Heath's first professional. He was tall (6ft 1½in), slim and sinewy (12st 6lb), dark-haired but perennially capped, with a chunky moustache whose downward contours gave him a misleading air of melancholy. He was outwardly serious, yet with an underlay of dry humour; a reserved, imperturbable, decent, modest man; economical with words delivered in a Scottish burr that had comfortably survived his migration to London; at times apparently uncommunicative yet full of commonsense and gentle wisdom. When asked for an opinion his reply would be frank and forthright. He appeared and was – oh, that terrible cliché – one of nature's gentlemen.

For those who knew golf – and despite its boom it was decades away from being a 'people's' game – he was a star. Women golfers also saw Braid as a role model. When *Ladies' Field* reported, with only slight exaggeration, that as a youngster weak off the tee he had gone to sleep one night a short driver and woken up a long one it was rumoured that many high-handicap ladies took to their beds for indefinite periods!

Proud father of two sons – James drives, younger brother Harry waits his turn.

---

[2] Equivalent to a two iron.

BRAID ON BOYHOOD

A match between amateurs and professionals took place at Elie, and among those who took part in it was Jamie Anderson, who was then Open Champion. To me then, at just nine years of age, he was the greatest man in the world, and I followed him about like a little dog, gazing with admiration at everything he did. Jamie seems to have taken some notice of me, and some little interest in me also. At all events, when we were walking side by side on the links, and he had seen me hit a ball or two, he told me very seriously that if I went in thoroughly for golf I should myself one day be the Open Champion. And I was only nine.

Great Golfers in the Making, 1907

Today's caddies' shed was Braid's showroom and workshop.

Two of Braid's clubmaking assistants stayed at the club for half a century.
Fry's Magazine, *1906*

By the terms of his contract the club had to provide him with working premises at least 36ft by 15ft to embrace a workshop, an office and a showroom. These quarters became a reflection of himself, the shop and showroom more rooms than show. He sold his best clubs for 7s.6d, members attending for fittings as though visiting their Savile Row tailors. Seven shillings and sixpence? Good heavens, you could get a club for half that price at Gamages in London! A Walton Heath member, though, would never stoop to such false economy!

Mr Braid, as every respectful Walton member called him, was a shrewd teacher and a capable clubmaker. It was no surprise that his contract absolved him from greenkeeping. Neither greenkeepers nor club professionals had yet achieved their rightful status, joint roles had for years been the norm at many clubs and certainly Braid had helped with the course at Romford. Most certainly Walton Heath could not ask him to be a greenkeeper – an Open champion indeed, consider the indignity!

What does seem surprising is that the agreement committed him to advise managing director Fowler on course maintenance and improvement. Braid already had dabbled in course architecture, but both men were proud and stubborn about their creations. Henry Longhurst, companion of Darwin in the Valhalla of golf's literati, once claimed in *The Sunday Times* that Braid had planned the Old course bunkers, and within a few months of his arrival magazines were reporting that the first nine holes of the New were being planned by both men. For all that, although they forged a partnership of mutual respect and while Braid certainly kept his eye keenly on course condition and presentation, not until 1935, when Fowler was nearly 80, is there any substantial evidence that James was intimately involved in major alterations or improvements.

Meantime the cast of characters at the club was now complete: landlord, directors, architect, secretary and professional. The clubhouse, the theatre where the plots were being hatched, was also nearly ready.

Two years previously, at a meeting on the heath, locals had vociferously opposed a plan by the Bonsors for a temporary clubhouse there. Cosmo won them over but building never took place. Instead, a piece of freehold land just away from the public heath on an area known as Lattice Meadow was found, and once a court had got rid of gypsies from the neighbouring field a partly prefabricated clubhouse, for which Cosmo probably paid £3,000 and which arrived 'carriage paid' at the station, was erected. And that is where it remains, much altered and much loved – and from time to time an agonising headache for the committee.

A Press release from Fowler derived national publicity. This bungalow clubhouse, built by the Norwich firm Boulton and Paul, would accommodate 500 gentlemen and 100 ladies and afford 'a lovely view of the heath and course.' It had brick foundations and chimneys, wooden walls and a tiled roof. Oil lamps supplied the light, but gas would not be long coming. Outside would be flower beds, a lawn and... anyone for croquet?

So the entire combined stage of club and course was now ready for curtain-up and on May 14, 1904, 'the great triumvirate,' the outstanding champions of the era, first bestrode it. Braid the local hero opposed Vardon and Taylor over 36 holes of match-play.

High Edwardiana! Vanity Fair! See the invited audience arrive! They come by special train from London... by hired brake from the station... by steed and carriage... in proud new cars at speeds of up to 20mph, dangerously close to the limit set by the 1903 Motor Act.

Imagine this select and sporty throng as it converges down country lanes to the clubhouse! Knights and lords... parliamentarians... the occasional general or admiral... well-to-do club members... gentlemen of substance and ladies of fashion! Also on the course are prominent

Five shillings an hour was Braid's teaching fee – but surviving invoice suggests he cut it to two for Fowler's daughter Phyllis.

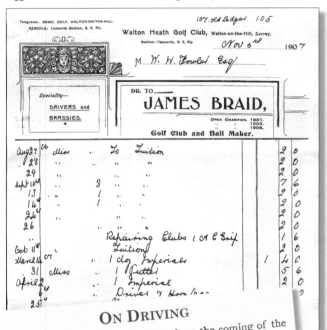

Great Golfers in the Making, 1907.

The Walton Heath Golf Club.

A SUCCESSFUL OPENING.

THE members of the Walton Heath Golf Club have every reason to be satisfied with the auspicious nature of the opening proceedings on Saturday last. The day was brilliantly fine, and the special train which the directors had thoughtfully provided at Charing Cross for the accommodation of their guests was filled with a distinguished company of golfers. Lord George Hamilton, M.P., Lord Walter Gordon Lennox, Mr. H. W. Forster, M.P., Mr. Guy Pym, M.P., Admiral Rose, General Moncreiff, Mr. J. B. Pease, Mr. Horace Hutchinson, Mr. Ernley Blackwell, Mr. Ernest Lehmann, Major Elliot, and many other well-known players, besides a large number of ladies, were present throughout the day, either enjoying a game over the new course or watching the play in the professional match. The latter was most interesting, since it consisted of a three-ball match between Harry Vardon, J. H. Taylor, and James Braid, who has now taken up residence at Walton Heath as club professional. Vardon was looking even better than he did a fortnight ago, and playing quite in his old inimitable style he beat his two opponents in decisive fashion. Taylor was in constant trouble with his putting, and finished the first round 3 down to Vardon and 2 down to Braid, the latter being all-square with Vardon. In the afternoon Taylor fell still further behind, and ultimately lost to Vardon by 6, while Braid also fell away and had to admit defeat by 3. The approximate scores were: Vardon, 76 and 80—156; Braid, 79 and 83—162; Taylor, 80 and 83—163.

Mr. W. Herbert Fowler, who was chief architect of the course, must be heartily congratulated on the result of his labours. His plan shows sound judgment and knowledge, and he has not failed to lay out the holes so as to give scope for every kind of shot.

Golf Illustrated, May 20, 1904

players... commoners exercising their rights and privileges... plus representatives of the *hoi polloi*, from itinerant caddies to villagers curious and critical as they observe a different world at play.

In the clubhouse some talk golf while others discuss wider-world topics: 'Have you read about this new motor car partnership of Rolls and Royce?'... 'Sad about Stanley dying, isn't it – you know, the chap who said "Dr Livingstone I presume".' The Bonsors supply liberal hospitality, proffered by steward Osborn, 25 years in the service of the Duke of Richmond and no mean golfer himself.

Even *Golf Illustrated* reported the day more as a social junket than as a match, leading on the luminaries present rather than on the trio of champions. On this brilliant day, disturbed only by afternoon wind, the one disappointment for the club was that Braid failed to win, Vardon finishing three holes up on him (one report said four) and six up on Taylor.

Cigarette card hero. Braid featured in 1912 Gallaher's series.

Affluent Edwardians watch Vardon drive off in the inaugural match.

But it had been a successful public relations exercise and Fowler, like a silent film producer with first-night nerves, survived to see his production, The Course, get rave notices. 'An up-to-date embodiment of all that a golf course should be,' wrote one reviewer. Best round of the day was calculated to be the 76 by Vardon and this was better than it reads considering the nature of Fowler's creation.

Conjure up a vision of that 1904 course and its setting. The all-round aspect is of open heathland. Trees? We can see scarcely any. There may be trees a century hence in 2003, but not now, not in 1904.

Now the course itself. Long at 6,424 yards; everything constructed in the grand manner. Fast-running, too – 'the fastest inland course in the country,' says Braid.[3] Inland? Yes, obviously. Yet the turf, communing with the winds, reminds one of sand-blown linksland. So, indeed, does the

entire out-and-back layout. It is reminiscent of the Old course at St Andrews – out to a distant point, then something of a loop before coming back home. Fowler, fervently in love with the 'auld grey toon,' will appreciate our compliment if he hears it.

The fairways, subtly domed, are 50 yards across, and balls not truly struck disappear from iron ground into 10 yards of semi-rough or, beyond, into heather taller and denser than it will be a hundred years hence. 'Fowler's graves' are steep burial grounds indeed; 'the bunkers may be a little too severe for the majority of players,' Braid admits. The greens are difficult to read, like a book to a person with fading sight, save when they disclose their subtle slopes and borrows to the evening sun and the shadows.

Longhurst once did what we have just done – tried to grasp what the original course must have been like. What, he asked Braid, would a goodish young golfer think were he to be magically transported back in time and set down on it? 'He'd be frightened out of his life,' said the old champion. Then Braid thought back to the rough and the untrammelled heather of that time and what they did for his sales of two-shilling balls. 'Yes,' he added, 'for a couple of years mine was a very good job!'

Slightly more than a month after the opening match and closely following the Open at Sandwich came the course's first open professional tournament. There was a

---

[3] *Golfer's Year Book*, 1905.

31

Below:
Vardon, winner of the 1904 match, in action against a backdrop of primitive, treeless heath. The green is that of the old fifth – where a drive on the fifth may land today. The bunker just visible, bottom right, is still there.

Left:
Braid bunkered at the 18th. When the architect needed a bunker wall he would try cutting heather fairly short, then use the sods as though they were turf. Thus, the traditional Walton Heath bunker was 'heathery'.
Golfing

Taylor putting on the first green. The cottage is long gone. Stonecrop, former home of Alick Renshaw, is there now.

Braid driving from the fourth tee. The posts alongside the gallops were still there until recently.
The Bystander

36-hole stroke-play event on the Saturday and the eight best scorers qualified for match-play. More than £100 in prize-money was on offer, with £25 for the winner – yes, as much as that. A hundred pounds then, the same as Braid's salary, would equate to £5,500 today and the winner's reward was half that of the Open champion.

Braid did not play and, while the other top men entered, the Open had sapped their adrenalin and the surprise winner was Rowland Jones (Wimbledon Park).

Braid of course had gone to Sandwich for the 1904 Open with the rest of them. By now using the rubber-cored ball like most players, he had a putt to win (or at least to tie) for the third time in eight years and for the third time he missed, sharing second place with Taylor behind Jack White.

The following year he began his inexorable climb to the summit. Not only did he win his second Open, by five strokes at St. Andrews, he again won the Match-Play – and about that, as it was held at Walton Heath, more later.

At Walton in July he returned a 70 that was regarded as a course record and in December improved on it with a 69 when playing in a four-ball against a Romford pair with everything holed out. 'There is no bogey for the course but it is generally estimated to be equal to a round of 82,' commented a golf writer. 'The handicapping committee would be quite justified in awarding Braid the phenomenal handicap of plus-12 or 13.'

We shall now leave James standing on the 15th tee one bitter day during the 1905/6 winter. Leave him? Yes, there will be plenty of time to catch up on the rest of his remarkable life and times at the appropriate chronological juncture because he will remain part of the Walton Heath furniture for another 45 years.

The drive he has just hit at the 15th will take its place in the Braid legend. The 15th we are talking about we now know as the 14th. Yes, it *is* a bit downhill, yes, it *is* playing down-wind and yes, the ground *is* frost-bound… but the ball has gone 395 yards! It is a distance almost unheard of, measured on the spot by an eminent engineer. 'It was so cold I could scarcely grip my club,' Braid explained, 'I feel sure that if I could have held it properly I would have driven very much further.'

Braid – flaunting his nationality in a studio portrait.

"I was told that James Braid always grips his niblick lightly when in the heather, but I have seen the Walton Heath giant shift a whole whin bush and that cannot be done with a light grip."

C B Macfarlane, *Evening News*, 1921

Chapter Four

'IT'S THE RICH WHAT GETS THE PLEASURE...'

No entry to anyone 'not received in general society'

THE LIST OF MEMBERS in 1904, with the course only just open and the paint on the clubhouse scarcely dry, shows 165 men and 52 women. Who were they? Where had they come from?

The men were an elite of titled gents and prosperous businessmen. The English aristocracy were tending to remain within their rarefied preserves of huntin', shootin', fishin' and racin'; golf clubs, on the other hand, were populated mainly by the successful upper middle class.

Walton Heath, however, was a bit special. Here were 217 leisure-proud Edwardians and new money would clink against old as the membership embraced the current wealth in professions and business. The general atmosphere, though, was distinctly one of high rank and impeccable social standing.

More than half the men, even some who owned local property, gave London addresses and impressive ones at that: Eaton, Belgrave and Cadogan Squares, elegant rectangular strongholds in Soames Forsyte and *Upstairs Downstairs* territory. Sir H.J.L. Graham was to be addressed by secretary Fowler at 'Royal Court, Palace of Westminster,' The Duke of Portland at Grosvenor Square, The Marquis of Dufferin and Ava at Cadogan Square, Lord Walter Gordon-Lennox in Princes Gardens. Others could be found at their West End clubs: White's, Guards', Cavalry... The Honourable Cecil Bingham, one of the Lucans, would be at the Turf in Piccadilly, The Earl of Dalhousie at nearby Bachelors'.

The ensemble boasted 26 dukes, lords, knights and honourables; a large band of MPs, a chorus of barristers, a trio of clergymen and a soloist King's Counsel. Of the 52 ladies 38 were wives, daughters or other relatives – a bevy

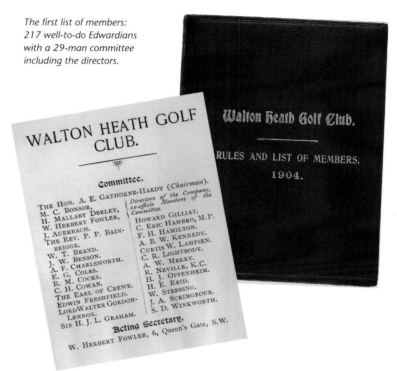

The first list of members: 217 well-to-do Edwardians with a 29-man committee including the directors.

uplifted by the presence among them of The Dowager Countess of Limerick and The Lady Florence Pery, contactable at the same abode in Queen's Gate Gardens.

Many were family or friends of founder members, joining in job lots to swell the ranks and fill the coffers. There were nine Bonsors (five men and four ladies), six Reids (all from Walton Oaks) and three Fowlers.

One or two came into the 'if-you-can't-beat-'em-join-'em' category, notably perhaps Harry M. Crookenden, surely the man who had wanted to prevent the Bonsors from buying the heath? Perhaps those with commoners' rights were automatically granted membership, though the 1904 rules do not say so. Frederick Colman, the mustard man, Cosmo Bonsor's antagonist over the railway, had died, but his relation Jeremiah soon joined and indeed presented the club with one of its first two trophies.[1]

Entry in Golfers' Year Book, 1905, by which time membersip had reached 350. The 1904 date included was really the opening date; the club was constituted in August 1903.

---

[1] The Colman Cup appears to have been played for only once, in 1907. It was recently returned to the club by the family of Frank Easterbrook, the winner. The other early trophy was the Bevan Cup.

33

Arthur J. Balfour, Prime Minister (1902-5) and great populariser of golf.
Cope's cigarette card, 1900.

8.—A. J. BALFOUR.
"Putting the most trying to the Nerves."

CHEAP – IF YOU COULD AFFORD IT!

To the Londoner of moderate means the game of golf is denied. Added to the expense of getting to the neighbouring courses are the heavy subscription fees of all the good clubs. To become a member of Walton Heath Golf Club it is necessary to part with twenty guineas, and the highest tribute that can be paid the club is that, to those who can afford that sum, it is cheap at the price.

Walton Heath is more than a golf club. It is a force in London golf, and it is a social club which can enter into competition with any in the West End. About a mile from Tadworth Station it stretches over a very fine piece of Surrey ground. If it is not as picturesque as Purley Downs, it is rather a better course to play on, being more level, and at the same time very sporting and equally dry.

To make Walton Heath the club it is cost upwards of £8,000.[1] It began its career when the rubber-cored balls came into general use, and whereas many of the older courses are much too short, Walton Heath boasts some very long holes indeed. The fact that there are now upwards of 420 male and 80 lady members of the club, including the Rt. Hon. Arthur J. Balfour MP, and half the inhabitants of Belgravia and Mayfair, proves that golfers have not been long in discovering the merits of the course.

[1] In 1911 the club said that £30,000, perhaps equal to about £2 million today, had been spent.

THE WORLD OF GOLF , 1906

As I was loafin' along the links, an' smokin' my pipe the while,
I seed a man who was goin' round with a most ubbrageous smile.
'E was knockin' the sand off 'is niblick-'ead, and I sez to 'im, 'Oo are you?'
Sez 'e 'Im a Golfer – a very fair Golfer – Golfer and Statesman, too.'
Now 'is work begins at Gawd knows when, an' 'is work is never through;
'E ain't no reglar sportin' toff, nor 'e ain't no professional too,
'E's a kind o' a giddy harumfrodite – Golfer an' Statesman, too.

Robert K. Risk on Balfour,
Songs of the Links (Duckworth), 1919

First 1903 share certificate, made out to one of the Freshfields.

The board of directors (Gathorne-Hardy, Malcolm Bonsor, Mallaby-Deeley and Fowler) were in complete charge. There was a club committee of 29, but the directors nominated it and, in both senses, sat on it. The first committee comprised the earliest debenture-holders and included, it is fair to assume, any men who had joined the Bonsors in financing the club.

Research into these debenture-holders reveals Cosmo's hand in it all. The W.T. Brand listed almost certainly represented the second Mrs Bonsor's family; John Benson was Cosmo's old partner in the railway projects; the Tattenham Park Estate (apart from Benson the only holder of five £100 debentures) was a company formed to acquire property in the area and Cosmo and Benson were two of its three directors. Among the rest, Ralph Neville became a judge, William Stebbing was a deputy editor and leader writer for *The Times* and Edwin Hanson Freshfield, whom we have already met, was many things.

To his professional clients Freshfield was a solicitor; to the lord of the manor, steward; within the club, which he had helped register, a shareholder; to locals, a prominent and perhaps eccentric figure. Legend says that his maid had to run a vacuum cleaner over his Sunday suit after he had put it on and, when attending him, carried a basket containing clean handkerchiefs, eau-de-Cologne and brandy. Or was that his father? To the eternal confusion of local historians, both were named Edwin.

Original first green in foreground. There was a laundry to the left where Stonecrop is now and the posts were for drying lines.

Walton Heath. 3.

Four Freshfields were among the club's first shareholders and they lurk behind the club's birth and infancy like shadowy, all-knowing spirits. But their knowledge is beyond our reach. Precious history went up in smoke when a V2 hit their offices in London's Old Jewry in October 1944.

The committee could elect new members – provided the board agreed and not too many black balls rolled out of the ballot box ('one in seven or two in any number shall exclude,' said the rules). Candidates needed merely a proposer and seconder, but nobody could enter who was 'not received in general society' – in other words no riff-raff! On the other hand 'princes of the blood, ambassadors, *charges d'affaires* and other distinguished persons' could be elected honorary members and those in the Diplomatic Service might be admitted without ballot provided they paid the subscription.

The club publicised special facilities laid on to seduce the members from the comforts of their London pads and the leather armchairs of their West End clubs:

> Arrangements are made for a through service of trains to and from Charing Cross. The tickets, to be issued by the club, will also be available from Victoria by changing at East Croydon. There will be a special train on Sundays, leaving Charing Cross in the morning and returning in the afternoon.

Before leaving, or at the station, these early members soon were able to speed their progress by utilising a recent innovation, the Post Office just having opened its telephone

system to subscribers. By this means they could arrange for a horse brake to meet them at Tadworth and Walton station. And so to the course, where, once off the first tee, they played with a speed that might shock or shame modern players.

The subscription, for the first 300 members at least, was five guineas and the entrance fee ten, while ladies paid two and three guineas respectively. As a writer in *The World of Golf* magazine made clear two years after the launch, when the entrance fees had risen to 15

Charles Dick was one of the club's outstanding early players. He won eight gold medals. Six are on display in the clubhouse.

The Sportfolio, 1896

and five guineas respectively, you got what you paid for and in this case it was a first-class club and course.

How were all these members recruited? The answer, I believe, was via the old boy network. That 1904 list bears the stamp of discreet but persuasive personal canvassing of acquaintances by the Bonsors, Fowlers, Freshfields and their like.

A few members of other local clubs transferred their allegiance, or joined Walton as an additional home; and was there also, I wonder, some thread leading from the Prince's club on Mitcham Common – long established, with at least 700 members? The evidence is circumstantial, contradictory and intriguing.

Consider the Walton hierarchy. Cosmo Bonsor was on the Prince's committee, chairman Gathorne-Hardy was a

> I calculate I could have repeated the Lord's Prayer and the Apostles' Creed between the time when he begins to address the ball on the tee and the final impact.
>
> Prime Minister Herbert Asquith, on playing golf with Lord Crewe, Walton Heath member and committee man.

Members of Parliament flocked to play at Prince's, Mitcham, before that club lost its exclusivity on the Common. Some of them had by then moved to Walton Heath or joined it as an additional club.

member there and Mallaby-Deeley ('the prince of Prince's') was that club's Gilbertian Pooh-Bah and eventual owner. Consider the character of the memberships. Prince's was a fashionable haunt of MPs; Walton Heath courted the same clientele and succeeded in seducing them. Gathorne-Hardy and Mallaby-Deeley, both MPs in their time, could have helped persuade more of their parliamentary friends into the Walton membership. Fowler's course on the downs was superior to anything Mitcham could offer and the area, as Cosmo and his colleagues had planned, was becoming an upmarket place to live.

But why should G-H and M-D help foster a club that in retrospect would seem a rival to their own? Did they despair of an end to their problems with the Mitcham locals who wanted use of their common? Did Mallaby-Deeley see Walton Heath as an alternative course for his members? A decade later he had plans to build one on Banstead Heath for that very purpose. Whatever the circumstances, from a list of 60 early Prince's members collated from various sources I find that at least 25-per-cent of them, including ex-premier Balfour, were, also or instead, playing at Walton before World War I.

Walton Heath, whatever its catchment area, was clearly for successful people. Those combined fees and subscriptions of 20 and eight guineas may sound cheap, but not when you realise that eight million people, a third of the work force, were bringing home 25 shillings (£1.25) or less a week. Add a set of clubs at seven shillings each, a canvas bag at the same price and balls at 10 shillings a dozen, to say nothing of a knickerbocker suit and accoutrements, payments to caddies, sustenance in the clubhouse and all the odds and ends of club life and you may imagine the plight even, say, of an Edwardian clerk. Joining and playing would have cost him probably £50 at least during the first year, perhaps a third of his wages. The miracle of the Industrial Revolution was over and the working man's income had declined in value.

As to the villagers, forget them. Golf was not a labourer's game – and even if it had been, how could a man consider applying for membership in a class-conscious society and when he was earning £1 a week, with his wife perhaps budgeting for the family's food alone on five shillings? As they were soon singing in the music halls, in these circumstances it is 'the rich what gets the pleasure.'

Walton Heath was not a local club, it was a London club. It was a country club for Londoners in much the same way as Mallaby-Deeley's second Prince's club at Sandwich would become an away-day bolt-hole for City gents seeking seaside golf.

Within a year a few of the more rebellious villagers were causing concern, standing in the way of golfers or actually trying to play. Freshfield approached Ralph Neville for advice and the KC had no doubts: anyone not exercising any rights of common vested in him was a trespasser and so, therefore, was anyone obstructing play or golfing without authority. A prosecution? Ah, that might be more difficult.

The villagers as a whole, though, could not be ignored. Some sincerely wanted to golf and accordingly members helped them form an Artisans club[1] with opportunities to play. Others were needed to work on the course and in the clubhouse and WHGC became the biggest employer in the district.

Caddies were also wanted – and were about to bring trouble.

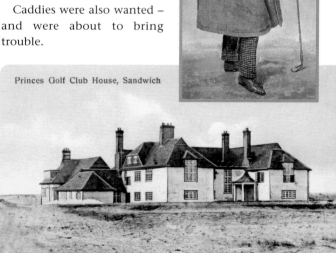

Harry Mallaby-Deeley, though a Walton Heath director, was a leading light at Prince's, Mitcham, at the same time and was starting a second Prince's club at Sandwich. Spy's cartoon of him was in Vanity Fair *in 1909.*

Princes Golf Club House, Sandwich

---

[1] Chapter 41.

Chapter Five

DEATH OF A CADDIE
'I struck at him with my iron … it caught his head'

Shillin' a day,
Bloomin' good pay.
Lucky to touch it,
A shillin' a day.[1]

K IPLING might have been writing not about soldier O'Kelley but of the first Walton Heath caddies. A shilling is what they earned for an 18-hole round. The caddiemaster collected an additional threepence – a penny as a booking fee for the club and twopence for the caddie's lunch.

Some of these caddies, though, did *not* consider that shilling bloomin' good pay, nor that they were lucky in other respects, and at the start of the club's second season this led to tragedy.

On Sunday, May 21, 1905, the caddies, or at least the older ones, went on strike. When stockbroker Charles Pilcher and barrister Reginald Coventry arrived to play that morning they found a crowd of them with other militants and hangers-on massed on the first tee. Boys were available but were reluctant to carry for fear of the rabble-rousers considering them scabs. A few crept furtively out on to the course before joining their players and Pilcher managed to find a teenager, John Smith, willing to carry for him.

When Pilcher and Coventry, apparently with another man, Arthur Kelly, went out again in the afternoon a mob 150 to 200 strong followed them, and on the second green, after Pilcher had complained, violence erupted. An assault on Pilcher and his caddie and what happened to Edward Earl, allegedly one of the assailants, was graphically described in the *Surrey Mirror*:

> The boy Smith was opposed by 150 hostile caddies, and in the ensuing fight Earl was hit on the head (*by Pilcher*) with a steel-shod club. The force of the blow was such that the club was broken in two and the steel head firmly embedded in the man's skull. A portion of the cloth cap Earl was wearing was also driven into his head.

Earl, unconscious, was taken to his home at Withybed Corner, Walton, by Pilcher and then rushed to Guy's Hospital in London.

The first upshot was that five Tadworth and Walton villagers, including the absent Earl, were charged at Epsom Pettty Sessions with 'unlawfully and wickedly conspiring,

Fishing-for-ball techniques on the Old course. One caddie succeeds by the 'toes' method; the other two take a dive.
Top: Golf Illustrated, 1913.
Bottom: Golfing, 1923.

combining and agreeing together to assault and beat divers persons' – that is to say Pilcher, Smith and Kelly. The prosecutor, Mr MacMahon, said that the members had only wanted to protect themselves and their caddies and that Mr W.J. Hart, for the defence, was prepared to consent to the defendants being bound over to keep the peace for six months.

Hart, however, stressed that while the defendants would consent to being bound over, this was against his advice. His defence would have been an absolute denial of any assault by them. Only Earl, whom he was not representing, had taken part, and had he been present in court and not in hospital would have been in a position to prove that the disturbance would not have happened at all had it not been for an act by Pilcher in the first place. 'I might say,' he added, 'that I have had instructions to apply for a cross-summons against Mr. Pilcher for assault.'

The reason the defendants were willing to be bound

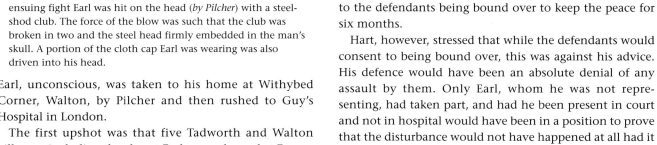

---

[1] *Barrack Room Ballads* (Methuen), 1892.

43

RULES
AS TO
EMPLOYMENT OF CADDIES.

1.—The Superintendent shall keep a General Register of all Caddies allowed to carry Clubs.

2.—Boys desirous of becoming Caddies must submit their names to the Superintendent, who will place them, if approved, on the Register, and allot each one a numbered badge.

3.—No Caddie under the age of 15 years shall be employed on Sundays.

4.—Badges shall be given out to all Caddies when engaged, which must be worn on the arm while engaged, and returned to the Superintendent at the end of the engagement.

5.—The Tariff for Caddies shall be 1s. per round of 18 holes, and 8d. for 12 holes or less. There will also be an extra charge of 3d. per round or part of a round, 1d. of which will be retained by the Club as a Booking Fee, and the remaining 2d. will be paid to the Caddie as luncheon money.

6.—A Member wishing to bespeak a Caddie for an afternoon round can only do so provided the Caddie is disengaged at the time wanted.

7.—If a Caddie is engaged in the forenoon and from any cause is not taken out till the afternoon, two rounds must be paid for.

8.—Members must engage their Caddies through the Caddie Superintendent only, and on no account pay them direct. All payments for Caddies must be made to the Superintendent at his office.

9.—At lunch time and at the close of play Caddies must clean the Clubs in the shed provided for the purpose.

10.—The Superintendent shall keep a daily register of all Caddies who have been employed and the Members or Visitors employing them, showing the payment made to each Caddie and the booking Fee, &c.

11.—The Superintendent shall, as far as possible, give equal employment to the Caddies, but Members may direct him to engage the Caddies they prefer.

Extract from 1904 members' book.

over, said Hart, was that the Bench had no power to deal with a charge of conspiracy, which would have had to be sent for trial. These villagers were poor men and could not have afforded to contest the charges. The Bench ultimately agreed that they should merely be bound over.

But what about Edward Earl, a local labourer with a wife and family, lying in hospital with a fractured skull, apparently recovering but still unaware of the proceedings? MacMahon asked that the summons against him be held over; Hart suggested it be withdrawn.

The Clerk: *'He might issue a summons for assault.'*
MacMahon: *'I do not wish to be prejudiced in the event of that taking place.'*

Eventually it was agreed that if the summons against Earl were withdrawn the Club members would not reintroduce it – provided the injured man did not take proceedings against Pilcher.

On July 2, six weeks after the affray, came tragic news: Earl had died. The club was now involved not just in an affray but, whatever the circumstances, in a death caused by a blow delivered by one of its members. Pilcher might be charged not with assault but with something far worse.

At an inquest at Southwark Coroner's Court both Pilcher and the club were represented legally, as was Earl's widow. Pilcher gave evidence personally:

When the crowd came on in a menacing attitude I mildly remonstrated with them. 'Now then, you men,' I said, 'you ought not to press us like that, why don't you clear out?' A boy named Bowyer then rushed at me and struck me several times about the chest and body. I put out my hand to hold him at arm's length. Bowyer struck me one or two more blows, but I swear solemnly that I never retaliated by hitting him.

The crowd closed round me and beat me with clubs and fists. My wooden club had been wrenched from my hand and to keep the peace I didn't try to recover it. They tried to get me down and used threats toward me.

While I was being struck on the back I turned to see who was hitting me and saw Earl coming toward me as if to strike me on the face with his fist. At that moment I saw my bag beside me, pulled out a club and struck at him with it. He ducked and the iron end caught his head. That was the only blow I gave and it was entirely in self-protection.

Smith, the young caddie whose willingness to work had been the underlying cause of the melée, said he was given a black eye and thrown to the ground, where the crowd continued to strike him. Club members described the struggle in detail. One of them, Stephenson Kent, explained that when he arrived on the scene he had tried to protect the caddie but was hit on the head, after which he heard some of the mob saying Pilcher had killed a man and threatening to lynch him.

Coventry, giving evidence with the practised fluency of a barrister, said that about 30 men had surrounded Pilcher, some with their arms round his neck. Yes, he had seen the fatal blow struck. Pilcher had raised his cleek above the heads of the crowd and swung it and Earl had been caught as he ducked. Pilcher then had tended Earl in every way possible.

Coroner: *'Are you of the opinion that Mr Pilcher did what he did in self-defence?'*
Coventry: *'Oh, perfectly.'*

The coroner, summing up, declared that the crowd was an unlawful assembly in law and that a man defending himself and causing death in an encounter with such an assembly could not legally be held guilty of anything more than excusable homicide. The jury found 'that the deceased met his death by a blow from a club hurled by Mr Pilcher in self-defence.'

So ended the tragic affair – of which not a word appeared in the club minutes.

That 1905 mob of between 150 and 200 were not all caddies and had almost certainly been swollen by militant supporters. Be that as it may, the amount of golf being played was necessitating a large army of bag-carriers. By 1911 some 20,000 rounds a year were being played; the

NOTICE

Regulations for playing golf on Walton Heath:
No person is permitted to play golf on Walton Heath except the following:
1. Members of the Walton Heath Golf Club
2. Members of the Walton-on-the-Hill Village Club
3. Before 9 a.m. and after 6 p.m. village boys under 15 years of age and caddies employed by the Walton Heath Golf Club.
By Order
Edwin Freshfield
Steward of the Manor

Notice agreed by lord of the manor in 1907

'AFFORDS A LOVELY VIEW OF THE HEATH AND COURSE'

1904

Times change! From the clubhouse in 1904 one had a widely publicised 'lovely view' of the heath. On the postcard reproduced above, the servant on the right of the group was identified by the sender as 'Edith' – almost certainly Edith Morgan, who retired 50 years later. Gradually the clubhouse would alter...

1911 or earlier. Bungalow to right was once lived in by the Holderness family, including Amateur champion Sir Ernest.

1911 (or earlier). Horse carriages still bring members to the club. The original steeple has disappeared.

Left: Original plan from Boulton and Paul advertisement. Entrance was from the verandah side.

1913 New ladies' wing – Above: the sitting room. Left: the dining room, with new additions. The Gentlewoman

1913 Re-developed ladies' quarters on left.

Girls as well as men ineligible for military service were called in as caddies during World War I.

following year the figure of 37,000 was being quoted. A hundred-and-thirty caddies a day were often present and 200 were catered for at a supper the club laid on for them around this time. Many tended to be small, perhaps coming from the racing stables around Epsom. Some walked up to 14 miles to and from their homes. Others slept rough on the heath and at times they were a necessary evil.

Complaints proliferated. In 1906 the local sanitary inspector protested that caddies were using a field near the clubhouse for improper purposes – a practice at least partly stopped by the club at a cost of £19, the bill for a lavatory. Soon, a policeman had to patrol near their quarters for three successive Sundays. As the years rolled by there was damage to the shelter behind the first tee when one or two took up permanent residence there… insolence to members… and caddies 'never to be employed again,' the banes of the lives of the caddiemasters, a few of whom were in turn a bane on the lives of the club committee.

Meanwhile a silent majority philosophically got on with their job of carrying, advising and club cleaning, thankfully consuming their bread and soup and even more gratefully pocketing their fees and tips. In 1908 some of these received their reward when the club introduced a category of 'guaranteed' caddies, selected largely on the basis of good behaviour on and off the course. They were retained on a minimum wage of £2 a month and took priority in going out. At first there were 25 of them; within five years there would be 50.

Privilege would soon be blended with discipline: the caddies and members of the green staff were expected to enrol in the Territorial Army. Fears of war were widespread and *Golfing* praised Walton's plan on two fronts, military and moral:

> This example will almost certainly be followed by other leading clubs and lead to a considerable addition to the enlistments for the coming year. What is perhaps even more important, the men will learn a little wholesome discipline, become physically well trained and lose something of the air of the habitual loafer that afflicts so many of them. A good deal of their somewhat abundant time will also be profitably and patriotically occupied.

The club directors subscribed to a new drill hall and set up a company to provide and maintain it. Alas, after a promising start the 'wholesome discipline' of the caddies' unit began to fall apart in the face of the enemy – innate laziness. Within four years a Captain Chetwynd Stapleton wrote complaining that the men lacked enthusiasm due to 'the liberal way they were treated by the club' and suggesting that they should be paid less. 'The board decided to action his proposals,' says the minute book.

The club's attitudes were sometimes influenced by wider social implications. Church and welfare groups, Edwardian do-gooders and local nuisances all applied pressure on occasions, complaining that under-age caddies had been hired and pointing to the evils of employing youngsters to carry golf clubs when they should be learning a proper trade. 'The club does not employ boy caddies,' *Country Life* would claim in 1914. Really? Well, they had certainly been available for hire. Boys were specifically mentioned in the first rules in 1904, when the only restriction was that under-15s could not be employed on Sundays; and the board later ordained that all Saturday caddies under that age were to receive 11d a round. In the future, members would be asked to use as few clubs as possible so as not to over-burden the many small boys and girls acting as caddies. On the other hand, many of the caddies were pensioners or reservists.

Caddies set out in mixed-golf company.

The club's treatment of its caddies was generally paternalistic. They could play early in the morning or in the evening; the suppers were annual events; their sheds were improved, though rarely before time; those who sought permanent employment were helped to find it.

In 1914, conscious that the demand for caddies dwindled in August and September when members were on holiday, the club planned to pay for 30 or more of them to go to Scotland or the south coast, where clubs might utilise their services.

This gesture was tragically nullified. World War One intervened and many caddies found themselves not carrying bags at seaside resorts but fighting in the mud of Mons, Ypres and other hell holes.

THE RIDDELL YEARS

SIR GEORGE ALLARDICE RIDDELL – after the painting by Sir William Orpen, RA. The signed 1919 original is in the Scottish National Portrait Gallery collection.

Chapter Six

THE GREAT DICTATOR
Out go the directors, in marches George Riddell

AT 3PM ON NOVEMBER 13, 1905, everything at Walton Heath began to change. Malcolm Bonsor, deputising for Gathorne-Hardy, took the chair for a board meeting at Freshfields' premises in Old Jewry. By the end of the meeting he and his co-directors, except for Herbert Fowler, were out and George Allardice Riddell, Sir Alexander Kennedy and Edward Hudson had taken over. Riddell, one of the earliest members and the solicitor who witnessed Braid's contract, would dominate the club for nearly 30 years.

What manner of man was Riddell, this tall, thin, stooping figure in old jackets and shabby trousers? Do you want the long version or the short one? You have no choice, it will have to be the long one. He was complicated, a man people admired, feared or despised:

> He is a man of great geniality and wide sympathies and enjoys the affectionate regard of all classes of golfers.   *Golf Illustrated*

> The more I discover about him the less I like him!
> *Jean Clew, local historian*

> Though in some ways a repulsive character, he was a very shrewd observer and certainly no sycophant.
> *John Grigg, author*[1]

> Riddell's god was wealth and he pursued it to the exclusion of all else.
> *John McEwen, editor*[2]

Stafford Somerfield, former editor of the *News of the World*, has left us the most critical account of this contradictory character in his book *Banner Headlines*.[3] Riddell said he came from Scotland; indeed once pointed out the Berwickshire house where he was born. Rubbish, apparently! Somerfield says that he was born, son of a struggling

'Brim-hatted, formal in stiff, high-winged collar... concentrating on his game'. Riddell drawn by Charles Ambrose.
Golf Illustrated, *1914*

photographer, in a small semi-detached house in Brixton, south London. His father died when George was a baby and the boy and his mother were subsidised by a kind uncle. Sensitivity about his upbringing left him with a chip on his shoulder and aggressive financial ambition.

He began as an office boy for his uncle's solicitor and at 23 was a senior partner, obsessed with raising capital to satisfy a huge interest in buying property. Somerfield quotes early signs of his ruthlessness toward occupiers he wanted to remove from houses: 'He harried them to the limit. His dictum was "When conciliation fails, crush... I can't afford mercy".'

He was a workaholic. The day he married he went to work, took an hour off for the ceremony, then returned to the office. Predictably, the marriage did not last, and when he became successful he saw to it that *Debrett's* and *Who's Who* ignored it, just as he got them to believe in his allegedly fictitious birthplace.

For Riddell the road to wealth began in Cardiff, through contacts he met as London agent for that city's corporation and some Welsh solicitors. In 1891 he helped journalist Henry Lascelles Carr, joint owner of the *Western Mail*, to negotiate purchase of the financially threatened *News of the World* and, aged 26, was appointed its secretary and legal advisor. There was no money, so he took 192 £10 shares from the other directors in lieu of fees. Soon he was managing director and proprietor.

'More than anyone, he came to be responsible for the financial success of the paper,' writes Somerfield. He bent rules, dismissed shareholders' meetings in short order, appointed sales agents throughout the country, began special distribution trains, dreamed up ideas and personally distributed handbills ('Good old *News of the World*!'... 'The best family newspaper'... 'Known all over the globe!'... 'All for a penny!').

[1] and [2] *The Riddell Diaries*, (Athlone Press).
[3] Scan Books, 1979.

Overwork, irregular eating and lack of sleep broke his health. Resting in a nursing home, he decided to cease work as a solicitor, confine himself to his newspaper proprietorship and change his lifestyle. He resolved to give up cigars. When telling a friend how he had done so he seemed unaware of the cigarette ash spilling down his waistcoat. More successfully, he promised himself fresh air and exercise. He took up golf.

When he, Kennedy and Hudson took over Walton Heath in 1905, Riddell was 40 and again married – to Annie, daughter of the kind uncle. He had masterminded the *News of The World* from a 51,000-copies-a-week paper that struggled to pay bills into a vibrant enterprise with

Bunkered by choice! The photographers w following the Bishop of London, hoping to see him play out of a bunker. 'No, take a picture of me!' said Riddell, keen to take t pressure off the bishop. It wasn't what th Press wanted, but they were happy once Riddell had ordered champagne for them
The World of Golf, 1

LORD RIDDELL AND WALTON HEATH

TO THE EDITOR OF THE TIMES

Sir,—I notice in the report of Lord Riddell's will a general statement that he was the founder of this club. As this is entirely untrue I shall be obliged if you will allow me to give you true particulars of how the club was started.

In 1899 my brother-in-law, the late Sir Cosmo Bonsor, consulted me as to the possibility of making a golf course on Walton Heath. I told him I was certain I could make a first-class course on part of the heath. In 1902 he bought the manorial rights and engaged me to lay out the course and form the club. In 1904 (May 11) the course was formally opened for play. I was appointed managing director of the limited company. This post I have held continuously till the present day.

In 1905, 18 months after the formal opening of the club, Lord Riddell, Sir Alexander Kennedy, and Mr. Edward Hudson purchased Sir Cosmo Bonsor's interest in the club and they became directors of the club. Up to that time none of them had any interest in the club beyond being ordinary members.

You will see that Sir Cosmo Bonsor was the founder of the club.

Yours truly,
W. HERBERT FOWLER.
Walton Heath Golf Club, Tadworth, Surrey.

The Times, January 22, 1935

staggering financial growth. He had spectacularly increased his holdings and was making a fortune.

Why the club board should sell out to the three men so soon is clouded in doubt, and the answer to the riddle, like much else, was lost in the bombing of the Freshfields' offices. The November 1905 meeting seems merely to have rubber-stamped prior agreements. We know that Riddell had written to Edwin Hanson Freshfield proposing terms and that the takeover was deemed advantageous to everyone ('We are all acting as personal friends,' said Riddell in his letter).

Gathorne-Hardy sent a note resigning because he had been appointed to a public office and Riddell was immediately chosen to replace him as a director. Before the meeting ended the resignations of Bonsor and Mallaby-Deeley were also recorded. Kennedy and, at a later date, Hudson, the only one not an original club member, were chosen as their successors and Kennedy was subsequently made chairman.

Only Fowler, managing director and secretary, had survived, but Bonsor was still the club's landlord. Money the company had borrowed from the Bonsors since the lease was drawn up was repaid, the three new men subscribing to a new debenture issue of £4,000 from which the cash was to be obtained, while Malcolm's shares were transferred to them.

Perhaps there were concerns about the club's finances? Perhaps that is why the directors, at a previous meeting, had shelved plans to alter the clubhouse and why Bonsor had agreed to forgo the first year's rent? Now that the railway and club were in place, possibly he and his father were content to recoup, remain members and await further increases in property values?

What we can conjecture about with more confidence are Riddell's personal motives for wanting to take over the club. His new enthusiasm for golf… a tie-up for the *News of the World*… the opportunity to make and entertain influential new contacts as he climbed the social and political ladders… his immense interest in local property investment… perhaps all these things jostled in his canny, acquisitive mind.

Whatever his calculations, with his two cohorts and Fowler at his elbow, Riddell was now set for an astonishing three decades of autocratic rule and at their first meeting the new regime made a confident start, agreeing £365 for a new dressing room and 15 shillings each for replacement lockers – which they would sell to members at £2.

Who were Alex Kennedy and Edward Hudson? Kennedy, 58 and recently knighted, was an eminent electrical engineer, while Hudson, 51, was in high-quality printing and passionately devoted to illustrating fine houses, paintings and other items of beauty. Hudson played off about 12 and Kennedy 16 – and off the course the two probably shared interests in music, photography and the exploration of archaeology in Petra, all pursuits of Kennedy's alongside Alpine-climbing.

Like Riddell, Hudson was described venomously by certain bitchy contemporaries, who deemed him dull, unattractive and a social climber. 'A gargoyle of a monstrosity,' said artist Dora Carrington charmingly. 'A typical minor Establishment figure with no general culture,' commented someone else.

'Huddy' owned *Country Life* and it was his dearest love: he controlled its policy for 35 years. The publication represented a genteel Edwardian existence, a rose-petalled concoction of fine art and architecture, refined furniture and décor, scented gardens, tennis on the lawn and golf in the country. It reflected the soft sunlight of an era of sweeping dresses and sumptuousness, the blessings of peace before the horrors of war. Hudson and *Country Life*  cultivated a close-knit coterie of friends and contributors: from Alfred Lyttelton, politician and sporting hero, and Horace Hutchinson, golf correspondent, to Gertrude Jekyll, garden designer, and Edwin (later Sir Edwin) Lutyens, architect.

Walton became part of that world. Riddell was on *Country Life's* board – a badge of rural culture to balance the banner headlines of his *News of the World*. The magazine afforded the club favourable mentions and carried advertisements for nearby villas. Affluent readers came to play, join and survey desirable plots, some of which were owned by, yes,

Above: The fourth board member: Edward Hudson, of Country Life*, as seen by cartoonist 'Mac'.*

Below: The Dormy House *– designed by Lutyens.*

Three of the four directors: from left to right, Kennedy, Riddell and Fowler.
The World of Golf, *1906*

George Riddell. Moreover, by 1906 the new directors had, in Riddell's name, commissioned Lutyens to design *The Dormy House* on land they had bought by the clubhouse, and almost immediately the same rising architect produced Fowler's *Chussex* on a plot owned by Riddell.

Christopher Hussey, a *Country Life* editor, wrote that these buildings, with two others, 'established the mode, almost by their own influence, of English architecture for a generation.' Pevsner, the German-born architectural historian, judged them 'sadly pedestrian.' To these opinions may be added that of Beatrice Broad, 40 years a member, who has a flat in *Dormy House*: 'One of Sir Edwin's *minor* masterpieces!' she suggested to me, tongue in cheek, as we stood in the truncated garden and studied the building's faded glories.

Building the *Dormy House* was a personal enterprise, not a club one. Riddell, Kennedy and Hudson, indeed, leased it to the club company of which they were directors at £300 a year (about £20,000 today), a figure reduced to £250 when the company bought the furniture and fittings for £950.

Riddell, Kennedy, Hudson and Fowler, media man, engineer, aesthete and banker-turned-course-architect, were unlikely bedfellows. Nonetheless they ruled the club together for 23 years until Kennedy died. As before, there were committees, but again the directors nominated and sat on them. The earliest minutes of the members' committee I have found date from 1909 and the sense of priority displayed by Messrs Lightbody, Cocks, Michie and Fowler under Kennedy's chairmanship was reassuring: their first decision was 'to purchase such wines, beer and spirits as may be necessary for the members.' Fowler, incidentally, was a teetotaller and Riddell rarely touched the stuff.

The committee dealt with golf, the welfare of the members and the election of new ones; the directors

Riddell shows the way at an Advertisers' event at Purley Downs in 1914.
Golfing

dictated policy and controlled the finances. Riddell's period in power embraced what we may still recognise as the most significant happenings in the club's first 70 years apart from the initial conception and the signing of Braid – and it has even been said, though never confirmed, that Riddell was involved in getting the great man to Walton. A second course, a new lease, challenge matches and championships, an enlarged membership replete with national celebrities, survival during a world war, royal patronage… all these are ingredients for future chapters. If there were any sort of pie, Riddell would have a finger in it.

Riddell's rise continued to match that of his newspaper. During his lifetime the *News of the World* circulation rocketed toward four million on its way to more than double that figure. He would become chairman, principal shareholder and proprietor, knight, baronet and peer – and the first divorced commoner to enter the House of Lords.

Golf had hooked him. Often he played four or five times a week. He would deal with work papers in bed, be chauffeured to Walton in his Rolls, play, have lunch, then be driven to his office in Bouverie Street off Fleet Street.

Playing frequently with Braid but increasingly with political friends, he cut a singular figure – brim-hatted, formal in stiff, high-winged collar, continually talking about all manner of subjects yet concentrating on his game and urging on his partners ('Great stuff, great stuff!'). Bernard Darwin remembered him 'putting with his right foot drawn far back, while he leered, or perhaps I should say scowled, at the ball over his left shoulder.'

Sir Hedley Le Bas – caricature by H.F. Crowther Smith in The Sketch, *1926.*

With Braid's help he got down to five. He liked to win and would wager on his ability to do so. He was willing to gamble on things if he could influence the outcome – but not unless, and that is why he shunned the Stock Exchange.

Occasionally the opinionated and dictatorial sides of his nature would spill over into his club life. A member who was boss of a brewery (Cosmo Bonsor perhaps?) once asked him if he would agree that the *News of the World* over-publicised crime. 'No,' stormed Riddell, 'We fight crime – and a lot of that crime is caused by your bloody beer!' Another day two young bloods swept into the grounds in a flashy sports car, saw a rather shabby, ageing figure and asked if he knew where the caddiemaster was. 'Yes, I do,' growled Sir George, 'but he doesn't want any more caddies.'

More serious was a feud that blew up between him and a prominent member. Hedley Le Bas was his friend and golfing consort and a fellow director on boards including those of George Newnes and the Caxton Publishing Company, but in 1915, with Le Bas in line for a knighthood, Sir George for some reason alleged in print that his colleague had in past times worked as a door-to-door book pedlar and in a billiards saloon. Le Bas and his family hit the roof and retaliated.

'Le Bas has proved to be a low blackguard,' *wrote Riddell in his diary on September 15.* 'Having offended him over some small matter he wrote me two blackmailing letters in which he threatened to expose my divorce proceedings and charged me with obtaining £500 from him by fraud three years ago. The £500 was part of a sum of £1,000 paid to Lloyd George in connection with the publishing of his "Life".'

Court action was threatened; Riddell, hoping for a baronetcy, feared that his reputation was at stake; the club became involved.

'Any chance of a reconciliation became impossible,' *recalled John McEwen, editing a collection of Riddell's diary entries.*[4] 'There is a story, impossible to confirm, that they chanced to meet on the clubhouse veranda and exchanged strong words, whereupon Le Bas seized Riddell and pitched him unceremoniously into some nearby bushes.'

A letter from Le Bas inflamed the issue. The board predictably took Riddell's side and accordingly Fowler wrote to Le Bas. I have before me a further letter written by Fowler on September 29, 1915:

Dear Le Bas,
I feel I must tell you that I signed the letter from the club company to you because I feel that no member of a club ought to write such a letter as yours of September 2 to a fellow member. It is an impossible letter from a club point of view and I am grieved you should have written it.

[4] *The Riddell Diaries* (Athlone Press).

I fear you have put yourself in a bad position and that your fellow members will consider you had no justification for going to such lengths. Many other friends of yours also deplore the bitterness with which you are carrying on this quarrel.

I should be very glad if I could do anything to help to arrive at an understanding, but if that is impossible please believe that it has caused me real pain to have to write to you as I did and now do. I have done so in the firm belief that I am thereby showing you real friendship.

Yours, WHF.

The bad blood continued to run. In their business worlds George Newnes Ltd eventually prevailed on Le Bas to leave its board and correspondingly Riddell withdrew from Caxton's.

That unsavoury incident apart, and give or take a few minor spats, golf and Walton Heath saw Riddell at his best and happiest. No doubt he used the club to further his own interests, but, helped by being its boss, he fitted compatibly into what was primarily a man's world.

He made Walton Heath something special. He invited the famous to join without interviews or payment, created honorary members on spontaneous whims and maintained a constant sequence of matches involving Parliament, Press, Church and the Law. It is said that he loved the place, where he spent more and more of his time, like he loved what Somerfield insisted was his imaginary Scottish homeland. When created a peer in 1920 he chose the title 'Baron Riddell of Walton Heath.'

'Baron Riddell of Walton Heath'. His crest includes a carrier pigeon holding a scroll; the arms embrace an ancient printing press; the motto reflects his thirst for knowledge.

Debrett's Peerage

He was Everyman's president, vice-president, captain, patron or host. A stream of societies (London Solicitors, London Press, Newspaper and Advertisers, Horticultural, Lucifers...), national associations (PGA, Greenkeepers, Stewards...), clubs (English, Scottish, Welsh)... the list of places where he held office, donated prizes or was guest of honour is a tribute to his enthusiasm, generosity and, in these circumstances, popularity. Visiting societies whose applications survived rigorous Walton Heath examinations almost swooned at the honour of acceptance, behaved in awe as Riddell distributed largesse and tended to write obsequious gratitudes ('Every member felt grateful to Lord Riddell for his lavish hospitality, his presence at

Presenting a set of clubs to the Duke of York (later King George VI) at the opening of the public course in Richmond Park in 1925.

Golfing

lunch adding warmth to the invitation and affording unmistakeable pleasure to all who were present').[5]

The man who for years refused to tip cab drivers and rode roughshod over employees and tenants felt sincerely for the poor and disadvantaged. He benefited medical centres and, directly or indirectly, his patronage of the Royal Free Hospital brought it about £1½ million. He helped those who wanted to play golf but could not afford to join clubs, co-founding the Artisan Golfers' Association, helping form the Walton Artisans and, with J.H. Taylor, leading the crusade for England's first municipal public course in Richmond Park, Surrey. Professional golfers were also hugely indebted to him and his newspaper.

He was a brilliant after-dinner speaker and had taken elocution lessons to rid himself of any south London accent. 'The poet,' he would begin at a mixed function, 'the poet tells us of

Women in our hour of ease,
Uncertain, coy and hard to please.'

He would then pause, peer over his spectacles, solemnly scrutinise his audience, then deliver his judgment: 'Uncertain, yes... coy, perhaps... but judging by their escorts here tonight, not hard to please!'

As a Liberal he would tell gatherings about two Conservative MPs in a fiercely contested match: 'As things grew more and more tense, one of them, attempting a crucial long iron shot, miss-hit it and sent an enormous divot through the air. He went to replace it but couldn't find

[5] *Graya*, Gray's Inn GS report, 1929.

We, the undersigned Directors of the Walton Heath Golf Club resolve that having regard to the greatly increased expenditure for Repairs and Renewals, Rates, wages, Materials &c. the Board in pursuance of the powers vested in them by the rules hereby increase the Entrance Fees and Subscriptions of Full members elected after the 11th September 1920 from £16.16.0 and £10.10.0 to £21 and £15.15.0 respectively, and of Lady members elected after the 11th September 1920 from £6.6.0 and £6.6.0 to £12.12.0 and £8.8.0 respectively, also that the Entrance Fee and Subscription of Supernumerary members elected after the 4th December 1920 shall be increased from £8.8.0 and £6.6.0 to £10.10.0 and £8.8.0 respectively.

Alex H.W. Kennedy
Hudson
Ethers & Hudson
W. Herbert Fowler

} Directors

Subs going up! Board decision, December, 1920.

it. "Where *is* the bloody sod?" he shouted, and his caddie gave him the answer: "He's up there on the fairway, sir".'

Or had they heard the one about the Walton Heath golfer, 'who in despair said to his caddie, "I can't even putt, I'm going to give up this game". "Oh, I wouldn't do that, sir," replied the caddie, "Sir John Simon plays a lot worse than you and he's a really *intelligent* person"!'

In later years, racked with worry over his health, Lord Riddell moved from his elegant house in Queen Anne's Gate to simple rooms in the dormy house, which by now he had bought outright from Kennedy and Hudson, making it his out-of-town home and re-christening it *Walton Heath House*. Bent-backed and haggard in pain, he was often grouchy and despondent.

But that is not how Jo Bryant, who joined in 1932, remembered him ('He was very sweet. "How's the golf?" he'd ask whenever he saw me'); nor Mrs William Crabtree, who recalled that he once asked her if she was a member. 'No, I'm a student and can't afford the subscription,' she replied. 'Go to the office and say that you are a member from today and that your sub will only be £3,' said Riddell.

This book has not done with Lord Riddell, not by a long chalk, particularly in the matter of the great figures who bestrode course and clubhouse at his urgings and whose worlds he infiltrated. That is a separate subject: I shall treat it

as such and Riddell will appear, so to speak, posthumously.

Because this chapter has tried to paint a picture of his contradictory and mysterious character, let us close it by pressing the fast-forward button and recording his death. 'After death there's nothing left but the grave,' this man who gave Sunday afternoon talks to the Christian Brotherhood had declared, 'and I don't want a lot of my hard-earned money spent on my funeral. You can dump my body in a bloody ditch so far as I'm concerned.'

He died, aged 69, on December 5, 1934. His newspaper shares alone were worth more than £1½ million and his fortune was valued at £2 million, more or less, which today might mean £85 million. Having acquired new holdings as the golf company's capital increased and through buying from his fellow directors, he held 83 per cent of its shares.

Fulsome tributes were spoken and printed. On behalf of the newspaper industry, Lord Beaverbrook:

> Only a man of great attainment could have achieved the results that made his services to the Press so substantial and so honourable. He gave more than his purse; he gave time and care, the dearest gifts of a busy man.

From the world of golf, a magazine editorial:

> He loved the game and did much for it… but of all the things he did Walton Heath must be accounted the greatest and most precious.

Some things about George Allardice Riddell we shall never know. On his instructions, says Somerfield, his wife burned every fragment of his private papers except his handwritten diaries, which were closed to the public for 50 years. From the *News of the World* many documents bearing his name were destroyed and three loads of evidence were taken to an incinerator, their demise witnessed by his confidential clerk.

As dusk approached one evening that winter of 1934/5, Baroness Riddell, who was seen at Walton Heath only rarely, arrived there with Twigg, his valet, carrying the casket of her husband's ashes. Legend, at least, says that, in accordance with his wishes, they made their way to the eighth hole, highest on the course and furthest from the clubhouse, and there poured his ashes on to the turf – and that his widow said:

> There, that's the end of him.

His fortune was equivalent to about million today.

Golf Illustrated, 7

A Whitehall Brush-Off

8. *Bouverie Street.*
Fleet Street.
London, August 8th. 1911.
E.C.

212493

My dear Mr Churchill,

    Herewith I send you the Petition in regard to the Walton Heath Golf Club. It is rather bald but I have no doubt it will serve the purpose.

        Yours very faithfully,

        George A. Riddell

To The Right Honourable Winston Spencer Churchill M.P.
His Majesty's Secretary of State for Home Affairs

The Humble Petition of The Walton Heath Golf Club Limited of Walton on the Hill, in the County of Surrey.

Sheweth

1. The Walton Heath Golf Club is admittedly one of the leading Golf Clubs in Great Britain.

*R*iddell, often out for personal advancement, had corresponding and perhaps related ambitions for Walton Heath. In 1911 he sought approval for it to be called 'Royal Walton Heath.' Hitherto this fact has remained virtually unknown, but now, with Robert Ruddell's esteemed help, I have unearthed official Government papers on the subject.

The petition was addressed not to Buckingham Palace but to one of the club's newest members – Winston S. Churchill. He happened also to be Home Secretary.

On August 8, 1911, Riddell sent Churchill two letters. One was personal, courting him with an invitation to golf. The other covered the petition. 'It is rather bald but I have no doubt it will serve the purpose,' wrote Riddell with a certain arrogance.

The 'humble petition' of The Walton Heath Golf Club Limited made seven points: Walton Heath was one of Britain's leading clubs; the course was the best inland and one of the world's finest; £30,000 had been spent on the club and its amenities; the course was a convenient and healthful centre for recreation, largely used by cabinet ministers, politicians, judges, civil servants, businessmen, lawyers and doctors ('no course in the world possesses a more influential and important membership'); important competitions were held there and societies accepted; Braid was the professional; and an artisans' club had been formed.

Finally: 'Your petitioners are desirous that His Majesty should graciously grant to them the right and privilege to use the title 'The Royal Walton Heath Golf Club'; and your Petitioners will ever pray – George A. Riddell, W.H. Fowler, directors.

Churchill apparently did his bit in support. 'Secretary of State is anxious to get it done unless there are any strong reasons against,' wrote a Whitehall official, passing the buck to others along the corridors of power. Those 'others' decided that there were strong reasons against:

Walton Heath has about 700 members and is no doubt very prosperous, but it does not appear to have a stronger claim than other courses round London (e.g. Woking, Byfleet, Sunningdale or Worplesdon) and compliance could create a rather awkward precedent...
Walton Heath has certainly no more claim to the title 'Royal' than the above-mentioned clubs and in my opinion they have none... they are not leading clubs like the R&A, Hoylake and Sandwich, which have championship courses and a voice in the management of the championships. Nor have they claims like the Irish and Welsh clubs honoured as representing the principal centres of the game in those countries. It

seems out of the question to confer the title upon them all because they are prosperous and have good courses and it would excite criticism and discontent if one was singled out which has no more right to it than the others...

One of the civil servants drew attention to a matter of principle:

In 1903 Hunstanton was refused on the ground that it was a limited company.

Another, commenting on the reference to Braid, at once praised him and indicated disdain of his master:

A decent man, who remains unspoiled in spite of this sort of thing.

The last words on the Home Office documents, apparently written to Churchill, are:

I have been corresponding with Sir G. Riddell about this. He had been under the impression that Sunningdale and certain other clubs had the title, and now that he knows the facts he quite agrees to let the matter drop.

A likely story! In retrospect, the request appears premature and arrogant – based on slender claims and without evidence, at the time, of any royal connections. Later the evidence would be far, far stronger.

CECILIA ("CECIL") LEITCH, Walton Heath's greatest lady player.
The Tatler, *1910*

Chapter Seven

CORSETS AND BOATERS TO BERETS AND BROGUES
— and Miss Leitch shows the ladies how to play

PRAY SETTLE DOWN with a gin and tonic on your veranda, ladies and gentlemen – yes, thank you, I will have one – and picture through the haze the lady members playing on the heath a hundred years ago.

The scene is colourful but decorous. 'When anyone is outrageously dressed it casts a slur on the whole society of lady golfers,' said May Hezlet, thrice British champion. They are wearing straw boaters decorated with ribbon, or perhaps caps or trilby-type hats. Blouses or shirts are high-collared and worn with ties. If your vision is of winter the jerseys may be a fashionable bright red and the jackets are sturdy Norfolk tweed.

Skirts? Avert your eyes, gentlemen. The creations of the 'nineties, long, awkward and conspiring with corsets to make a free swing an impossible dream, have been beginning to give way to mini-skirts, five inches off the ground if you please! The hem may be banded with leather to save the material from mud, and round my lady's waist may be elastic, which she can lower to just above the knees to prevent embarrassment as well as impeded action. 'Otherwise a sudden gust of wind might prove fatal at the critical moment,' warns a fashion writer.

These ladies will have been accepted grudgingly by some of the male members, for that was the norm. The objections, wrote John Lowerson,[1] stemmed from the women's supposed weakness, their short hitting and 'slowness of play made worse by chatter' – plus concerns on the one hand about de-feminisation and on the other the distraction caused by a shapely feminine swing.

Thus was born the legend of The Lady Golfer. 'Yes,' Henry Longhurst once observed to me, 'Mary Queen of Scots was the *first* lady golfer to be beheaded.' The emphasis ominously implied that Mary, who reputedly played in Scotland, might well not be the last.

The women of Walton seem to have avoided the worst excesses of this male resentment, probably because so many of them were invited or coerced into membership by husbands or relatives. Also, once the New course opened it was easier to escape each other.

Early reference books state that the Walton Heath

Fashions for spectators and players at the club's open meeting in 1908.
Illustrated Sporting and Dramatic News

Ladies' Club was not founded until 1906, and that must refer to some formalisation or affiliation. We have already established that by 1904 52 ladies were in membership and the total grew to more than 80 within a year. Anyway, there is nothing epoch-making about a start-of-the-century birthdate. English women had been playing golf, as distinct from putting games on what members were pleased to call hen runs, at least since the 1880s.

But the Walton ladies were soon catching up, and their guiding administrative force was Fowler's wife Ethel. Mrs Fowler was the first secretary and, after nine years, lady president – a position, so far as I can see, never again filled. Mrs F was a useful player. She won the Tod-Stewart medal at the St Andrews Ladies' Club meeting and at Walton achieved a notable double-first – in 1905 the club's first hole-in-one, scored at the then 12th, and the following spring the ladies' first gold medal.

[1] *Sport in Britain*, ed. Tony Mason (Cambridge University Press), 1989.

Man v Woman

It was a gimmick but it made golfing history – a match between Harold Hilton, already twice Open and Amateur champion, and Cecilia Leitch, a 19-year-old girl from Silloth on the Solway Firth. They played 72 holes, the first 36 at Walton Heath, the second at Sunningdale.

It was not the first man-v-woman match, but this one, starting on October 11, 1910, was hyped to unprecedented levels. The Ladies' Field, whose idea it was, called it a 'Test Match' – a test of ladies' golf against men's; more specifically of Hilton's pronounced judgment that the difference between an amateur champion and a lady champion playing off men's tees was nine strokes a round. That would be Cecilia's allotment: a stroke at every even-numbered hole.

The gimmick caught the public imagination. Feminism was topical and added spice to the brew. Hilton was a sporting hero to a degree utterly unattainable by amateur champions of today. Miss Leitch, never mind that she was known as 'Cecil,' was a comely teenager less than half his age who had reached the British Championship semi-finals at 17 and captivated the golfing public by her derring-do.

The crowds turned up at Walton on foot, in cars and via special trains. How many? Two thousand or so said the Morning Post, 2,500 to 3,000 thought The Ladies' Field, up to 4,000 reported Golf Illustrated. All seemed to agree, first, that the gallery was one of the largest ever to watch the sport in the south of England and, second, that it was ignorant and unruly.

At the opening hole Miss Leitch's ball hit a pram and at the third she was put off by a dog. People crossed fairways, talked during backswings and cramped the players. Not surprisingly, while both had moments of brilliance, they also suffered phases of mediocrity.

But by heaven, it was exciting! Miss Leitch fought adventurously, unwilling to temper aggression with caution when facing bad lies or improbable carries. In the morning, at the 457-yard 17th (now the 16th), she found a heavy lie just off the fairway but struck a brassie (equal to a two wood) past the pin, missing it by inches, and achieved her first win of a hole where she did not receive a stroke. Four down after 13, she had it back to one by lunchtime.

In the afternoon Hilton won the first two holes, then lost the next three and was down for the first time at the ninth. By the end of the day he was one up –

and it would have been all-square had Cecil not missed a four-footer on the final green.

Reportage matched the advance publicity. Readers were told of Miss Leitch's 'cream serge skirt striped with blue… her white blouse… a green tie with red in it… blue stockings and tan shoes… her hair done with a comb or two, securely but artistically fastened'. As for Hilton, one magazine described him, 'with his constant cigarette,' as 'a picturesque figure'!

After a day's rest the pair re-joined battle at Sunningdale in rain and a strong north-easterly. Cecil, five down with 15 to play, suddenly engaged top gear while Hilton stalled. She won seven of the next nine holes, squared at the 10th and eventually won the 72-hole match by 2 and 1.

Hilton, admitting to have been beaten 'fair and square,' took consolation in that the result justified his judgment: the difference between their total scores for the 71 holes was calculated to be 36, or nine shots a round – just as he had predicted.

The ladies, the *Golfing Annual* made clear, were 'a branch of the men's club.' They may have had initial input as to whom they would like to run their affairs, but it was the male board who officially nominated their committees and the women's proposals were sometimes 'revised' by Riddell. They had to go cap in hand to the directors for anything they wanted.

Nonetheless, the board including Mr Fowler did not unreasonably withhold permissions from the section including Mrs Fowler. In cases of disagreement, what tensions at *Chussex*, where Herbert was outnumbered by Ethel and daughter Phyllis! Young Phyllis was a rising member of the section who reduced her handicap from 16 to six in three years and would win the spring gold medal one rain-soaked day in 1912.

In 1907, the ladies were admitted to the dormy house. That year, too, the men permitted them their first annual open meeting and dipped hands in pockets to pay for some of the prizes. Fifty-five entered and a notable winner emerged – the aforesaid May Hezlet, with 94 against a bogey of 91.[2]

The women were making their presence felt. In 1910 the directors agreed that all applicants should be proposed or seconded by a lady before going to the board for approval; handicaps appeared on members' lists, a sign that the female of the species, though not as deadly as the male, was being recognised as a golfer and not merely as a matrimonial appendage; soon she had new quarters in the clubhouse.

The 1910 LGU Year Book listed 71 members with handicaps and a 13-strong committee including Malcolm Bonsor's wife and a Mrs Thornhill, no relation to current members John and Jill. There were match results, too – a win at Purley Downs and home-and-away encounters for a second team against Mitcham. The subscription for new members had risen to four guineas and before long it would be five. Weekday visitors had to fork out a shilling.

No captain was listed until 1912, but once in office Mrs. Allom, a left-handed golfer, a rare species then, promptly asked Riddell for ladies' tees. Her successor, Mrs Dick, had even had the audacity to complain that the board's annual monetary contribution to the ladies was small compared with those paid by other clubs and a request for £30 was timorously put forward.

Numbers kept increasing. By 1914 they would have risen to 235 and provisional membership only was available. Newcomers included two who would add character to the section, live to a ripe age and become female counterparts of Wodehouse's Oldest Member. Phyl Foster, a talented artist, joined in 1913 when she was 17. Joyce Spurling, who played golf and hockey for Kent and was a member of Blackheath and Mid-Surrey, had arrived two years earlier and stayed until she died, aged 95.

Cecil Leitch 'played with the fearlessness of a girl who had learned her golf in seaside winds'.

LGU Year Book, 1910

At first, Miss Spurling would walk to the club, carrying her clubs. Occasionally, from the station, she might take a horse-cab driven by the infamous 'Grimey' – so called for obvious reasons and who once drove his passengers into the village pond. Two years before joining she had been taken to the States with three other girls by the man behind 'Silver King' balls. They stayed with the Curtis family and there is even a legend, of dubious authenticity, that this inspired the beginnings of the Curtis Cup.

The first notable competitors had also arrived – among them Miss Barker (five gold medals in four years), Mrs Hughes and Mrs Johnstone (later Lady Stevenson), who on home ground won the second official Surrey championship. But the most consistent winner was the Old course, a tough handful for a lady.

> The course was never planned for her. The very formation of the bunkers impresses on our minds what an impotent thing a lady golfer is compared with a professional and one can only return from a round over the Old course humbler and wiser ... it is almost audacious to talk of Walton Heath as it strikes a lady.[3]

So, with feeling, wrote a woman columnist, and it is a fact that after 10 years only two players had beaten 90.

By now, though, at the end of 1912, two sisters had joined who were destined to perform great deeds. One of them was Edith Leitch, who had had won Walton Heath's open meeting four years earlier and was already an England player. Her younger sister, also an international, was the 21-year-old Cecilia ('Cecil' as she was called), who two years previously had won the much hyped man-v-woman match against Harold Hilton.

They came from and frequently represented Silloth (Cumbria) and it has been said that when Cecil came south she regarded Mid-Surrey as her golfing home. However, in her book *Golf* she suggested that her favourite London courses were Swinley Forest, Sunningdale, Walton and Addington. This being the Riddell era, both sisters

---

[2] Bogeys were considerably more generous for both sexes in the old days.
[3] *Golf Illustrated*, March 14, 1914.

First national amateur championship on the heath – the English Ladies' event. Play at the second hole, Old course.   Golf Illustrated, 1914
Left: 1910 fashion statement.   LGU Year Book

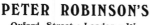
were promptly made honorary members; nevertheless they were genuine participants before and after the war. Within a year Cecil had won both the spring and autumn gold medals. Both entered from Walton Heath in several national championships.

Would you like a few figures to emphasise Cecil's supremacy over normal mortals? How about her round of 80 on the Old against a par of 86? How about her handicaps? Top men rated her scratch by their standards and, at a time when the LGU declined to recognise any women's mark better than scratch, Walton Heath made her plus-five. Oh, by the way, she once won a 36-hole Canadian championship final by 17 and 15.

She played with the fearlessness of a girl who had learned her golf in seaside winds, swinging gracefully, achieving abnormal length with her woods and hitting superbly with the irons. George Duncan, when Open champion, noticed that, contrary to the general rule, she stood rather open, with the ball in line more with the right heel than the left. 'One of the few women who could hit downwards, always taking a divot from just in front of the

ball,' observed Duncan. 'First of the Amazons,' reported Enid Wilson, golfer and journalist, in a phrase apt in the matter of strength but misleading about the person.

In June 1914, the year of the war, Walton Heath received an accolade: its first national amateur championship, men's or women's. It was, in fact, the first English Close Championship held by the LGU. Could Cecil win?

Well, she made a bad start. In the qualifying competition a confrontation with a bush earned her double figures and she scored 95. Her second- and third-round matches in the championship – one against a leading contender. the other against a virtual unknown – both went to extra time. In her semi-final the crowd saw the real Cecil Leitch. Off the men's medal tees, whose first-nine par was 38, she went out in 37 and proceeded to win by four and three.

In the 36-hole final she met Gladys Bastin, a promising young player from Woodcote Park, who had just shattered illusions of an all-Leitch climax by beating Edith in the semis. Miss Leitch began the day by driving into the pond (as did her opponent) but, after an intensely hard match, ended it in triumph, winning by two and one.

It was the first of her two English titles, and by the time her career ended she would have added four British championships and, for good measure, five French. She was without a doubt Walton Heath's greatest lady player, and her international career, during which she won 29 of 33 matches, spanned from 1910 to 1928.

EDITH GUEDALLA (née Leitch) – champion like her sister.
Golf Illustrated

But she was not the only star between the wars. Sister Edith (Mrs. Herbert Guedalla), whose 10 international appearances spanned quarter of a century, won the English Close championship in 1927. What other club, asked a golf writer, has included an Open champion (Braid), an Amateur champion (Sir Ernest Holderness), a British Ladies' Open champion (Cecil Leitch) and an English Close champion? It was Riddell, said Edith, who had encouraged her to continue playing when she was on the point of giving it up for a career as a singer.

Music? Edith shared that interest with another of the club's top players – Amy Patey, a member also at Worplesdon, who twice represented Scotland. Players and wartime soldiers, it was reported, 'will not readily forget her singing.' This, incidentally, was said as a compliment – we are talking here about an associate of the Royal College of Music, not Madame Edith of *Allo, Allo*.[4]

Different days! Impromptu soirees were held after championships and leading players took part. Miss Gladys Bastin would tickle the ivories and Mrs. Stubbs ('the Kentish nightingale') might sing, while an additional attraction reported was 'Miss Sant and her drum' – though what she did with it is not recorded.

Later, Nancy Halsted was another good player and, as an innocent bystander, was witness to an incident that shook

Gloria Minoprio, with her single club and scandalous trousers, precedes Nancy Halsted at Westward Ho!

traditionalists to the core. A murder? A sex scandal? A divorce? No, it was something far more unusual. Gloria Minoprio, from Littlestone, Nancy's first-day opponent in the 1933 English Amateur Championship at Westward Ho!, arrived in black pullover, cap and… trousers! And was using only one club!

Never had such things happened. Oh, dear, what a to-do it caused in the world of cloche hats, berets, cardigans, sturdy brogues and skirts below the knee! Miss Halsted was not put off balance, but only beat her elegantly slim opponent at the 15th on her way to reaching the semi-finals. The LGU 'much regretted this departure from the usual,' while Eleanor Helme, the *Morning Post* correspondent, having noted Miss Minoprio's chalk-white face, scarlet lips and distant expression, likened her to 'a stage Mephistopheles or executioner.'

> A statement has been circulated that the Walton Heath Ladies' Club had refused to adopt the new system of handicapping of the Ladies' Golf Union. The Walton Heath Club desires it to be known that its members voted for the retention of their system of handicapping for their own competitions only and that they adopted the system of the governing body for open events.
>
> *Golf Illustrated*, 1921

Cecil Leitch's predominance was followed by that of the amazing Joyce Wethered, about whom Bob Jones eulogised 'I am doubtful if there has ever been a better player, man or woman.' She, too, became a Walton Heath member but probably only a grace-and-favour one, and we must resist any temptation to 'claim' her because Worplesdon was her acknowledged home. She did win one of her Surrey championships on the heath, though, and returned a magnificent 78 in an open meeting in 1922.

The same qualification must be made about Pam Barton, who held the British and American championships in the same year. She was not elected a Walton Heath member until late in 1938. Then the war came and by 1943 she was dead at 26, killed when her boy friend's plane crashed as he took her for a post-dance joy-ride.

Walton Heath had been affiliated to the Ladies' Golf Union since 1909, 16 years after the union was founded,

---

[4] For the benefit of readers many years hence, *Allo, Allo* was a TV comedy series set in occupied Europe.

supporting it yet prepared to do battle with it. In 1925 they had a genuine spat, 'strongly objecting' to the union's lowering of the Old course par from 80, which the club had considered too stiff, to 79.

Like a bullied child threatening revenge through her big brother, the ladies said they would tell Riddell. They then urged a reversion to a par of 80 and asked for Miss Benton, the LGU handicap manager, to be replaced. Net result – the LGU agreed 80, but Miss Benton kept her place.

Walton Heath's winning Pearson Trophy team, 1924.   The Sketch

In 1931 club and union were again in dispute and not quite for the last time. The LGU had decided to alter the scratch scores of both courses as they needed stiffening. Stiffening? Good heavens! In the past 10 years of open meetings and club competitions the scratch scores, currently 80 (Old) and 79 (New), had never been broken by a member except for Miss Wethered on the Old, where the ss had been equalled only by Mrs Crosthwaite. The club probably lost on this occasion because an undated surviving postcard confirms 79 and 78.

Competitively, Walton Heath were often formidably strong between the wars, with players like Crosthwaite, Patey, Mrs Cruise, Mrs Heriot Glen and Vivienne Falconer, who played for Scotland in 13 home internationals in a 24-year span from 1932. The club were well represented in the Surrey teams that won six consecutive English county championships in the 'twenties and three more in the 'thirties. As for inter-club matches the ladies of Walton were among the most powerful teams around London and often more enthusiastic about them than the men.

But there were peaks and troughs. In 1924 Mrs. R.J. McNair, writing in a golf magazine, bewailed a general lack of interest:

> There used to be tremendous rivalry, and clubs such as Prince's Mitcham, Woking, Mid-Surrey, Walton Heath and Wimbledon had splendid fights. Moreover there was much competition as to who could entertain their visitors best.

In that case the Walton ladies' complaint to the steward about stale cakes for tea, minuted in the 'thirties, assumes a new enormity!

Mrs. McNair blamed the increasing number of open meetings and competitions, and certainly Walton Heath's enthusiasm graph showed sudden ups and downs. In 1926 low-handicappers were reluctant to play. In 1931 the club played 19 matches, losing only four; six years later they were struggling to raise teams. Higher handicappers were similarly inconsistent. Having won the Pearson Trophy in 1923 and 1924, three years later they could not gather a strong enough team to enter. By 1930 they had won again. In 1937 they withdrew halfway through the series, again because they couldn't raise a side.

The club had not entered in 1926 either, but for other reasons. The previous year, trying for a hat-trick, they had written to the organisers about Leatherhead players 'teeing their balls through the green'! When the trophy committee said their protest was too late the Walton ladies replied first that they had not protested, only questioned, and secondly, apparently throwing a sulk, that they would not play the following year.

Less competitive were some of the women made honorary members in acknowledgement of their celebrity status. The Mrs. Chambers and Miss Ryan elected in 1920 were surely the illustrious tennis stars – Elizabeth Lambert Chambers, in her day the world's finest player, and

SHOULD WOMEN WEAR PLUS-FOURS?

Sir, – I have read your recent article on "Should women wear plus-fours?" with great interest, and my regret is that the writer was not more decidedly in favour of this costume for ladies.

I think they would play golf with far greater freedom if they wore plus-fours or the divided skirt as recently advertised. I see no reason why they should look less graceful than the ladies who ride astride or the winter sports lady in her becoming costume of a tunic and jumper over a divided skirt. I hope the day is not far distant when all lady golfers will feel strange in the old-fashioned clinging skirt as worn today.

Lucy, Lady Holderness (Walton Heath)

Golf Illustrated, 1925

Elizabeth Ryan, winner of 14 Wimbledon doubles titles. The Gladys Cooper of 1926 was almost certainly the stage and film star.

In the 'twenties, in a microcosmic reflection of the national voting equality gradually granted to all women over 21, ladies' golf sharpened yet softened its image. Gone from the golf periodicals were the condescending advertisements and articles like 'Getting rid of female moustaches.' By 1926 they were carrying beauty hints from Miss Cooper, publicity for smarter clothing, features on shopping and physical exercise, even nude photographs of the female form (back-shots only, of course, and in the finest possible taste). Corsets were becoming 'waistline garments, a joy for the golfer,' while the Charnaux belt guaranteed 'scientific aid to your swing'.

In 1927 the club ladies' increasing self-confidence showed when they sought a bigger say in their own affairs. In future, they proposed, two committee members should retire each year and their replacements, plus the captain, should be elected by the ladies at their own agm. Riddell, by invitation, presided over a ladies' committee meeting, listened to the proposals and said all the right things. 'You ladies take more interest in the club than the men,' he flattered. 'And as you feel the proposals would be for its betterment I see no reason why they should not be agreed.'

But his wily lordship would not completely lose control of the ladies. The names of candidates for the captaincy, vice-captaincy and committee should be submitted to the board before going to their agm, he insisted. Also, he did not want retiring officers and committee ladies to be eligible for re-election for a further year. Enthusiastic that half a loaf was better than none, the ladies' committee agreed the terms, which were implemented at what they termed their first general meeting – chaired by Riddell.

The lady elected captain at the following year's meeting (November 1927) was Mrs. Hill – 'a golfer of renown,' said Riddell. She repaid the compliment by proposing a ladies-v-men match the following summer and the directors approved.

First casualty of the not-for-another-year rule for re-election was the formidable Lady Holderness, four times captain and mother of the club's outstanding male player. This took away some of the cachet of the committee, which before her non-election had included three ladies of title. She remained a stalwart of the section but was not above the law. She would once suffer the ignominy of disqualification in a monthly medal for taking her dog with her, transgression of a rule passed the previous year. Or have I done her an injustice? Perhaps this was the younger Lady Holderness, wife of the champion?

In 1928 Walton Heath hosted the England and Wales

ENID WILSON, *later golf correspondent for the* Morning Post *and* Daily Telegraph, *won the 1928 English championship at Walton. She beat Dorothy Pearson by nine and eight in the 36-hole final.*

Golf Illustrated

county finals, followed by a second English Close Championship. This was won by the girl who called Cecil Leitch an Amazon – the future journalist Enid Wilson, then a tall, strong 18-year-old from the Midlands.

The section continued to grow in size and prestige. In 1923 a limit of 250 had been put on the membership, vacancies to be filled by low-handicappers though possibly also by local residents. The following year the ladies had their own secretary, Les Cocker, presumably the club's long-serving steward. Their committee ran a tight ship: in 1929 the balance was £1-16s-7d.

The relationship with the men's board and committee continued to progress as well as could be expected within the context of golf club traditions. 'It wasn't easy at weekends,' a lady member from the 'thirties told me. 'We grumbled because our starting times were limited; the men complained that we held them up.' What else was new?!

'Gentlemen don't play with their servants'

In February 1906, Herbert Fowler, disdainful of the increasingly popular four-ball format, led Walton Heath's launch of a foursomes competition. What a hullabaloo that caused! The tournament was The London Foursomes, open to all clubs within a 30-mile radius of Charing Cross. Each could enter one pair, either two amateurs or one amateur with the club professional. Letters to the Press were fired off – mostly anonymous and starkly revealing of class attitudes. Two examples:

> Nothing but harm to the game can result from this close association of amateurs in public competition with professionals. – *signed 'Pure Sport.'* [1]

> I quite admit the professional's excellent qualities, but nothing will spoil him sooner than taking him out of his proper station and treating him as on an equal footing with those who are his superiors socially, educationally and financially. Gentlemen do not usually play and bet with their servants, nor have them in to lunch and tea. – *'Conservative.'* [2]

Riddell broke into print with an indignant and high-minded response, the 1906 competition went ahead and the crowd at Walton for the 36-hole final was reputedly the biggest ever seen at a match in the London region. It 'served to completely deplete the village of Tadworth of provender fit for human consumption,' wrote Harold Hilton, then carving a career in journalism. 'By two o'clock there was hardly a crust to be found.'

In the first year of the London Foursomes, Braid and Fowler, representing Walton Heath, had to play one of their matches against Royal Wimbledon on Wimbledon Common. Here, of course, it is necessary that golfers must make themselves conspicuous by wearing red coats. The lockers of the club were ransacked to find one of these flamboyant garments to fit the mighty Braid. He appeared on the course in a coat several sizes too small for him.

Golf Illustrated, Jan. 17, 1913

The winners were Mid-Surrey, J.H. Taylor and Sidney Fry, the English billiards champion, upsetting Walton's Braid and Fowler by nine and eight. These finalists had been predictable and it was clear that the format was faulted – not through any social stigma but because clubs who had champions as professionals held an advantage from the start.

Woking, Byfleet and Sunningdale promptly planned a rival event – for amateurs only. Walton, with its baby kidnapped and put into different clothes, had little option to an 'if-you-can't-beat-'em-join-'em' policy. 'We'll abandon our tournament if we can join yours as joint promoters,' said Fowler, and the clubs agreed.

So in 1907 The London Amateur Foursomes began and none too convincingly: 27 clubs entered whereas 40 had been anticipated. Golfing blamed geography and inadequate transport: 'To golfers on the far north or east of London, Sunningdale, Woking, Byfleet and Walton are almost as inaccessible as seaside links.' Three years later, when the event was held on the heath, the point was repeated: 'Walton Heath's inaccessibility is not on a par with its quality.'

In spite of all this a record 35 clubs entered that 1910 event. Could Walton

Amateurs and professionals together – to some people a distasteful sight. The 1906 London Foursomes finalists: from left: Braid, Fowler (runners-up), Fry and Taylor (winnners).

win on home terrain? No, they couldn't. They lost in the final to Home Park. An icy March east wind blew over the heath, colder than anything Hilton had known: 'It was painful to play and one felt quite sorry for the couples who survived to the final stages.'

The foursomes, though, became firmly established, the carrying of the massive shield appropriately a job for two strong men. Meanwhile, the excluded London professionals shed few tears because bigger opportunities were beginning to come their way – and notably so at Walton. For a select few there were the challenge matches; for more of them the News of the World *Match-play Championship, a show that would run and run and eventually make the heath its permanent home.*

From the start, though, the balance between professional and club golf at Walton was delicately poised. When the first challenge match was proposed in 1906 the board agreed, but only so long as it wasn't on a Saturday. Weekends were sacrosanct for the members.

---

[1] and [2] *Golf Illustrated*, March 2 and 23, 1906.

Chapter Eight

FREE FOR ALL AS WINNERS *TAKE* ALL
High stakes in the challenge matches

I MAGINE IF YOU can the crowds massing on the heath for the old-time challenge matches: vociferous and unruly, golfers and gamblers, *cognoscenti* and *hoi polloi*, Frith's *Derby Day* scene transferred three miles and a furlong from Epsom Downs to the canvas of Walton Heath. As late as 1969 Henry Longhurst was still describing such crowds: 'a mixed assembly of knowledge-able golfers, courting couples, girls on horseback, babies in prams and innumerable dogs – all attending the free spec-tacle on the heath.'[1]

Yes, they were free shows for one and all, because it was impossible to charge admission to the open heath. Yet the biggest stars in the game were appearing. To watch Braid, Vardon, Taylor and their like at Walton was akin to being given the best seat in the house to watch Ellen Terry at the new London Coliseum or, for the less refined, Marie Lloyd at the Metropolitan in the Old Kent Road. To a general public not yet quite on terms with the jargon of handicaps and bogeys, these matches presented a simple, under-standable plot: one champion fighting another for big money.

Personal backing in challenge matches was a continuing tradition into which Riddell had now entered. The first such match proposed for Walton, in 1906, was to be between Braid and Vardon on the one hand and George Duncan and Charles Mayo on the other. They would contest 72 holes of foursomes, the first 36 at Braid's Walton and the second on Duncan's course at Timperley, near Manchester. The stakes were £50, the same as first prize in the Open.

The piquancy, the popular appeal in all this was that established champions were being challenged by upstarts. Braid and Vardon, both 36, had between them captured seven Open championships; Duncan and Mayo were in their early twenties and neither had won a really big event. However, in the match-play championship earlier in the year Duncan, a policeman's son from Aberdeenshire, had beaten Braid and reached the semi-finals, while Mayo, back from a sojourn in America, had got into the final. Now they fancied their chance of a famous victory.

_____
[1] *The Sunday Times.*

Cartoonist's view of Braid/Vardon v Duncan/Mayo.   Golf Illustrated

A big, excitable, ill-disciplined crowd turned up at Walton on the first day and one of their number may even have affected the result. Not surprisingly, the scoring was higher than expected.

Duncan and Mayo played with the precocity of young pretenders, George hitting his shots with characteristic speed and Charles pleasing the crowd with his cheerful, laid-back manner. Braid and Vardon, close friends, progressed solemnly, earnestly discussing shot after shot. At the then short sixth, Vardon, fearing he might not stop his ball on the green, deliberately put it in the left-hand bunker nearest the hole, confident that Braid would explode it close. 'He did not fail me,' said Harry.

The younger pair, two down after the first 18, were all-square after two holes of the second round, courtesy of rare mistakes by Braid, but eventually stood two down with two to play. If they had a chance of levelling before the move to Timperley it was lost at the 35th. 'A good drive of Duncan's was intercepted by an out-of-place spectator and deeply found a side bunker – so deeply that the incident cost the young men the hole. Hard luck truly.' So reads a contemporary report. Vardon went on to hole a long putt at the final hole, so the veterans finished the Walton stage four up.

Braid and Vardon emphasised their superiority at Timperley. The strain told on the youngsters and by the end of the 72 holes the masters had beaten the pupils by nine and eight.

Not everybody approved of these winners-take-all arrangements. It may have been a free show at Walton, but such was not the case at Timperley and letters to the press attacked the principle of charging the public half a crown when the losing pair would be out of pocket. In actual fact Duncan and Mayo had been backed by a third party. One writer complained about the 'outsiders who now attend these matches for business purposes and are even admitted to the clubhouses' – a sentiment that strikes a chord with those of us who abhor the proliferation of hospitality tents unless we are invited into them.

Three years later Duncan and Mayo tried again. A few things were different: Taylor came in as Braid's partner, the stakes had increased to £100-a-side and Burhill replaced

The Big Foursome for £200.

George Duncan.   J. H. Taylor.   James Braid.   C. H. Mayo.

Timperley. The result, though, was pretty much the same. This time Burhill staged the first two rounds and the second half at Walton spluttered and died like a damp squib. Braid and Taylor arrived five up, the play was only average and the crowd probably enjoyed as much as anything a comedy of errors at the eighth:

> Mayo pulled his tee shot into a bunker, where it lay in a pool of water, while Braid pulled his even worse into the gorse. While Duncan was playing out of the water Taylor played a left-handed shot from under a bush which went right across the course amongst the spectators. Then Mayo again pulled into some very thick gorse, from which Duncan failed to get out. Impaling himself in agony in the middle of a gorse bush, Mayo broke his niblick. The ball glanced out at right angles, bounced off a lady and almost hit Taylor, who was watching the proceedings with keen interest.[2]

Braid and Taylor won by eight and seven. 'The effect will probably be that the Triumvirate will be left severely alone for some time to come,' a writer conjectured – and he was right.

In 1911 came a strange contest – strange, that is, because of its location. Here were two middle-aged Scots, Andrew Kirkaldy and Ben Sayers, disputing supremacy not at St Andrews and North Berwick whence they came but at Sunningdale and Walton Heath. They were fierce rivals. Seventeen years previously they had fought an epic and emotional match on their home territories, Sayers

Charles Mayo (left) and George Duncan – upstarts challenging champions. Marsuma cigarette cards, 1914

---

[2] *Golf Illustrated.*

winning on the last green at St Andrews by two holes. That was in 1894, years before either Sunningdale or Walton were created and when such a match on a southern inland course would have been unthinkable.

Now this was to be a return match on neutral terrain. Would the old boxing adage that 'a good big 'un will always beat a good little 'un' ring true? Sayers was only 5ft 3in and comfortably outreached and outweighed.

Also in the tradition of boxing, the return fight ended in anti-climax. The weather for much of the time was cold, damp and misty; Sayers was 54 and Kirkaldy, over-weight and cramped by rheumatism, 51. Although both played some fine golf and Ben was only one up after the first 36 at Sunningdale, the Walton Heath finale again became a procession. Sayers was six up after the morning round and won by six and five. Kirkaldy praised Sayers to the hilt, then added: 'Wait till I get twa stone off and then we'll have anither match. But none of these southern courses, Benny knaes 'em too well!'

That same year, 1911, the club hosted another match-play event, but this time a tournament – the first *Sphere* and *Tatler* Cups Foursomes for £350 prize-money. Sixty-four individuals qualified regionally, but then partnerships were drawn from a hat. Such a lottery might be all good fun for Walton Heath's dinner foursomes, but somewhat less so for a national champion who might find himself saddled with a no-hoper. In the 36-hole final Sandy Herd and his partner Bradbeer beat Taylor and Hambleton eight and seven and, not surprisingly, the event was short-lived.

Going to one of the holes, I had a chat with Braid, who said to me, "The day is fine, the course is fine, everything is fine except the golf." Now that really seems to me to sum up the situation to a nicety. The putting at times was ludicrously bad and it was amusing to hear "W.G." on the subject. With all possible emphasis – and the great cricketer can be emphatic – he said, "Why, you don't see ME miss putts like that!"

Braid/Taylor v Duncan/Mayo report, Illustrated Sporting and Dramatic News, 1909

The challenge matches so far had not lived up to their advance publicity either, but better things were to come. Of all the matches for which the heath provided a stage the closest was the 72-hole, £100-a-side contest in June 1913 between Duncan and Ted Ray. The pairing was a 'natural': Ray the reigning Open champion versus Duncan the Match-play champion.

Over two rounds at Walton, then two at Sunningdale they waged a battle characterised by brutally long hitting – particularly from Ray, although on the first day at Walton Duncan drove to within 30ft of the pin at a 14th hole measuring 350 yards. The position see-sawed dramatically, Duncan playing with the urgency of a man who wanted to go home early and Ray, biting on his pipe, pugnacious in response.

George, three up after the 11th in the morning, was himself three down at that same 11th in the afternoon. The pendulum then swung again and by the end of the day they were locked together. The approximate scores were Duncan 79+77, Ray 80 +77. At Sunningdale, with the match all-square coming to the 71st, Ray drove out-of-bounds to go dormy-one down but saved himself at the last, striking a huge drive, then hitting his second to within three feet of the pin... after 72 holes it was a tie.

During World War I golf matches were more exhibition than challenge, more charity than winner-take-all, and in the 'twenties the fashion tended to die. Challenge matches would not return as a Walton Heath feature until the late 'thirties.

TOM VARDON – Harry's younger brother. In the first News of the World *Match-Play final played at Walton Heath he found Darwin was right: 36 holes against Braid at Walton was like playing Zeus on his home course at Olympia!*

Illustrated Sporting and Dramatic News, *1905*

Chapter Nine

IT WAS A KNOCKOUT!
The Match-Play Championship starts a new pro era

THE *NEWS OF THE WORLD* Match-Play Championship in effect replaced Walton's challenge matches or at least would comfortably outlive them. What Riddell's newspaper had come up with in 1903 was a whole series of matches encapsulated into a three-day tournament. In all but name it was the British championship.

The professionals were to qualify via regional stroke-play events, and 32 survivors, theoretically the best pros in Britain, would come to courses around London for the match-play knockout. All matches would be of one round until the 36-hole final.

It was a wonderful chance for the professionals, particularly those below the top rank. Champions might be making £400 a year but those below first-class were probably pushed to earn £150. Total prize-money in the Open was £115, but the *News of the World* was offering £200, including £100 and a gold medal for the winner, and within a year or so it would be £240.

News of the World editor Emsley Carr joined Riddell as a member of Walton Heath, but Fowler's course was not yet open for business. The 1903 championship went to Sunningdale, where Braid won, and that of 1904 to Mid-Surrey, where Taylor triumphed on his adopted home course.

The championship first came to the heath in October 1905. That year at St. Andrews Braid had won his second Open, so Walton Heath members to a man and woman now desperately wanted to see him become the first golfer to take the Open and Match-play titles in the same year.

He had an agonising first match against Herd, who had beaten him by one hole at Mid-Surrey. Now, at Walton, Herd drew all-square at the 14th... at the 17th and 18th Braid missed four-footers for wins... they went to extra time. At the 19th Braid again had a putt to win. It was about nine feet... it hung on the lip... then dropped.

Braid reached the final against Tom Vardon, Harry's younger brother from Royal St George's. After three holes Tom was two up and play at the fourth was, to quote Braid, 'a strange business':

> Vardon pulled his second about 50 yards wide of the green, whereas I placed mine about three yards from the hole. It seemed certain that it was going to be my hole, but my opponent played his third beautifully and got just inside me; then in some extraordinary fashion I managed to take three putts and lost the hole with a five to a four.

Three down! But Darwin once surmised that to play 36 holes against Braid at Walton was like playing Zeus on his home course at Olympia. From now on Braid constantly

Braid at the 15th in 1905, watched by an uncharacteristically sedate gallery.
Illustrated Sporting and
Dramatic News, 1905

Strokes and Flirtations

Walton Heath's love affair with match-play was punctuated by flirtations with stroke-play and other dalliances. In the 'twenties there were putting competitions, with up to £500 at stake and 400 entrants including most of the top professionals. A long-driving contest was added. One year Ted Ray came along to watch, was invited, coconut-shy-style, to try his luck, took off his coat, borrowed Sandy Herd's driver and won the prize.

The first notable stroke-play tournament, just after World War I, was a 1919 PGA Victory Tournament for southern professionals – in effect, the region's qualifying phase for the News of the World event taken out of context. The top players entered, playing one round each on the Old and New courses, and most of them in their rustiness found both a handful. Predictably Braid won, but even he took 79 and 76 and

finished only one stroke ahead of Kirby, a little-known professional who was playing with a silver plate inserted in a leg wounded during the war. It was Braid's last tournament win at Walton.

On the New in the autumn of 1934, a few weeks before Riddell's death, came the inaugural £500 Dunlop-Metropolitan tournament, a four-round relation of the established Dunlop-Southport event. Open only to those who had done well in sundry tournaments during the year, it was the precursor of the Dunlop and subsequent Masters championships. Ernest Whitcombe, oldest of three golfing brothers, successively scored 69, 69 and 68 to establish records for the New and, despite a last-round 77, equalled Henry Cotton's record championship total of 283 achieved in the Open that summer. Cotton was down in ninth place, 11 off the pace.

Whitcombe's scores were made despite the fact that the New had been stretched to a yardage variously reported as 6,600 or 6,726. The waspish sports writer E.M.Wellings complained that 'the Walton Heath people were not content to allow the course to stand on its merits. The Old course was called on to redress the wrongs of the New. Tees belonging to the Old were employed in several places and other tees were cut in unexpected positions – an unnecessary and harmful undertaking.'

Whitcombe's 68 might have been even lower had it not been for a dog which ran off with his ball at the fifth. The dog's lady owner recovered the ball and replaced it in the rough, although many spectators thought it had finished on the fairway. Whitcombe played it from the heather and took five – having changed the ball on the green because of the dog's teeth marks.

The
famous
17th
hole

E. Ray.
runner-up

James
Braid
driving

T. Williamson
judges
an approach

Braid
and
that
Niblick

The Open Champion
on the green

An innovation

Frank Reynolds cartoon portrays the 1911 championship.
Reproduced by permission, Illustrated London News *Picture Library*

kept his ball in play while Vardon was too often in the heather. The Open champion won by four and three, finishing with a moment of panache as he hit the flag with his approach.

Braid, for that year at least supreme at both stroke- and match-play, accordingly received his £100 and medal from the *News of the World*, plus offerings from the club of a type that were to become a regular custom over the years: an illuminated testimonial to mark his Open success, a £90 cheque, plus a silver tea service for his wife. 'Braid tried to say what he felt,' a reporter wrote, 'but he cannot speak in public with the same fine length he can drive from the tee, so his thanks were brief – but everybody understood.'

No such celebrations occurred when the championship next came to Walton. The *News of the World* event had appeals similar to those of the FA Cup: the knockout format and the potential for giant-killers. In 1909 the giant-killers struck with indecent haste: Braid, three times the winner by then, and Taylor, the defending champion, were ousted in the first round! The pro with the audacity to humiliate Braid on his own territory by four and three was Jack Rowe from Royal Ashdown Forest.

Two years later, again at Walton, there was nearly another upset for the club's hero. In the semi-finals Tom Williamson, from Hollinwell, who had never previously survived the second round, led him by two holes with three to play and succumbed only at the 22nd. Braid's admirers had a shock of a different type when they saw their man approach the first tee for the final. He had abandoned his trademark cap and homespun trousers for a Homburg hat and neat light suit. This, one spectator observed, gave him the look of an ambassador's secretary.

His opponent was Ted Ray, destined to win the following year's Open – and who also, as usual, wore a brimmed hat. The two had contested the first final at Sunningdale in 1903, when James won by four and three, but that was as nothing compared with this 1911 encounter.

The championship was anyone's until the third hole of the last round, where Ray, well placed with Braid in the rough, topped into the bunker guarding the hole. Braid won it and became rejuvenated. As for Ray, everything began to go wrong and his putting, shaky all day, broke down altogether. With nine holes to go he was six down and doomed.

At the 10th Ted suddenly re-found his touch – five down, eight to play. At the 12th Braid pushed an iron shot into sand and Ray again won – four down, six to go. At the 13th Ray pitched superbly and holed the putt – three down, five left. The *News of the World's* Taylor described what followed at the 14th (now the 13th):

> Braid suddenly became inoculated with the germ of bad putting that had been worrying Ray. He got well on to the green with his second and looked to have a half for the asking. Short with his approach putt, he gave the next a lusty chance, eventually finding himself called upon to hole one from about a foot.
>
> I have never yet found Braid in a hurry to play a stroke when a tremendous issue hung upon its successful accomplishment. Even Homer sometimes nods, and now we see Braid in a fearful hurry to hole this one... I think the memory of that missed putt still rankled when he duffed his chip out of the rough into the bunker at the 15th and Ray holed a beauty for a four after hitting two tremendous wallops straight down the course.

Ray was now one down with three to play, but when he pushed his drive at the 16th into a bunker it looked all over and Taylor left for the clubhouse. Twenty minutes

A suitably deferential bow for Riddell from Reggie Wilson, winner in 1923.
Golf Illustrated

Braid, 57, making his last appearance in a final, against Archie Compston.
Golf Illustrated, *1927*

later, alerted by distant cheers and ashamed of his defection, he returned. Ray had halved the 16th and won the 17th, so the match was all-square with one to play!

> Ray pushed his drive into the rough, whilst the 'old man' hit one of his specials, as straight as a die. Edward 'houcked' out, though, about six yards from the hole, but James put his inside.
>
> Remembering how beautifully true Ray had been hitting his putts lately, it was quite possible that he would end a memorable day by doing the disappearing trick again. He struck the ball as true as a hair, and from the back of the hole, where I was placed, I thought it was there; but it came to a stop about three inches short. Jimmy did not hurry over his putt this time. He did not try to play to the gallery by attempting to hole it. He took the greatest care to lay it 'stony.'
>
> It was all over, and the cheers that now broke out must surely have gladdened the hearts and lightened the limbs of the two gladiators. We escorted the tired pair in triumph to Braid's shop, where James flung himself down, dead beat, into a chair. 'This match has made me properly shake,' he said.

The 1911 final had added lustre to a championship that had gone from strength to strength. Within its first three years the Press had acknowledged it as 'second only to the two big championships (the Open and the Amateur) and in some respects more interesting than either.' The qualification process, with a southern bias, had its critics, but entries had risen from 120 to 400 and the prize-money from £240 to £400, the first-round losers now collecting a fiver. By 1912 eight of the ten events had been won by Open champions.

Braid in the bracken, Compston in the clear – but only for a moment. Archie's brassie shot found the bracken, too. Golf Illustrated, 1927

Not so many years ago English crowds followed decorously at the heels of the players. They comported themselves like earnest students of the game. Now we pursue the performers in the hope that they will provide us with something thrilling.

The World of Golf, 1913

Another man destined to win the Open took the title when the club next hosted the event, George Duncan beating Braid three and two in 1913. This, though, was a sub-standard championship. The field was poor and on the first two days it rained so much that it was impossible to play from some of the bunkers.

Let us now travel ahead a decade and a half through the Riddell era, leaving behind the horrendous years of World War I and two more Walton *News of the Worlds* – those of 1919, in which Abe Mitchell beat Duncan, and 1923, when the finalists, to the surprise of one and all, were Reggie Wilson, the winner, and Tom Renouf. If that top-of-the-bill duo lent an element of ironic humour to the show, one of the supporting acts from Blackpool provided a unique cameo of slapstick comedy. In his first-round match against Duncan, Simpson, from the Knott End club, asked for the pin to be removed for his 12-foot putt and his caddie duly moved away with it. Simpson then putted straight for the flagstick, which the caddie was holding six yards away from the hole.

But now it is 1927. Sixteen years have passed since Braid's last win. He is 57, yet he qualifies in style. Surely he can't win? Or could he? His supporters point out that last year at Mid-Surrey Herd had won at 58.

He reaches the final. 'There were visions of such rejoicings as the heath had never seen,' writes Darwin. His opponent will be the 34-year-old Mancunian giant Archie Compston, Ryder Cup player, runner-up in an Open and already once the winner of this championship.

The Old course in wind and driving rain is no place for a 57-year-old faced with 36 holes against such opposition, particularly when he has already, before breakfast, walked all round it to check that everything is up to the club's standard. He wins the first two holes, but it is too good to last. Compston forges away to win by eight and seven.

According to Longhurst, the club in those days declined to have a rule permitting players either to clean balls on the green or to pick out 'suckers' – the course was claimed to be dry and in such good order that one never got mud on one's ball, nor found it half-buried. On the 12th green, to the club's embarrassment, Compston found his ball settled in something of a hole during one of his matches and sought relief. 'We don't have plugged balls at Walton Heath,' said the referee. So he had to play it as it lay, which meant practically digging it out.

Longhurst claimed later that Archie used a niblick, a sort of sharp-edged sand wedge, and 'not only hacked out half the green but took two similar practice shots first;' and that years later, when he asked James what he thought of Compston, 'Braid, a wise and taciturn man, looked at me for a moment and, slowly shaking his head, said, "Tst, tst".' It was Braid's last final.

'The mole who ventured to raise a mound at Walton Heath' – Bateman cartoon.
© H.M. Bateman Designs

Chapter Ten

SOMETHING OLD, SOMETHING NEW
The second course – created by Fowler, untouched by heavy hands

WHAT IS NEW? Walton Heath's New course – or anyway half of it – is over 95 years old.

> We hear that it has been decided to go ahead without delay with the construction of a nine-hole relief course, *reported Golf Illustrated* in *1905*. What with one thing and another it is evident that Walton Heath is destined to be a great centre of inland golf in the very near future. It has ambitions and is pursuing them wisely and with certainty.

The new baby, conceived a year after its elder brother began life, was born after a two-year pregnancy on October 19, 1907. The birth was celebrated in conjunction with the autumn medal, when a handicap competition against bogey was played over a composite course combining eight of the new holes with ten of the Old. The contestants faced an intimidating first drive – straight over the Dorking Road.

The nine holes relate to the first four and last five of the present-day course. 'They are quite first-class, full of variety,' a writer assured the readers of *Nisbet's Golf Year Book*. Well, he would, wouldn't he? He was, after all, the architect – Herbert Fowler again. Less inviting to prospective visitors out for a good time was Nisbet's hotel recommendation: 'Tattenham Park (Temperance).' That was all very well for Fowler: as I have said, he was a teetotaller.

This 3,062-yard course was indeed a relief. There were now nearly 500 men and over 100 lady members. On Sundays, those coming by rail from London had often found the tee booked and queues forming, so the Club had ruled that, while locals and those coming by car could fill the early starting times, alternate slots after 10.20am would be reserved for the train contingent. When big crowds arrived on the same train, members not wanting to play the same nine twice were given the option of playing the composite 18. Cutting-in induced rising blood pressures.

Lord Mayor of London Sir David Burnett opens the 18-hole New course. The club, an old-fashioned scare-headed wood, was borrowed from Braid and can be seen in the clubhouse today.

Golfing, 1913

Yes, the nine new holes were a relief but they were still not enough, and within a year there was talk of extending them to 18. At first it seemed possible that the Lady of the Manor of Banstead Heath might offer land, but various bodies objected and the club abandoned negotiations.

The directors were haggling with their own Lord of the Manor, Malcolm Bonsor, over a renegotiation of the club's lease: although a member himself he was sticking out for £620 p.a. for a 70-year extension. When the club sought more holes he couldn't agree. He felt a responsibility to those with commoners' rights and indeed to all the people he had allowed to walk, ride and even 'practise with aeroplanes.'[1] The club, he said, would first need to persuade those folk who might feel their rights or privileges were in jeopardy.

It wasn't easy. Arthur Bray, a club member living at The Hermitage nearby, feared the worst and argued that an agreement he had with Fowler and the City of London Corporation would be broken if the club boundaries were extended. Others shared his concerns and the wrangling dragged on between 1909 and 1912. The locals and the corporation between them confronted the club with conditions: limits on the number of members and the acreage of any extra ground (sufficient for nine holes only); membership and green-fee concessions to residents; careful picking and strict supervision of any extra caddies.

The club eventually accommodated the objectors. Provided all objections were withdrawn, it would not, for a

---

[1] Steward Freshfield in a letter to City Land Committee, 1912.

WALTON HEATH GOLF CLUB. Sown September, 1912, opened for play October 9th, 1913.

THE SIXTH GREEN.
1st 18 holes sown September, 1903, opened for play May, 1904. 1st 9 holes of 2nd Course sown September, 1906, opened for play May, 1907.
2nd 9 holes of 2nd Course sown September, 1912, opened for play October 9th, 1913.

This course was sown from start to finish with

CARTERS TESTED GRASS SEEDS

Carters

90% of the new courses in the United Kingdom have been sown with CARTERS Seeds under the CARTER System.

Seedsmen to His Majesty the King. RAYNES PARK, LONDON, S.W.

HIGH HOLBORN

Cutting the bracken, breaking up the ground by steam plough and preparing bunkers and greens, After all that, seed was sown – supplied by Carters, who were quick to advertise their achievements. Country Life

period of 80 years, have more than 36 holes, nor more than 800 full male members; 25-per-cent of membership vacancies would be reserved for residents of Walton parish; Sunday green fees would be reduced for visitors introduced by local members. Agreements were signed with individuals, the club was granted an 80-year lease at £550 p.a. dating from 1910 and Fowler proceeded with his creation of nine new holes.

Fowler remembered how, when he built the Old course, native grass had grown through and eventually superseded the Dutch fescue he had sown; therefore on both nines of the New he had hoped merely to clear the heather and bracken and let the natural grass come of itself. For some holes this proved possible and only a heavy roller and mowing machine were needed. In other areas the massive carting away of the top spit of earth for sale to carnation growers – one of the practices now virtually banned by Bonsor – meant that Fowler had to plough, cultivate and sow. The seed came from James Carter, as it had for the Old.

A steam cultivator is doing splendid work in breaking up the ground and tearing out the bracken and heather roots, *Fowler reported[2] in September 1912*. As soon as this is done the ground will be heavily manured and sown. With ordinary luck the turf should be ready for play next summer.

Fowler explained the 6,400-yard layout he envisaged and it corresponds almost exactly with today's – with one mysterious exception. The seventh, he declared, would be the best hole on the heath, a double dog-leg measuring about 500 yards:

The fairway, after about 200 yards, bends to the right, and after another 150 bears away to the left. The green, splendidly situated, is long and narrow, with bunkers guarding the right and left fronts and a narrow entrance between them.

That hole, it would seem, was never built. We can only guess that it would have taken him too far – beyond the gallop that runs behind the present green and exceeding the limits agreed by Bonsor and the commoners. Fowler thus lost 100 yards off his seventh, but he compensated by lengthening the eighth.

Eventually, on October 9, 1913, Walton Heath became one of the few clubs to boast two full-length courses. That day the official opening took place after a Match-Play final in which George Duncan had beaten Braid. The Lord

---

[2] *Country Life.*

*Today – view from behind the
13th green of the New.
Photographer: PATRICK WEBB*

*Yesterday – Braid (c1930) plays
his tee-shot to the short second.*

NEW COURSE

○ EXISTING HOLES

○ ORIGINAL NINE HOLES

● FOWLER'S MYSTERY HOLE

ORIGINAL 9 HOLES
(Presently 1-4 & 14-18)

1	311
2	120
3	481
4	233
5	395
6	349
7	502
8	306
9	365
	3162

GRAPHIC COURTESY OF

strokesaver
GOLF'S No1 DISTANCE GUIDE

© 2003 DuCam Marketing (UK) Ltd. Trade mark Strokesaver

Mayor of London, Sir David Burnett, having borrowed one of Braid's clubs, hit the first, ceremonial shot – and to his worshipful relief it soared as straight as an arrow. Braid then presented him with the driver – an old-fashioned scare-headed wood which one can see in the clubhouse today.

The course had only just opened for business when World War I halted progress. Afterwards it soon gained respect, not least because of its variety of angles to the wind. It also had critics. A few felt particularly that hazards placed behind greens encouraged players to be short rather than bold with their approaches.

The New has remained virtually untouched by heavy

hands for 90 years, or at least since 1914, when Bray forced the club to make a different green for the third and alter the fairway of the fourth. The drive over the main road, increasingly dangerous with the increase of traffic, was predictably abandoned, probably in the 'twenties, but the only other significant change would not come until 1937. That year the short 12th on the Old would be abandoned and its green become that of the 14th (New), replacing the original which had been further left and shorter. This lengthened the 14th by 30 yards and created more room for the tee shot on the next hole.

We may perhaps leapfrog our time frame at this point, because since then precious little has happened to disturb

Heather and heaven, New course style. The fourth fairway seen from the bunker beside the third green.

Photographer: KEN MACPHERSON

Traditional...

c1930: Three pictures of the same bunkers on the 11th (New). Above, the traditional Walton 'heathery' look.

Spoiled...

c1953: The bunkers have been shorn. Out of character, say the traditionalists; no natural blending into the heath's landscape.

...Revived

2003: The bunkers restored to their old-time glory.

doned second. The New would be stretched to 6,586 yards, with an sss, like its neighbour, of 73.

The thought of losing the 17th shocked Fowler diehards. Was this not Darwin's 'most ingenious and teasing hole'? Was it not the hole another specialist writer[3] had considered one of the greatest he had played, a hole which, irrespective of season, wind or ground condition, demanded

a tee shot controlled into one spot – and one spot only will do. And the greatness of the hole is that in all circumstances this one spot may be found by the right shot. From this one spot the second is sublimely simple. From anywhere else it is undiluted hell. I am prepared to salute this hole as the creation of genius.

The members would approve the New course proposals by 250 votes to 62, an 80-per-cent majority, but the alterations were not made. They were pre-empted by outside forces in a bitter local struggle that will be explained in chapter 36. Those members who had voted for change remained frustrated; traditionalists felt that destiny had saved their hero's masterpiece. 'Fowler may have made the odd error when making his first course,' one of them told me 'but, with his added experience, not on the New.'

The Old has hosted 23 Match-Play Championships and

Architect Tom Simpson, later to become a business partner of Fowler, drew this plan and landscape of the short sixth on the New. The drop to the left of the green used to be steep compared with the present manicured slope. The Architectural Side of Golf, by Wethered and Simpson (Longman), 1929

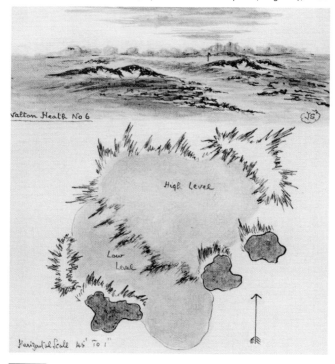

Fowler's original concept. There have merely been minor tinkerings. Today's 16th tee was moved from the right to the left of the 15th green, again creating space and length; bunkers made redundant by modern hitting have been filled in or emptied; one heather-faced Fowler original in the middle of the ninth fairway would be abandoned by a majority vote in 1998. A large, deep hollow at the front of the 15th green which continually flooded was filled in with sundry flotsam and jetsam – including member Keith Birdseye's old car, which had been used on the course for some years.

In the mid-1980s, dramatic changes would be proposed, aimed at improving holes and eradicating congestion. 'Even courses as great as those we enjoy have to change to keep pace with the development of the game,' said the committee. The second hole would be abandoned, two new holes would be built and the 16th and 17th would become one monster of 540 yards. There would be a new 18th tee, the fourth would be shortened to 220 yards to restore the number of par-threes to three and the 10th to 140 to provide a short hole the same length as the aban-

[3] 'Brer Rabbit' in *Golf Illustrated,*

The view from the 18th (New) tee, then and now.

Photographer: PETER CHORLEY

a myriad of illustrious events both amateur and professional. The New has contributed holes to the composite Ryder Cup and European Open courses, been used for qualifying rounds of the Match-Play and shared events with the Old, but it has staged only one big professional championship on its own and that was in 1934 – the first Dunlop Metropolitan Tournament. Perhaps a life out of the headlines and growing up in an elder brother's shadow are why it has remained so untouched by heavy hands and by successive management and green committees.

To revert to my genealogical analogy, and casting the

club as parent, the Old has basked for a century in the traditional love for one's first-born, but the New is gaining similar affection and encouragement to achieve renown for the family. It is growing up: thanks to new back tees it now has a championship length of more than 7,000 yards. The parent, it is clear, wishes it to win a place alongside big brother in the hallowed halls where, courtesy of journalistic enterprise and sundry travelling experts, the world's top 100 courses reside. The New, say its most fervent admirers, could be the ugly duckling whose merits are about to be recognised.

NEW v OLD

FRANK CARRUTHERS (*Golf Illustrated*, 1919)
Goodness knows, the Old course is hard enough, but Mr Fowler has contrived to make the New harder still. Braid puts the difference at two strokes.

CECIL LEITCH (Her book *Golf*, 1922)
The New is the more interesting of the two courses and calls for a greater variety of shots.

BERNARD DARWIN (Writings in 1920's and 1930's)
The New seems to show Mr. Fowler in rather a lighter vein. On the Old he makes more direct frontal attacks on us with his big cross-bunkers. He shakes his fist at us more openly. Especially when the wind is against us on that long flog outward we are more directly conscious of his hostility. The New is just as difficult: in some ways more difficult, since there is no series of comparatively easy holes as there is coming home on the Old. But there is more variety, more tacking this way and that and, in a way, more fun.

'TWO INFERIOR COURSES!'

Having suggested to a certain member of the Epsom Golf Club that he ought to visit Walton Heath, and having learnt that he had acted on our suggestion, we inquired what he thought of the golf there. We have not yet recovered from the reply – 'Two rather inferior courses!'

Golf Illustrated, 1927

CHARLES AMBROSE (Artist/writer, in magazine, 1927)
Mr. Fowler himself prefers the New and many good judges agree with him. When he laid out the Old the idea uppermost in his mind was to follow the way of the Old Course at St. Andrews. Later he perceived that a more irregular arrangement might break too long a sequence of shots with the prevailing wind, or against it, and on the New he varies direction much more.

HAROLD HILTON (*Golf Illustrated*, 1927)
While there are several who would hold that the New is better than the Old, I cannot bring myself to agree.

HENRY LONGHURST (*Sunday Times*, c1934)
The New course is every whit as good as the Old as a test of golf – some say even better – but one may be forgiven for saying that it has not yet quite the same amount of character.

SIR PETER ALLEN (*Famous Fairways*, 1968)
The New, good as it would be anywhere else on its own, is just slightly inferior by comparison with the Old – and about three shots easier – so that it gets scant praise and less than it deserves. If you can play 36 holes in a day, try both.

W.F. DEEDES (*Daily Telegraph*, 1997)
Good judges say that the two Walton Heath courses make the best pair in the country. Certainly I have no preference: both are a delight.

THE FUTURE PRIME MINISTER AT PLAY

It is 1915. World War I is a year old... the club is in its zenith as the golfing playground of leading politicians and other notables... David Lloyd George, Minister of Munitions, is within a year of becoming Prime Minister. Artist Michael Brown poses him about to play – although with his back to the green – on the then 17th hole (now the 16th) of the Old course. Watching him (from left) are Braid, Fowler and Riddell.

The name of Brown, an Edinburgh artist, became synonymous with the golf scenes that were featured on Life Association of Scotland calendars for 25 years. This painting, used for the 1916 calendar, was the last of them.

The original watercolour was purchased by the Club's endowment fund, with the generous support of a number of members, in 2001.

The windmill, like the green and bunker, still exists, but is now within the gardens of a house, The Millfield, now converted to offices.

Chapter Eleven

'THE WAR IS BEING CONDUCTED FROM WALTON'
Lloyd George, Churchill and Co. make the Club a political annexe

'WE MUST MAKE the British people understand that we are at *war*,' thundered Lord Kitchener in 1914, three days after the start of World War I, at a meeting attended by Sir George Riddell. 'They should give up playing and watching games,' the Minister for War continued, '*War* is the game now!' Two days later Riddell was playing golf at Walton Heath.

What is more, he was accompanied by David Lloyd George – Chancellor of the Exchequer, soon to be made Minister for Munitions and destined to become Prime Minister.

The scene no doubt would have incensed Kitchener had he witnessed it. So would the knowledge that not long ago, as war threatened, Winston Churchill, First Lord of the Admiralty, had been golfing on the heath once or twice a week for a year. 'The war is obviously being conducted from Walton's 19th hole,' someone said after Lloyd George became prime minister of the coalition government in 1916. 'Clearly, far more of the business of Britain was done on Walton Heath than in the House of Commons,' another author commented in retrospect.

Angrily as Kitchener might have fixed these golfing politicians with the same stern eyes and pointing finger of his recruiting posters ('Your country needs YOU'), Lloyd George and Churchill could have mounted a spirited defence. Walton Heath had become their haven; a safe house, a refuge for relaxation, where the fresh air might clear the mind, the game act as therapy and the clubhouse serve as a chamber for chat among friends and colleagues.

And there was a phalanx of those friends and colleagues. On the eve of war the membership included four past or future Prime Ministers (Balfour and Bonar Law as well as Lloyd George and Churchill), the Chancellor and First Lord, the Home Secretary (Reginald McKenna), the Secretary of State for War (Jack Seely), the Lord Chief Justice of England (Rufus Isaacs), the Financial Secretary to

Lloyd George in action.

the Treasury (Charles Masterman), the Parliamentary Under-Secretary for the Home Office (Ellis Griffith), the Secretary of State for India (the Earl of Crewe), a former Conservative Lord Chancellor (Lord Halsbury), the Liberal Chief Whip (Percy Illingworth), his predecessor (Alex Murray) and two of Lloyd George's private secretaries, plus others.

The Club boasted at least 24 MPs and 21 members of the Upper House and no party had exclusivity. Cosmo Bonsor, Gathorne-Hardy and Mallaby-Deeley, leading figures when the club began, all became Tory MPs. Now the Liberals were in power and had joined Walton Heath in droves. One day, Riddell and Seely, both Liberals, bumped into Bonar Law, who had recently succeeded Balfour as leader of the Conservatives. 'We were wondering whether it would be consistent with the decencies of political life if you and your partner were to play a foursome with us this afternoon,' said Riddell. Law smiled, but disappointingly made an excuse!

Churchill, who crossed the floor of the House twice in his career, had defected to the Liberals. He and Lloyd George once arrived at the final hole all-square. 'Right,' said Winston, 'Now I'll putt you for the premiership.' So the story goes – and as it was told by a clergyman[1] it may even be true!

There are no prizes for guessing the prime mover in mobilising this political invasion of Walton Heath. Bonsor may have helped begin it, but Riddell emphatically took over – as he took over almost everything and everyone he touched. Golf had become a fashionable fad for parliamentarians and Riddell manipulated the situation to his and the club's advantage.

He had first met Lloyd George as a solicitor, almost certainly through Lascelles Carr and the *Western Mail*.

---

[1] The Rev G. Borlase, *History of Walton-on-the-Hill*, 1929.

Now, helped by his rise at the *News of the World* and increasing wealth, he reeled in the dynamic Welshman as his prize catch and as a result soon had the ear of other leading politicians.

More to the point, they had *his* ear, for Riddell was consumed with curiosity about them, thirsted for information from them, revelled in their company and hung on their every word. As he was nobody's political rival great figures divulged opinions, even secrets to him that they would have reserved in other company.

Riddell persuaded Lloyd George, then 44, to join the club at the end of 1907. He became his audience, listening post, sounding board, informant, occasional adviser and general confidant. His Rolls could be placed at the politician's disposal and so could his elegant London house, 20 Queen Anne's Gate. Early in their friendship he gave him a gold watch, but later it would be a car and between times he built him a house – *Cliftondown*, which was promptly bombed and damaged by the Suffragettes a few days before its completion.

At golf Lloyd George was steady rather than stylish but

Lloyd George playing with (top) Charles Masterman, Financial Secretary to the Treasury.   *Golfing, 1914*

Which paper do you read?

*L*loyd George, following play between George Duncan and Reggie Wilson in the 1913 *News of the World Match-Play Championship, stood a trifle too close to the action. The Press rather relished this but could not agree on the detail. The* Daily News *stated that the player concerned was Wilson and that the referee had courteously requested LG and a friend to 'stand just a little further away, please.' If you read the* Daily Express, *the Chancellor was 'sternly ordered' to move and the golfer he stood behind was Duncan. Anyway, LG, 'with a graceful bow, retreated' – according to the* Daily News.

no pushover, particularly when partnered and protected by Braid. He was playing off 15 when war broke out and claimed that he once got down to 13. That is quite believable – particularly if you trust his word on golf more than many did in politics. 'I could never hit a long ball at golf,' he said, 'but, unlike what might be imagined, I was always straight!'

Above all he was enthusiastic. On the day of a big debate in the Commons prime minister Asquith showed surprise at seeing his chancellor in golfing gear – 'but I told him I'd be back in time to take part.' In October 1918, when he was prime minister and sweating on peace, he phoned Riddell and invited him to lunch at 10 Downing Street. 'One o'clock sharp,' he stressed, 'so that we can go to Walton and play golf.'

The only day he would not play, in this country at least, was Sunday. Indeed, he did not actually play with Riddell that day during the first week of war. August 9 was a Sunday so he compromised: he walked the holes but left his clubs indoors.

One day in March 1915, keen for an antidote to the bulletins from the trenches, he was avidly looking forward to his Saturday game and Sunday rest at Walton when a message arrived from Buckingham Palace requesting his presence at a Saturday meeting with King George V. '*Damn* the King,' he said. When he sent back a reply that he had planned to go away but that if the king wanted to see him he would of course cancel, the monarch said that he certainly would not wish to interfere with the chancellor's weekend. 'God *save* the King,' said Lloyd George.

When he was prime minister his golfing schedule was inevitably disrupted and he might go three or four months without playing. He would come to Walton but remain in his repaired *Cliftondown*, secluded with his then mistress, Frances Stevenson, and imagining that he could hear the guns from the French battlefields. On the afternoon of June 7, 1917, he walked across to the eighth hole and there apparently heard the explosion caused by the blowing apart of the Messines Ridge, timed to take place at a particular hour.

When he did get out on the course impromptu and protracted political conferences would take place on fairways or greens. Did any impatient members, Conservatives perhaps, ever try to drive through him? No such breach of etiquette or patriotism is on record; I mean, would a Walton Heath man *ever*...!

Some did bristle at their prime minister's warped sense of priorities. One day LG joined Riddell, who was playing in a three-ball. A big battle was raging and he had been unable to relax. There were lengthy conversations. Then a detective arrived with a reassuring message from the Front. This made LG happier but not the three-ball behind. 'Look here, old chap,' said one of them, 'Are we playing golf, or are we not?'

If Riddell and Walton Heath were profiting from the presence of Lloyd George, LG was profiting from Walton Heath. He was, in the view of journalist-author Frank Owen, 'making full use of golf... not only for exercise but

Lloyd George. 'A champion of golf although scarcely a champion golfer' was a magazine's caption for this picture. Golfing, 1913

Churchill. Golf, he said, 'is like chasing a quinine pill around a pasture.' On another occasion it was 'a game whose aim is to hit a very small ball into an even smaller hole with weapons singularly ill-designed for the purpose.'[3]

for developing political friendships, mellowing opposition and generally extending his personal activities.'[2]

Churchill, who joined in 1910 when he was 36 and home secretary, was by contrast often a reluctant player, inclined to regard golf as a mere adjunct to conversation. At times he had to be dug out from the clubhouse, where he might be studying the trial of Charles I or rehearsing aloud the proclamation he was to deliver at the investiture of Edward, Prince of Wales. Golf took low priority in his life. Lloyd George said that he had never met anyone with such a passion for politics and that after his marriage ceremony Winston began discussing world events in the vestry, oblivious to the need to escort his bride Clementine from the church.

But even Churchill recognised the game's therapeutic qualities. 'My Darling One,' he wrote to Clemmie, 'I shall be back tomorrow between 11 and 12 and I thought it would do us both good to play a little golf at Walton Heath.'[4] Once, on an afternoon of sunshine and showers, he called his playing partner to his side and recited:

Why am I loth to leave this earthly scene?
Have I so found it full of pleasing charms?
Some drops of joy with draughts of ill between;
Some gleams of sunshine 'mid renewing storms.[5]

[2] *Tempestuous Journey* (Hutchinson, 1954).
[3] *The Wicked Wit of Winston Churchill*, by Dominique Enright (Michael O'Mara Books), 2001.
[4] *Speaking for Themselves*, ed. Mary Soames (Doubleday), 1998.
[5] Robert Burns, *Stanzas in prospect of death.*

Walton Heath Golf Club,

WALTON-ON-THE-HILL,

EPSOM.

21 / III / 10

DEAR *Madam*

I have the pleasure to inform you that you have been Elected a Member of this Club.

Your Entrance Fee is £ 5 : 5 : –

Annual Subscription ... £ 4 : 4 : –

I enclose Banker's Order, which please fill up for

£ 4 : 4 : – , and return to me with Cheque for your Entrance Fee. ✗£1 = 1 = sub

£ 31 May 1910 –

I enclose Book of Rules and List of Members.

Yours truly,

W. Herbert Fowler

Mrs. Winston Churchill

Mrs. Churchill elected.   *Churchill Archives Centre, Cambridge*

Did the doctors recommend Mr. Lloyd George to take up golf? If so, they will be pleased to learn that his handicap has been reduced to 15. A decade ago, the Chancellor of the Exchequer was a 24 man. There are people who say that even now he is the very limit.

Golf Illustrated, 1913

Another day Britain's most notorious war leader picked up a worm from the fairway and tenderly placed it on some bracken. 'Poor fellow,' he said, 'If I'd left you there some ruthless boot would have trampled on you.'

According to the novelist Somerset Maugham (credentials as a golf critic uncertain), Churchill was not only a reluctant player but a poor one – an assessment that will perturb those readers who play off 18, as Winston claimed to do. Braid, reluctant to describe his game, awarded him a place in golf history, apparently declaring that the great man actually invented the greensome. Perhaps Sir Frederic Hamilton, club chairman in a later era, was alluding to that format when he said that 'by selecting Braid as his partner Churchill was able to win a fair proportion of his matches while not unduly hampering the efforts of others.'

Churchill and Lloyd George both found time to serve on the club's wartime committees and were made honorary members. Clemmie also became a Walton Heath member. With the ladies' membership virtually full, she was offered only 'provisional' entry. How embarrassing. Imagine Riddell's reaction! She was rapidly fast-tracked into the permanent category.

Bonar Law was less robust than Churchill and LG, more prone to personal and professional pressures, and Riddell once found him with tears coursing down his cheeks. He did not play as much as he might have done, but for all that claimed to have accepted the leadership of the Conservatives only on the understanding that he would continue life in his own way: 'I like my golf, it keeps me in health and I don't mean to give it up,' he said. Out on the heath he told a partner that he didn't know how he could have withstood the strains of life without it.

How are we privy to all these conversational titbits? Through Riddell, of course! The clubhouse, the fairways, the dormy house and *Cliftondown* joined Downing Street, Queen Anne's Gate, country houses, the Savoy dining table and the plush seats of his Rolls as venues for talk with the great, the good and the not-so-good. Strikes, conspiracies, scandals, budgets, Ireland, the war – these were the topics. And everywhere Riddell was listening, memorising, transcribing; nibbling up morsels for the *News of the World* and later repaying the talkers, who didn't seem to mind, by publishing three volumes of his diaries. He gave instructions that the full, handwritten versions should be kept from the public until 50 years after his death – and then came a fourth book,[6] edited by Professor John McEwen.

The diaries are overwhelmingly political, but viewed in a golf club context the gossip quoted elevates criticism of members by fellow members to an art form! Thus, 'Winston has acted like an extravagant boy given a bank account for the first time' – Lloyd George at the club, referring to Churchill's demands for the Royal Navy. 'Lloyd George is a nice man but the most dangerous little rascal who ever lived' – Bonar Law during a golfing day. 'Masterman is incompetent... unfit to organise a Sunday School' – Riddell's own comment. As for Robert Donald, *The Daily Chronicle* editor and playing partner of the politicians, he was eventually seen by Lloyd George as 'an enemy who must be destroyed,' and his newspaper, which had been critical, was bought from under him.

The spice, the ingredient that for years established the club's character and lent drama, intrigue and secrecy to the place, was this gathering of great political figures using

[6] *The Riddell Diaries*, Athlone Press.

Walton Heath as an extension of their offices and debating chambers. Longhurst recalled how this character reached its zenith during that first world war:

> ...a kind of political eminence which has never been, nor is ever likely to be, attained by any other golf club in the world...Historic decisions were made there, Cabinet ministers appointed and the fate of millions decided.

Dispatch boxes were locked in the safe as the great figures went out to play. At least one political secret was unwittingly disclosed here and found its way into the headlines. For most of the time, though, we may be sure that such disclosures were delivered in huddles and hushed tones in bar or lounge, in the isolation of heath and heather, within the privacy of Riddell's room in the dormy house or at meetings and dinners at *Cliftondown*.

Secrets? Consider Lloyd George, covered in soap suds after a game, being told by Churchill that he had let drop to Riddell that he was leaving the Home Office and going to the Admiralty ('You must tell no one!')... Churchill reporting that, with war on the horizon, our ammunition stores were practically unprotected... LG saying that unless our military methods changed we would be beaten and admitting that the public could not be told the truth... and as late as March 1918, on 'Black Saturday,' having to rush back to London, confiding that the Germans had broken through our lines and that the Third and Fifth Armies had been defeated... all these disclosures were whispered at Walton.

Melodramatic thoughts arise. What if a spy had infiltrated the membership? What if the clubhouse had been 'bugged'! What might our enemies have learned! Mercifully, on November 11, 1918, Riddell's diary records 'Armistice Day. Peace at last.'

What a vibrant membership this was! These were interesting men, with stories to recount and the intelligence and wit to tell them well. It is circa 1913/14. Enter the clubhouse. Conjure up a composite scene like the old paintings in which all the worthies are present at one time.

Exercising his renowned wit may be F.E. Smith, the future Lord Birkenhead, soon to become attorney

Lloyd George's 'People's Budget' of 1909, introducing new taxes on the rich to strengthen the Navy, was rejected by the Conservative majority in the House of Lords.

> The gods of Finance, the Press, the Stage, Politics and the Peerage assemble here. There is an air of wealth about the whole business of the day, which does not exactly add to your peace of mind if you come down in a rattling £170 two-seater which you have bought second-hand on the instalment plan. But the actual golf, if you can forget your own miserable banking account, is glorious.
>
> Dell Leigh, *The Bystander* (1926).

general... and the central figure in the group over there is Rufus Isaacs, KC, or Lord Reading as he will become, the Lord Chief Justice. He is Jewish and therefore, having avoided the 'one-black-ball-in-seven-or-two-in-any-number' that spelt exclusion to applicants, a rarity in a golf club at this time. Earlier, out on the course, he has been bewailing the bad lies that have afflicted him. 'Bad lies?' Lloyd George exclaims, 'As a cross-examiner, you should be an expert at them!' Should you see the two in muffled discourse with Murray, the former Liberal chief whip, the subject may even be the Marconi insider-trading affair controversy, in which all were involved.

This pre-war atmosphere is convivial – less exclusive than in the country houses where the Victorian political

Flemwell's cartoon was entitled The Little Brother of the Poor *and its caption quoted Lloyd George's fellow club member Bonar Law in 1913: 'When the lights are put out and he goes home, after a most eloquent tirade against the evils of luxury, he probably does not deprive himself of any of the little comforts to which any of us are accustomed.'*

elite had sought recreation. But it is not riotous. There is a considerable teetotal influence; Lloyd George, Law and Isaacs, to name but three, join those who, like Riddell and Fowler, drink little or not at all.

But not all these men in this composite clubhouse scene are politicians. If the entire membership were to be lined up you could now find 21 dukes, marquesses and earls, nine barons, three baronets, 22 knights, two bishops, an admiral and four clergy. A host of them, like many of the parliamentarians, have been attracted in through the board's special deals variously described in the minute books, where Mr. X is a 'special' member, Colonel Y is 'honorary' and Sir XYZ has been 'elected without fee.'

That group in the corner includes Press lords and newspapermen (Sir Max Aitken, Sir Harold Harmsworth and others)… this one embraces Lord Knollys, private secretary to George V… over there sits the Lord Mayor of London… and the Bishop of London is there, too. Heroism is also represented, indeed anticipated. Sir Ernest Shackleton's election has been minuted on July 4, 1914. Six months hence, with *Endurance* crushed in the Antarctic ice, he will be drifting on ice floes prior to his 800-mile open-boat

journey to South Georgia and the crossing of its mountainous interior. Admiral David Beatty will lead the Battle of Jutland and command the Grand Fleet.

The less recognisable figures? They are probably merely golfers! High status seems as important as a low handicap. Look at your membership book. According to this only half the 758 male members have handicaps – which can not be completely true but emphasises that Walton Heath is not exclusively concerned with golf.

Nevertheless some top internationals can be spotted, past heroes resting on their laurels. Horace Hutchinson was twice Amateur champion and now, at 54, writes prolifically and perceptively about the game, not least in *Country Life*. Edward Blackwell, it is claimed, once drove from the 18th tee at St. Andrews to the clubhouse steps with a gutta percha ball, and according to who tells you the story that meant 340 or 366 yards and the longest-ever strike with a guttty. The erudite John Low, whom we have met in connection with Fowler, had the temerity a few years ago to predict that Americans would soon be invading and perhaps winning on British courses ('Already I hear the hooting of their steamers in the Mersey').

Two of the group are younger. John Graham has several times been leading amateur in the Open and can still win the Amateur title his talent deserves. How are we to know that he will be killed in the war? As to Bernard Darwin, his literary career has scarcely begun and he plays off plus-two. He will eventually bring his tally of England appearances to eight; also go to the States to report the first Walker Cup for *The Times* and find himself whisked into the team as captain when Robert Harris, another Walton member, falls ill.

One senses the hand of Fowler in attracting some of these golfers, but the prime recruiter of the fashionable and famous has obviously been Riddell. Other clubs can have the runners-up and also-rans of life; the Walton Heath policy is elitist. The members have to be the best; everything first class.

This multi-charactered membership forms a web, and its strands cross, tying together different factions: a collusive network, well hyped from without, strong within its own boundaries and profoundly influencing the area and people outside them.

We have met the politicians… The Press barons, editors and writers are their potential allies or enemies and mutual interests are involved. As the politicians ascend, businessmen in the club find important jobs. One is Stephenson Kent. When he gave evidence in the case of the dead caddie back in 1905 he was described as a coal contractor; surely he is the same Stephenson Kent who will become director-general of munitions labour supply under Lloyd George's premiership (and, incidentally, warn the government that the country is on the verge of revolution)? Another businessman member, James Stevenson, will also go to the ministry of munitions and eventually become *Lord* Stevenson.

Occasionally, in this mishmash of more than 900 male and female members, individuals may find that their interests and ambitions conflict. Will not McKenna, the home secretary, be a factor in the Riddell-Le Bas feud previously described? Le Bas, so it is reported, has allied himself to McKenna in his rivalry with Riddell for Lloyd George's friendship. McKenna lives in a Lutyens house

Sir Ernest Shackleton. Within a few months of being elected he would be drifting on ice-floes, his Endurance *having been crushed in Antarctic ice.*
Golf Illustrated, *1914*

and is thus also part of the *Country Life* clique – which is yet another thread in the web, endowing the club with prestigious publicity, touching it with aestheticism and conspiring with it to influence the village.

I should, perhaps, complete the story of Lloyd George and Riddell. After the war LG appointed his friend Britain's press liaison officer at the various peace conferences and it was at this stage that their association ended.

Their partnership had benefited both, probably in equal measures. The politician had received largesse, hospitality, inside information about others' thoughts and actions, sensible opinions and invaluable advice on press and publicity; Riddell had been swept up the ladder, making valuable contacts, garnering privileged information and

Reginald McKenna, the Home Secretary.
More Pages from My Diary
(Country Life), *1934*

progressing through knighthood and baronetcy to peerage. There was huge opposition to his peerage because he was divorced, but his friend bulldozed it through. The payment-for-honours scandal was weighing heavily on Lloyd George's flowing white mane, but nobody could show that Riddell doled out to anyone for his honours, despite nudges and winks from the cynics.

They fell out over international politics (LG bitterly anti-French and anti-Turk, Riddell the opposite), assisted by a deteriorating personal relationship (Riddell perhaps a little too big for his boots, LG autocratic and sensitive to criticism). The first rupture came in 1920 and, if you believe tittle-tattle, was rendered incurable once the politician's dog – according to whom you listen, a black chow or Bill

the Airedale – pinned His Petrified Lordship to a chair for an hour while LG strolled in his garden in ignorance.

After 1922, when Lloyd George lost the premiership, they rarely met. The *News of the World* had supported Bonar Law in the election and some felt, perhaps unfairly, that Riddell now had less time for his old friend. LG sold *Cliftondown*, which had cost Riddell £2,000, for £7,000, moving first to Chobham, then Churt. The cord between him and Walton Heath loosened and lengthened, though his son Gwylm was soon to join the club, and the directors decided that he should come off the committee. Riddell and LG apparently played their last games not on the heath but at clubs like St. George's Hill, Coombe Hill, Burhill and Hindhead.

THE SPICE OF LIFE

It does not seem to be the least necessary to play golf if you are a member of this famous club. Indeed, people have told me that it is often a distinct disadvantage, as it occupies valuable time which could and should be more profitably employed in the clubhouse. Moreover, there is only one Sunday in each week.

But if, as a budding politician, you are an aspirant for an Honour, an elegant KBE for example, the channels towards such dignities are tortuous and tedious until you join Walton Heath. After which, in careful hands, things become noticeably easier. It is as well to join also if you desire the editorship of a moribund newspaper which is about to be sold and to take on a new life and policy. Most certainly you must immediately join, at all costs, if you want to become an advertising manager, the latter post, as everyone knows, being far the more important of the two.

If, having joined as a young and nervous MP, because it is the correct thing to do, you happen also to be a scratch player, it is advisable to keep this gift in the background as much as possible. When playing round, under political observation, it is as well to fluff your drive at about every second hole, or pull the ball into the rough and take five to get out. Because it is conceivable you might one day be asked to play with a Cabinet Minister. And if, from sheer force of habit or ignorance, you played consistently accurate golf and beat him eight up and seven to play, as you would, you might find that your political career thenceforward had never thoroughly shaken off this blemish. Men do not forget these things...

Lord Riddell chatting to the Secretary.

Mel, *The Tatler*, 1932

But they are very justly proud of themselves as a club are the Walton members. Have they not also got on their members' list that well-beloved Peer who wears two pairs of trousers on wet days and consistently burns the back part of the outer pair before the smoking-room fire; and then, having a super-tax beyond the dreams of most of Lloyd's underwriters, complains that golf is becoming too expensive?...

When I was last at Walton Heath I really enjoyed my day, largely because snow hid the face of the country, and beyond the half-dozen congenial idiots who padded round the course with a red ball, there was no golf. Thus one was able, without feeling one had missed a game, to plunge for the day into that cauldron of life, the clubhouse, wherein the great and the little games are so assiduously played.

The little game is merely Bridge, which any mediocre man may indulge in. But the great games are those which, on inclement days, are played in low tones in the deep armchairs by keen-eyed, rather tired-looking men. Dynasties are set up by them, or swept away. Large blocks of shares are moved about the market. A constituency is 'arranged for' over the post-prandial coffee. Or a big political-cum-newspaper move is set upon its ponderous way by those two potentates in the corner.

It is here that Things Happen, and are known at Walton Heath long before you open your querulous newspaper on the Monday morning. And as you return somnolently to town on the Sunday evening in the big limousine, you feel you have, for a brief space, been allowed a glance into the inner working of the nation.

The fact that you may not have played a round of golf is a matter of no moment .You have seen Life.

E.P. LEIGH-BENNETT, *An Errant Golfer*, 1929

The long-whiskered Doctor

*C*ricket was represented at Walton by its colossus:

The long-whiskered Doctor, that
 laugheth rules to scorn,
While the bowler pitched against him
 bans the day that he was born.[1]

W.G. Grace's Test career was long gone: he was 58 when he joined, having been encouraged to do so by George Beldam, cricketer, golfer and pioneer sports photographer. Although he golfed elsewhere, at Royal Mid-Surrey for example, he probably played at Walton more than almost anywhere.

In November 1906, soon after he arrived, he played in the club's first recorded match, winning both his single and foursome against Home Park. Journeys to the club in Riddell's open Rolls, with Darwin and others as fellow passengers, became regular outings. Darwin recalled that Grace, with his flowing beard, was recognised by everyone they passed, so that the trips were transformed into something of a royal progress.

From the start he hit the ball characteristically hard ('I hate defensive strokes,' he used to say as a cricketer, 'You can only get three off 'em'), taking the club back upright and bringing it down on the ball with tremendous force. Braid said that his length came purely from muscular force and remarkably strong wrist action. Darwin thought him an excellent putter but that his weakness was iron play.

When he had his driver in his hand one perceived that here was a ball-hitting genius who had come to golf a little too late, but with an iron he seemed a very ordinary mortal. There was a favourite nondescript club of niblick ancestry (*made for him by Braid*), which he called his 'cleaver' and used in all possible situations, but it was not, in my recollection, very effective. It has always been said that good iron play is the hardest thing for a late beginner to learn and I have always thought of W.G. as providing sound evidence of that truth.[2]

Unabashed by such criticisms and practising assiduously, the 'long whiskered doctor' played enthusiastically in matches, helped Beldam to win the foursomes knockout tournament in 1910 and at 65 had a handicap of 10 compared with the 18 off which he had played against Home Park. No evidence suggests that he had 'laugheth the rules to scorn' on the golf course and Darwin, many times his foursomes partner, said that to play with him was exhilarating:

He played golf with a mixture of keen seriousness and cheerful noisiness peculiar to him. It was never, as he played it, a silent game: there would come from him, periodically, immense shouts of laughter, or loud greetings to some friend playing another hole. And yet all the time he was trying as hard as he could to win. No one ever extracted a greater poignancy of enjoyment from the holing of a long putt. There is still remembered a very long and curly one holed for a half at Walton which caused him to lie down and roll on the ground in ecstasy.

Once, partnering Riddell, he noticed one of the caddies removing a glass eye. As the old music hall line used to say, it came out in the conversation. Riddell had not noticed the removal and was somewhat shaken when next he looked at the caddie. 'I'm sure he had two eyes at the last hole, now he's only got one,' he whispered to the Doctor. 'Nonsense,' replied Grace, 'of course he's got two. That's the trouble with you teetotallers, you only see half of what's there.'

Grace captured by photographer G.W. Beldam and giving the lie to critics who said he had no follow-through.

Golf Illustrated, *1909*

[1] Francis Thompson, *At Lord's*.
[2] *W.G. Grace* (Duckworth), 1934.

Pankhurst trial opens

Mrs Pankhurst leaves court surrounded by admirers and policemen.

Feb 25. The trial of Emmeline Pankhurst on bomb charges opened at Epsom Court today. The suff-ra...te de... ...at pale-faced but stro... ...at ...me ...al ...idents

but workmen had been due to start only 20 minutes after the bomb went off. The explosion was so

---

ALLEGED PLOT TO MURDER THE PREMIER.

MAN AND THREE WOMEN CHARGED WITH CONSPIRACY.

DOCK PROTE...

FULL STO...

SENSATION:
Premier Lloyd George who w... be poisoned by ... "plotters" ... how the Expres... told shocked readers in the Fi... World War

---

he secrets ...ehind PM murder plot

BY ALEX HENDRY

A BIZARRE plot to assassinate David Lloyd George was a government ruse to discredit peace campaigners, it is revealed in secret papers released yesterday.

The plan was to plant a poisoned nail in one of the First World War prime minister's shoes so he would die within six seconds.

The incident led to a sensational Old Bailey trial in which a Derby mother was sentenced to 10 years in jail.

linked to pacifist and Left-wing causes, had been tricked into the plot so that those campaigns would be discredited.

What provoked concern was that Wheeldon and her fami... were convicted on the e... of a police agent. Alex ... who was never produced ... to be cross-examined.

The jury was told he ha... friends with Wheeldon a... within a week she was tell...

played. He was to dip a nail into the poison then put it in the PM's shoe so that when he pul-led it on it pricked his foot, delivering the fatal dose.

Because there were so many prickly bushes in the course

MRS. PANKHURST SENT...

THREE YEARS' ... SERVITUDE...

A DISORDERLY SCEN...

The trial of Mrs. Pankh... inciting certain persons ... an explosive in a buildi... with intent to destroy or dama... cluded at the Central Criminal Court y... Mrs. Pankhurst, who conducted her own defen... was found *Guilty*, with a strong recommendation to mercy, and Mr. Justice Lush sentenced her to three years' penal servitude. She had previously declared her intention to resist strenuously the prison treatment until she was released.

A scene of uproar followed the passing of the ... A number of women repeatedly ...... and in the excitement ......male sympathizers

There were ... voice struck up ...w." Mr. Justice otest against such emonstrators that, he should have the e, however, fell on nd continued uproar ...arseillaise." removed isorder. Mrs. Pank... e stood calmly in the ...pers, was vociferously Court for the cells. It uiet was restored, and who made the demon-ney desisted he should

com... After furthe... nesses who took shorthand notes of speeches by the defendant, Mr. Bodkin (who, with Mr. Travers Humphreys, prosecuted) closed the case for the Crown.

MRS. PANKHURST'S SPEECH.

...she did not desire to give ...addressed the

2 BROKEN HATPINS AND WRAPPING PAPER FOUND

WHERE UNEXPLODED BOMB WAS FOUND

BROKEN WINDOW

WALL CRACKED HERE

SUPPOSED PLACE OF ENTRY

WOMEN'S BOMBS FOR MR. LLOYD GEORGE

EXPLOSION AT HIS GOLF VILLA.

GUNPOWDER AND PARAFFIN.

MRS. PANKHURST'S BOAST

"We have blown up the Chancellor's house."

Mr. Lloyd George's new country house at Walton Heath, near Epsom, was seriously damaged, though not destroyed, by the explosion of a bomb at six o'clock yesterday morning.

It is assumed to be the work of Suffra-gettes. Mrs. Pankhurst, speaking at Car-diff last night, said:

In M... they have put...Minister

Chapter Twelve

BOMBS, GUNPOWDER, POISON!
Lloyd George's house attacked – and dastardly deeds in the clubhouse?

BOMBS IN Lloyd George's house... a plot to murder him at the Club... threats to vandalise the greens... an attack on the clubhouse... gunpowder, poison, canister bombs! Even worse: the future prime minister debagged on the course! These were the stories that made melodramatic headlines – or rumours – just before World War I.

The suffragettes, frustrated by failure to achieve full voting rights for women, had chosen the preserves of male-dominated sports as battlegrounds. Wimbledon and Henley were targeted and so was golf. In their latest demonstrations the women had fired the Manchester club's pavilion, thrown acid on a course at Leeds and vandalised greens at Bradford Moor. Nearer home, Woking were advised that they were immune because they had suffragettes in membership. Walton Heath and its two courses were potentially high-profile targets, particularly because of Lloyd George. As chancellor of the exchequer and a future prime minister he was personally at risk merely because of who he was and what he stood for.

Early on February 19, 1913, Riddell's bedside telephone brought him alarming news: part of the house he was having built for LG and which was almost finished had just been 'blown to smithereens' by suffragettes. 'We have blown up the chancellor's house,' boasted Emmeline Pankhurst, their leader. 'Why?' asked someone. 'To wake him up,' replied Mrs. P.

She was not totally accurate. For one thing *Cliftondown*, as it would be named, was not the chancellor's house but Riddell's. Sir George had commissioned it for his friend but had not yet presented it to him. Secondly, the house was not completely blown up: you can see it today, renamed *Pinfold Manor* and standing near the club in Nursery Road. Still, a seven-pound canister bomb placed in a linen cupboard severely damaged various rooms. *Golfing* magazine, in

The first time Lloyd George broke his vow not to play on the Sabbath was on a friend's private course – where he was suddenly approached by two women in somewhat masculine garb. 'Give us the vote, you wicked man!' they shouted. 'Go away,' said Lloyd George. The situation looked ugly...until he realised the 'suffragettes' were his playing companions' wives in disguise.

Riddell's diary, 1913

its own idea of a lyrical phrase, described Mrs Pankhurst as 'an old lady whose opponents accuse her of harbouring a stray inhabitant of an apiary in her headgear.'

The house had been empty and Lloyd George on the Continent when the bomb exploded. He pointed out that, had the bomb gone off slightly later and if another that failed had exploded, 12 workmen might have been killed and the damage rendered much worse. Home Secretary and club member Reggie McKenna was determined to prosecute Mrs. Pankhurst, hunger-strike threats notwithstanding: she had not planted the bombs herself but admitted responsibility for inciting her followers to do so. She was duly arrested, tried at the Old Bailey and sentenced to three years' penal servitude.

But did she also conspire to place gunpowder in the clubhouse? It has been said that there was a plot to do so in the club's 'tea pavilion.' It has further been suggested that Mrs P was personally involved and that before her 'dastardly deed' could be perpetrated she was arrested and committed to Surrey Assizes.

This affair seems little known and reports are confusing. One version suggests the date as February 24, 1913, just under a week after the attack on *Cliftondown*, and another as some date that

Cliftondown. Bomb caused severe damage.

Victims of World War I

The Great War of 1914-18 claimed Walton Heath's head greenkeeper and the man whom, as lord of the manor, we may perhaps call one of the Club's co-founders.

Peace was eight months away when, on the night of March 9, 1918, Captain Malcolm Bonsor of the Norfolk Yeomanry led his company, under heavy Turkish machine-gun fire, in an attack on a Palestinian mountain. He was shot through the heart and died instantly. His colonel of regiment paid tribute:

> Everybody is heartbroken. His men loved him. Danger? He didn't know the word. Hill or dale was taken with a sort of philosophical cheerfulness that was simply undaunted.

He was 39. His legacy to Walton lay in his and his father's insistence on first-class courses, his ecological policy for the heath and his conscientious dealings with villagers and commoners which established a balance of interests with the golf club. 'The practices and traditions he established remain relevant and important today,' says club member Ian Huntington, who has written[1] on the subjects.

The greenkeeper was Tom McNeice, a friend of Braid in Scotland and brought down south at his request. Highly respected, he sat on the Greenkeepers' Association executive committee. A private in the Middlesex Regiment, he was killed in France in 1916.

No roll of honour exists to tell us how many other members or employees died, but the story of a survivor, Colour Sergeant Herbert Savage, a local headmaster and an artisan, reminds us of the horrors. On July 1, 1916, first day of the battle of the Somme, he and his mates of the East Surreys went over the top kicking footballs. Their Captain Neville had bought the balls, believing that they would take the men's minds off the terrors facing them. Neville was killed; Savage was awarded the Meritorious Service Medal. One of the balls is in the Queen's Museum, Clandon Park, near Guildford.

Back home, practice trenches stretched from the edge of the courses to Kingswood church. The club did its best for the war effort: pig sties were built and vegetables grown. Members on active service were not charged subscriptions; caddies and green men in uniform were paid a few shillings a week and women and girls worked in their place.

Shortly before the war the board had estimated a cash deficiency of nearly

Tom McNeice – killed in France.

£2,000 and the company's capital was increased to £15,000 by a new share issue. Toward the end of 1914 the club's net profit was £340 as against £1,291 in 1913 and soon descended into losses. Entrance fees, £1,600 in 1914, totalled £170 in 1916; subscriptions fell from £8,832 to £6,405. Soon, all directors' fees were suspended. For three successive board meetings in 1916 only Fowler was present and the clubhouse sometimes echoed – but even then certain guests were not welcome. Up went a notice:

> Objections having been raised by members to naturalised persons of enemy origin using the club, the committee beg to give notice that members may not introduce such persons as visitors or temporary members.

If you saw strangers they were probably officers stationed nearby who had been granted use of the club's facilities, or new members who eventually began filtering in at increased subscriptions – 10 guineas for men, six for ladies. There were a few military events and even a visit from a group of American professionals who had been over to play before the war. Alec Smith, the 1906 US Open champion, was among them and, speaking at a PGA dinner after the golf, hoped that the day would come when a representative match between the two countries would be arranged.

But for the members there were no gold medals, no prizes, no official matches. After 1914 not a ball was hit in competitive anger until 1919.

[1] Dissertation, The History of Walton Heath as Common Land.

month 'after her release from a three-year prison sentence' – but she was not sentenced until April.

One thing is certain: no action against her was taken. Edwina Varley, editing her History of Leatherhead in 1988, wrote: 'Her committal to the Surrey Assizes after a night in Leatherhead, where it is said the chief of police gave up his bedroom for her, led to the dismissal of this particular case.' I suspect that if any such deed took place it happened after the Cliftondown bombing but before she was sentenced for it and a handwritten entry in the assizes book for June 1913, while not mentioning the crime, seems to support this. It notes that Emmeline Pankhurst 'had been tried, committed and sentenced to three years' penal servitude at the Central Criminal Court, and upon proof of the certificate of such committal all recognizances are discharged.'

Meanwhile the vandalising of courses was continuing. 'The suffragettes damaged greens at 12 courses, from Sheringham on the Norfolk coast to Sandwich on the Kent coast,' wrote historian Roland Quinault[1] in later years. But did they ever come to Walton Heath? It has always been accepted that the greens were guarded day and night, but nothing in the minutes suggests an attack. However, Quinault is unequivocal: 'The sixth to tenth greens were vandalised, although the course had been guarded by 100 caddies specially selected for their strength.'

Lloyd George and Riddell outside Cliftondown.

The relationship and confusion surrounding the bombing, vandalism and gunpowder plot seems even to have inspired a thriller, *Dance in Blood*[2] featuring 'Nell Bray, The Suffragette Sleuthess'! Certainly an additional real-life plot involving Lloyd George – an attempt to murder him – sounds like a stage melodrama and not a very good one either.

By now, the country was at war and Lloyd George was prime minister, but the affair had nothing to do with the suffragettes. The central figures were a police agent, Alex Gordon, and a Derby woman, Alice Wheeldon. When the case came to court the jury were told that Gordon had infiltrated a group comprising Mrs Wheeldon and some of her family, that she had told him of her plans to murder the politician and that she had invited him to become the hit man – or, to be specific, the poisoner.

The assassination was to be at Walton Heath Golf Club and Gordon was told first to get a job as a caddie. Mrs. Wheeldon sent him a message, hidden in a meat pie, instructing him to meet the person who was to supply the poison. He was then to dip a nail in the poison and place it in Lloyd George's shoe, so that when he put it on he would prick his foot. Death would come within six seconds and nobody would notice the puncture mark because such wounds were frequent at the club through members catching themselves on the prickly bushes!

At the Old Bailey Mrs Wheeldon was sentenced to 10 years and, after an appeal was rejected, distinguished herself in Aylesbury prison, according to reports by the governor, by going on a hunger strike and threatening to rip out the eyes of warders. One of her daughters and a son-in-law received lesser sentences.

Within 10 months Wheeldon was released – by order of Lloyd George. There had been something phoney about the case; in particular, police agent Gordon never appeared and could not be cross-examined. Suspicions that the family had been set up developed. They were closely linked to pacifist and left-wing causes and many people believed that they had been tricked into the case so that these campaigns would be discredited. Secret papers released in 1997 suggest that it was a government ruse to discredit peace campaigners.

Which leaves us with the case of the debagging? It is referred to in a book by former professional Dale Concannon,[3] who quotes a report that it happened to LG when he was playing at Walton. Did it really occur? Was the report accurate? Or was someone caught with his trousers down? Concannon tells me his information came from a parliamentary source but that he was never able to track it down specifically.

Finally, let us return to the *Cliftondown* bombing for a postscript. During the war Lloyd George introduced Riddell to Mrs Pankhurst. Riddell told her that she had been convicted on the evidence of a reporter on his *Western Mail* who had covered her inflammatory speech in Cardiff the evening after the bombing. In return Mrs P confirmed that she had not known it was his house. 'I hope it was well insured,' she said. 'The insurers would not, in fact, pay,' replied Riddell, 'But that doesn't matter. In those days the blowing up of Lloyd George's house was an event of importance. Today the blowing up of an entire town counts for nothing.'

---

[1] *Land and Society in Britain, 1700-1914*, ed. Negley Harte and Roland Quinault (Manchester University Press), 1996.
[2] By Gillian Linscott (Virago Books), 1998.
[3] *Golf – The Early Days* (Salamander Books), 1994.

Chapter Thirteen

THE IMPORTANCE OF ERNEST
Holderness – what a player he was!

HOW MANY AMATEUR champions of the last 10 years can you name without diving into the reference books? I am addressing not the knowledgeable coterie of golf historians but the average, youngish club man or sports enthusiast. The answer, surely, is not a lot.

Before World War II our Amateur Championship was one of the 'majors.' When Bobby Jones achieved his grand slam in 1930 it was by winning the two Opens and the two Amateurs, British and American. When lives were more leisurely and before professional prize money soared and tempted, amateurs *stayed* amateur and the champions became stars, lionised by artists and cartoonists and often afforded more publicity than the professionals. Several names still strike chords: John Ball and Hilton, both of whom won Opens... Freddie Tait, killed in the Boer War and recalled at Walton by the Tait Bronze... Cyril Tolley, Roger Wethered, Jones.

But where in most people's memories is Sir Ernest William Elsmie Holderness, Bt? The *cognoscenti* recall him – though less vividly than they do his contemporaries Wethered and Tolley – but for others the answer is pretty well nowhere. Even to many young members at Walton, where his membership spanned 55 years, he is not much more than a posh name on the honours boards.

Yet Holderness was twice Amateur champion... played six times for England... was in three Walker Cup teams... won five President's Putters, thrice beating Tolley... became president of the English Golf Union. At Walton Heath he won 18 gold medals... the Surrey amateur championship... and, with Noel Layton, another international, two London Foursomes. At least six times he equalled or beat the Old course amateur record, the last such achievement coming when he was 59.

He was born in India, where his father Sir Thomas was a high flyer in the Civil Service, but learned his golf at Dornoch, north of Inverness, where the family had a

holiday home. There he would conjure up shots over flower beds and banks, while on the majestic, windswept links he would play not only as per the card but, in the quest for unusual challenges, by sundry intermediate routes – from the first tee direct to the eighth hole, for example. Imagine that today!

At Radley School, complications having occurred during an operation for appendicitis, he had to give up robust team sports and applied himself seriously to golf, modelling himself on Vardon. During World War I he was rejected for the Army.

He first came to notice in 1909 as an Oxford freshman and four years later was offered membership at Walton, where Braid would apply the final polish – not through formal teaching but merely by playing with him. And at a slightly later date, mother came, too – 18 handicap, a force among the ladies and a considerable influence on her son.

Ernest's prime was in the 'twenties. When he won his first Amateur, in 1922 at Prestwick, 20,000 people ('a tense, heaving phalanx of humanity,' someone wrote) followed his final against the Scot John Caven, whom he beat by one hole. He won again in 1924.

I am sorry Sir Ernest Holderness has been beaten in the Amateur Championship, for it would have been a wonderful record to be the winner three times in four years.

I think the General Strike must have played some part in his downfall, for though he is not actually in the Home Office department which deals directly with strikes, every clerk in the office was pressed into emergency service in addition to doing his ordinary work.

The Home Office must have been during that week a very bad training ground for the Amateur championship.

Writer in *Daily Sketch*, 1926

ERNEST HOLDERNESS, Bt. – Oil painting by James Quinn, 1925.

Sir Ernest's medals were presented to the Club by the Holderness family and unveiled in August 2002 by his daughter, Margaret Southwood. The 38 medals include those for his two Amateur Championships, five for President's Putters, two for London Amateur Foursomes and 14 won at Walton Heath.

From left at the unveiling: Sir Martin and Andrew Holderness (grandsons), Pamela, Lady Holderness (daughter-in-law), Jane (granddaughter), Margaret Southwood (daughter), Philip Truett (club archivist) and Charles Harvey (2002 captain).

Holderness was a quiet, modest man. He was also the archetypical amateur, working full-time at the Home Office, practising in the evenings, using holiday time to play in championships, sometimes arriving only on the eve of his first match and reporting himself unable to spare the time for any Walker Cup match in the States.

'What a player he was! Walton Heath never had a member quite like him,' Laddie Lucas, Walker Cup player of the 'thirties and 'forties, once recalled. He was correct on both counts. The club had had many fine players – internationals like C.E. Dick, with his eight gold medals, and Angus Hambro, first man to win one with a score below 80 – but none was as outstanding as Holderness. What a player indeed!

> The best amateur Britain has produced in 15 years. For direction in driving, accuracy with irons to the hole and steadiness in putting he is superior to either Mr. Tolley or Mr. Wethered.
> *R.E.Howard, golf writer, in 1924, year of Ernest's second Amateur victory*

> He had that simple and, in the best sense, elementary sort of style that enables a man to leave his clubs for a year or two in the attic and, on retrieving them, play from memory.
> *Henry Longhurst*

> He had an extraordinary knowledge of the stroke and swing and taught me more when we were at Oxford than anyone in my lifetime.
> *Roger Wethered*

> He was like a spring. He wound up, let it go and never missed.
> *Cyril Tolley*

Unlike Wethered and Tolley Holderness was slightly built. He was not a long or dramatic hitter, but with strong, flexible wrists, whipcord timing and lowish trajectory could pull power out of the bag when needed: in the morning round of that Prestwick final he drove from the 18th tee to the clubhouse railings, at least 300 yards. 'One never expected to see him hit a huge shot, but neither did one ever expect to see him hit a crooked one,' said Darwin.

Perhaps one reason his name has not quite retained the charisma of that of his two rivals is this essentially undramatic orthodoxy. Another, maybe, is that he has always seemed such an establishment figure: senior civil servant and, from 1924, baronet – succeeding his father, who died after collapsing at Walton while escorting Lady Holderness and her playing partner from the 18th green to the clubhouse. 'A Very Important Person in the Home Office, which is perhaps why he has never been known to smile,' Charles Graves wrote cruelly in *The Bystander*.

But in his day Sir Ernest, too, was a star: eulogised in print, feted at dinners, invited to write for magazines and newspapers. Interest in him and his family sometimes made golf periodicals look like society glossies. On front

Bobby Jones a member

*T*he world's greatest amateur was a Walton Heath member. For at least 13 years the lists included:

Jones, R.T., Atlanta Golf Club, Georgia, USA.

Yes, we are talking of Bobby Jones – epitome of sportsmanship, perhaps the most revered figure in the history of golf. His connection may have begun in 1926, the year of his first Open Championship. No membership roll from that year has survived, but he was certainly listed in 1927 and thenceforth until the war.

Bob, as he preferred to be called, was more honoured invitee than normal member, but he certainly played on the heath during the 'twenties. In 1960, R.B.Dunwoody, a prominent member, presented the club with a picture of his doing so. Where is it?

THE DEMON HOLE-CUTTER OF WALTON HEATH

The unfortunates who competed on the opening day of the 1925 Surrey Amateur Championship at Walton Heath caught it hot and strong in the newspapers. 'The most difficult course in the world,' thundered one critic, 'would hardly justify the appallingly high scoring that was the rule yesterday, and with very few exceptions the exhibition of golf was miserable.' (Holderness took 80 on the New; Noel Layton 93 on the Old; at least one eminent player tore up his card; others failed to qualify). I was playing myself and amassed scores of 83 and 90, including one ten and three sevens.

What was wrong? How can one account for the 'miserable' golf? The reply is, ask the greenkeeper, or whoever was responsible for cutting the holes and placing the teeing-grounds.

Any course laid out by Mr. Fowler is quite difficult enough to extend any amateur from normal tees with the holes cut somewhere in the centre of the greens. It is pitiful to see a fine hole, depending upon its perfect length for its beauty, ruined by some ignoramus of a greenkeeper whose one idea is to make his course as

long and as difficult as possible. Perhaps there are greenkeepers who are also good golfers; if so, I have not met them.

Sir Ernest Holderness did not blame anybody but himself for his own performance. Naturally he would not. All he said was that most of the holes were cut so near the hazards behind them that nobody dare risk being 'up'; they were frequently cut in very tricky places.

Whether the cutting of holes and placing of tees should be left to a man who is not an expert golfer himself is so doubtful and at the same time so important a point that clubs would do well to give it more attention than it seems to get. Any club – just as surely as any woman – likes to be admired and liked. Every greenkeeper worth his salt likes people to admire and like his course, and to want to come again. If he worries them too much they will not want to come again.

The cutter of the holes, in a heroic attempt to show all and sundry what a great golf course his is, lamentably defeats his own object.

CHARLES AMBROSE, Magazine article, 1925

Holderness's 'simple and, in the best sense, elementary style' stop-framed in 1925. Golf Illustrated

covers Lady Holderness was portrayed, all ball gown, pearls and boa feathers, and his fiancée was featured in riding gear. Inside pages carried wedding-day pictures of their prominent guests, including Braid resplendent in top hat.

Holderness wrote course descriptions, instructional pieces, humorous essays, even short stories, and might allude to anyone from Aristotle and Epictetus to Thomas Hardy and the Duke of Wellington. In one article, *Confidence*, he attributed some of his success at match-play to following the philosophy of Jones, who taught himself to play purely against 'old man par':

> The road to confidence is to learn how to play every stroke to the best of one's ability and to take each stroke as it comes without looking further ahead at the scoreboard.

Yet Holderness did *not* always exude confidence and was occasionally humiliated. In the 1926 Amateur he lost in the second round to a 17-year-old boys' champion, Robert Peattie, and his Walker Cup record was poor: no wins and

two defeats in singles, two wins and one loss in foursomes. During the 1930 match, his last, reporters painted a painful picture of his 10 and 8 defeat by George Voigt. 'I would never have believed he had so many bad shots in his bag,' wrote one of them. 'I am sure he has never swung so fast. To see such a fine golfer in such straits was pathetic.'

He was sometimes unwell and often short of practice, but one senses that his failures were inextricably bound up with his personality.

> His only failings appeared to be a certain lack of physical and temperamental stamina. That he takes a great deal out of himself when playing is most plainly evident.   *Hilton*

> Nobody could believe he finds any pleasure in the experience. There is an almost deathly pallor on his face. He looks drawn and anxious.   *Howard*

A friend of the family described him thus:

> He was highly strung and nervous and sometimes couldn't sleep during the course of a competition. His mother became

High Societies

It wasn't just the membership that reflected Riddell's professional passions and ambitions, it was the character of the visiting teams and societies. Editors and journalists, barristers and solicitors, politicians and bankers arrived to play. Bishops and vicars came, too. If your society was not based on one of these professions or vocations you were hard pressed to get a date.

Lords versus Commons, Commons v Bar, Church of England v Press, Parliamentary Press v Commons, London Press v Provincial Press, Parliamentary Mixed Foursomes... these were just some of the contests attracted to Walton. A Press society played there as early as 1905; by 1907 the Commons were playing the club and London's solicitors were opposing the Press.

Members and strangers mingled and overlapped in these events: Prime Minister Balfour, the Bishop of London, Sir Robert Donald the editor, Gilbert Jessop the cricketer, artists like Harry Rountree and Clement Flower – who painted The Triumvirate, *a copy of which inevitably hangs in the clubhouse. Oh, what days! Carefree competition, the best of company, Riddell's hospitality, lunches at the club, dinners at the Savoy!*

The Parliamentary Handicap
In 1924 a new era of parliamentary association began. The Parliamentary Handicap, open to everyone at Westminster from peers to doorkeepers,

had begun in 1891 on Tooting Bec Common – described by Lord Newton, a competitor, as 'a confined area intersected by roads, frequented by perambulator-wheeling nursemaids and tramps' and containing hazards such as street lamps and 'forbidding gorse clumps whose recesses, for various reasons, were best left unexplored.'[1]

The Handicap later migrated to some of the finest courses in the land, but shortly before World War I the event had been abandoned, to quote a contemporary report, 'owing to the strength of feeling aroused in the party struggles of the time'! This probably was not so much because of any possibility of fisticuffs between different persuasions but because of the suffragettes, who were reported to be planning to attack the event.

Two future prime ministers, Balfour and Bonar Law, had won the Handicap and both were Walton members. So was Angus Hambro, also a winner (off plusfive) and largely responsible for reviving it. Nevertheless, for many years the event was never brought to the heath.

At last, in 1924, it came – and the members were not best pleased, more than 50 signing a protest against both courses being reserved on a Saturday, the first day of the tournament. There were 100 entrants but not a single cabinet minister. 'To such depths of gloom has golf been plunged by a Socialist Government,' complained writer R.E. Howard in a magazine. In

1926 the event returned, weeks before the end of the General Strike. Who won? Why, the Minister of Labour, Sir Arthur Steel-Maitland!

From 1931 Walton became the event's home for 37 successive tournaments; add the four played in the 'twenties and you get a total of 41. Winners would include the future Lord Brabazon of Tara, Sir John Simon when Foreign Secretary, Selwyn Lloyd, later to be Foreign Secretary and Speaker, Lord Balfour of Burleigh, former Walker Cup captain Laddie Lucas, sundry backbenchers and clerks, a gallery correspondent and a police constable. The name the Parliamentary Golf Association really wanted to see on the list was that of the Prince of Wales – but that is another story.

The Lucifers
Some of the biggest and grandest affairs at Walton from the late 'twenties were the gatherings of the Lucifer Golfing Society.

The Lucifers decided to form themselves into a sort of golfing Mecca, aiming, via friendship and hospitality, to bind together in spirit players from all over the world – or, as things turned out, at least those in the British Empire. They began an annual competition open to all overseas players with handicaps of 18 and below. The first, in 1928, was held at Sunningdale, but thereafter, wooed by Riddell, the meetings came to Walton Heath. The Lucifers saw their aims as:

> A first step on a road that, winding through the field of sport, may lead us on to the great uplands of world peace and unity... Golfers from every part of this great association of free peoples, meeting annually to dispel jealousies and doubts under the shadow of a game that calls forth many of the highest qualities of sportsmanship.[2]

Mrs Cecil Norton, winner of the 1913 Ladies' Parliamentary Handicap, drives off the eighth tee.

Golf Illustrated

[1] *The Parliamentary Handicap, a short history,* revised 1991.

[2] From report and speeches at 1928 meeting.

Whoops! Sir John Inskip, the Attorney General, achieves an air shot on the first tee in the 1933 Parliamentary Handicap – and under the eyes of The Prince of Wales! Starter James Braid, like the ball, remains unmoved. The Prince, conceding six shots, won by seven and five. Golfing

Against this backcloth of international idealism huge numbers entered the meetings, stayed in Lucifers' houses and were entertained at banquets at the Savoy. In 1936, the trophy, adorned with the figure of Lucifer and two lions emblematic of the Empire, would be won by the 19-year-old Bobby Locke from South Africa.

The banquet speeches, though witty, were delivered with missionary-like zeal, but at Walton the affairs dissolved into something far less formal:

> This Empire Overseas Meeting is the jolliest of all meetings. It represents two days of sheer fun, even unto complete schoolboyishness. The competitors meet and greet each other with a perfect sense of camaraderie. For two days they swap experiences, joke, laugh and make merry.[3]

Captain Carlton Levick, organising meetings in the 'thirties, knew his men. While orthodox notices urged against slow play in fairness to others, he appealed to his players on different terms:

> Please walk quickly between strokes so as not to delay your next drink.

The relationship between the Lucifers and Walton Heath remains close. Memberships overlap, matches and other events are played and the Overseas Meeting, now re-named the Commonwealth Tournament, continues.

[3] Golf journalist E.M.Cockell, 1931.

Lloyd's

Another way to get a date in the early days, of course, was through old acquaintance – always provided that one's society sprang from a respectable professional background. Lloyd's, the first 'company' golf club in England, fitted the bill professionally and socially. Moreover it had among its founders Sidney Boulton (apart, incidentally, from John Franklin-Adams, great-grandfather of Walton Heath's centenary year captain). Boulton subsequently became Lloyd's chairman. Meanwhile, more importantly, he was a member of Walton Heath.

Boulton and his colleagues certainly held their 1906 autumn meeting on the heath – and Lloyd's still play their spring event there today. Since Walton Heath became a members' club Lloyd's has provided seven of its captains.

Today's biggest

Today's largest visiting society, playing both courses, is that of the Livery Companies, who play for the Prince Arthur Cup. Livery Companies, Seniors, Hazards, London Solicitors...all are modern equivalents of the old-time visitors.

his trainer and disciplined him strictly. He took to smoking a pipe and this seemed to calm his nerves. He liked to play serious matches in silence. One day he was drawn against a voluble American. He stood it for a few holes, then, finding it upset his concentration, said: 'You go up your side of the fairway, I'll go up mine and we'll meet on the green'. He was highly intelligent and by nature kind, generous, shy and retiring. I think he was inclined to be imposed on by more forceful characters.

One senses that he was happiest amid the familiarity of Walton Heath – plus-three, often without a caddie and carrying about five clubs. Even there he was reserved, says Brian Pope, the old English rugby international and pre-war member, 'a very quiet man who didn't much use or drink in the clubhouse.' Tolley recalled 'a lovely man – strict with the young, but gentle, caring and never wasting a word.'

He continued to play after World War II and won the last of his 18 gold medals in 1949. Sadly, toward the end of his life – he died in 1968 aged 78 – he suffered badly from arthritis like his role model Jones.

Comedy of Errors

*H*olderness's 1921 London Foursomes quarter-final, in which he partnered Noel Layton against defending champions Mid-Surrey, remains one of the classic matches in the event's history – three down with six to play, they won by two and one – but their final against Addington was notable more for eccentricity. At the third, Addington's Mr. Mellin hit one of the Walton caddies with an atrocious drive so took the hole by default. At the fourth, nervous and confused in trying to get out of the rough, his

partner Mr. Hooman played two shots in succession so this time it was Walton Heath who won the hole. Holderness and Layton, having beaten Addington four and two, won again in 1926, once more enjoying home-green advantage, but it would be almost a quarter of a century before the club next won the trophy.

Championships

*T*HE RIDDELL YEARS encompassed a golden age of amateur golf. At Walton there were few competitions apart from those for the gold medals, where, progressively, Dick, Holderness, Layton and Harry Braid came to dominate, but the club hosted men's and women's national championships, matches and the very best of societies.

The first big amateur event for men was the English Championship of 1926, only the second of its line, and it has a link with today's membership. The losing finalist, RAF champion Cecil Hayward, was Prue Riddiford's father. Moreover, her son Martin married into the family of the man who beat him, Thomas Froes Ellison, from Hoylake!

Long before that, in 1913, more than

Ellison and Hayward in 1926.

a decade before the EGU was founded, a County Golf Unions tournament for Daily Mail cups and embracing representatives of shires as far away as Fife

and Caernarfon had come to Walton. 'It is a course that makes you think before every shot,' said the Welsh runner-up, Rowley, after losing a 36-hole final to a 19-year-old from Somerset. 'For my part I prefer something a little easier.'

There were international trials, Surrey championships and matches on level terms between the county's amateurs and professionals. In 1924 a minor sensation was caused when James Braid and J.H. Taylor were both beaten by their gentlemen opponents. Braid contributed to his one-hole defeat by Addington's eminent Robert Harris (who was also a Walton Heath member) by holing his adversary's ball as a result of a stymie.

Match Milestones

A potted history of Club matches during the Riddell years:

First recorded match: At home against Home Park, November 13, 1906. With W.G. Grace's help, Walton Heath won by eight matches to three.

First against a university: Eleven days after the Home Park match, against Oxford. Thick fog. Club won comfortably.

First against Cambridge: February 15, 1908. Another easy win.

First against Artisans: July 25, 1907. Club won 8-0.

First defeat: Glamorganshire, playing at home, won 9-3 in July 1907, reversing result of match at Walton.

First loss to a university: Oxford won 5½-4½ in 1911.

First match v Oxford and Cambridge Society: March 1914 but abandoned through rain. Next played 1920, club losing 12-4.

Oxford v Cambridge: 1912 match would be played at Walton, said Press. It wasn't: Cambridge chose Prince's, Sandwich.

New opposition: Sunningdale, St George's Hill, Mid-Surrey among 10 fixtures in 1920.

Best-ever teams?: Britain's outstanding amateur champions played during 'twenties: for example, in 1920 Roger Wethered and Cyril Tolley for Oxford, Ernest Holderness for club alongside Harry Braid (Scotland), Bernard Darwin and Noel Layton (England). Three years later, Walton's top three, Layton, Braid and Tipping, were all internationals. ('A team of only moderate strength,' reported a golf periodical).

Halved in one? Nearly! In 1922 against Oxford, Stanley May holed in one at 12th; his opponent's ball landed four inches from pin.

1928: Harry Braid (left), son of James, plays J.H. Taylor, Jr.

Stormy weather: Oxford's matches blighted by weather during 'twenties. In 1923, temporarily suspended due to poor visibility; 1924, curtailed by rain; 1928, five matches abandoned in snowstorm.

Japanese visit: Club beat Japanese Golfing Society 5-1 in 1926, Sir Emsley Carr diplomatically losing.

Sons of famous fathers: In 1928, Harry Braid (WH) beat J.H. Taylor junior (Oxford).

Universities only? For 10 years until 1932, with two exceptions (Irish Golfing Zingari and the Japanese visit), only university fixtures were recorded in match book. Fixture with Royal Lytham then listed.

Won 47, halved 2, lost 13: Summary of club's 62 recorded results up until 1932. Defeats (six) had exceeded wins (three) only in 1920.

First defeat by Cambridge: Would not come until 1935, 27 years after first fixture. Score was 9½-8½ – though newspapers gave four different ones! Holderness beaten by 19-year-old Laddie Lucas – his third singles defeat against a university in 22 years.

Chapter Fourteen

CHIP OFF THE BLOCK
Harry Braid – son of the champion

IN 1923, when Sir Ernest Holderness was at his peak, someone wrote to the golfing press and, camouflaged by a pseudonym, dared to nominate Walton Heath's three greatest players. One was Holderness and the second Noel Layton, his London Foursomes partner.

The third was the baby boy whom I recorded in chapter three as being christened Harry Muirfield Braid and, in 1904, arriving at Walton where his father was starting his new job.

By 1920 the champion's son had grown into a massive 18-year-old chip off the old block. He had his father's height, the same huge hands and feet and, at plus-two, much of his talent. Inevitably, the hype began:

> Skilful beyond his years … Out-driving his father on occasion … The same snappy wrist action at impact, the same drawing in of the club after it has gone through… *and then*, Braid's son to play in Amateur Championship.

Fittingly, the 1920 championship was at Muirfield, scene of his father's first triumph in an Open, but fate dealt the teenager a cruel and uncanny hand. Out of 165 competitors his first opponent was Holderness!

If Harry had nerves, an incident early in the match must have tautened them to snapping point. Watching Holderness play, he accidentally let his club slip from his grasp and it fell on top of his ball. This was counted as a stroke and he lost the hole. Shaken, he lost the next hole as well.

Then, pulling himself together, he counter-attacked – and coming to the final hole Holderness was only one up. Braid pushed his drive, and as he played his second the

Postcard message from James Braid as he prepared to watch son Harry in his second Amateur Championship at Hoylake in 1921. Harry lost to Darwin in the fourth round.

grass turned the club and his ball finished 50 yards wide of the green. Holderness was always going to get a four, so only a miraculous shot could keep Harry alive. It almost happened: his pitch finished two feet from the pin. The youngster had lost by one hole.

The professional's son, never mind that he had been to Whitgift School, was at that time still a Walton Heath Artisan and had been entered in the championship as such. Later that year, though, he was elected an honorary member of the golf club. The directors saw this not only as a gesture to Harry but as an additional 50th birthday present for his dad. In a brief speech James said he felt deeply touched, it was a unique honour for an artisan.

Harry – his action from strike to follow-through.

CHURCH V PRESS

Once a year the more or less heretical representatives of the London Press come into close contact with the Church. The annual golf match between the temporal and the spiritual powers took place at Walton Heath on Friday last. And the newspaper men are all the better for the association, as a more genial and jolly set of sportsmen it would be hard to meet than the Bishop of London's team.

If there are black sheep from the church point of view, among the journalists, there are dark horses among the golfing clergy; they always play above their handicaps.

The Bishop encourages the clergy by his example. As a patron of golf the Bishop has done for clergymen what Lord Balfour did for politicians 30 years ago. One of the cheeriest members of the Bishop's team is the Rev. H. Must, who is almost scratch. He acts as honorary chap-lain at Pentonville Prison, and entertains his opponent on the round with accounts of his experiences.

One advantage which Church golfers have over the laity is that they are able to exercise greater patience and self restraint. They do not fall back on language to add to their discomfiture in case of difficulty. There are tantalising incidents in almost every match which sometimes provoke expletive exclamations and occasionally the Bishop has been heard to relieve his feelings by saying, "tut-tut." On other occasions, when the ball, instead of taking the wrong turning which it should have done because of its misdirected start, comforts its owner by unexpectedly doing the right thing, the Bishop's partner would say, "That one had the episcopal blessing." The pressmen, I think, thoroughly enjoyed their uphill fight with the parsons, and the Bishop's team went home happy.

SIR ROBERT DONALD, newspaper editor and member c1920

Harry Braid in 1978.

The son was promptly recruited into the club team, taking his place and winning against Oxford – a university side headed by Tolley, the 1920 Amateur champion, and Wethered! However he maintained his allegiance to the Artisans and he and his elder brother James junior, a scratch man himself, represented them in an 18-a-side foursomes match *against* the club. In the top match Harry and his partner Bennett beat Holderness and Edgar B. Beck by seven and six. In later years he would become for a long period the Artisan club's president.

Originally most people had expected that Harry would turn professional, but he never did so. For one thing, like his brother, he had made a promising start in business; for another it was said that James had adopted the same attitude to his son's future as his parents had taken towards his and that he had not wished him to rely on golf for a living. Later in life Harry said he could not recall ever having a lesson from his father – almost incredible and partly contradicted by the photograph on page 28. Whatever the truth, the champion's judgment about his son's career proved correct: Harry became chairman of the Johnnie Walker whisky company and a director of Distillers and in 1967 received the OBE. His brother was a director of the Walker company.

He was twice selected for Scotland against England and played in more Amateurs, reaching the last 16 at Deal in 1923. But further opportunities were limited – business took a hand and so apparently did his health. 'Harry Braid, son of the Old Man, would probably have been the best amateur in the country if he were not delicate despite his huge physique,' *The Bystander* conjectured in the 'thirties. Longhurst recalled playing with him when he was 55 and out of practice yet still able to hole St. Andrews in 71, with two threes, 15 fours and a five.

Meantime his golf was largely confined to Walton. There he hit the ball prodigious distances, won six gold medals, the last when he was nearly 60, and equalled the Old course record of 74. His *annus mirabilis* would come in 1935, when he took both gold medals, became the first winner of the Prince of Wales' Challenge Cup and played one of the finest rounds in the club's history.

In the autumn meeting he and E.B. Tipping had tied, but in the replay Braid returned 67 (34 out, 33 in), nine strokes better than Tipping and five less than Holderness's record. The card showed eight threes, seven fours and three fives; he single-putted nine greens and had 11 birdies. For all that, it was not recognised as a record because some of the competition tees were not in place.

Harry was successively committee man, captain, long-serving company director and honorary life member. By the time he died, aged 79, in 1980, his membership had spanned 60 years and his memories reached back to the days when, as a tiny boy, he watched the golfers arrive at the station from London and pack themselves into the old horse brake for the final trek to the course.

Chapter Fifteen

Good and Bad News for the Village
Did the media sensationalise local problems?

A T A POLITICAL MEETING held in Walton a few years after the Club was formed, a Free Trade tub-thumper was passionately promoting the policy of international trade without restrictive tariffs as the panacea for everyone's woes. Having waxed lyrical about the air of prosperity in the village he spread his arms and confidently asked his audience, 'Now to what is all this due?' Before the desired answer could be given a shout came from the back of the hall: 'The Golf Club, you fool!' Collapse of stout party.

The heckler had a point. Golf, following Cosmo Bonsor's railway, was revolutionising the village and continued to do so into the 'thirties. The Rev. Granville Borlase, rector of St Peter's, who told the story in 1929,[1] continued thus:

> House after house has been erected by those whose main desire is to be adjacent to a good golf course. What has happened at Walton has, of course, happened all over Surrey and in many parts of the south of England. The advent of golf and the motor car has entirely changed the nature of the country village. The agricultural labourer has almost disappeared. Within a year or two of the laying out of the course, new residents with their attendants began to outnumber the old inhabitants – in fact the population rose from rather over 800 in 1907 to about 2,000 in 1927.

These new residents tended to be Very Important People. The *Country Life* image of a comfortable existence away from London found communion with these successful Men About Town and George Riddell pulled many of the strings. Around the time he took over the club he had begun to acquire land: notably in Deans Lane, in the area that is now Nursery Road, near Borlase's church and along Chequers Lane. He apparently bought for a song and sang all the way to the bank.

On Riddell's sites and those of others, most notably between 1905 and 1915, innovative and attractive small country houses rose to accommodate the eminent newcomers. *Country Life* and other glossy publications helped publicise them. It was, writes David Metcalfe, an authority on the history of local architecture, 'all part of the hype about Walton Heath Golf Club that in turn created the right sort of image of the area and benefited Riddell.'[2]

Edwin Lutyens, having designed *The Dormy House* and

Chussex, c1920 – Lutyens-designed and lived in over the years by, among others, Fowler, Sir Hedley Le Bas and current member Robin Marsh.
Photographer: Kate Pragnell

Chussex, proceeded to bigger things elsewhere, but other respected architects came to put their stamp on Walton. Not least of them was Percy Morley Horder – or 'Holy Murder' as he was re-christened by a fellow architect who knew what it was like to work with him. Several of his houses were commissioned by Riddell or built on land sold by him, so Horder was not too proud in 1912/13 to turn temporarily from designing fashionable edifices and to work on modest extensions to the clubhouse.

Lloyd George's residency at *Cliftondown* was a coup for the area and many of his friends and colleagues, some of whom we have already met in the clubhouse, also took houses. They included Sir John Simon, in his time home secretary, foreign secretary and chancellor, and Charles Masterman, financial secretary to the treasury – for whom Riddell provided *Churchfield* on the corner of Nursery Road and Breech Lane. Churchill, Chief justice Rufus Isaacs and Liberal chief whip Percy Illingworth never followed through with their plans to live here and it would be

---

[1] *The History of Walton-on-the-Hill and Walton Heath*, 1929
[2] *The Architectural Development of Walton-on-the-Hill* (Walton-on-the-Hill and District Local History Society), 2000.

Circa *1905 and the Deans Lane view has a significant addition. The notice is advertising land for sale. Now the railway and golf club are in place the property developers are moving in.*

interesting to know why, but over the years came a constellation of heavy hitters from various walks of life: MPs in abundance... knights by the dozen... eminent surgeons, barristers and bankers... newspaper editors including Sir Robert Donald and Sir Emsley Carr, industrialists like Sir Frederick Bowater, leader of the British paper-making industry... Sir Anthony Hope Hawkins, who wrote *The Prisoner of Zenda*...The Earl and Countess of Londesborough, landowners in Yorkshire...

> Among the growing places that encircle London and are something larger and richer than villages while they escape the reproach of the name suburb, Walton Heath takes a high place – *so said a typical article in the Press.* It was a microcosm of Edwardian and later England at work and play, *says Metcalfe.*

The Daily Chronicle, *August 12, 1913.*

But not everyone in the village was happy. There were three problems: class, rising costs and shortage of accommodation for the workers.

Walton was split by strong class divisions for several decades as newly rich invaders assumed the roles of small estate-owners.

Villagers blamed increasing costs on their new, upper-crust neighbours and in 1914 one of them went to court about them, appealing against a rate assessment. *Golfing* reported thus:

> Is the popularity of Walton Heath as a residential district attributable to the golf course? Or to cabinet ministers who there do congregate? That question cropped up at Surrey Quarter Sessions last week in an appeal against the rate assessment of a house in that neighbourhood.
>
> Mr. Cecil Whiteley, for the appellant, said that there was only one reason why land had gone up in the parish. That was the fact that one or two cabinet ministers, whose names were not usually associated with the increased value of land, had bought houses there.
>
> The respondents argued that the great things which governed house rent at Walton Heath was the golf course, which had attracted very distinguished patronage.
>
> And we are suffering for it, *interjected Mr. Whiteley.*
>
> It has attracted rare and refreshing fruit, *retorted Mr. Lailey, the respondent's counsel,* On these links one can play cheek by jowl with two or three cabinet ministers who take their ease in this very charming neighbourhood.
>
> For our own part, *'Golfing' editorialised,* we never watch cabinet ministers playing. We are too much afraid of spoiling our style. The appeal was allowed, with costs.

Some were unhappier still. 'Hovels of Walton Heath', the *Daily Chronicle* had shouted, illustrating its story with a photograph of a derelict cottage:

> The neighbourhood of Walton Heath has been 'developed' by the erection of beautiful residences for rich and leisured golfers, but no provision is made for the working classes. Within a few yards of Mr. Lloyd George's new house and the golf course, where leading politicians of both parties play, there are over-crowded, insanitary hovels that are undermining the health of working men and blighting the lives of their children.

The Vicar of Kingswood was quoted as saying that a family of 12 were inhabiting a two-roomed cottage (5s a week rent) in a deplorable state of disrepair with open spaces between its brick and woodwork, and that a station porter, married, with five children, could find no accommodation except a three-shillings-a-week stable in which to lodge his furniture.

> All round the neighbourhood, within easy distance of the course, houses have been springing up which are let from £100 to £300 a year, *said the Rev. Arthur Wethered,* Some are empty for the greater part of the year and are only used as weekend residences. Their existence means that more workmen are required as gardeners, labourers, artisans, chauffeurs and

SENSATIONAL COTTAGE DESTRUCTION

Great sensation is being caused in the district of Tadworth and Walton owing to the action of a celebrated titled lady landowner who, it is said, has ordered the demolition of two cottages situate in the hollow near the Walton Heath golf links because they obstructed her view of the links. The cottages, we understand, are now let at the rental of six shillings per week, and the tenants have been compelled to find other homes owing to the action of the owner of the property.

Coulsdon & Purley Record, February 1916

servants, but no houses have been built for them. We cannot expect the land speculators who build for the rich to recognise their moral obligations towards the workers brought to the neighbourhood by their enterprise.

The workmen and caddies, unable to find accommodation nearby, walk from three to seven miles to their work. The effect of this one-sided 're-development' of a district like Walton Heath is to enhance the value of land so much that cheap houses for the workers become impossible. Lloyd George, the chancellor, has an object lesson at Walton Heath for the justification of his increment tax. Land which less than 20 years ago was valued at £50 an acre now sells for £800. Some sites have brought over £1,000 an acre. Values have doubled within the last few years.

The club itself suffered from a dearth of local accommodation for staff. There are those who contend that Riddell had seen the destruction of nearby cottages in the interests of villa building so the problem was self-inflicted.

However, Riddell had bought land and built houses for employees off Chequers Lane and in Meadow Walk. Metcalfe points also to the Riddell Hall as further patronage by him and the club.

Certainly the shortage of working-class housing was an on-going problem. In 1919, a year after the war, the club was writing to the local authorities challenging them with it and pointing out what Riddell had done at his own expense. Ten years later Borlase was reporting that more houses had been built in Walton, helped by subsidies under the housing acts, than in any place of the same size in the Reigate rural district – 36 of them by Riddell with the co-operation of the district council.

Overall, the changes wrought by the club had 'made' Walton-on-the-Hill. If they brought problems they also provided tangible benefits which local historians have recognised:

There were new opportunities for permanent or regular work at

The changing village. Fine new houses advertised by Harrods and other estate agents.

99

the club and the new villas. Wages were higher than the old agricultural and labouring pay. The younger women, too, found employment in the large houses and additional opportunities came through the increasing range of local shops.

Jean Clew (local historian)

The coming together of ambitious businessmen and the golf club created the conditions that have given the village its special character. The protection afforded by conservation-area status means that Walton retains much of that character and let us hope that the future will be as kind as the past.

David Metcalfe

Against these judgments must be put the view expressed by the club's own Phyl Foster:

It's turned into a blooming suburb!

Robin Marsh, club member and chairman of the Walton-on-the-Hill and District Local History Society, can take a balanced view:

I think past criticisms about life in the village have been exaggerated. For centuries, Walton was a small village with an agricultural community somewhat isolated from the county surrounding it. The arrival of the railway was a cultural shock to that community and the development of Walton, Tadworth and Kingswood that followed the establishing of the golf club reinforced that cultural change. Of course there was a wide social gap between the members and most of the villagers, but such divisions were generally the case in England before World War I.

I believe that, because there were so many high-profile politicians and businessmen with luxurious houses in Walton, the media went out of their way to pander to their readers by seeking stories of class divisions and poor local housing. *The Daily Chronicle* surely exaggerated about those 'overcrowded, insanitary hovels.' A study of maps does not reveal where the implied large numbers of such dwellings would have been located.

I have heard people today saying that large areas of common land and many cottages were sacrificed. To my knowledge, less than a handful of cottages were lost – perhaps as few as two.

For a final, reassuring reminder let us return to the words of rector Borlase in 1929:

Walton also has one priceless possession in the heath, which will ever preserve some portion of the old natural beauty of the place. Though the line of houses may enclose it on every side, the genie of the heath will ever say, 'So far and no further'.

The end of Riddell

*L*ord Riddell, says David Metcalfe, the local architectural expert, was the most significant influence on Walton's development from 1905 until his death in the 'thirties, by which time the most important parts of the village and its environs had long since been developed. I have already recorded his date of death – December 5, 1934. He died in Walton Heath House, the former dormy house that he had made his second home.

The chief beneficiary of his will, which revealed his £2 million fortune – a sum we have calculated as equal to nearly £90 million today, much the same as Cosmo Bonsor's – was his wife. Apart from sundry charities he remembered his political friends with whom he had spent so much time at Walton Heath and elsewhere. There was £1,000 each for Lloyd George and Churchill and a similar amount for LG's Frances Stevenson.

To Edward Hudson, of Country Life and the golf club board, he left £100 'to purchase a souvenir of our long friendship.' He did the same for Sir Emsley Carr, News of the World editor and long-time club member, to whom he also bequeathed his gold watch.

More significantly, more touchingly, just as he acknowledged countless workers at the News of the World, so he remembered the servants of the golf club. In considering the figures, remember that they would be worth more than 40 times as much today.

He left £1,000 to James Braid, apparently for his 'discretion' although the copy of the will I possess does not include that phrase. Certainly Braid had been privy to all manner of confidential information disclosed by politicians in his hearing; perhaps also the phrase had something to do with Lloyd George and his sojourns at Walton with Frances, his then mistress.

To Twigg, personal valet and dormy house steward, Riddell bequeathed £2,000. His chauffeur, Webb, received a legacy of £500, plus a £300 annuity, while his son got £100. Payne, the head gardener, was left £1,000.

Braid's long-serving clubmakers, Horseburgh and Brown, each received £200 and there was £100 for 'each servant, greenkeeper or other employee, male or female, at the golf club with three years' service.' Predictably there was some jostling for qualification among the caddies, and apparently a judge's wisdom had to be called for to decide who were genuine, employed 'regulars' and therefore entitled to benefit.

Perhaps significantly, Fowler's name is not specifically mentioned among the beneficiaries, at least not on the copy-documents I hold (the will and two codicils). Fowler had been the club's managing director and Riddell's fellow board director for the past 30 years and conjecture about the closeness or otherwise of their personal relationship during that time is a fascinating and fruitless exercise. One thing seems certain: in the circumstances that I shall reveal later, Fowler could have done with some money.

But what about Walton Heath Golf Club? Riddell virtually owned it. What would happen to it now?

THE CARR ERA

*Three generations of Carrs.
Above: Sir Emsley, caricatured
in* The Bystander *and
painted by George Harcourt,
RA. The portrait, presented
to him during the war in
Churchill's presence, formerly
hung in the clubhouse.
Above left and left: Sir William
Carr, 20 years club chairman;
presenting the Match-Play
trophy to Peter Thomson. His
nephew Clive Carr (with
1968 Ladies' British Amateur
Championship winner Brigitte
Varangot) succeeded him.*

Chapter Sixteen

LIFE AFTER RIDDELL
Sir Emsley Carr takes over and things begin to change

WE NOW ENTER the 'Carr' years. I almost wrote 'the *News of the World* years,' but that would have been inaccurate and premature although understandable.

The Carr dynasty, or at least the men who concern us most, were newspapermen: talented editors and journalists with noses for news or businessmen behind the scenes. Additionally in the blood there has been a passion for sport – particularly golf.

The Carrs' connection with the Club resulted from one thing leading to another. The seeds can be traced back to the Victorian day when George Riddell met Henry Lascelles Carr on the *Western Mail* and helped him buy the *News of the World*. As we have seen, Riddell reigned dynamically on that paper alongside editor Emsley Carr, a nephew of Henry L, and after Riddell had contracted the golf bug Emsley (later Sir Emsley) promptly joined him as a member of Walton Heath. This union in turn gave rise to the *News of the World* Match-Play Championships regularly (and in time exclusively) staged at the club and, off the course, all manner of financial transactions.

Now, at the end of 1934, Riddell had died and only two directors from his era remained: Fowler and Edward Hudson. Moreover Hudson would soon leave the scene. In May 1935, after 30 years as a director, he sent a touching little note: 'Many happy memories... afraid my golfing days are over... you might ask Anderson (*the secretary*) to have my clubs sent to me.'

But he and Fowler had by then elected a new director and chairman – Sir Emsley Carr, the *News of the World* editor (a post he would fill for half a century), a two-handicapper in his prime and still in single figures at the age of 67; a stalwart, stocky, plus-foured figure with six

The Carrs well represented at the 1926 English Amateur Championship: Sir Emsley (next to Braid), 'Wash' (in white shirt) and Betty Carr. On right is Jo Bryant (neé Moorcroft).

sons and two daughters. He succeeded Riddell as chairman of the *News of the World* and now, after a brief stopgap spell by Hudson, he had followed him as chairman of the golf club.

Since Sir Emsley joined in 1905 an unbroken line of Carrs have strolled through Walton Heath's history, casting an impressive haze of Cambridge blue. Prominent among them have been three of his sons – Walter Copley (whose initials brought him the nickname 'Wash,' which could have been worse), his twin Horace (who was customarily called Harry) and the youngest, William.

Sir Emsley once bet all three that Braid, over the course of a round, could beat their best-ball score hole by hole and they accepted with the abounding confidence of blues, which they all were, and a certain hint of arrogance. Braid won – and the silence at the dinner table at *Wonford*, their Walton home, that night has taken its place in the family's folklore. The quiet was broken only by Sir Emsley, who was in insufferably fine form!

William (later *Sir William*) would become chairman of the club for 20 years after World War II and be succeeded by his nephew Clive, at one time deputy managing director of the *News of the World* and yet another blue. 'Wash' at one time sat on the club board. He was a stockbroker, not a newspaper man, and a golfer good enough to win the German Amateur. Tragically, both he and his twin Horace were destined to die during the war. The line of golfing Carrs continues today: Horace's sons Clive and Richard, his grandson Michael and Sir William's son William junior all play on.

But consider the position in 1935. Riddell had died holding 83% of the club shares. What would happen?

First, to enable the club to carry on business, Riddell's

Membership in the 'thirties remained distinguished, with more than 100 titled men and other prominent figures.
Left: Sir John Simon, Foreign Secretary and member, holds the umbrella while his partner, the Japanese Ambassador (right), gets wet in a 1935 match against U.S. Ambassador Norman Davis (far left) and Naval Attaché Admiral Standley – a relaxation from the disarmament conference they were attending. Result? The Americans lost.

Right: Sir Emsley and Lady Carr with Cecil Purdey the gunmaker, also a member.

executors – his widow and the public trustee – loaned money. Next, Lady Riddell offered the membership, as a body, first option on the shares, plus the Dormy House and adjacent Nursery Field. Carr and his board felt they could not promulgate this offer: they anticipated a price of £40,000 and feared members' resignations. Instead, when the public trustee insisted on some promulgation, they told members that anyone interested in buying shares should contact Fowler.

The outcome was that 23 members willing to guarantee the price were found and Carr, with Edgar B. Beck and Frederic Hamilton as fellow trustees, completed the purchase for £32,800, 38% (3,787) of Riddell's shares going to Sir Emsley. Capital was increased by the issue of a further 10,000 shares at £1.7s each and the same 23 members took these up in proportion to their original purchases.

The company was back in business. It still was not a private members' club in the fullest sense, but from Riddell's virtual one-man proprietorship things had shifted to a broader, albeit limited shareholding basis. The minutes of a *News of the World* board meeting on May 22, 1935, show how important for the club that organisation was becoming:

> The chairman reported that he had entered into a joint guarantee on behalf of the company for the purchase of Walton Heath Golf Club and *Dormy House* from the executors of the late Lord Riddell and a cheque for £3,320 had been paid by the company on account of the purchase price. Mr Dods, of Smith, Rundell, Dods and Bocket, submitted for the board's approval draft documents carrying out the arrangement by which Sir Emsley Carr was to offer to holders of ordinary shares in the company a quota of the late Lord Riddell's holding in the company which he has purchased from the public trustee.

The club's new directors, Carr, Beck, Fowler, Hamilton and Sir Henry Strakosch, were impatient to get cracking on new plans, but times were difficult. Britain was in the grip of the Depression. More than two million were

unemployed and a magazine appealed to golfers and golf clubs to donate all the unused clothing and footwear lying in their locker-rooms (Walton Heath replied that they already distributed clothing to the needy in their own locality). War was feared and the club's accounts would show significant losses as it approached.

Meanwhile Beck told his colleagues that 'it would be a great shame to give the impression that Walton Heath was on its uppers.' He urged waiving of the entrance fee to members' children and those within three years of leaving university or public school; it was to these younger people that the club should look for the support it needed.

Finance apart, the club's prestige was high and the membership replete with the 'quality.' The 1937 list includes a hundred-odd lords, knights and other title-holders, plus, incidentally, a somewhat esoteric supporting cast embracing Baron Parlmstierna, Count Raczynski and, wait for it, Baron Franckenstein.

Among a continuing abundance of MPs (some encouraged by concessions on joining fees), Sir John Simon, an 11-handicapper, was a member when foreign and home secretary and was chancellor of the exchequer when he assumed the captaincy in 1939 – succeeding one lord, Russell of Killowen, and preceding another, Lord Ebbisham.

But much needed to be done. The clubhouse demanded expensive work; the dormy house was a problem; the directors wanted new tournaments and the members more competitions.

Then there were the courses. 'Judging from remarks one hears, the most important point we have at the moment is to get them into first-class condition,' the ubiquitous Beck told his fellow directors. 'It is the common talk around that Walton Heath is in bad condition, which is, compared with other clubs, a true statement.'

Already, though, Sir Emsley had announced headline news…

Chapter Seventeen

A Prince Becomes Captain
People ask, 'Why not *Royal* Walton Heath'?

S IR EMSLEY CARR made a spectacular start to his six-year reign. In May 1935, within minutes of being made chairman, he announced that the Prince of Wales had agreed to become the Club's captain. The members recognised this not only as an honour but as a hint that under the new regime things were going to change. In 32 years under proprietorial control Walton Heath Golf Club had never had a captain, only a chairman.

Edward, Prince of Wales (later King Edward VIII and even later Duke of Windsor) had first played golf at 13, but his sporting passions were steeplechasing and hunting. When his mother, Queen Mary, urged him at least to give up steeplechasing to reduce the risk of accidents and permit him more time to help his recently ill father, George V, he 'reluctantly abandoned the one pursuit that gave outlay to my competitive spirit… and for relaxation I turned increasingly to golf.'[1]

In 1921 Riddell had arranged to have the Prince and his brother the Duke of York (later King George VI) elected honorary members. 'He accepts the invitation with pleasure,' stated a letter on the Prince's behalf from St. James's Palace. Another, from Buckingham Palace, said that the Duke of York 'gladly accepts the privilege, which he hopes to avail himself of as often as he can.' The Duke once played tennis at Wimbledon but was less keen on golf than his brother, for whom it became a lifetime obsession.

It has been said that Edward first came to the club after an equerry had asked Bernard Darwin's advice about a teacher who might improve the Prince's game. Darwin said he knew just the man, a teacher well qualified but also patient and tactful – James Braid. Helped by the

champion, Edward got down into single figures. Not least of the club's treasures is the letter handwritten by him in 1930 and accompanied by a scorecard:

Dear Braid,

I am very pleased with this card and hope you are. I was very unlucky at the last hole, as a good second with a spoon pitched in the rough just a few inches over the green, and with the chance of breaking 80 I couldn't stand the nerve strain and fluffed the chip and took two puts (*sic*). But it was great fun and I only wish you had been playing round with me. Will phone you one day soon and we must have another game.

Yours sincerely,

Edward.

Letters accepting honorary membership.

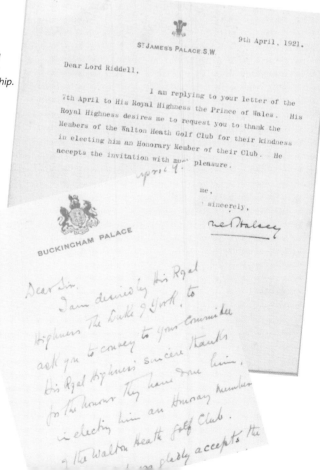

---

[1] *A King's Story, the memoirs of The Duke of Windsor* (Prion), 1998.

Royalty on the Walton Heath courses became almost a routine sight. The Duke of Gloucester came to play, Prince Arthur of Connaught became a member and on one day at least an illustrious foursome was on view, the Duke of York and Braid losing two and one to the Prince of Wales and the Argentinian Jose Jurado. That was in 1931, the year Jurado lost the Open by a stroke.

Jo Bryant, looking back 70-odd years, remembered coming across the brothers playing when she was out riding on the course. 'No-one took special notice of them, they were just like ordinary members,' she told me.

'The Prince was quite a pal,' said Phyl Foster, characterful pillar of the ladies' club. 'He would land his plane near a big house owned by some friends of ours behind the school at Kingswood, opposite the church. One day he was expected but didn't come – he'd disappeared with Mrs Simpson!'

The villagers basked in reflected glory, agog at reports that he might live in the area, but he went off to Fort Belvedere at Sunningdale and residents who had envisaged the loss of servants, gardeners, peace and quiet breathed again.

In 1933 Prince Edward, for the second year running, reached the last four of the Parliamentary Handicap. His semi-final was to be played at Walton and his adversary was Lady Astor, first woman to take her seat in the House of Commons. There were whispers that she had bribed her quarter-final opponent with a fiver to lose so that she could ensure playing the heir to the throne – later reported as 'a disreputable story' in the Parliamentary Golfing Society's history but as a fact by Bill Deedes in *The Daily Telegraph*.

Depending on which report you trust, the Prince played off 11 and conceded her ladyship seven strokes or was off 12 and conceded six. He was perturbed by the big crowd of spectators who had arrived to watch what was supposed to be a secret, while she, finding herself in the lead, had pangs of guilt and apprehension at the thought of beating the future king.

In the event no such treason was committed. Lady Astor, one or two up at the turn, again depending on whose report you read, ultimately lost by two and one. The Prince then lost in the final at Coombe Hill to George (later Viscount) Lambert.

Two years later Sir Emsley approached him about the captaincy, first in a private conversation and then, on May 11, in a suitably proud and dutiful letter:

> As chairman of Walton Heath Golf Club (*he was anticipating his election by a couple of days!*) I desire to present my humble duty to Your Royal Highness and beg to inform you that it is the unanimous wish of my colleagues that Your Royal Highness should do the Club the great honour of being its captain for the ensuing year.
>
> The Club, as you may know, has been called 'the St Andrews of the South,' not only because it was originally laid out by Mr.

THE PRINCE V THE LADY

The eagerly awaited match between the Prince of Wales and Lady Astor in the semi-final round of the Parliamentary Handicap was played yesterday and the Prince of Wales won by two up and one to play.

It was known that the match was to be played at Walton Heath, but nobody knew exactly when. Rumour said that both combatants had been practising in the morning and that Lady Astor had then departed for luncheon to an unknown destination. Next, the Prince was discovered still busily practising with so many balls that the putting green seemed as if it had been visited by a snow storm in miniature.

Finally, a little before 3 o'clock, Lady Astor reappeared. She reproached James Braid with having put the tees too far back for her, and these remarks were received with the most perfect tranquillity.

The battle began with two excellent tee shots straight down the course. The Prince was driving with great fire and dash, and Lady Astor, though naturally not so long, displayed a ruthless and mechanical precision of hitting, well deserving of the modern term 'grooved.'

Lady Astor became two up at the eighth, but the Prince won his first hole at the ninth and turned one down.

Then began the most dramatic period of the match, during which, for hole after hole, Lady Astor seemed to have her foe in her grip only to be robbed of her prey. Finally, at the 15th,[1] the Prince recovered cruelly well from a hooked second, holed a long putt and took the lead.

Now for the 17th,[2] a hole all in favour of the long-driving man. The Prince hit a very fine tee shot and could have got up in two; he topped his second into the heather, and it seemed that anything might happen. Poor Lady Astor had threaded her way skilfully past bunkers but could not beat a six, and the Prince made no mistake with his putt.

He wanted a four for 87, but the scores do not do any justice to an extraordinarily interesting and exciting match. There were moments in it which, as Mr. Slurk remarked, 'curdle the ink in one's pen.'

[1] This 15th is now the 14th.
[2] This 17th is now the 16th.

BERNARD DARWIN, *The Times*, June 30, 1933

The Prince of Wales during his match with Lady Astor.
Illustrated Sporting and Dramatic News, *1933*

Herbert Fowler on the lines of that great course but because of the great tradition it has established since its formation. As the home of the Parliamentary Golfers it occupies a unique position in the golfing world, a position which will be still further enhanced when, by becoming its first captain, Your Royal Highness will bestow upon it your invaluable and exalted patronage.

A reply came back rapidly from St. James's Palace to the Carrs' home, *Wonford*:

The Prince of Wales wishes me to acknowledge the receipt of your letter of the 11th instant. His Royal Highness wishes me to say that he will be very pleased to become the first captain of the Walton Heath Golf Club.

The letter was signed 'P.W.Legh, Equerry' – surely The Hon. Piers Legh who was a member of the club!

Not only did the Prince accept the captaincy, he also presented a trophy for annual competition – the Edward Prince of Wales's Challenge Cup, still played for today on the New course as a match-play event between 16 qualifiers from a handicap stableford. Fittingly, the first winner was Harry Braid, and HRH sent his congratulations, saying that he was particularly pleased in view of his high regard for James.

The rest of the story is inextricably bound with monarchal history. In January 1936, eight months into his year of captaincy, Edward was proclaimed King on the death of his father. Thus Walton Heath had a reigning monarch as captain – an honour almost but not quite unique.[2]

In December that year Edward abdicated the throne and was succeeded by his brother, who in May 1937 was crowned George VI. Even before his coronation the new king, via a letter from the keeper of the privy purse,

granted the club his patronage. 'Patron His Most Gracious Majesty The King' are the first words in the 1937-8 rule book and membership list.

Ever since then, on and off, the question has been asked, 'Why isn't it *Royal* Walton Heath?' More than 60 clubs are or have been 'Royal.' You could find them in Africa, Australia, Canada, India, Malta, England, Scotland, Wales, Northern Ireland, the Republic of Ireland and elsewhere. If we can have Royal Perth, Royal Dornoch, Royal Dublin, Royal Jersey, Royal Cromer, Royal Mid-Surrey and all the rest, why not Royal Walton? The Royal and Ancient *Golfer's Handbook* has stated:

The right to the designation Royal is bestowed by the favour of the Sovereign or a member of the Royal house. In most cases the title is granted along with bestowal of royal patronage on the club.

Let us put matters into perspective. Edward Prince of Wales was at some time captain of many clubs – by 1936 the Press were listing a dozen of them. Neither was Braid his only teacher and friend: in the 'thirties he studied under Archie Compston and in the early 'twenties had got to know Taylor at Mid-Surrey. Indeed, that club, through its centenary history,[3] has laid claims to have been the Prince's 'home' course.

For all that, the story of Walton's royal connections is

---

[2] For example, the prince also became monarch while captain of the Royal Burgess Golfing Society of Edinburgh.
[3] *Characters and Kings* by Peter Ryde, 1992.

The former Duke of York, later George VI
Jackson's 'Pageant of Kingship' cigarette card.

The Prince of Wales at Walton Heath.

hugely impressive, so, again, why not 'Royal'? Since Riddell's ill-timed and abortive request in 1911, captains and committee men have several times considered applying for a fitting and happy ending to that story.

In 1977, I am assured, captain Sir Patrick Macrory told his committee that the accolade might be arranged through a suitable contact, but his suggestion brought a somewhat negative reaction ('We've been plain Walton Heath for years, we don't need any change now,' seemed to be the majority view, apparently). In 1991 the committee considered applying and the letters from the palaces accepting membership for the prince and duke were needed. Embarrassingly, they had gone missing. They were found in the cellar several months later. In January 1995, on David Barber's suggestion, the board agreed that

the matter should again be explored, but three months later, by which time secretary James had circulated details of how they might go about it, a decision was deferred.

There is no evidence of an approach in the 'thirties, when the royal connection was so close and topical. Were Carr and his men inhibited by knowledge of the 1911 rebuff or by the fact that Walton Heath was still not, in the fullest sense, a members' club? If those were problems why would George VI grant his patronage? Did the abdication and perceived tainting of Edward's character affect the issue? Did the passing of time make any approach to the Palace seem an anachronism?

Walton Heath has been outstandingly 'royal' – in character even if not in name.

The Prince of Wales driving in a Parliamentary Handicap at Walton. Golfing, 1933

The present Duke of York – Prince Andrew during a Sunday morning game in 1995.

Chapter Eighteen

THE OLD ORDER CHANGETH
New brooms sweep away some of Fowler's work

THE NEW BROOMS of the Carr era were ready to sweep clean on the Old course. Well, not entirely clean, not by any means, but sufficiently to wipe away several of Fowler's sacred creations.

Let us go back to 1904. The rave reviews granted the course following its opening continued, but not even Fowler could get everything right first time round and soon minor criticisms began to be voiced.

Harold Hilton, the former Amateur and Open champion, criticised the greens: too difficult, he said, with grass unequal in texture and growth. He thought the voracious bunkers ('Fowler's graves') well placed and fair – with one exception. He had been to the 1905 *News of the World* championship and seen Sandy Herd beaten by Braid in the first round. At the 17th[1] Herd had played an almost perfect approach, only to see his ball run with the swing of the ground into the right-hand bunker. Hilton felt the sand was too near the green: 'I have no love of an artificial hazard which penalises a well played shot.'

Fowler himself was continually plotting improvements. He duly adjusted the 17th, not by moving the bunker but by banking up the green so that, while the sand still devoured slices, truly hit balls would stay on the green. 'His brain is teeming with new bunkers to be placed where the myriad niblick shots of the unfortunate have thinned the rough country at the sides of the course,' wrote one newspaper correspondent. Fowler was thinking not so much of the champions as of you and me:

> I found that 70 yards[2] was rather too narrow, especially on the long holes, and we have by degrees widened the course in many places, but only by cutting or burning the heather and leaving the ground rough... I think it better to put in bunkers as hazards for wide shots. Where the heather is strong you may get an impossible lie perhaps only a few feet off the line and there is also the annoyance of losing balls, temper and time, whereas being in a bunker is looked on as one of the ills of golf which are to be expected.[3]

More bunkers went in, but nothing was done significantly

'The second shot at the 17th hole' – by Harry Rountree. It is now the 16th.
Golf Courses of the British Isles, *by Bernard Darwin (Duckworth), 1910*

to affect the course's overall length. In 1907, fourth year of its active life, the Old measured 6,322 yards off the medal tees, about 100 yards less than originally. The figure is bound to be accurate because it was calculated by Sir Alexander Kennedy, a man with the precise mind of an eminent engineer. It was he who had immediately confirmed Braid's drive at the 15th two years previously at 395 yards.

That year, 1907, the club produced for members what today we might call a primitive 'strokesaver' – a rudimentary plan with brief hole-by-hole details (yardages, distances to hazards, 'pits' and so on) and a stroke index. Judging from Horace Hutchinson's praise in *Country Life*, this was a rarity if not an innovation. Those distance details, he suggested, would at least end the speculative claims as to the length of those 'enormous carries' the members were so prone to romance about between the luncheon and the liqueur.

Soon, though, some of the carries and certain of the holes were not enormous enough. When Fowler conceived them the old 'gutty' had been about to give way to the rubber-core and he took this into consideration in his grand design, but within a decade the game had changed dramatically. Shades of today! An unholy alliance of new

---

[1] Today's 16th.
[2] Reported width of Fowler's fairways, but actually including semi-rough.
[3] *Golf Greens and Greenkeeping* (Country Life), 1906.

The 10th (Old) then and now. Right: This green was new when played in the Match-Play final in 1913. It was, in turn, abandoned in 1939. Below right: In the 1938 match against Oxford they played to it, but the replacement, soon to be opened, can be seen to the right. Bottom: Braid's view of the old green; in colour, how it looks today.

balls and machine-made clubs meant that players were hitting further. By 1915 Fowler was saying:

> All these factors have moved in the direction of making the game easier and it is becoming a vital question whether some steps should not be taken to limit the so-called improvements. Practically every shot is simpler. Iron shots in particular and getting the ball to rise quickly out of bad lies and over steep faces are now comparatively easy.[4]

Another factor was involved – an advance in greenkeeping aided and abetted by improved machinery. Greens were better, bad lies on fairways became rarer and Fowler had to re-think some of his philosophy. He had generally been against cross-bunkers, but now:

> We want more cross-bunkers in addition to the flanking ones to curtail the long drivers from getting nearer the green than a certain distance to play their approaches.

A new water service to both courses, estimated at £8,000, had been ordered in 1914, but then came World War I and Old and New inevitably suffered. Greenkeeper Samuel Ashton, appointed to succeed McNeice, killed in the war,

faced a stern challenge when peace came, as did Sid Saunders, who began a 32-year reign in 1922.

In the 1920s critics began deigning to write under such headlines as *How I would alter Walton Heath*. W.H. Ricardo, a good-class amateur, weighed in with body blows that wounded Fowler painfully below the belt:

> I am going to be iconoclastic and Bolshevik when I say that I can see no merit in the course as a test of golf. On most holes there is some atrocity that would not be tolerated on a modern course in the form of either a badly placed sand trap or a cross-bunker that entirely obscures the hole.[5]

Less extreme critics found common ground on certain points. They found holes two to eight monotonous in direction and scarcely any holes demanding a pitch. There were feelings that players on the edge of the rough were still being punished as harshly as those 30 yards into it, could get away with topped approaches and were being encouraged to play short by hazards placed immediately at the back of greens. One critic, writing in 1924 and camou-flaged by a pseudonym, complained that the course was 'growing fat':

> Many courses have been ruined through over-feeding and it would be a pity if Walton Heath, long famous for its turf, were to suffer a similar fate. A great effort should be made to retain the native fineness of the turf which clothes the barren heath.[6]

When it came to appraising individual holes the critics showed a distinct lack of unanimity. Hilton, who had joined their ranks, thought the fourth was the second best hole of all and that 'the bunker placed in the centre of the course makes the long hitter view the situation with anxiety and have to steer his way to have an easy second.'

---

[4] *Golfing.*
[5] *Golf Illustrated.*
[6] *Golf Illustrated.*

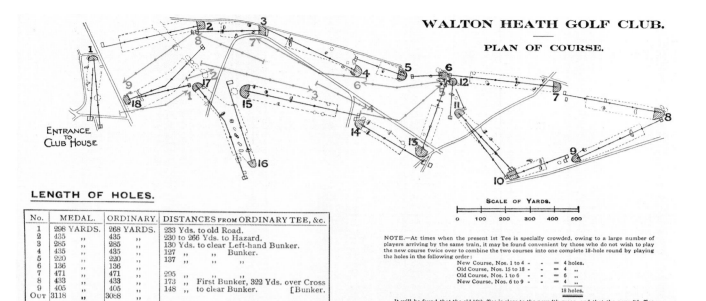

WALTON HEATH GOLF CLUB.

PLAN OF COURSE.

SCALE OF YARDS.

0   100   200   300   400   500

NOTE.—At times when the present 1st Tee is specially crowded, owing to a large number of players arriving by the same train, it may be found convenient by those who do not wish to play the new course twice over to combine the two courses into one complete 18-hole round by playing the holes in the following order :—

New Course, Nos. 1 to 4	=	4 holes.
Old Course, Nos. 15 to 18	=	4 ,,
Old Course, Nos. 1 to 6	=	6 ,,
New Course, Nos. 6 to 9	=	4 ,,
		18 holes.

It will be found that the old 15th Tee is close to the new 4th green, and that the new 6th **Tee** is close to the old 6th green—arrangements which were made specially with a view to the playing of the above round.

LENGTH OF HOLES.

No.	MEDAL.	ORDINARY.	DISTANCES FROM ORDINARY TEE, &c.
1	298 YARDS.	268 YARDS.	233 Yds. to old Road.
2	435 ,,	435 ,,	230 to 266 Yds. to Hazard.
3	285 ,,	285 ,,	130 Yds. to clear Left-hand Bunker.
4	435 ,,	435 ,,	127 ,, ,, Bunker.
5	220 ,,	220 ,,	137 ,, ,, ,,
6	136 ,,	136 ,,	
7	471 ,,	471 ,,	295 ,, ,, ,,
8	433 ,,	433 ,,	173 ,, First Bunker, 322 Yds. over Cross
9	405 ,,	405 ,,	148 ,, to clear Bunker. [Bunker.
OUT	3118 ,,	3088 ,,	
10	255 ,,	255 ,,	133 ,, to clear Left-hand Bunker.
11	352 ,,	337 ,,	233 ,, to Road.
12	160 ,,	160 ,,	
13	338 ,,	318 ,,	257 ,, ,, [Right.
14	353 ,,	327 ,,	128 ,, over Pit, 200 Yds. First Bunker on
15	503 ,,	503 ,,	193 ,, over 2nd Pit, 300 Yds. 1st Bunker on Right, 413 Yds. 2nd Bunker on Right.
16	376 ,,	376 ,,	320 Yds. over Cross Bunker.
17	457 ,,	437 ,,	115 ,, to Fair Green from Medal Tee, 300 Yds. over Cross Bunker.
18	410 ,,	410 ,,	100 ,, over Hazard, 350 Yds. over Bunker
HOME	3204 ,,	3123 ,,	(220 Yds. to carry Bunker from Short Tee)
Total	6322 ,,	6211 ,,	

The 1907 plan issued to members – earliest depiction of the original layout. Red lines indicated the first nine holes of the New course.

'Could any trap be worse placed?' sneered Ricardo. To Hilton the 13th of that time was 'a good hole of the simple drive-and-short-approach variety;' another correspondent judged it the worst on the course. The short 12th was unanimously found wanting and an unnamed 'Golf Architect' urged that the 15th was 'crying out for improvement as a real three-shotter.'

All these opinions were actually a compliment to Walton Heath, for no such space would have been given to lesser courses. Even when 'Brer Rabbit' (*nom de plume* of a respected golf writer) wrote in 1933 that the modern ball had robbed the course of some of its terrors and altered the

The 10th attracts us with its new green, though somehow one never passes the old one without a shudder to think of the London Amateur Foursomes players who called a half after each side had made four attempts to find the bottom of the tin with putts of dimensions which certainly shrank a few inches in every fresh journal which shouted over the discomfiture of the golfing giants.

Golf Illustrated, 1913

character of at least six holes he had to concede that Fowler's work had been that of a genius and that the Old still represented the hardest inland test he knew.

In spite of the various criticisms, for more than 30 years no significant changes had been made apart from a 100-yard stretching of the original 10th before World War I, which gave it the green shown at the top of page 110. But now, by the time the Carr era began in the 'thirties, something had to be done. Steel shafts and new balls were achieving even vaster distances. In the 1934 *News of the World* championship professionals were reaching parts where their predecessors could not reach and Braid, in ripe middle age, had reputedly been driving the 13th through the gap, 338 yards and uphill.

But it wasn't just distance. The professionals, feeling their feet, were shying away from traditional features on courses they felt old-fashioned. There was also the course's condition for the club to worry about. As we have noted, board member Edgar B. Beck had urged his colleagues to make this a priority. 'It is the common talk around that Walton Heath is in bad condition,' he had said. Fortunately, Carr and others of the new order were hell-bent on stamping their imprint on things.

There were problems in the way of changes. Money was one; agreements limiting the golf area of the heath were another; extensions on the Old were constrained by the existence of the New; nobody wanted to offend Fowler.

But Fowler himself had realised the need for certain changes. He was now nearly 80 and in failing health, but the first alterations came under his direction. Behind him stood Braid, 14 years younger, architect of a huge number of courses, man of wisdom and *eminence grise*.

Overleaf: The Old and the New – the pride of Walton Heath in 2002. Photograph: REALISTIC

Immediately above: The old 11th green (left of the present 12th green) with the original short 12th in the background (now the 14th green of the New). Top: The new 12th green in use for a Surrey-v-Sussex match in 1938. Right: New secretary Captain Tippet, who was to make revolutionary course changes, gets an early taste of Walton's rough.

When the changes came they arrived in a torrent. Between 1935 and 1938 nine holes were banished, altered, extended, grafted together or transposed.

In 1935 came the initial operation, with Braid the consultant and Fowler apparently the surgeon. The hole for surgery was the 15th (which we now know as the 14th). The wish of the anonymous 'Golf Architect' for a 'real three-shotter' was granted: from 503 yards it was transformed, with a new green as he had suggested, into a monster of 560.

In 1936/7 proposed changes referred to a sub-committee comprising Sir Emsley Carr, Fowler, Braid and Beck were implemented. They killed off the roundly criticised par-three 12th and compensated by conceiving a new short hole and inserting it before the 18th. As a result the old and universally praised 17th became the 16th and thus was formed the last-three finish we know today. Losing the 12th necessitated other re-numberings, all the old holes from 13 to 16 going back one digit.

The making of the new short 17th had another reason apart from its hoped-for merit as a golf hole. Formerly there had been a long, rough walk from the 17th green to the 18th tee – against tradition, which, stemming from the days when one teed up a few club-lengths from the previous hole, decreed that greens and tees should be adjacent. Insertion of the new short hole would eradicate the problem.

The hole was built with bunkers at the sides of the green only and with quite a wide grass bank at the front. Not until Sir William Carr's reign as chairman in the 'fifties and 'sixties would the bunkers be extended to run along the front.

With these 1937 changes, the old 337-yard 11th disappeared. It was to be fused with the abandoned short 12th and played to the latter's green, making a bogey of 460 yards. 'A very fierce hole it should make,' surmised Darwin – but apparently others were disappointed.

In November 1937, a month after the new holes had

J.H. Taylor putting on the old fifth green. The bank and bunker are still there, but now to catch a drive off the fifth tee.

been favourably reviewed, the board were approving further, urgent alterations involving that 11th as well as the 10th, 12th and 13th. Two new greens, for the 11th and 12th, were to be started at once and six extra men engaged for six weeks.

By some horticultural miracle, amateurs in the Metropolitan Shield were playing the new holes seven months later. The 11th, far from being 460 yards, had suddenly become a par three of 185 for the members and just over 200 for big events; the 13th, previously a par four of 355 yards, grew into a five of over 500; the 12th, a dog-leg extended to 370 yards for big occasions, had a dramatic baptism as we shall see later.[7] Off the back tees the course measured nearly 7,000 yards.

In 1938 yet more plans, revolutionary ones, were hustled in. Braid's views were ascertained, but by now another character had appeared on the scene – Captain

Tippet, the new secretary, a first-class golfer and a man with ambitions in architecture. Prior to his appointment he may even have proposed or been involved in the 1937 changes, but certainly these 1938 plans were his. By this time Fowler was in a nursing home, probably recovering from a heart attack suffered on the steps to the locker room of that time.

So far, changes had been confined to the homeward nine; now, under Tippet, the outward half was to be altered. Again the reconstruction was deemed urgent: new greens were to be sown within a month, at the end of August. The aims were stated as including the avoidance of playing into the sun, but the real need was to nullify two of the criticisms: that holes two to eight extended roughly in the same direction to the far end of the course and that two shortish holes, the 260-yard bogey-four fifth and bogey-three sixth, were played in immediate succession.

All this was to change. The fifth and sixth would merge into one par-four and the 480-yard seventh would be banished. Instead of continuing straight up the hill as that hole had done, a new par-four sixth and a short seventh would zig-zag, one bearing half right and the other half-

Reminder of the old short sixth – plus the long-abandoned seventh stretching up the hill, with (smaller picture) players on its green.

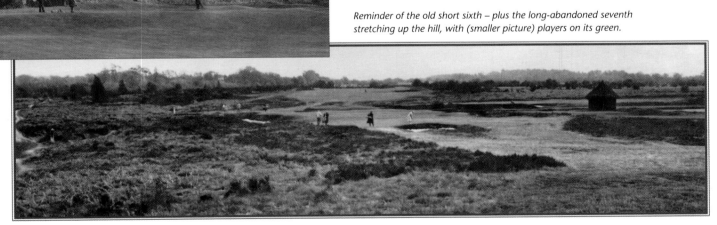

[7] Chapter 19

left. 'The new holes will add needed variety to the course and render it once more the finest inland test of golf in the country,' *The Illustrated Sporting and Dramatic News* predicted.

But traditionalists were shocked. The sixth was the fabled 'Port Arthur' – the starting point for Fowler's design and a jewel in his crown; a hole exempt from criticism except by those who found it impossible! A hole described thus:

A hole of monumental greatness   *Brer Rabbit*
                                                    (*Golf Illustrated* contributor)

If there is a better short hole I do not know where it is
                                                    National newspaper

One of the classic short holes of inland golf
                                                    Bernard Darwin

Port Arthur – now not captured by the Japanese but killed at Walton Heath!

In four years the course had been suddenly and radically changed. Even before Tippet's new holes opened in **September 1939**, the month World War II broke out, Charles Graves launched a withering attack in his *Daily Mail* column:

Walton Heath was the first club to introduce a roadhouse flavour to its club premises. It has now gone further. It has so altered the unique character of its Old course that Lord Riddell must be shifting in his coffin. It has suppressed most of its best holes. It has elongated its more inferior holes. Briefly, it is a mess.

Most people did not share Graves' opinions. 'The new holes are extremely popular,' chairman Carr told shareholders. He publicly thanked Tippet for designing and constructing them and awarded greenkeeper Saunders a tenner on top of his customary £15 annual bonus. Even the neutral Press seemed to approve them, only nostalgia qualifying their praise.

I find it difficult to think of the Old course being subjected to any radical changes, *Brer Rabbit had written*, but it has undergone one and in my humble opinion it has improved the course.

The two most gorgeous holes in the early days were the short sixth and the 17th and I must be allowed to shed a private tear that they are now changed, *wrote Darwin*. That superb 17th is now the 16th. It is just as fine a hole, but it no longer occupies the most critical of all places on a course, where it challenged even the Road hole at St Andrews.

The committee realised that their courses left as they were 35 years ago were fine tests but that if they were to remain in the top flight they must be modernised, *said Henry Cotton, expressing the professionals' viewpoint*. They completed alterations to make the Old course the best inland test in the country.

Moreover, with more money being spent, its condition had improved. Once wartime birch and scrub growth that

The Greenkeepers

*T*he two greenkeepers during the Carrs' era served the club for a total of 57 years.

SID SAUNDERS reputedly helped make the course as a youngster. He was head greenkeeper at Cooden Beach (Sussex) for 10 years from 1912, having previously been at Bexhill (Sussex), and in 1922 began 32 years' service at Walton Heath before retiring in 1954 through heart trouble. Seen at the Savoy Hotel for the club's 50th anniversary.

FRED DULAKE was an ex-Royal Navy man. 'He was so good,' Jo Bryant told me, 'Yet we had been arrogant enough to be a bit sniffy because he came from Chipstead, not one of the famous clubs!' He used to ride round the course on his bike and comfortably outlived the Carrs' and News of the World eras. He died in 1978 – a few months before his intended retirement after 25 years' service. He is remembered by a seat near the 13th hole presented by the Artisans. Seen above astride a new Triplex mower and with (right) a youthful Clive Osgood.

Above: rare vintage view of long-skirted lady and caddies approaching the 18th with the dormy house and clubhouse in the background.
Left: The short 17th before the gap in front of the green was closed.

from here that they played in *News of the World* championships at that time.

William Carr, taking office in 1949, eight years after his father's death, would prove a provocatively active chairman. He involved himself in standard scratch scores, wanting to apply for an additional stroke on grounds of course difficulty and to bring the sss from 73 to 74, and was restrained from doing so by his committee. In 1967, having seen American 'target' golf, he was instrumental in the installation of a new automatic watering system reaching all greens. Walton Heath was one of the first clubs in Britain to have such a system and this one cost about £19,000. Perhaps Carr had also been stung by the words of Bobby Locke:

> All American courses have watered greens and nearly all have well watered fairways. The result is that American players learn to pitch not for the green but for the flag. On too many British courses you cannot do that... Walton Heath is a case in point. Time and again when the ground is hard you have to pitch short and trust to luck, you just dare not play a long second for the flag.[9]

If Carr did indeed act on such strictures, he must have been disillusioned four years later to find the course criticised as uncharacteristically lush. Rather like an alcoholic on a cure, it was made to dry out and even then the body took a long time to recover.

In 1967, the year the water system was installed, a far worse innovation exploded in the club's face – the great motorway saga. The course changes it might force were planned as the *News of the World* era drew to a close – but a new-look club would implement them.[10]

was endangering its heathland character had been cleared, the conditioning continued to be praised – feathers in the cap for Saunders, who retired in 1954, and increasingly for Fred Dulake, who succeeded him.

For some years after World War II would-be reformers generally resisted temptations to tinker further and when that resistance gave way the results were not unanimously praised. Sir Peter Allen made it plain in print that he did not much like the extended re-bunkering of the 17th which had removed the small gap by which one might just run on, nor the scheme for the second in the mid-'sixties. 'The second,' wrote Allen,[8] 'had a great gully of humps and heather right across the fairway about 250 yards from the tee. You played short, of course, then usually had a full wood shot off a hanging lie to get you anywhere near the green. Now two-thirds of the gully has been smoothed out and the hole is not as challenging for the ordinary player as it was.'

Another idea was to play the third (then and now a par four) as a three off a new tee, thus freeing the former ground for use on the 18th of the New. This explains the tee well forward and at the back of the second green. It was

8 *Famous Fairways* (Stanley Paul), 1968.
9 *Bobby Locke on Golf* (Country Life), 1953.
10 Chapter 32.

OLD SAYINGS

HAROLD HILTON, (*Golf Illustrated*, 1925 and 1926)
It is not the length of the course which supplies the difficulty, neither is it the peculiarities in the approaching, nor the trickiness of the greens. It is the heather – and what may happen to the player if he visits the heather. Once he has passed through a sad experience in this way he is for ever after in mortal dread that there may be another disaster.

It is, perhaps the most health-giving course in Britain, for even on the hottest of summer days one can fill one's lungs with the best quality of British air. On a raw, cold day, however, when the wind is blowing strongly from the east, there is often too much of the bracing element.

GUY CAMPBELL, (*Golf Illustrated*, 1933)
What a fine course it is, to be sure... and what turf! Short and sweet and tough through the fairways, shorter still and keen and true on the greens themselves. 'Ah, yes' I can hear someone say, 'but all this is the eye-wash side of the business; what of its playing qualities?' The answer comes quick and pat. Its qualities are those of a great course.

PATRICK DICKINSON, (*A Round of Golf Courses*, 1951)
Walton Heath seems to be very like James Braid, for it is strong and modest, positive and forthright, yet never ostentatious. Walton Heath, by saying nothing, will give you its opinion of your golf. If you ask for an opinion you will get one and there will be no mincing matters. It seems to move with the long, slow, loping stride, never hurried, of its genius. It moves you along slowly and inexorably. It says, 'Your business is to play round, not even stopping for lost balls – because you should hit straight; nor to admire the view – for your business is to concentrate. You are to keep going. Golf is a game of flowing rhythm, of a steady resolve, it is not over till the ball is in the bottom of the hole and you have lost or won or put down your final score.

BERNARD DARWIN, (Club Handbook, 1937)
There is no more charming place on a fine sunshiny day, none where the air is fresher and more cheering, none where the sky seems bigger. It is a place where it is good for us, alike for our game and for ourselves, to play golf.

BOBBY LOCKE, (*Bobby Locke on Golf*, 1953)
I must face it that Walton Heath is not my course. It is an extremely exacting test of golf... It is a course I have never been able to master.

SIR PETER ALLEN, (*Famous Fairways*, 1968)
Altogether Walton Heath sets as strict an examination in golf as any in the United Kingdom and is certainly the hardest inland course in the country. One thing is certain: if you play regularly at Walton Heath, any other course you go to will seem easy.

THE BEST?

BERNARD DARWIN (*The American Golfer magazine*, 1929)
Comparisons are dangerous, but in some ways Walton Heath has always seemed to me the greatest and most formidable among inland courses. It is not perhaps the prettiest and most engaging and it can be bleak; but beyond all possible doubt it is great and demands greatness in the playing... A better course to my thinking even than Sunningdale.

JEROME TRAVERS, (winner of 1915 US Open, (*Country Life*, 1914)
Of the London courses, I saw Woking, Mid-Surrey, Sunningdale, Walton Heath and Stoke Poges, and I should place Walton Heath first and Sunningdale second. What I particularly liked at Walton was the turf, which seemed in some way more like seaside turf.

TED RAY (*Inland Golf*)
Sunningdale I consider to be indisputably the finest inland course I have ever played over. Ganton I would place next in merit, with Walton Heath a good third.

BRER RABBIT (*Golf Illustrated*, 1933)
Walton Heath offers the sterner test and Sunningdale, because of its more taking landscape, the more enjoyable one.

NICK EDMUND, (*Golf Links*, Jan/Feb 1999)
Because of television, the West course at Wentworth may have become more widely known and Sunningdale has always been more strikingly scenic, but Walton Heath remains the purest of all England's great heathland layouts. Put it this way, if one were given the task of showing an overseas visitor just one example of a classic heathland layout, then that person should be taken to inspect the Old course at Walton Heath.

What was so special about Fowler?

Philip Truett, Walton Heath's archivist, worships at Fowler's shrine. As a layman to whom one hole looks like any other, I asked him to define what made his man so special. This, edited, was his reply:

Fowler looked at the task of laying out a course completely differently from the professional-golfer architects. They had other duties to fulfil, but a gentleman had time. He studied all aspects of construction and maintenance and knew time was needed for proper surveys of the land. He did not build courses according to the fashions of the time, with their gun-platform tees, rampart-like bunkers and square greens – a terrible symmetry. He laid them out using the natural contours of the land, blending in his hazards with the surrounding countryside.

Where, now, are Fowler's lost gems?

*W*ere Fowler put down on earth today, would he recognise his Old course? Some people say no. Others vehemently disagree and present convincing evidence.

The configuration remains much the same as ever. Eight holes are Fowler originals: the first four, plus the 14th, 15th, 16th and 18th. Surviving features at the fifth, eighth, 10th and 13th would stir his memory. That leaves six holes that are not his originals, but he would have known five of them before he died. Only one entire hole, the ninth, has been built from scratch since then. What might disorient him are the trees. Long gone are the vistas of uninterrupted open heathland.

But where do Fowler's lost gems lie? How can we find the sixth, the first hole he pegged out? What of the others destroyed in the 'thirties?

Photographs show fragmented features of these holes, but the only complete representations of them – or at least those on the outward nine – come from a board game, Henry Cotton's Tee Up, marketed in 1938, just before they fell victims to change.

Join me if you will on an exploration to find them. Bring your imagination – and your funeral attire.

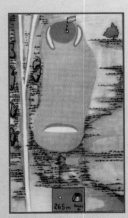

The fifth: Fondly remembered. Died in 1939, when its green was sacrificed in an operation to fuse it with the sixth. It then measured 265 yards.

Imagine it by standing on the back tee of the present fifth, from where it was played. Look at the right-hand drive bunker – its original right-hand greenside hazard. Another bunker lay to the left and there was one in mid-

fairway at 137 yards. Its epitaph may be found by past-tensing Darwin:

A short hole... but when the wind blew strong in our faces too long for us to entertain any great hopes of reaching the green... The green was right to left and a series of graduated horrors awaited the pulled ball: a mere bunker for the moderate sinner, a tract of wet ruts and hoof marks for the rather more criminal and a waste of heather for the utterly depraved.[1]

The sixth: Sorely missed. Nicknamed Port Arthur after that supposedly impregnable Russian port. Died, 1939, in the operation involving the fifth, to whose successor it has bequeathed its green. It measured about 150 yards from a tee identifiable on flat ground to the left of today's fifth fairway at a long drive distance. From there, mourners may find Darwin's tribute affecting:

The green is undeniably of adequate size, but it is ringed, save in front, with bunkers deep and horrible and the ground draws unmistakably towards them. Often, as we stand in a frenzied attitude, trying to steer the ball to safety with vain gesticulations of the club, we see it light upon the turf and breathe a sigh of relief. Alas, we were too hasty! The ball trembles and totters for a moment or two in a state of indecision and then, as if magnetically drawn towards Scylla on one side or Charybdis on the other, slowly disappears from our sight.

Once in the bunker we ought with ordinary fortune to get out, but the ball must be made to drop wonderfully dead, scattering showers of sand, or else it will run gently and deliberately into the bunker on the other side. It is one of those holes at which, were the fates amenable to a compromise, many a stout-hearted player would

write down four on his card and proceed to the next tee with the ball in his pocket.[2]

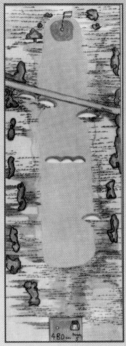

The seventh: Left for dead in the 1939 upheavals. Ran 480 yards straight on up the hill from the old sixth. Duck hook off the eighth and you may find your ball in uncharacteristically lush grass to the left of the start of the fairway. This was the old, double-tier green. A coal post, now deep in the trees, was at its back.

The eighth and ninth: Met violent deaths – one buried alive, the other decapitated. But these atrocities were to come years later and will be described in chapter 32.

When Cotton's game came out the back nine had already been changed, so no diagrams exist to describe the originals. But explore...

Find an old double-tier green for the 10th, hard up against the Gallops, the line of which is still there behind the trees... a platform tee for the 11th from when it played down the valley with the line on Kingswood church... remains of the bank that ran right across the 13th with one narrow gap... the original green of the 15th...

Explore! Take my informant, archivist Truett, as your guide. Wallow in history!

[1] and [2] Golf Courses of the British Isles (Duckworth),1910

CLASSIC CHALLENGE

The historic 1937 challenge match over 72 holes between Henry Cotton, the Open champion, and Densmore Shute, United States Match-Play champion. It was billed as for the world match-play title and lived up to its advance publicity.

Left: Cotton and Shute shake hands in the rain before the start under the eyes of referee James Braid.

Golfing

Above: Cotton approaches the 18th in the third round, having hit his ball over the green and under a car. Obviously there was room to park there in those days.

Right: Big crowds on the second hole. They watched the match free and saw enthralling golf from both players.

Chapter Nineteen

KING COTTON
Champions, challengers and Walton's most celebrated shot

I N 1937 THE DRAMA of the old challenge matches returned after nearly a quarter of a century and it was a simple task to cast the leading character – Henry Cotton.

By July that year, when he was matched with Densmore Shute from the United States, Cotton was a national sporting hero, the man who had broken a decade of American domination of our Open three years previously and had just repeated the dose by winning at Carnoustie. Shute, winner of our Open in 1933, had for two years been America's match-play champion, the USPGA championship not yet having converted to stroke-play.

The two-day match promised valuable publicity both for the Club and the *News of the World*, for whom Cotton was now writing. Sir Emsley Carr's paper, seeing it as a spectacular adjunct to its match-play championship, put up £500 in prize money (worth £20,000 today) and stipulated that all 72 holes were to be played at Walton. 'The match of the century!' shouted the headlines, 'For the world match-play title!'

Among the spectators was young Ronnie Watson, who, with the club's blessing, had begun playing on the heath when he was 13 and to whom Cotton was a role model. He watched and prayed for his hero in more than one match at Walton and last year, in his eighties, he recalled for me 10 seconds of youthful agony:

I desperately wanted Henry to win and dogged his footsteps

Henry Cotton as painted by John Berrie.
Royal and Ancient Golf Club
of St. Andrews

as closely as I could in the vast crowds. At one particular green I was directly behind him as he prepared to putt. Then, horror of horrors, I saw the way he was lining up. I knew that green, I knew how that putt would break and I knew he'd got the wrong line! I thought, 'Should I tell him?' He putted – and missed!

When the match against Shute was made, Cotton fans like Watson feared that their man might arrive drained from his efforts at Carnoustie. They need not have worried, he won by six and five. *The Times* correspondent was ecstatic:

I am trying to cultivate the art of deliberate understatement when I say that I have never seen better golf than Cotton played in this match and particularly in the second part of it. His first three rounds were 71, 70 and 69 and he was four under fours in the fourth round when he won at the 13th.

Reporters paid tribute also to the Open champion's big hitting, not least at the seventh, a hole measuring some 490 yards that would soon fall victim to course changes. In the third round Cotton reached the green in two with a four iron from a heathery lie. *The Times* called it miraculous.

To these reports and Henry Longhurst's eulogy (page 122) may be added three pieces of trivia. First, at the 10th hole Shute's drive somehow wrapped itself in a lady spectator's skirt; Braid, the referee, turned her round and round until the ball dropped. At the 18th on the morning of the second day Cotton hit his approach over the green and under a car: obviously there was room to park there in those days.

Finally, after the match, Captain Tippet, the club secretary, wrote almost apologetically to chairman Carr about the expenses incurred – £133, which covered payments to 37 caddies, nine policemen, extra phone lines, catering for the Press and entertaining the American Ryder Cup team to lunch and tea! 'I should also like to pay a little overtime to my green men, who started at 5am each day and worked until the match was over,' he ventured to add.

NO FINER SETTING, NO BRAVER LOSER

For sheer concentrated brilliance the Cotton-v-Shute match at Walton Heath will not be surpassed as long as the game is played.

Perhaps I may say a word about the course, so that those who were not present may better appreciate the true significance of the golf these two men produced. I say 'two' because, although he lost by 6 and 5 (which is not a tremendous lot over 72 holes), Shute played well enough to have beaten almost everyone in Britain and nine out of ten of the world's first-class professionals.

The Old course has always been among the sternest tests in inland golf. Walton from the ordinary medal tees was, however, as nothing to the Walton that one saw presented to these two experts. New tees were seen to have been prepared for them away back in the undergrowth, in one case even on the back of one of the greens on the New, and the course totalled what we have now come to expect of a championship links – nearly 7,000 yards.

It was in absolutely spotless order, giving the impression of having been specially brushed and polished for the occasion, and altogether presented one of the finest tests of inland golf that I have ever seen. No finer setting could have been found.

I have often been engaged in wordy warfare on the subject of the excessive length of the golf ball, deploring the fact that it has now become virtually impossible to find a course that compels the expert to produce a complete range of shots. Let me at once acknowledge that Walton was indeed such a course... and produce all his shots Cotton certainly did – one after the other for nearly four rounds.

Shute can crack the ball as far as the rest of them and can produce a fine snap with his hands and wrists at the critical moment. Yet beside Cotton he became like a man struggling to keep up with a giant. He hung on like a leech until the last putt was holed and his heart must have warmed to the tremendous ovation he received for his gallant display. (He was given a special consolation prize of £100).

Both here and at Carnoustie Cotton won because he could hole the putts. But I shall still take leave to say that Shute left the impression of being the safer man at all distances up to six feet. Cotton from five feet is still inclined to remind the less reverent spectator of a broody hen. However, results presumably justify methods. We should not criticise the hen for being broody; our only just ground for complaint comes if she fails to hatch out the eggs.

HENRY LONGHURST in *Golf Illustrated*

Friendly pre-match line-up disguises the fierce rivalry that existed between Cotton and (third from left) Locke.

Almost exactly a year later, in July 1938, Cotton was challenged from South Africa. In London-born Sid Brews, several times their champion and runner-up to Cotton in our 1934 Open, and a 21-year-old prodigy named Bobby Locke who had just turned professional, the South African interests believed they had a pair who could beat Cotton and anyone he cared to nominate in a 72-hole four-ball.

They put their money where their mouths were to the tune of £500.

The *News of the World* accepted the challenge, again stipulating that Walton Heath must be the venue. The man chosen to partner Cotton was Reginald Whitcombe, professional at Parkstone (Dorset), and the match assumed extra magnetism when, shortly beforehand, Reg won the Open at Sandwich – on a day when the wind wrecked the exhibition tent, blowing out its contents and reputedly twisting and breaking steel-shafted clubs.

Spice was added to the mix by an element of 'needle' between Cotton and Locke. The young South African, twice leading amateur in the Open, had just beaten Henry in winning the Irish Open, whereupon, according to Locke, Cotton told him he was a lucky young fellow. 'I did not forget that,' Locke wrote subsequently. 'I had decided for some time that Cotton was the man to topple. I felt I could do it and now I was really after him.'[1]

'More than 8,000 saw the closing stages of a match of bewildering fluctuations and thrilling incidents,' wrote *The Daily Telegraph*'s George Greenwood. 'As an entertainment for which there was nothing to pay it was almost ideal, except for the time taken.'

_____

[1] *Bobby Locke on Golf*, (Country Life), 1953.

Locke approaching the 10th.

The time taken? Good heavens, it was disgraceful! On the first day, three hours 40 minutes and three hours 55 minutes for rounds of competitive four-ball! Today even two-balls take four hours, with the crowds behind fences – which they weren't in 1938! Anyway it was considered slow then and Locke was unanimously chastised as the sinner.

Locke admitted that he deliberately took his time on the first day, studying every putt from all angles and gaining satisfaction from the pressure he sensed he was putting on Cotton. However, although the newspapers complained of his 'funeral-procession golf,' he said he saw only scant reference to Cotton's behaviour. According to the South African, Britain's hero had kept everyone waiting on the tee for 20 minutes before the first round and 25 before the second and had neither explained nor apologised. 'As far as I was concerned, the gloves were off!'

Brews and Locke led by two holes after the first day. After 10 holes of the third round, with Locke crawling up to second gear, they had lost that lead and at the 16th it was the home pair who were two up. With a round to play Cotton and Whitcombe led by one.

Locke squared the match at the fourth with a masterly brassie shot drawn over the heads of the crowd, and at a bogey-five eighth measuring 440 yards he put his side ahead. He and Cotton were the only players on the green. Locke putted to within inches for a four; Cotton, trying for a three, ran four feet past and missed the return. The next three holes were halved.

Now came perhaps the most famous stroke in Old course history. Nearly 50 years later, when Cotton was Surrey CCC's guest at a Test match, he recalled it while talking with Walton Heath member Ken Ohlson and shed new light on what happened:

> Going up the 10th I said to Reg, 'We're in trouble. When we get to the 12th, the dog-leg, you drive conventionally down the middle – I'm going over the trees for the green.'

The 12th hole was almost brand new; professionals were playing it for the first time. Dog-legged from left to right, it measured 370 yards that day and the gambler's line Cotton envisaged meant a carry of about 280. The wind was at his back, but the venom of the terrain he would have to carry can be assessed by studying contemporary descriptions: 'wild country'…'a belt of trees and shrubs and impenetrable trouble'…'a sea of bracken up to your neck'…'a jungle of bracken and heather'…

Whitcombe played safely on to the fairway. Cotton, who could not see the green, ordered spectators out of the way and let fly. When the players approached the green they found his ball just short of the apron and within 40 yards of the pin.

Henry told Ken that the club he chose for his second was a four-iron, that the chip stopped on the very edge of the hole and that Locke, who had walked there while the putt was running, actually eased it in, telling him to pick it out quickly! As a result, many of the crowd thought he had made a two, but it was a birdie-three and it won the hole. Scarcely credible!

Brews escaping from the rough.

The tee-shot has taken its place in golfing legend – Locke called it the greatest he had seen – but Braid, refereeing, saw it in a wider context. 'The drive was a grand 'un,' he said quietly to Cotton as they left the green, 'but *the* shot was the run-up.' Cotton agreed: it would have been so easy to have taken four after the catharsis of the tee-shot.

The 12th would become known as 'Cotton's hole' and meantime it proved the turning-point. The match was all-square with six holes to play and now Whitcombe, who had generally played second fiddle to his partner, came to life. Two great woods at the par-five 13th and vital putts thereafter helped put the Englishmen two up with three to play and they held on to win by two and one. Energies drained by the events of two long days, each pocketed £250, while the *News of the World*'s Sir Emsley Carr presented the South Africans with £100 apiece as a reward for their efforts.

The better-ball figures of this extraordinary match, played over a course of 6,905 yards with a bogey of 78, were calculated as Cotton/Whitcombe 67-65-67-66=265; Brews/Locke 67-62-70-67=266.[2] Young Locke was the player of the match and for long periods was on his own, playing against the opposition's better ball. This slim 21-year-old would reappear, somewhat bulkier, after World War II to win our Open four times – only once less than Braid.

Cotton and Locke would play one more challenge

The last big challenge match. Fred Daly on the tee.

match at Walton after the war – a 36-hole four-ball in September 1952, when the *News of the World* backed Henry and the Ulsterman Fred Daly against the *Sunday Dispatch*'s Eric Brown and the South African. There was £500 for the winners and £200 for the losers, but the contest was a let-down. Locke and Brown, playing as poorly as their opponents (eight under fours) played well, won only one of the 36 holes, the first, and were beaten by eight and seven.

Long before the end the crowd were beginning to leave the course – a sad scene to signal the closing pages of the club's catalogue of money matches.

The 1952 match was an anti-climax. Big crowds came (this was the fourth green), but many left before the end.

[2] Some assessed the South Africans' second-round score as 63.

End of the cosy life

efore her death in 2002, Mrs Jo Bryant, whose association with the club spanned 72 years, painted me a word-picture of life at Walton Heath in the 'thirties – for her and her friends a life of blissful leisure bereft of responsibility.

Some members had suffered sorely in the Depression, but not others: 'I had three horses and rode or played golf all the time. I didn't work; oh no, it's a terrible thing but we almost looked down on people who worked in those days!'

She also kindly gave me permission to

quote from her diaries, which reflect that cosy existence:

Rode. Practised golf... Daddy and I went for a walk over Walton. Saw the Prince playing in Parliamentary Handicap. Taken to the Berkeley for dinner. Got home about 3am...

Rode in morning. Played golf with Daddy. We had a row with a four-ball...

Rode. Played in a Pearson Trophy at Epsom – our only winner. Dinner at Great Eastern Hotel, then went to see Jack Doyle fight at Earls Court.

'There was precious little social life at the club in the old days,' said Jo. 'Nobody really stayed on – it was very much a golf club. But there were all sorts of socialising and entertaining in the houses. Everybody seemed to have their butlers and servants.'

These comfortable life-styles ended with World War II. Jo went into the WRNS – and for security reasons was not permitted to continue her diaries. At Walton the only serious golf for the ladies would be monthly competitions in aid of the Red Cross.

Chapter Twenty

BOMBS ON THE COURSE
World War II – the Club suffers and survives

'GOSH, BOMBS all over the show!' said Phyl Foster, the long-time member, recording her memories in old age.[1] 'Seventeen bombs in a line over the golf course, most famous club in England,' wrote a Serviceman on the back of a postcard. Such were recollections of Walton Heath during World War II.

Nobody has been able specifically to confirm for me the 17 bombs recalled by the soldier who had been billeted nearby and none is mentioned by Cyril Hewertson in his 1979 club history. But the course was certainly hit. The map reproduced on page 126[2] is one piece of evidence; personal memories, although surprisingly vague, form others.

During the blitz on London, which began in September 1940, planes on their way home may have off-loaded their residue of bombs; then came the pilotless V1 doodlebugs; and finally the V2 rockets, approaching at far beyond the speed of sound.

The map suggests that high explosives in 1940/41 dropped on the north-east corner of the courses, probably in the vicinity of the first, second and third of the Old, and seems to explain the crater to the right of the 16th (New), to the side of the former gallop where a sliced drive might finish. This, though, is claimed to be a doodlebug's imprint.

Angus Lloyd, who lived his boyhood in grandfather Beck's house on the edge of the heath, recalls at least two strikes in the summer of 1944. Walk the eighth hole on the New, he says, and in certain conditions you may still distinguish a change of colour where a missile exploded; another, according to Angus, struck the former ninth of the Old.

The doughty Phyl Foster was living at *Priestmere* when an incendiary bomb dropped one night. She rushed out

Sir Frederic Hamilton – steered the club through war years.

with a stirrup-pump to put out the flames. Her cook was understandably shocked. 'Oh, good gracious, Miss Phyllis,' she gasped, 'you've nothing on over your nightie!'

Canadian troops camped on the heath to the edge of the course, the military took over the Riddell Hall as well as the Dormy House and the Captain Mainwarings and Sergeant Wilsons of the local 'Dads' Army' used the clubhouse as their HQ and weapons store.

The club carried on as best it could. Things had been looking good. In four years the membership had increased from 798 to 1,021 and the new holes on the Old course had been paid for out of revenue. A really good 1940 had been anticipated – but when war was declared on September 3, 1939, a board meeting held that very day had to re-think all plans.

As in World War I, the courses and clubhouse would be kept open but official competitions would cease. Members unable to use the club could become 'non-playing' and pay three guineas per annum. Secretary Tippet urged rigid economies, including reduction of staff. Wives of servants who were called up were granted 10 shillings a week. Thoughts of moving the clubhouse across the Dorking Road were shelved and a match between amateurs and the Ryder Cup team was cancelled, the encounter arranged for Florida itself having been abandoned.

Membership plummeted; 200 were lost almost immediately. In 1941, when the war had taken a disastrous turn, chairman Sir Emsley Carr died, Tippet had re-joined the Army, the steward was on munitions work and at times it seemed that the place was falling apart. Ironically, the luncheon room was over-crowded at weekends, to the degree that afternoon rounds were being delayed or curtailed and the number of guests had to be restricted.

In January 1942 at least £1,500 was needed to clear debts and enable the club to carry on until May 31, end of the

---

[1] Walton Local History Society newsletter.
[2] Provided by Ted Bond, former green man.

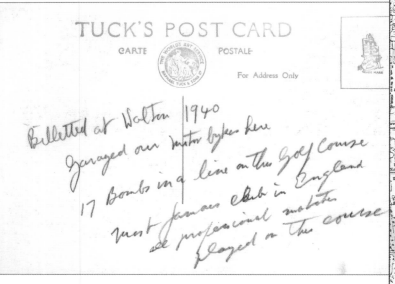

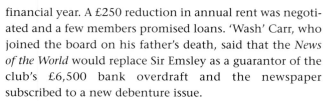

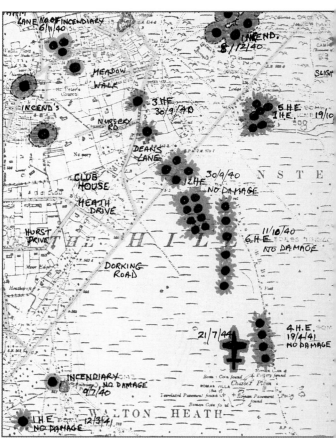

Two pieces of evidence purporting to show where bombs fell – a postcard sent by a serviceman and a map supplied by a former green-staff member.

financial year. A £250 reduction in annual rent was negotiated and a few members promised loans. 'Wash' Carr, who joined the board on his father's death, said that the *News of the World* would replace Sir Emsley as a guarantor of the club's £6,500 bank overdraft and the newspaper subscribed to a new debenture issue.

One of the members who offered loans was Sir Frederic Hamilton, who had succeeded Emsley Carr as chairman. He had joined in 1904 and as a debenture holder was on the first nominated committee. Now, against the backcloth of war, he would emerge as a giant in Walton Heath's history.

Hamilton, son of a doctor, was a multi-faceted character: Cambridge graduate, lawyer, journalist, politician, businessman and political prisoner; a man deeply involved in the intrigues of late-Victorian South Africa.

He had gone to South Africa in his twenties and eventually became editor of the *Johannesburg Star*. The flashpoint of his life came when he met and befriended the English-born entrepreneur and politician Cecil Rhodes – prime minister of the Cape Colony, controller of 90-per-cent of the world's diamond production, ambitious for a British colony stretching from the Cape to Cairo but frustrated by a barrier to expansion in the Boer republic of the Transvaal. The liaison led to Hamilton's getting involved in the Jameson Raid affair.

A plan existed for Leander Starr Jameson, a doctor in the diamond mines who grew close to Rhodes, to invade the Transvaal from Mafeking at the end of 1895, his raid to coincide with an uprising of disaffected British workers there. Rhodes was involved in its early planning. Hamilton, a member of the political Reform Committee but apparently against the use of force, was sent to see Rhodes by a worried Joseph Chamberlain, secretary of state for the colonies, in an attempt to diffuse the situation. In later years at Walton he would vividly describe how he and Rhodes sat together awaiting the outcome of the latter's attempts to halt the enterprise.

The raid took place. Jameson invaded with 600 men, the uprising never happened, 16 died and after four days the mission ended in failure. It tightened the tensions that would eventually lead to the Boer War. Meanwhile it was difficult for the public to know whose side people had been on, who had changed their minds, who had been caught in the middle and who were guilty of what.

Rhodes, attacked for complicity, resigned the premier-

Dumping ground

*G*eoff Womersley, DSO, DFC, a member since 1987, was controlling RAF bombing operations in 1942 when a Wellington bound for Italy lost an engine over the south coast. It had to return to its base in East Anglia, more than likely Mildenhall, and had to get rid of its bombs.

Walton Heath, it seems, was part of a so-called 'dumping ground' and this is where the crippled bomber dropped its bombs.

'Dad's Army' at the clubhouse. Left: James Braid, commanding officer Dr. Candy (Tudor Davies's father-in-law) and Sir Frederic Hamilton at a Home Guard Christmas lunch.

of the character recalled by Lady Macrory:

A man who fought hard and argued strongly but who was also ready to listen and give with a generosity for which it was said that 'he seemed almost to disclaim responsibility.'[3]

One day in 1945 the clubhouse was silent in celebration, closed to mark the end of the war with Germany. Then plans began to be made for the future as the members gradually returned. No memorial exists, nor have any minutes survived, to suggest how many never came back.

ship and Jameson was imprisoned. Hamilton, judged to have been some sort of collaborator, was fined £2,000, jailed with other Reform Committee members and released after four months on condition that he did not engage in politics for three years.

He returned to Britain and concentrated on dealing with his financial and mining undertakings in South Africa, Australia and elsewhere. He resisted pressures to stand as a Liberal candidate but remained a significant figure behind the scenes. His houses – *Homefield* in Walton, for instance – became venues for much intellectual chat with prominent politicians.

He enjoyed bridge and chess, which he could play at much the same speed as his golf. The dawdles of his fourballs in the 'twenties inspired those who stood and waited to bestow on him a nickname at once satirical yet affectionate: 'Fleet-footed Freddie.'

By the time Hamilton was made chairman he had been knighted for services to the National Liberals and was 77; when he resigned he was past 80. By then, clear in thought, judgment and explanation and helped by a committee which now included James Braid, he had steered the club successfully through the remaining war years. In 1944, 'in some slight recognition of the immense debt the members owe you,' he had been elected captain.

His portrait in the clubhouse, presented to him by the members, reflects much of his strength as a chairman and

At a board meeting in 1946 some surprise was expressed that there had been comparatively few applications for membership. Two possible explanations were offered and one was the temporary hangover of petrol restrictions. The other was more socially significant:

Heavy taxation and the general position of the country had seriously affected the classes from which, in pre-war days, members of the more expensive clubs were mainly drawn.[4]

Things in life were changing and would continue to do so. So would the character of golf club memberships. For better or for worse golf would never again be quite the same.

Lloyd's Golf Club had accumulated funds of over £1,000 by the end of 1945. Instead of making a refund of wartime annual subscriptions, it was unanimously agreed to give a donation of £100 to a number of 'first class courses' to help with restoration work on the understanding that the club would be allowed to hold one of its meetings annually at such a course, if so desired, at a green fee of five shillings a member. The chosen clubs were Rye, Royal Cinque Ports, Sunningdale, Berkshire, Littlestone and Walton Heath.

One Hundred Years Without a Course (Lloyd's Golf Club History)

---

[3] Walton Local History Society newsletter.
[4] Board minutes, May 17, 1946.

Chapter Twenty-one

THE SUCCESS AND SADNESS OF HERBERT FOWLER
Wartime death brings an end to an era

IT IS TIME we returned to the subject of William Herbert Fowler. We left our detailed scrutiny of him in 1904,[1] when he had been made managing director of the company and his original course had opened for business. Since then he has lurked in the background during almost every chapter. Now, in World War II, there are valid albeit sad reasons to pick up the threads of his story, some of it triumphant, some distressing.

The architect

Walton Heath may have been Fowler's first course, but it immediately established his reputation. Darwin said that it was 'a stroke of genius to see with his prophetic eye a noble golf course in the expanse of Walton Heath.'[2]

'God builds courses and the less man meddles the better for all concerned,' said Fowler with uncharacteristic humility, but clients from near and far, unable to approach the former, were soon seeking the services of the latter. Before World War I, on his own or in partnership, he embarked on at least eight courses, from Surrey to Yorkshire and from Devon to Wales.

In 1913 he went into partnership with another architect, Tom Simpson, with whom he had already worked. Simpson was wealthy, independent, multi-talented and a touch eccentric. Eccentric? Club committees were not altogether comfortable when they saw their potential designer arrive by chauffeur-driven Rolls, clad in cloak and beret and brandishing a riding crop. 'Too artistic, a friend

> There is one outstanding fault — the descent to the seventh hole and consequent climb up to the eighth. To the young and athletic this may be of small importance, but to a large number of players it must be almost intolerable. I was so blown after playing them that I did not hit a shot for two holes. If the seventh was a very good hole I would say less about it, but I consider it a very *bad* hole.
>
> Fowler, writing to Southerndown Golf Club

Flashback to 1904. Fowler putting on the sixth green (today's fifth) of the Old course he had just created.

Illustrated Sporting and Dramatic News

of the nobs!' said one secretary, 'Architecture is just a hobby for him!' Admittedly Simpson was a barrister who could afford not to practise and to indulge himself in golf instead, but behind the mask of rich eccentric he was a sound and serious architect.

In February 1920, when he was 64, Fowler arrived in New York to set up an American outpost for his and Simpson's company. They began advertising their plasticine models of holes that they would design and others could implement:

> The better 'ole is never a blind hole, it must be seen to be appreciated! Every contour and trap, almost every blade of grass can be seen before construction starts!

From New York he made the long trek by rail to the west coast ('The journey passed quickly,' he said of his five-day return via Chicago. 'I made eight models and darned all my socks').

Out west he was responsible for, among others, the Los Angeles Country Club's south course and the city's Ambassador Hotel layout, took co-billing for Burlingame and made plans aimed at improving Pebble Beach. Back

---

[1] Chapter 2.
[2] *Golfing*, Jan 7, 1914.

RBERT FOWLER – portrait by Sir James Gunn, RA, 1935.

129

Fowler the architect. Surveying the terrain for a new course and (above) at work with partner Tom Simpson.

Pacific Golf and Motor, *1920.*

east he was responsible for the spectacular Eastward Ho! links at Chatham, Massachusetts.

At home Fowler and Simpson next combined with two other architects, Arthur Croome and John Frederick Abercromby. Together or apart they created, added to or changed a myriad of courses in Britain and Europe and Fowler laid out, among others, Saunton (Devon), The Berkshire (red and blue) and Cooden Beach (Sussex). There were upmarket personal clients, too, like Lord Louis Mountbatten, for whom Fowler and Simpson collaborated on a private practice course, and Viscount Northcliffe, who commissioned them to design a par-three layout at Sutton Place, near Guildford.

Fowler's reputation continued to be that of a master craftsman carving out big, testing courses. When, in 1914, Fowler opined that the game had become too easy a hornet's nest was stirred. 'Fowler and company have gone mad,' declared Walton's own Riddell. 'The ordinary golfer never finds golf too easy, he usually finds it too difficult. The fashionable golf architect is an ingenious and interesting creature, but he is apt to forget that courses do not exist just for the benefit of the crack players.'

However, as we have seen, Fowler was trying to counter the changes in the game caused by the rubber-cored ball, new clubs and improved conditions. He always denied that he was biased in favour of the top players:

> We are businessmen and do not lay out courses for the benefit of our health. If we consulted only the one per-cent of those who play we would soon cease to have a business because no one would recommend us. We lay them out for the benefit of all and sundry. If any one class receives more consideration than another it is the 12-handicap man, who is perhaps the mainstay of most clubs.[3]

---

[3] Fowler/Simpson company brochure.

Fowler's 50

*F*owler, alone or in partnership, has been credited with work on the following more than 50 courses. Where an associate has been recorded his name is included. The total could eventually turn out to be more.

BEFORE WORLD WAR I

Abbeydale (Yorks), Bull Bay (Isle of Anglesey), Delamere Forest (Cheshire), Shirley Park, Walton Heath (Old and New), West Surrey, Woodcote Park (Surrey), Yelverton (Devon).
Alterations: *Westward Ho!*

AFTER WORLD WAR I

IN BRITAIN:

Abbeydale (new course), Beau Desert (Staffs), The Berkshire (red and blue), Blackwell (Worcs), Bull Bay (second time), Cooden Beach (Sussex), Cowdray Park (Sussex) with Simpson and Abercromby, Knole Park (Kent) with Abercromby, Saunton (two courses) (Devon), West Kent (old course) with Abercromby. Private courses for Viscount Northcliffe (Sutton Place, Surrey) with Simpson, Lord Louis Mountbatten (Adsdean), Mortimer Singer.

Additions, alterations etc.: *Aberdovey (Gwynedd), Bradford (Yorks), Broadstone (Dorset), Cruden Bay (Aberdeenshire), Ganton (Yorks) (no proof), Hallamshire (Yorks), Huddersfield (Yorks), Lindrick (Yorks), Manor House Hotel (Devon) (possibly with Abercromby), Royal Lytham (Lancs), Southerndown (Glamorgan).*

IN EUROPE:

San Sebastian (Spain). Probably more in association with others.

IN UNITED STATES:

Ambassador Hotel, Burlingame (with Harold Sampson), Crystal Springs, Lake Merced, Los Angeles CC (all California); Eastward Ho! (Mass).

Additions, alterations, advice etc: *Del Paso, Lincoln Park, Menlo, Old Del Monte, Pebble Beach, Presidio, Riverside, San Francisco Municipal, Sacramento, Sequoyah, Allegheny, Olympic (SF), Capitola.*

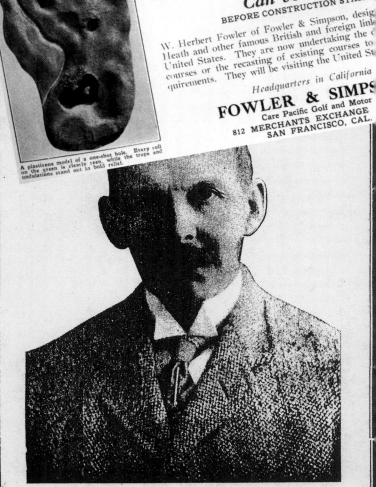

In the 'twenties a good-class course might be made for between £5,000 and £8,000, or £10,000 to £15,000 with a modest clubhouse. However, Shirley Park, on which Fowler and Simpson worked in 1913, had been priced at £25,000 including a clubhouse and accoutrements. The architects charged fees at six-per-cent of the total and £1,000 in the early 'twenties would be worth over £23,000 today. Fowler's return was good – while it lasted.

The pundit

Fowler's deluge of letters to the Press flooded on, the topics ranging from stymies and lost balls to weeds and worms, from weak committees to moss and muck. He made some sparks fly at R&A meetings, too. Sometimes committees and publications supported his opinions, but not always. When Herbert objected to bogey as a basis for competition, an editor accused him of 'blasé ignorance.' When Fowler's views were repeated the editor's reply was merely 'Rats!' – the equivalent, you may think, of singing *Colonel Bogey* to him today.

> It seems to be considered a *sine qua non* that all championships must be played over a seaside course, *wrote Fowler in 1908 in an extension of his eternal argument that the closed-shop rota of the same few favoured courses should end.* This view cannot logically be upheld.

The editor of *Golf Illustrated*, recognising Fowler's allegiances and ambitions, was suspicious:

> In these days of syndicates and proprietary clubs there are a large number of players interested in the commercial success of courses and it would be highly improper to allow any such persons any voice or say in the choosing of greens for the championships.

Walton Heath *was* then a proprietary club and Fowler, its managing director and architect, *was* interested in its commercial success. A decade or so later he gave full rein to advocacy of his own course:

> In England no championship has yet been held on an inland green, yet there is 10 times more inland golf played than at the seaside and many of the finest tests of golf and best greens are found on inland courses. Walton Heath, for example, is the course par excellence which has shown up the weak spots of even the greatest masters of the game.[4]

Fowler in the 1930s.

Apart from Walton Heath there was Westward Ho!, where he had learned the game and altered the course. Submerging his affection for St Andrews, he once wrote that it could not be compared with Westward Ho! as a test of golf.

By no means everything for which he campaigned came to pass. He would have been apoplectic in heaven when four-balls were inserted into the Ryder Cup matches. A national-course project he supported came to naught. The Open has never been played inland.

However, during or after his lifetime some of his pet hobby-horses did find their way into the winners' enclosure. They included rule changes like the abolition of the stymie and the substitution of stroke-and-distance for loss-of-hole when a ball was lost in match-play. As early as 1912 the closed shop of the Amateur roster squeezed creakily open for slightly wider business with the inclusion of his beloved Westward Ho! As for playing the championship inland, it has happened only three times, always at Ganton and the first occasion 23 years after Herbert's death.

His most significant influence was in changing the way the entire game of golf was controlled. From the early 1900s, when he was elected to the R&A's green committee, he had vociferously campaigned on the subject and his missives to *Country Life* and the game's periodicals, summarised below, foreshadowed fundamental changes at the top which, when they came, embraced him personally:

> It was in 1888 that the R&A gave to the world the Rules of Golf.[5] Since that time all clubs all over the world have played the game under these rules… The R&A, then, is the only authority which attempts to control the game, and it may be of interest to consider whether the club should not be asked to go further and take charge also of both championships (*then managed by separate committees of club delegates*).

Fowler was urging that the R&A should, via a committee of members, take over the entire game:

> There are strong feelings that the club does not sufficiently take the lead… and a desire that it should step forward and show the golfing world that it is not only capable but also willing to assume a more direct control of the game… There is one great difficulty in the way, and that is to find a means of satisfying the R&A that there is any necessity to wake up and assert its authority and position.

Such changes came about after World War I. The case for a supreme ruling authority was put to the members and a 16-man championship committee emerged. One of the 16 was Fowler; another was Hilton; among the remainder

---

[4] Golf magazine in US, 1920.
[5] The R&A actually became responsible for the rules in 1897. Originally each club had its own.

Fowler playing his Old course in its first year, 1904. Top left: at the 18th in the bunker, its face revetted with heather sods. Top right: the 17th tee, with horse-drawn roller in the distance and wire netting (to keep rabbits away) in foreground. Above: the second green. Note the new 'sweeping' machine and Castle House, home of the Allom family.

Illustrated Sporting and Dramatic News

were three others who numbered Walton Heath among their clubs: Darwin, John Low and Robert Maxwell, all part of the close-knit camaraderie in the upper echelons of amateur golf.

Even then Walton Heath was not entirely happy. Described in the Press as being 'as powerful and representative an organisation as exists in London golf,' the club wrote to the R&A complaining that the ruling body's committee men would be voicing only personal opinions and that the principal clubs should have direct representation – the old order restored but in accordance with modern developments. It is tempting to imagine Riddell as the signatory.

For a time Herbert contented himself with writing on greenkeeping topics such as 'Weeds and their removal' and 'Autumn work on the course,' but when someone criticised Westward Ho! in 1925 the riposte he delivered filled three-quarters of a magazine page and 10 years later, when he was 79, came his indignant letter to *The Times* refuting the claim that Riddell had founded Walton Heath.[6]

---

[6] Chapter 6.

At Walton Heath

Heaven knows how he managed it, but for all the travel, the writing, the designing, summer stays in St Andrews and committee work for the R&A, Fowler's day job remained managing director at Walton and he held it down for nearly 40 years. Darwin called him 'an instinctive despot with a touch of genius,' while to an American writer he was 'an autocrat who ruled the club with an iron fist.' He had been the club's secretary for its first eight years; he had created the New course as well as the Old; he had introduced the London Foursomes; with his high profile in amateur golf and a sense of publicity he had helped bring prestige and big names to Walton Heath.

And of course there was his own golf. The display cabinets at *Chussex* must have chimed from within at every nearby footstep so many trophies, medals, replicas and prizes had he collected. He had carried off the R&A's Jubilee Vase and Bombay Medal... the Kashmir Cup... names redolent of the Raj and the game's imperial history; had plundered gold and silver at clubs from Sandwich to Muirfield, Walton to Westward Ho! He won that Kashmir Cup twice in succession at Royal North Devon and, when 64 and recently recovered from illness, took the Franklin-Adams gold medal at Royal St. George's.

On the heath he won the 1912 spring gold medal, playing off plus-two; represented the club in numerous matches; secured a notable victory in the first and apparently only Hudson Cup competition,[7] when he beat O.C. Bevan 6 and 5 in a 36-hole match in which both players were plus-one. At 71 he was still able to play off four in the autumn meeting and he claimed 12 holes-in-one.

He was, except for one brief period, virtually ever-present at board and committee meetings during 37 years, and sometimes, notably during World War I, he *was* the board and committee, a lone figure making the decisions, dictating the minutes and signing them as correct. He served as a special constable during part of that war and conjectured that, as a course he had helped design in Germany had been transformed into an airfield, it might now be launching Zeppelins or airplanes to bomb him!

When a man serves his same masters for nearly four decades they clearly have confidence in him. Equally obviously, during such a period there is bound to be at least the occasional falling-out, and one surviving letter, written to Riddell, shows Fowler angry and resentful:

My Dear Riddell,

Your letter of yesterday has filled me with amazement. I have never had such a letter before and trust I may never have such another. You surely are not suggesting that I have purposely tried to deceive you? I had no idea the matter had reached such an acute stage, nor that you were meditating making such absurd accusations against my personal honour.

The spat concerned finance – and it was finance that would ultimately deal Fowler a disastrous hand.

Receipts for his various club subscriptions (including £3 to the R&A in 1914) have survived and so have some of his personal accounts and expense-claims at Walton, dating back to 1908 and detailed to the last penny. There are accounts for his dinners (invariably '4s 6d plus one Perrier'), meals for his wife (including 1s 6d for claret), her dormy and club account ('14 weeks at four guineas, plus fires four shillings, cards seven shillings'), 'Mrs. F's caddie £1-19s-4d' and 'maid's room and fires for four weeks, £6-8s.' These details indicate an efficient, tidy, canny mind, which is no more than you would expect from a former banker.

In the wider world he was an inveterate investor: Argentina, Australia, Canada, India, Russia, the States… real estate and railways, oil, copper and gold. Documents I have viewed reflect his wheeling and dealing: commission from companies to whom he brought business… an offer during World War I of two dollars a weapon on a possible sale of a million rifles involving an American steel company and the Russian Government…

Yet in 1928, with the Depression threatening, came a

Fowler joined various top clubs all over the country. Receipts for his subscriptions survive.

tragic echo of his financial problems at the turn of the century. Darwin's 'erratic genius' was bankrupt. He had liabilities of £6,563 against assets estimated to produce £634, a deficiency of £5,929 (or more than £200,000 in today's terms).

Fowler, then 72, told the court at London's Carey Street a sad and surprising story. He claimed that since the golf-design business in which he was one of four partners was dissolved at the end of 1927 he had not had an occupation, that various ventures had failed to yield him profit, that he lived in a flat and that he had not owned any furniture since 1916.

In 1924, he explained, he had been invited to become managing director of two companies, one of which had an option on gold-mining properties in Canada. The promoter needed finance to cover expenditure until he received a large sum for some property he owned. Accordingly, the bank had granted Fowler a £5,000 loan on the guarantee of two of his co-directors and this had gone to the promoter. Eventually he found that the promoter was not a property-owner at all and the gold mines were never bought. The guarantors were called on to repay the bank's loan and one of them had now obtained judgment against Fowler in respect of it. He was declared insolvent because of the promoter's misrepresentation and the company's inability to obtain finance; he had also incurred more than £2,000 of debts.

Not a word of this bankruptcy appears in the club minute books and a settlement was probably made, but research suggests that he had experienced problems for many years. At a meeting as early as 1914, when the board routinely considered their list of debtors, he suffered the indignity of being confronted by his own name.

The Kidd Medal

*T*he Kidd medal was given to the club by Herbert Fowler. It was awarded to Thomas Kidd when he won the 1873 Open Championship – the first to be held at St Andrews. It is the second oldest surviving champion's medal.

On a waterlogged course Kidd's 36-hole aggregate was 179, the highest so far recorded. He appears, wearing the medal, in the illuminated address which the Walton Heath members presented to James Braid, the winner, to commemorate the 50th anniversary Open in 1910 and which hangs in the clubhouse. Kidd appears immediately to the right of Braid at the top. Not for him the fortunes of a modern champion. He spent most of his subsequent summers as a registered caddie and player at St Andrews and died when he was 35.

At the time of writing the medal is on loan to the British Golf Museum at St Andrews.

Right: Extract from Fowler's bankruptcy papers.

He had clearly moved out of *Chussex* and the flat mentioned was obviously in the dormy house. The board had decided he could continue to use it only if he gave a charge on either his company shares or *Chussex*. In 1922 he sold his 1,000 shares in the club to Riddell. As to the house, a deed of charge was duly executed. Two years later the charge was 'to be released on payment of £1,100, the balance, about £170, to remain as a debt without security.' The picture emerges of this proud man humiliated by bankruptcy and over a number of years struggling to repay loans to the club.

The previously ever-present Fowler was missing from all committee, company and shareholders' meetings for nearly 18 months spanning the cathartic bankruptcy hearing of July 1928. That year he was not re-elected to the R&A's championship committee and after 1931, whatever the reason, he was no longer a member of that club. But normal service was resumed at Walton and he continued

Fowler, a keen gardener, at Walton Heath in 1936. In those days the club regularly exhibited at the Chelsea Flower Show.

to vote on financial and all other matters – and this at a time when the conventional penalty for bankrupts in clubs and societies was expulsion. Walton Heath's own rules at the time declared:

> If the name of any member shall be officially published as a bankrupt he shall, *ipso facto*, cease to be a member of the club. Upon application to the committee stating the cause of his bankruptcy any such member may be re-admitted by the committee if a majority of two-thirds be of opinion that his character as a man of honour has not been affected.

Fowler, of course, was managing director rather than member, but anyway if he owed the club, the club in a different sense owed him. In 1935 his portrait was hung in the clubhouse. That year the minutes recorded that the managing director's remuneration was to be increased to £25 a month with free meals at the club, and two years later, 'Dormy House rooms (Mr. Fowler) not now being charged.'

He continued to chair the committee, the last occasion being in July 1939, and at 83 attended the directors' meeting on September 3, the day war was declared. A few weeks later he was in a nursing home and on April 14, 1941, he died. He left £365-8s-3d – perhaps £10,000 today.

PAST AND PRESENT

Moderns (guess who!) seek to establish themselves alongside characters such as those Mel depicted in
The Tatler in bygone days.

Chapter Twenty-two

A TOAST TO THE CHARACTERS
— especially the eccentrics!

THE CHARACTERS deserve consideration in this history alongside the champions and chairmen – by their very nature they demand it. They are an endangered species. They tend to be vociferous and insufferingly cheerful or extremely controversial and sometimes impossible. The outstanding breed are the eccentrics.

My favourite eccentric from Walton Heath's 100 years? This is an apt time to present his credentials, because he is part of the period, a pillar of the club before, during and after World War II. We have already met him briefly as one of the syndicate of members who ran the club after Riddell's death. May I reintroduce Edgar B. Beck.

My man was a good golfer, board director, committee man and character. His slowly intoned testimonial to the Old course has entered folklore: 'In wintah and summah this course plays bettah than any othah.'

Beck was a wealthy man and a big noise in business, but would go to the office in holed, threadbare suits, not giving a damn about what people might think. He owned 200 golf clubs, all lined up in racks at his home, and more than 200 pipes, about 25 of which might be within reach at any one time.

He always owned the newest Bentley but never mastered the art of driving. Accurate reversing was a closed book. When members heard clashing bodywork and splintering glass from the direction of the car park they automatically observed, 'That will be Beck.'

So, 'That will be Beck,' said Phyllis Foster, something of a character herself, hearing those familiar sounds as she played bridge and knowing that he had recently taken delivery of the first Bentley automatic. Two hours later she emerged to find that it was her car that had been shunted into a wall and rendered undriveable.

Beck? He had simply gone home. She phoned him. 'You've crashed my car,' she announced. 'Yes,' he replied.

Edgar B. Beck – character No. 1?

'Well, to start with, I can't get home,' she complained. 'I see. Get a cab and send me the bill,' was the reply.

His indifference, like the damage, was unintentional. Would he not have gone into the clubhouse to report the accident? Highly unlikely! 'Oh, well, whoever owns the car will contact me,' he would have decided, and at that stage he would admit guilt and pay up. He would not have considered his behaviour in any way unusual or discourteous. He saw things, well, differently!

He took up golf at 30, was scratch within two years, got down to plus-two for a time and was still scratch when past 60. In committee he was opinionated and controversial, not least where ladies were concerned.

In 1937 Mrs Joannides, the lady captain, complained that he and colleagues had ruined her team's match against Royal Wimbledon by starting in front of it both in the morning and the afternoon and holding up her ladies so badly that they had to abandon their round on one course and transfer to the other. The committee judged his behaviour 'inexcusable and a grave breach of the rules and ordinary courtesy.'

Beck denied everything, even claiming that he was at a meeting in London at the time of the match. Soon afterwards he resigned from board and committee and announced that he wished to sell his 500 shares. Both resignations were accepted with regret.

But characters like Edgar B. Beck are not easily put down. Six years later he was back on both committee and board and remained a director into the 'fifties – and even then was not above holding up a ladies' match, this time against the WRENS. He was playing in a three-ball with James Braid! He died in 1958, mourned by the board as a man 'zealous for the club's welfare and active in its services.'

Beck did not stand alone as a character. Judging from Charles Graves' feature in *The Bystander*, extracts of which I reproduce (page 139), the club teemed with them in the Carrs' era.

Can any members of more recent times rival them?

Edgar Beck looks on as Braid, aged 74, drives off the 11th tee. The effects of sun and cloud typically captured by Walter Poucher, eminent photographer of mountains, who was a member. He was also a prominent perfumer and something of an eccentric himself: he used to wear perfume and make-up in the mountains – somewhat to the consternation of his colleagues! He presented his photographs of the course to the club during the period from 1942 to 1975.

I wondered whether Angus Lloyd, Beck's grandson and having been brought up by him, had inherited his traits. Well he *considers* himself an eccentric and certainly has *one* eccentricity. It is not so much that he is a member of nine clubs but that he has noted every round he has played since 1949, when he was 13. The count at the start of 2003 was 7,065 rounds, an estimated walking total of 31,000 miles or round-the-world-plus!

The name of Caryl Thain, Ken Ohlson's father-in-law and a leading light from the mid-thirties until he died, still with a single-figure handicap, in 1969, has been suggested

Caryl Thain.

to me. He lived at *Boxdale* in Deans Lane and the parking of cars during *News of the World* championships caused him profound grief.

One day he found a large car blocking his exit. When the owner returned hours later Thain was present, an apparently idle observer. The car would not start. After prolonged efforts, the driver asked him if he could use his phone. 'I'll start it for you if you give me a £10 note for charity,' said Thain. The driver handed over the note – whereupon Caryl casually

took the car's rotor arm out of his pocket!

Do I hear the name of Mike Easby? He won two Portuguese Open Amateur championships in successive years (1957-8), a feat that resulted in his being known as 'Portugueasby' and, if you believe bar talk, encouraged him to exude such confidence for a third success that he took his portrait with him to present to the golf association – and that, having lost in the final, he brought it back home. This is the stuff of legend: contemporaries swear by it, but son David (who owns the portrait) douses the story with cold water. Father Mike, he says, was more notorious for the alacrity with which he would show all and sundry his cuttings books.

Other candidates are proposed: Irvine Edwards, writer, artist, golfer, resplendent in his Bentley, inveterate gambler on the Stock Exchange... Lord Castlerosse, full of Irish gossip left out of his newspaper column... Alick Renshaw, to whom we shall come in a later chapter... and Richard ('Stinker') Murdoch, the comedian. Murdoch was in single figures and good enough to win the James Braid Cup in 1959, but once played a foursome with Dai Rees, Max Faulkner and Ken Bousfield on a match-play championship practice day when there was a big crowd of spectators, not all of them well informed. At the final hole 'Stinker' fluffed a chip. 'Cor, there's one bloke who won't win,' said a man behind him. I am sorely tempted to nominate my esteemed mentor Philip Truett on account of his passion for hickory, knickerbocker suits, cigarette cards and all things old in golf and his complete disinterest in most things modern.

But in modern times the strongest candidate must be John Junor, former editor of the *Sunday Express*. Like Beck he had a huge array of clubs, from hickory putters to Big Berthas – bought, usually, in vain hopes of miraculously improving his game above the average. He would play – at alarming speeds and with occasional gamesmanship – in snow, storm or tempest and for 10 years his excuse was 'Curly,' the scruffy caddie who carried for him from the early 'seventies. JJ plied him with money, food, drink and firm and fervent friendship. Of Junor – and Curly – more later! Meantime...

Max Davidson (*Junor's features editor*) was about to play a shot with a seven iron. 'If you play a seven you'll be far too short,' said JJ, 'I'm going to play a five.' 'I'd rather play a seven,' said Max. 'Well I've played this course before and you haven't and I'm telling you to use a five,' replied JJ.

So Max did as he was told and his ball went straight over the green and into a bunker at the back. He turned to JJ, busy lining up his shot beside him, and said ' What club are you playing?' 'A seven,' said JJ with a malevolent grin.

Home Truths – Life Around my Father, Penny Junor (HarperCollins), 2002.

THE 'TADWORTH TERROR' AND OTHERS

I have not asked Mr. Beck's opinion of the course alterations, but I should like to do so. Although over 60, he is a scratch man who always plays down to his handicap. His first name is Edgar, but nobody ever dares call him by it. Small and clean-shaven, he is a very big noise in John Mowlem and Company, the contractors.

Noel Layton

Near the top of the back-markers of the club one must put ginger-haired, spectacled, light-hearted Noel Layton. Despite his insouciance on the course, he wins medal competitions more consistently than any other amateur in the country. He doesn't mind playing anybody or anything, and shouts with laughter when he misses a shot. But this occurs very seldom indeed.

Very good off his handicap of five is Sir Pomeroy Burton. Known as 'Pom', he and huge, benign Colonel Rolleston (known as 'Rowley') are probably the two most popular members of the club. Sir Pomeroy was brought over by the late Lord Northcliffe from the United States and was an immediate success in his newspaper organisations. Today, he has retired from all that and has a chateau at Antibes, a town house in Charles Street, off Berkeley Square, and a country house near Reading. He belongs to 13 or 14 clubs and is one of the few short-handicap players who still wear plus-fours.

John Bealey, one of the younger members, is a great friend of mine. He is very good-looking, and dresses and addresses the ball with equal dash. He never seems to get bored, has a very pretty wife, uses extremely whippy clubs, drives an eight-litre Bentley, sometimes gets depressed by his cards and has the most attractive flat in London.

Another regular is Mr. G.S. Fort, a remarkable gentleman, whose exact age is always a matter of keen speculation. It is known that he rowed in the Varsity boat over 60 years ago. And yet it was only quite recently that he stopped letting people step on his stomach to show how good his abdominal muscles still were. Fairly recently, too, he was struck full pitch on the head by a ball and yet was playing next day as though nothing had happened.

'Ole' Haley' Mr. G.S. Fort

Then there are Davy Davidson, 'the Tadworth Terror;' 'Scotty' Legge and his repertoire of anecdotes; Gerald Russell; Claude Liddell, who always clicks his heels before putting; David Stacey, whose wife has a poodle so beautifully trained that it remains motionless until you are about to putt – when it walks gently into your vision; Stanley Colman, with his Wellingtonian nose, white moustaches and encyclopaedic knowledge of sport; and last, but very important, Sir Emsley Carr and his sons, Horace, 'Wash,' and William, all former blues.

One cannot conclude without mentioning Cocker, the charming steward, and John in the changing-rooms, who will always rake you up a pair of mittens or dry socks when wanted and has a marvellous way of sympathetically soothing the ruffled nerves of defeated players.

Cocker, the steward   *John, of the dressing-rooms*

CHARLES GRAVES, *The Bystander*, 1935

Highlights and failures

*D*uring the 35 Carr years the old Match-Play Championship continued to enthral and the challenge matches of the 'thirties were classics. Curiously, though, Walton Heath appears to have put the kiss of death on tournaments it hosted - not guilty of wilful killing, you understand, but a helpless presence at the death bed!

The old-established Daily Mail tournament came in 1950. It featured a wonderful fourth-round 71 by Bobby Locke and ended in a three-man, 36-hole play-off in which Charlie Ward beat Locke and the Australian Ossie Pickworth. Yet the tournament died out. The 36-hole Smart Weston tournament, played over both courses in 1964 and 1965, then died in infancy.

Amateur innovations announced by the new directors to promote the club proved short-lived. In 1936 the Metropolitan Shield began, low-handicappers contesting 36 holes of stroke-play before 16 advanced to match-play. It did not survive the war. Neither did the Morning Post tournament. Previously held elsewhere, it came to Walton in 1937, involving, on both courses. 36 survivors from a nationwide entry of nearly 30,000. The worthy winner was R.L. Bramwell, from Penzance, but in the era of Cotton and company it was not easy for a newspaper to excite readers about a chartered accountant who played off 13.

Of sterner stuff, traditional and unstoppable, were the national championships staged over those 35 years. One of them, the national Artisan Championship, was held on the heath eight times during the era. In 1956, when Doug Sewell (Hook Heath) won the title, contested over both courses, the rain was continuous. Twelve years later the English Stroke-Play was curtailed to three rounds. Michael Bonallack profited: after a first-round 69 he had begun 6-5-5 and was five over par after 16 when the second day was abandoned. He began both the last two rounds 3-4-3, four-putted the 11th (three, it is said, from two feet) and won by five strokes. Second was Walton Heath's own Bill McCrea. That year, 1968, was hectic: additionally Walton staged the usual

1968 washout

Match-Play and the Ladies' British Amateur. The other national championship had been the men's English Amateur, returning in 1958 after 32 years and with Sewell conquering again, beating David Procter by the widest-ever margin of eight and seven.

Meantime, competitive golf among the members ran unevenly. In Riddell's time, according to Don Allom, a member nearly all his life, the club had organised only four men's competitions – the gold medals, a singles knockout usually at Easter and a mixed foursomes bogey event on Boxing Day.[1] Anything else was run by 'The Heathens,' formed before World I, said Allom, by his father and 11 others thirsty for competition. Each annually gave a box of balls to be played for monthly on Sunday mornings.

After Riddell died the Heathens were asked to form a competitions committee. They accordingly disbanded and presented the club with their trophies – those for men's and mixed foursomes, plus the Bruce Cup, which had been their autumn challenge prize. The club, until the cost struck home, gave nine-carat gold medals for the monthly competitions. Six, including five won by Allom, can be seen at the club.

A 1937 fixture card shows many

> Soon after I was elected in 1949 I was played into, twice, at the 12th (Old). Accordingly I tore a strip off one of the offenders, whom, as a new member, I did not know. He turned out to be the future Sir William Carr, the club chairman!
>
> Jack Rae (captain, 1986)

matches and competitions, but this new enthusiasm seems to have waned after the war; the 1953 list recognises few competitions and only the university matches. The custom then, and not only at Walton, was friendly, social match-play, not least in foursomes. The competitive card-and-pencil approach came later, stimulated by TV and Press popularisation of the game at top level.

Sir William Carr, proud of what at times seemed his own private club, was nevertheless, according to contemporaries, comparatively disinterested in competitions and matches. In their desire for more a 'Sods of Surrey' group began playing their own matches, all away from home.

Still, there was plenty of incident. Cambridge had beaten the club for the first time in 1935... Two years later, T.S. Winton, one of their new blues, returned 70, seven under the scratch score for the Old, and Locke, as a 20-year-old amateur, helped a South African team beat the club 4-2... In 1953 Allom and Michael Easby, seven up after eight against Cambridge's John Gillum and Gordon Huddy, lost eight of the next nine holes and were beaten. Individually, in 1968, Michael Bryant set a New course record of 67 and a squad of formidable players, led by Tony Slark and John Thornhill, were riding high.[2]

Oh, one other thing. When Colin Walpole approached Carr with the idea of starting the annual open invitation meeting the chairman seemed puzzled why anyone would want to do such a thing but gave luke-warm approval. The event was aimed at being different; the prizes not cups, cutlery and glassware but caviar, smoked turkey, Plymouth gin and other tempting titbits from Fortnum and Mason hampers. It came in more than £200 over budget – Carr was not pleased. Then letters flooded in from contestants, congratulating him and his club on such a fine affair – Sir William was *very* pleased!

[1] The ladies had their own competitions. The Riddell and Lord Marshall Cups date from 1926; the WH Ladies' Challenge Cup (whose records end in 1968) from 1923.
[2] Chapter 25.

Chapter Twenty-three

LADIES' RULES? *WHAT* RULES?
Times begin to change – for golf and for women

WITH HUSBANDS and sons, or at least the lucky ones, safely back from World War II, what did a few difficulties at the golf club matter? Quite a lot it would seem.

More than anyone, Mary Morison, captain immediately before and after the war, had held the ladies' section together in the interim, but soon after normality resumed in 1946 she and her members were complaining to the board. Their quarters were shoddy, the men were using their lounge, they weren't getting value for their subs, the secretary couldn't give them enough time and their committee would find it impossible to carry on unless they again had their own paid help. A year later they couldn't even find a captain and carried on without one, committee members chairing meetings in turn until reluctant debutantes were persuaded to accede to the throne.

There were other problems. The understanding that candidates for membership should be considered by the ladies before their applications were submitted to the men's committee seemed to have been forgotten, while the restrictions on playing times formed subject matter for continual debate.

The ladies' committee, you may think, were corporately playing the role of the demanding housewife and the board that of the harassed husband – determined not to be henpecked, sincerely concerned about his finances and wary of disturbance of his traditional life with the chaps.

Both sexes won a few and lost a few and the marriage was sustained by compromise. The ladies regained their lounge but failed to get a paid secretary; their quarters were periodically upgraded but rarely before time; the membership process was reinstated but certain playing restrictions remained.

Since before the war, though, the best lady players had achieved a significant break-through. Those with handicaps below 14 were permitted to play without restriction and were regarded as full members provided they paid the same subscription as the men – the first step toward equality perhaps!

In 1949 and 1951 an awkward situation arose in respect of the ladies' annual matches against the Artisans: they were not permitted to entertain their opponents in the clubhouse and return their hospitality. Embarrassed, one of their number, Mrs. Murray, offered her house and the ladies provided food and a barrel of beer.

In 1952 the women found that new yardage and stroke-index details had been painted out from the LGU tee boxes. Phyllis Foster, the captain, claimed that one of the directors had ordained this, without consulting the men's committee, because 'such markings were unsuitable on a course of such high standing as WHGC.' Off went another protest to chairman William Carr.

These are the happenings that leap from the minutes and incline to distort the general truth. There was no deep-rooted enmity between the ladies and the men and sometimes it was individual militants on both sides who precipitated problems. In the post-war economic climate the directors certainly had financial constraints, quite apart from long-cherished traditions.

So, in their own way, had the ladies, and they spent with housewifely thrift. They received annual grants from the main club for prizes and major expenses, and one year, when £114 had been incurred in replenishing the stock of prize spoons, there was a loss of 19 shillings and five pence, nearly a pound for heaven's sake. 'And we must not allow this state of affairs to continue,' warned Mrs Falconer, the hon. secretary.

Annual ladies-v-men matches were already established,

Top: Ladies' gold medal, played for at their Autumn Meeting.
Above: Ladies with low handicaps who paid the same subscriptions as men wore this brooch when playing as proof that they were regarded as full members.

Two Days, Three Records

Competitors in the 1954 Spalding Tournament. Winner Jean Donald is one from left, second row.

A ladies' tournament diary

*I*t is 1955. For the second year running the 72-hole SPALDING TOURNA-MENT for women comes to Walton. For more than half-a-century it has been the claim of Walton Heath's ladies that the standard scratch score for the Old course has never been beaten by a regular playing member. For over 40 years they have said the same about the New.

Within one day those claims become history. The scratch scores are 76. On July 13, after a long spell of dry weather, Elizabeth Price, future British champion, returns 73s on both Old and New.

Next day Miss Price repeats her 73 on the Old and goes on to win with 295, while Gabrielle Keiller (Walton Heath) breaks the day-old record for the New

with 72. It is a stark contrast to the previous year's Spalding at Walton, when Curtis Cup star Jean Donald won with 318, including rounds of 79 and 82.

1964-5: The HOVIS TOURNAMENT is held at Walton, again in successive years. The winners are Margaret Nichol (314) and Marley Spearman, twice British champion (304).

1968: The LADIES' BRITISH OPEN AMATEUR CHAMPIONSHIP. Many Curtis Cup players, including seven Americans, enter, but the third time winner is Brigitte Varangot. In an all-French final against Mme Robin she is two down at the 12th but hits a massive drive over the trees and gets a three; one down at the 18th, she plays a superb wood to the green for another three to stay alive; at the second extra hole she wins with a five to a six – a shabby end to an exciting match.

Nancy Holder (neé Halsted), three times a gold medallist before the war and winner of three more afterwards, with her father Denis, then 91. He was still competing in the Burhill Family Foursomes when he was 93. He was an eminent doctor and for 20 years a member of Walton Heath. Riddell made him an honorary member after a police lunch!

although at times the tradition lapsed, the women claiming that the men had not challenged them as was the custom. The ladies also pursued a passion for mixed foursomes, which had become a natural extension of the game ever since the handicap system had enabled the sexes to play together and which, as one historian[1] put it, had joined 'the range of respectable matrimonial stalking grounds of the more affluent middle classes.'

Some but not all the requests for foursomes events were approved. The mind boggles at a men's committee minute of a much later date (1981), which reported that a certain mixed fixture would not be revived, it having been abandoned some years previously 'after unacceptable behaviour from some entrants'! When the women sought

[1] John Lowerson in *Sport in Britain*, ed. Tony Mason (Cambridge Un. Press), 1989.

Pearson Trophy winners in 1962. Standing, from left: Mesdames Webb, Dove, Williamson, Reed and Miss Moorcroft; seated: Mrs Pope, Lady Costain, Mrs Lewis.

Women actually worked! More did so now than ever before. It would not be long before a 'business ladies' group, most of whom could play only at weekends, would spring up – and be eyed by the male committee, determined to avoid clubs within the club, with the same suspicion as they applied to their own burgeoning mid-week veterans of the time.

The repercussions of war were slowly changing and improving the lot of the lady golfer. Equality? The vote? Hold hard! We may have been entering the 'sixties and the talk in Carnaby Street may well have been of mini-skirts, flower power and free love, but golf clubs were still hanging on to their tattered straight lace and proud masculinity. 'Powder room' on a ladies' door was more than Walton Heath could bear; it had to be changed to 'cloakroom.'

And certain ladies had been wearing trousers in the dining room! There were complaints, and questions as to the rule. There wasn't one, but a notice went up requesting ladies to desist. Jo Bryant, then captain, said that this was at the express wish of Sir William Carr.

It then emerged that the ladies didn't *have* any rules, or that if they had they had never been documented.

permission for an open meeting and an invitational four-somes they were told they could have one or the other, not both; if they wanted three events they were granted two. Half a loaf was always better than none.

Generally, things were on the up. On the courses, the heady days of the Leitch sisters were past and Viv Falconer remained Walton's lone international, continuing to represent Scotland until the mid-fifties, but in 1951 two members reached the last four in the English champi-onship at St Annes – Miss McCloughry and Gabrielle Keiller,[2] who went on to lose the final – and the following year Pamela Davies[3] won the title at Westward Ho! The club continued to contribute formidable players to the Surrey teams – not least Shirley Allom, who took six gold medals at Walton – and in 1962 a 20-year-old Jill Thornhill won her first county championship.

Membership grew: limits were imposed and reached and gold-medal entries increased. In 1963 the clubhouse quarters were re-built and enthusiasm was such that the following year 74 ladies, a post-war record at least, attended their agm – or perhaps they just wanted to know why their subs were going up from 20 to 25 guineas.

The 'more affluent middle classes' alluded to by the historian were now rather less affluent, and this was the case at most clubs. Meantime democracy hammered away at half-closed doors and finance committees stretched out their palms. The days when Jo Bryant and her friends did little but ride, play and socialise were gone.

[2 and 3] All three players ceased their playing memberships soon after these achievements. Mrs Keiller retired from competitive golf in 1955 after the death of her husband despite being short-listed for the 1956 Curtis Cup.

Good news for 21-year-old British golfer Vivien Saunders – whose handicap was last week reduced to plus four, the stiffest on record for a British woman.

Earlier this year the Walton Heath Golf Club in Surrey turned down her application for member-ship.

According to club rules, this carries with it a ban on visiting the club as a guest. Which, in effect, had barred her from practising on the course – where the British Women's Open Championship will be held in June. But now the club secretary says: 'Miss Saunders will be able to practise here before the championship.'

Why was Miss Saunders – runner-up in last year's British women's championship – refused member-ship? 'I don't know,' she says. 'No comment,' says the club secretary.

Sunday Express, December 1967

Chapter Twenty-four

THE OLD CHAP IN THE TIN HUT

The ageing Braid – 'a wonder of the golfing world'

OH DEAR, this chapter, which concerns James Braid, could be very difficult! Difficult for me, that is, and possibly boring for you! Surely everyone already knows everything about Braid? Walton Heath members do not need reminding that he was the first man to win five Opens and in his heyday perhaps the greatest player of all, nor that he was their professional for 46½ halcyon years.

Another problem is the man himself. Even Longhurst, rarely lost for a sage or witty word, confessed that he found it difficult to write about Braid, dour and tactful old Scot that he was.

Infuriatingly perfect, too: kind, modest and wise. He offers no element of controversy, no whiff of scandal… a journalist's nightmare!

Ah, well, let us progress, and hope that research and recollection may breathe life into things!

The Prime of Mr. James Braid

*B*raid's Open Championship achievements in the first 12 years of the 20th century. He had already played in five Opens (once runner-up, once fifth, once sixth, twice tenth) and would continue to compete in the championship after World War I. * = Tied.

Year	Score	Position
While at Romford		
1900	322	3rd
1901	309	1st
1902	308	2nd*
1903	310	5th
While at Walton Heath		
1904	297	2nd*
1905	318	1st
1906	300	1st
1907	318	5th*
1908	291	1st
1909	301	2nd*
1910	299	1st
1911	305	5th*
1912	303	3rd

The champion

You will observe from the statistics that James won all his five championships within 10 years (1901-10). Between 1899 and 1912 he never finished out of the top five, achieving five firsts, three seconds, two thirds and four fifths. If we add his four match-play championships in nine years we have impressive evidence for the case that for several years Walton Heath indeed possessed the world's greatest golfer.

The first tee at Muirfield, 1906. Braid on his way to his third Open Championship.

Under cross-examination we may break down and reluctantly concede that on comparison of entire careers Harry Vardon's counsel has even more convincing evidence – six Opens and the United States Open as well – but the jury will be out for a long time!

Statistics bore me. They mislead. They omit to tell you why Braid never won in America while Vardon did. He never went there, and the chief reason was motion sickness: if he was afraid of crossing by ferry from Campbeltown to Islay, how could he face the Atlantic? Car travel also made him sick and he travelled many thousands of miles by train – a walking *Bradshaw*, a familiar figure well-wished by stationmasters, ticket-collectors and porters the length and breadth of the land.

Neither can statistics and results convey styles,

‌MES BRAID, painting by Sir James Gunn, RA, c1925.

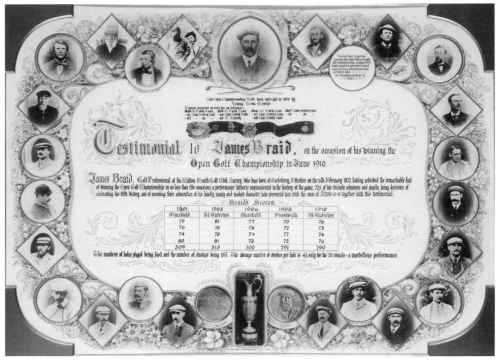

Testimonial presented to Braid by '205 of his friends, admirers and pupils,' with a cheque for £200, to commemorate his fifth Open – a record at the time – and in 'admiration of his kindly, manly and modest character.' It records that he averaged 4.2 strokes a hole over the 20 rounds involved in his victories.

characters and emotions. They cannot describe Braid's pride after victories as his son James drove him home from the station in an open carriage through cheering crowds of members and villagers, nor the manner of his play.

Braid in competition was indeed a sight to behold. If his long, slow, loping strides between shots were symptomatic of a perfect temperament, his action and style when striking revealed his confidence and boldness. Horace Hutchinson referred to the 'divine fury' of his hitting; Darwin called it 'appalling in its ferocity, rhythmical in its majesty.'

There were occasional big hooks and wild hits into the rough, but he was supreme at recovery. The scribes' lyricisms were stretched to exaggeration: he could 'remove tons of sand and acres of heather' through his union of strength and technique. Running shots? He could play them like a master.

At first he was a poor putter, but he made himself a good one, deadly from middle distances. The Walton greens helped; so did playing with Fowler, a demon at that devilish art; so did discarding his cleek for an aluminium putter. He was never a *natural* putter, though. He was always thought suspect over short ones and this vulnerability worsened with age.

But it wasn't only age, it

Dark glasses under an uncharacteristic brimmed hat – protection for his eyes against bright light.

Golf Illustrated, 1913

was eyesight. Lime had got into his eyes when he was a joiner and he suffered to varying degrees ever afterwards. He could not stand bright light – perhaps another reason why he shunned the States and tried to resist the French Riviera.

He always remained a fine player – did he not reach the match-play final at 57? By that time, though, he had long since revealed another string to his bow…

The architect

According to John Moreton, author of *The Golf Courses of James Braid*,[1] Walton Heath's professional designed more than 170 courses, re-modelled another 150 or thereabouts, re-bunkered several others and, overall, influenced more than 350 courses. However, the numbers are almost certainly incomplete. As soon as Moreton publishes an apparently definitive list of Braid's work, more crawls out of the undergrowth.

His designer shoes have left their large, distinctive prints on layouts from Brora in the north of Scotland to Mullingar in the middle of Ireland and from Southport and Ainsdale on the Merseyside linksland to Gleneagles at the gateway to the Highlands. His work can be identified on windswept ogres such as Carnoustie and inland beauties like Blairgowrie. You can find 'Braid's Hill' at Routenburn, 'Braid's Bunker' at Northamptonshire County, 'Braid's Brawest' at Gleneagles and 'Braid's Last' at Stranraer. Severe bunkering was his hallmark; some say he invented the dog-leg.

He managed to fit in all this work alongside his club and other commitments because of his method, which was a marvel of economy of time made possible by instinctive

[1] Grant Books, 1997.

decision-making, immediate planning and the laying-off of construction work to others. He would arrive at a station, be taken to the club, conduct a survey, return to base the same day or overnight and often complete his plans on the journey – an immediacy made possible by his accurate memory and a talent for reading topographical maps. The recollections of club historians have a common theme:

> EXETER: The wizard Braid came; walked round the park once; nodded comprehensively; departed; and in a few days back came a rough sketch plan of all 18 holes. He had them in his head.

> MULLLINGAR: Braid was taken to the proposed site. He demanded an axe and 36 pegs, ordered the committee to leave him to get on with his job and strode off into the scrub. When he emerged he had sketched a masterpiece.

His saviours were those who implemented his plans and actually built the courses, and prime among them was John R. Stutt. The old champion was in his fifties and Stutt 23 years younger when they began working together, but they blended perfectly.

Any tampering with his plans was anathema to Braid. If anyone criticised his work he would deliver a dignified but crushing response. At Mullingar in Ireland he faced a committee delighted with his course but critical of one hole, the 190-yard second. It was impossible, they said, to stop a ball on its elevated green. 'Give me a club, any club you like, and three balls,' said Braid. He then struck the balls one after the other and every one stopped on the green.

At another club members of a certain handicap complained about a cross-bunker 50 yards short of the green. 'Just where a good second shot would finish,' they complained. 'A good second shot?' repeated James, 'Why, a good second shot would be on the green – and a man

Gleneagles Hotel and his most celebrated course.

who canna reach the green has naught to gain by trying to carry the bunker!'

Fowler has been called a genius by fervent devotees, but such munificent praise has not generally come Braid's way. 'By the 'twenties Braid was considered a most competent architect,' state the authors of *The Architects of Golf*,[2] and even Darwin, his biographer and friend, qualifies his tribute: 'I should not say that he was very imaginative or subtle in the designing of a hole – and it is possible to be too subtle for ordinary human nature – but he had what the golf architect needs, a good eye for country and, as in everything that he touched, a temperate judgment and a fund of plain common sense.'[3] Henry Cotton, though, said that 'Jimmy was a great architect and could see a golf hole in a wilderness'.

The limits to which Braid could bring his architectural skills to bear at Walton Heath were inevitable. Perhaps, occasionally, it was a trifle frustrating for him. Asked what he thought of some improvements proposed for the New he apparently said, 'You mean the *alterations*'.

The club pro

His fidelity to Walton Heath was unquestioned and here, in his rosy retirement from competitive play, he spent increasingly more time.

At times he had a staff of seven, including Will Brown and Robert Horseburgh, the clubmakers he had fetched from Scotland and who, known to all and sundry as 'Bob and Brown,' served him for a lifetime.

The members to a man respected him and his assistants revered him. As for the local boys like Fred Faulkner who caddied when they could and were allowed to play after 6pm, 'Mr. Braid' was 'almost a god.' They called him 'Jimmy' behind his back as a token of their affection and to kid themselves that they were the great champion's buddies. When they heard senior members address him as 'Braid' they instinctively felt it discourteous.

'Bob and Brown' with their boss; Will Brown (left) and Robert Horseburgh.

[2] *The Architects of Golf*, by G.S. Cornish and R.E. Whitten (HarperCollins), 1993.
[3] *James Braid* (Hodder and Stoughton), 1952.

Memories of the champion. The 'Orion' putter (1913) was among the very few patented clubs Braid endorsed. Books by and about him were numerous.

Nobody ever seems to have criticised Braid without incurring the wrath of Walton Heath and the whole of Scotland. When someone wrote to *Golf Weekly* saying that Braid had reduced him to tears during a lesson, John Thornhill immediately broke into print in protest. 'He was a very kindly person who was always interested in the golf of lesser mortals,' he wrote.

Braid's strictures, indeed, tended to be soft-spoken, with a certain delicacy and half-hidden humour. Swings were not harshly and peremptorily dismissed by the usual 'Too quick!' or 'Too slow!' His observations might be delivered wittily, almost deferentially. 'What did I do wrong?' Brian Pope asked him after slicing off the first tee. 'You took a little longer than you usually do, sir,' said Braid, politely.

It was not 'Keep your head still' but 'Tut, tut, tut, I'd no swear that you looked at that one!' – or, notably, when he spotted premature forward head movement, 'You'll ha'e to remember, Mr Jones, that ye ha'e to hit the ba' with the

heid of the club and not with your ain heid!' If you had marred your lesson with several bad shots the worst he might announce was 'Well, I'd say that was verra guid – on the whole!'

True, he did not suffer fools gladly and the more caustic comments attributed to him were reserved for that category. 'Ah, I see your problem,' he eventually told an exasperatingly unresponsive member, 'You're standing too near the ba'.' 'When I address it?' asked the pupil. 'No,' said Braid, 'After you've hit it.' The old stories are always best!

He was, in fact, an excellent teacher of the old-fashioned school. He didn't fill minds with technical gobbledygook but taught basic principles simply, respecting players' natural games so far as he could. Ross Whitehead, later to join him as an assistant and to reach a match-play championship final, remembered that he took him to the 18th and set him up on the up-slope of the cross-bunker so that his left shoulder was much higher then the right. 'That is the feeling I want you to have every time you address the ball,' he said.

Irvine Edwards once asked him for a single tip for young players. His response was that, while they should certainly concentrate on the ball, they should not do so to the extent that they became immobile. 'Many of them try too hard and are straining,' he said. 'They should have a firm grip with the left hand, in fact with both hands, but at all costs they must avoid tension.'

Braid's action analysed in 1923, when he was 53.   Open Air magazine

FOURSOMES WITH BRAID

I recall very clearly what pains James invariably took over his play, studying his putts as if the fate of empires depended on them and never allowing himself even the suspicion of a slack or hasty shot.

I used to think that this was part of a deliberate system, adopted because he felt it dangerous to lapse even for a moment into anything like carelessness. No doubt also he conscientiously felt that he must give nothing under his best to those who took him out to play with them.

But I feel now that there was one supreme reason, the simplest of all, for this high standard of care, namely that he loved playing golf so much for its own sake, that no matter how unimportant the match, it would never enter his head not to try his hardest.

He always tried to play his best and never showed by word or gesture the faintest sign of disappointment if he did not. Perfect golfing manners could not further go.

Day after day people wanted to play with James and he was ready and willing to play with them. I had a notion that he laid down for himself one rule of abstinence, namely never to play more than two rounds a day, but I am told that I was wrong and that he certainly did on occasions play three.

Moreover he played in all sorts of weather and Walton can be as bleak a spot as need be. No wonder he was one of the pioneers in the matter of mackintosh trousers.

How he avoided growing stale I cannot imagine, but he was very strong and liked playing golf much better than doing anything else.

BERNARD DARWIN, *James Braid* (Hodder and Stoughton) 1952

It has been said of some celebrated person – perhaps of several of them – that nobody could be so wise as So-and-so looks. As regards golfers, I feel inclined to transpose the aphorism and say that nobody could look so wise as James Braid is. There is nobody whose every word and action is so redolent of sagacity. He has a great twinkle of humour, too, humour such as the Scots call 'pawky,' and many other admirable qualities, but one thinks of him first and foremost as a man of extraordinarily cool, wise judgment.

Bernard Darwin, *Playing the Like* (Chapman and Hall), 1934.

With that, said Irvine Edwards, the ageing Braid put on his cap and sauntered off to play his second round of the day. Perhaps because of his Scottish upbringing he would never teach on Sundays, but normally nothing would stop him from playing seven days a week, even in advanced age.

In his prime, reports of his deeds at Walton had caused no surprise – even his memorable 70 in a gale in 1908 and a remarkable 67 five years later despite his eye trouble and the after-effects of flu…

> But look at him now! Past 50, and if there's a sight worth travelling far to see it is Braid playing iron or niblick shots from the rough on his own adopted Walton Heath – that is, of course, when his partner has put him there. *So wrote Andrew Kirkaldy,[4] successor to Old Tom Morris as the R&A's honorary professional.*

> See him in winter, sniffing the frosty air on the heath and then, with that characteristic bend of the knees, giving the wee ba' a buffet which would please a man a quarter of his age! *So wrote Edwards.*

---

[4] *Fifty Years of Golf: My Memories* (T. Fisher Unwin), 1921.

When he was 50 he went round the New in 66, two strokes lower than the previous best. The following year he was made an honorary life member, a rare honour for a professional then, but if the directors felt he was about to rest on his laurels as a player they were 30 years wrong.

The stories of his feats continued as the lanky figure bulked towards portliness and the moustache matured from charcoal to snow. At 68 he surpassed himself on the New with a 64… When he was 78, by which time birthday challenges to beat his age had become a cherished tradition, he celebrated with a 74 on the Old… A year later he achieved his 18th hole in one… It was claimed, outrageously, that he had done every hole on both courses in two!

One day an American tourist turned up looking for a game and was directed to the tin-roofed workshop. Braid said he would go out himself but, self-effacing as ever, did not reveal his identity. A few hours later, after a sound drubbing, the visitor was describing his round to his friends: he was amazed, he said, at the golf 'the old chap in the tin hut' had played.

> I can see him now on the first tee, with his cap well down over his eyes and wearing his tweed jacket and trousers, *wrote Golf Illustrated's Tom Scott years afterwards.* He never wore plus-fours. Perhaps he thought, modest that he was, that this new-fangled fashion would not suit his tall, ungainly figure.

Doug Smith, once an assistant to Cotton, a stickler for smartness, remembers his boss sending him to Walton to play with Braid: 'There was I in my Daks slacks, Pringle jumper, Lotus shoes and with my tour bag and caddie; and there was Braid in his baggy trousers and baggy cap with a wee pencil bag under his arm. He was 79. He went round in 76, I took 82.'

This tall, stooping, ruddy-faced complexioned old Scot is one of

the wonders of the golfing world, *wrote Cotton*[5], The older he gets the easier it seems for him to go round in his age or less. *Irvine Edwards concurred:* That golf cheers his heart is evident.

'The lanky figure bulked towards portliness and the moustache matured from charcoal to snow.' The skills, though, never left him. His 64 on the New, the card signed by Sir Emsley and 'Wash' Carr, was achieved when Braid was 68 years old.

Well, perhaps it was *not* immediately evident, for his demeanour remained solemn, like that of a man bored with his work. The revelation was in his play. No matter how insignificant the occasion, he played almost as if money and titles were at stake. He loved it. If the weather was bad enough to prevent play he would brood, grow restless and continually search for a break in the clouds or a thaw of the snow.

He knew the courses as intimately as his front room in Meadow Walk. 'Aim on yon church spire,' he told a visitor one foggy morning, 'Ye canna see it today but that's your line!' On such a day Irvine Edwards played his last game

with him on the New. At hole after hole Braid struck approaches through impenetrable fog and invariably they found his ball a few yards beyond the holes.

Lord Simon, an illustrious member, once said that if the College of Heralds were ever called on to devise a coat of arms for Braid, his shield should be emblazoned with *'a royal tigre proper on a field vert, with supporters in the form of coneys cherchant in a warren'* – that is to say 'a right royal tiger who was always on the fairway surrounded by rabbits looking for their balls in the rough'!

Braid took his own pawky Fifeshire humour out on the courses and also to the first tee, where he conducted many lessons and acted as starter. Once, in a foursome, he played

---

[5] *News of the World.*

150

starter – for a wet Parliamentary ndicap.

a rare poor shot at a par three, leaving the ball on the edge of the green. His partner, a promising girl, promptly holed it for a two. 'I'm glad I put you dead,' said James.

In another mixed four-some his young partner, a bubbly musical comedy actress, kept topping their ball into the heather and Braid just as regularly kept hitting tremendous recovery shots back on to the fairways. Eventually she put him in an impossible place. He removed the greater part of a young tree but the ball moved only a few yards – nobody else could have moved it at all. 'Oh, Mr. Braid,' exclaimed the sweet young thing, 'Thank goodness even you make mistakes sometimes!'

When World War II began in 1939 he was 69. In March that year he had lost his wife. It is said she never saw him play in a championship and would sit by the window at home awaiting messages from the shop or elsewhere. He took consolation from his sons' successes in life.

The war changed Braid's life. In 1941 he was elected a director of the company; the following year his name appeared for the first time on the minutes of the club committee and henceforth he was almost always present at the meetings. In 1950, his 80th year, the R&A elected him to honorary membership.

February 6, 1950, dawned. His birthday. A day for great-coats, mackintoshes and layers of swaddling as barriers against the wet and the wind. In those conditions Braid went out yet again to try and equal or beat his age. Astonishingly, it seemed that he might do so. But at the final hole the wind was so strong that he had no chance of carrying the cross-bunker in two. His third was ensnared by the side bunker and the 80-year-old holed out in 81.

He was guest of honour at a celebration dinner. The last of many presentations was made to him, his health was drunk and reluctantly, nervously, he rose to respond.

Words fail me, *he said, according to his notes which survived the evening.* Although it is becoming the fashion for orators to become golfers it does not follow that golfers can become orators, and it is easier for me to pitch the rubber-core than to pitch a tale.

I need hardly say that I am most grateful and proud to be thus honoured by the members and other friends who have helped to subscribe towards this most beautiful salver and cheque. I have been a fairly lucky man since I came to the Walton Heath club. I was in at its beginning and have seen it grow into one of the leading clubs in the country. It has been my pleasure and privilege to attend to the wants of the members for a long time now and I hope to do so and to play for a bit longer still.

It isn't often I've seen so many members together. It takes me back to my own early days when the Open Championship was a real meeting. Everybody stayed in one little area and got to know one another a lot better. Nowadays the cars whisk everybody away and one half of the players don't know the other half. Thank you again, ladies and gentlemen.

Teeing off on his 79th birthday.

Even after that reports of his deeds continued to be published. Advertisements for clubs bearing his name but actually made in St Andrews claimed that the octogenarian had returned a 69 when testing them on the Old at Walton, while Darwin assured his readers that the last two rounds James played were in the low 70s. Perhaps these were half-truths. Towards the end members would affectionately concede him missable putts.

On November 27 in that year of 1950 Braid died following an operation and he was buried in St Peter's churchyard. The tributes flooded in:

James was like a fine piece of durable Scottish tweed – unembroidered, never spoiling. *George Duncan*

He loved his job, he loved playing and teaching, he loved his wooden, tin-roofed building… He was the person everyone at Walton Heath turned to for help or guidance.

Henry Cotton

He had the dignity and gentleness which sometimes show

On his 80th birthday, with Sir Ernest Holderness and Bernard Darwin.

themselves in a great man who is master at his craft but who feels nothing but sympathy and interest in others much less skilled. He was incapable of any unkind word and every golfer who knew him loved him.

Lord Simon

Jimmy was the last representative of that worthy race of Scottish professionals – the Dunns, Morrises, Parks, Kirkaldys and Fernies – who are immortalised in golfing history. Among this gallant company my dear old friend, by his life and achievements, takes as by right an outstanding, honourable place.

J.H. Taylor

Modesty, dignity, reticence, wisdom, kindliness... but I think there is another epithet that would come to most people's minds. They would call him, almost instinctively, a great man.

Bernard Darwin

He left £29,000. That would be worth more than £500,000 today and it was more than any other British professional had left. There was little money and no pampering when he turned professional. The most he received for winning the Open was £50 and during the 1900 championship he and Taylor had to share a bed, nightly rubbing each other down with embrocation. When things improved, unlike many professionals he looked after what he earned, saving and investing on the advice of friends and contacts.

He was a canny Scot. He knew it and, eyes twinkling, basked in the knowledge. 'Do you think I ought to get one of the new wedges?' a distinguished visitor asked him. 'If you are thinking of buying it from me, sir, I would say yes,' said James. On a society day a sports-goods firm sent him two balls to give to every player. Bad for his business? 'Oh, no. I waited till all the players had been to my shop and bought balls, then gave them their free ones on the first tee!'

Yet he could be spontaneously generous, helping young professionals or older ones on hard times. His last words of advice to a meeting of professionals just before he entered hospital for his operation were not to be greedy: 'Take care you don't cut your own throats.' He had significantly supported the formation of the PGA, served on its

committees and was six times captain. The Great Triumvirate helped raise the status of professionals – and not least by their own dignity and conscience.

Today the clubhouse is a Braid shrine. There is the 'Braid Room,' opened by son Harry in 1974... the driver James used in the 1901 Open... baffies, mashies, cleeks, brassies, spoons... his old desk... replicas of medals... illuminated addresses and testimonials... the 1905 Spy cartoon... one expects to see him emerge from his old shop and lope his leaning way towards us.

Were he to do so he might tell us when he was first allowed in the clubhouse. No evidence exists to suggest what the policy was before the 'twenties. What is clear is that Braid was enthusiastically welcome in the clubhouse thereafter. At most courses the members' quarters were out-of-bounds to professionals, but Braid was special and, as we have seen, became an honorary member.

Even so, says Faulkner, Braid would for years have considered entry a privilege dependent on invitation. Darwin writes of his using the back door and, unless specifically requested, lunching not in the dining room where his portrait hung but in the secretary's room. He would seldom if ever go into the bar on his own, no matter his penchant for a dram of whisky, but would wait to be asked.

One final point needs stressing. This ploughman's son, whose passions were confined to his family and golf, who read only newspapers, golf reports and wild west stories and whose evenings might be spent playing billiards and darts at the village club... this man became regarded as a friend and confidant by eminent politicians, high-flying businessmen, even royalty. 'I see in the paper that you were sitting next to the Prince of Wales at the Lucifers' dinner,' his daughter-in-law Violet once said to him. 'Oh, no,' replied Braid, 'The Prince of Wales was sitting next to *me*.'

James Braid boring? How could I have suggested such a thing! I apologise!

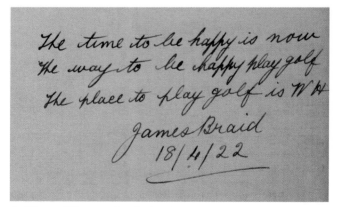

Braid's own little poem of contentment.

Chapter Twenty-five

THE DAY OUR MAN NEARLY BEAT NICKLAUS
Slark and Thornhill carry the flag

THEY ARE OCTOGENARIANS now, but from the post-war 'forties to the swinging 'sixties, they were the powerhouse of Walton Heath's golf. One is John Thornhill, still a regular at the club. The other is Tony Slark, inevitably nicknamed 'Cutty' and, though seldom seen in action these days, with claims to be the club's oldest playing member in terms of years of membership.[1]

Thornhill may lean a little more than in his heyday and Slark has an arthritic right knee, but both can still swing with a hint of their old panache. John finds comfort and companionship with the mid-weekers, playing off the blues on the '50p-and-buy-your-own-tea' basis. Tony does not so much play as practise, hitting up to 40 shots a day for exercise near his home at Reigate Heath in the summer before going off to South Africa for the winter.

Their friendship was forged at the Kingswood club and on the 8.10 train to work in London. Tony had been at Walton Heath since 1945 and John was elected two years later: Braid, acting as a one-man handicap committee, promptly gave him four on the strength of one card. That year Slark won his first gold medal. By 1950 John had reached the last four and Tony, for the second time, the last eight in English championships and the pair were up and running with a vengeance, often in harness but also as individual thoroughbreds.

For 10 years John was scratch; Tony achieved plus-one. Their triumphs came at county and regional levels, but nationally they made impressive inroads and dented sundry reputations.

In the 1950 English Championship at Deal, Thornhill knocked out two Walker Cup players, one present, one future, before losing his semi-final to the eventual winner, John Langley. The Press soon took notice. 'He will tackle anyone anywhere and is always full of fight,' wrote *The Daily Telegraph* man. 'Is there a better non-international in England?' asked *Golfing* magazine.

And was there a better sportsman? On the first day of the 1958 Amateur Championship at St Andrews John came to the 18th all-square with the Australian Tom Crow

Slark (far left) and Thornhill, winners of the massive London Amateur Foursomes shield in 1951, having beaten Lionel St.J. Scott and G.H.T. Chalcraft at Sunningdale. Scott later joined Walton Heath and became captain.

and both had putts of just over a yard. John missed and his next was conceded. Crow also missed – and then, in a rush of blood born of disgust, dragged his ball away.

'That's your hole and the match then,' he told John, having realised the enormity of his deed. 'I don't play golf that way,' said our man and, under the raised eyebrows of the R&A members in their clubhouse, he walked to the 19th tee. Their match ended four holes later and John was the loser. Moreover he received a rocket from Gerald Micklem and Raymond Oppenheimer, pillars of the amateur establishment, for 'abandoning the rules of golf.'

The peak of Tony Slark's career came when he reached the semi-finals of the Amateur at Muirfield in 1954 and he also got into the quarter-finals at Formby three years later. Both times, yet again, he lost to the eventual champion – Australia's Doug Bachli and Scotland's Reid Jack respectively.

At Formby he knocked out three current or future Walker Cup players: Gordon Huddy, Philip Scrutton and Michael (now Sir Michael) Bonallack, who at that time was poised to become the outstanding British amateur of the 'sixties.

The Walton pair both had titanic matches against Bonallack in championships. Tony's win at Formby was by one hole, and when they met in the last 16 of the English

---

[1] Oldest in years of continuous membership is Robert Allen, who joined in 1938 and is non-playing.

Two years later he came close to beating Jack Nicklaus. This was in the 1959 Amateur at Royal St George's, when Jack was a stocky, crew-cut college boy making his first appearance in Britain. Having impressively consumed the week's aperitif, the 36-hole St George's Grand Challenge Cup, Nicklaus was among the favourites to demolish the main course. Slark recalls their third-round encounter:

I remember Jack hit one absolute socket with an eight- or nine-iron, but even then he could play terrific golf. At the 16th I drew all-square, but three-putted the 17th to be one down with one to play.

At the 18th Jack seemed to be all over the place, but, playing to the small green, I caught the lip of a bunker. I then left myself a six-foot putt for a four to take the match to extra time… my ball rimmed the hole. Nicklaus also got a five so won the match. Ultimately he lost in the semi-finals to Bill Hyndman, the United States Walker Cup player.

Jimmy Irvine Edwards shakes hands with Slark at celebrations of Tony's feat in reaching the semi-finals of the Amateur Championship in 1954.
Golf Illustrated

Amateur at Hoylake that year their contest was even tighter. 'I stood dormy-two up,' Slark recalls. 'Then Bonallack won the 17th and 18th, so we went to extra holes. At the 20th I had a putt of about 12 feet for a birdie and Michael faced a chip from a very bad lie through the green. He proceeded to hole it… and, in shock, I missed!'

Bonallack won the second of his five English titles at Burnham and Berrow in 1963, but his first match was almost his last – it was against Thornhill. John, two down at the 11th, fought back to be one up after 17, where he holed a 35-footer for a two. He then cut his drive into the sandhills and Bonallack went on to win at the first additional hole.

Slark had a wonderful 1957 and finished second in the Brabazon Trophy, the English Stroke-play Championship, at Moortown (Leeds).

Tony was once selected by England and was unlucky never to play in the Walker Cup. In the clubby atmosphere of the times, did the facts that he was a teetotaller and not always around socially hinder his chances? More than one person has assured me that they did.

Neither Tony nor John was inordinately long off the tee, but they compensated with accuracy. 'I was a good iron player but couldn't putt,' claims Slark. John played great fairway woods and had a formidable short game.

In partnership, once they got their teeth into an event they wouldn't let go. They won the London Amateur Foursomes two years running (1950-51), a feat achieved only once previously, and Thornhill helped secure the massive shield again two years later, though this time for Kingswood. John has played in six London finals, more than anyone. In 1957 the head of his driver came off and finished 80 yards away – 'without unduly affecting the stroke,' noted a reporter.

Again in successive years they won the open amateur

ONE BETTER THAN COTTON

In a Lloyd's Golf Club autumn meeting in the 'fifties I partnered Steve Tredinnick, an England international, in a stableford foursomes. When we came to the 12th Steve's somewhat aggressive caddy addressed our party: 'This is the hole, gents, where Cotton drove the green in the famous match against Locke and Brews'.

I had read Cotton's *This Game of Golf*, so knew Henry had not driven the green but, having cleared the corner of the dog-leg, played a run-up stone dead to get his three. Foolishly, I decided to correct the caddy. 'He drove the green,' he insisted, 'I saw it with my own eyes!'

It was Steve's honour. The tee shot at the left-to-right dog-leg posed him a major problem as he had a pronounced draw, but, starting the ball miles to the right and over the wildest possible country, he controlled it to such effect that it landed on the fairway just over the corner, got a favourable kick and finished on the edge of the green.

I found myself facing a putt of perhaps 30 feet, which, incredibly, I holed for an eagle two. 'How many eagles have you seen at this hole, with the second shot being a putt?' I asked the caddie. He declined to answer.

JOHN GILLUM (post-war member)

foursomes tournament at Fulwell (Middlesex), returning one remarkable 70 on a day when the wind blew John's umbrella to shreds.

Apart, they were just as tenacious, and not least in those major mixed foursomes events where a veneer of happy families and high handicaps camouflages ferocious rivalry. In a Burhill Family Foursomes final Thornhill and his 30-handicap mother, Nell, were four down with five to play but won. Next year, when they won again, their semi-final opponents were Tony and his mother Doris (28 handicap). The match went to the 19th, by which time the two matrons were well nigh exhausted.

Both men won the Worplesdon Mixed Foursomes title, Slark in 1954 (with 'Bunty' Stephens, six times a Curtis Cup player) and Thornhill, after his prime, in 1975. Another foursomes event to fall to John was The Antlers at Royal Mid-Surrey, one of those little publicised competitions about which the public know nothing but which embrace some of the best of amateur golf. He won it with Scrutton in 1954.

As individuals John and Tony won, between them, three Surrey championships in eight years. In the 1955 event at West Hill John beat Doug Sewell, inflicting on the Hook Heath artisan and future Walker Cup player his only defeat in four successive county finals. It was another of John's

Tudor Davies, seven times a Welsh international.

> I met a man at Walton Heath who always fines himself by drinking a pint of beer for any putt he misses from less than two yards. The other day he was condemned to drinking five pints – what hard lines on a blazing hot day. After lunch he had another. 'You forgot one?' I hazarded. 'No,' he said, 'this is just on account for this afternoon.'
>
> *Golf Illustrated, 1938*

charges from behind: three down after six, he played the next 11 in six under fours to win by two and one. He and Slark helped Surrey (whose captain and president John became) to the inter-county title in successive years.

They had picked up the flag for Walton when Holderness's race was nearly run and pre-war gold-medallists like Harry Braid and Sir Richard Costain were past their best. A young Ian Caldwell was breaking through to Walker Cup class but leaned increasingly toward Sunningdale. Tudor Davies did not join until 1954, the year he made the first of seven appearances for Wales, and Bill McCrea, an outstanding Irish international and subsequently club secretary, not until 1957. Jimmy Irvine Edwards, Michael ('Portugeasby') Easby and others played their parts, but they were character roles in the shadow of the two stars.

In the 1962 West of England championship three of the four semi-finalists were from Walton: McCrea, the winner, Thornhill, whom he beat in the final, and Slark. It was with McCrea and assistant professional George Will that Tony and John took the 36-hole Hudson Trophy Foursomes at South Herts, and when they won the Fulwell Foursomes those two consecutive years the runners-up both times were Irvine Edwards and Caldwell.

At Walton Heath, such was the duo's domination that between them they won six spring gold medals in seven years in the 'fifties and nine of the 14 autumn events leading up to 1965. Thornhill altogether won 11 gold medals and Slark eight.

Tony's competitive career lasted into the 'eighties and in 1985, when he was 63, he finished second in the English Seniors Championship.

The Thornhills and Slarks make an illustrious quartet. Tony's wife is the former Ruth Porter, three times an English champion and Curtis Cup player. As for John, he married a certain Miss Jill Woodside in 1962. He would continue to win club competitions for many years, but so far as championships were concerned that year effectively sealed one career and launched another. It was the start of the Jill Thornhill story.[2]

---

[2] Chapter 37.

Chapter Twenty-six

CRAFTSMAN SUCCEEDS CHAMPION
Harry Busson – 27 years as pro, 16 more as clubmaker

LET ME NOW INTRODUCE James Braid's successor – and prepare for the handshake because the man has a grip like his workshop vice. Yet his hands are sensitive, even artistic.

'Next to my father,' says Ken Macpherson, who ultimately in turn succeeded him, 'Harry Busson was the most unforgettable man I've ever known, the most talented, the funniest, the most knowledgeable on all aspects of golf, the most...'

But we run ahead of time. This is Busson described at a ripe age – silver haired, making woods at his bench with Beethoven for background; an anachronism, an old craftsman.

Let us flick back the calendars to 1951, when Walton Heath offered him the job. He was 43; of medium height and build; when playing he often wore glasses. In Braid's shadow he seemed an insignificant golfer, but that suggests he couldn't play which is far from the truth.

Harry, or James Henry as he was christened, was the elder son of the greenkeeper-professional at Water Orton (a village near Meriden at the centre of England) who later became pro at Brockworth Park, Gloucester. At 16 he twice holed in one during one round at Painswick. Busson senior, influenced by his own struggles to get jobs and soured by the poor rewards and low social standing of club pros, was set against his sons making golf their career. Just as the boy Braid had become a joiner, so young Busson began making wooden patterns for metal castings at a firm that manufactured milling and grinding machinery.

The turning point came in 1928 when the professional at Formby, on Merseyside, needed an assistant. This time his father did not stand in Harry's way. For one thing Formby was a respected club; for another the professional was Willie McEwan of the historic Bruntsfield and Musselburgh clubmaking dynasty.

Harry went north, promptly won regional assistants'

Harry the tournament professional.

events and, subsidised by the members, played in the 1929 Open, probably the only man in the field to have made all his clubs himself. Thus began 20 happy years at Formby, a period split by one visit to America at the invitation of the wealthy mother of a youngster he had met during a boys' championship.

'One regrets that this young player is transferring his abilities to the other side of the Atlantic,' wrote a northern writer. 'It is time something was done to keep young players of such brilliant promise at home, where they are decidedly needed.' It was just dawning on our people that the Americans might be at least as good as us in the Ryder Cup and soon, indeed, they would be beating us eight times in nine matches.

As the young man set off for America in 1930 McEwan wrote to him as a father might write to a favourite son:

> You have hardly been out of my thoughts for many minutes together. I know it will be a great wrench leaving home, but keep a stout heart. I'm sure there is a good time in front of you and a year or two is not very long to think about when you will return full of beans (and dollars)!

Within two years Harry received a cable telling him that McEwan had died following a heart attack on the course and offering him his job.

His sojourn in the States had coincided with the start of the Depression, but he had obtained posts in New York and Florida and his golf had improved. Back home it

> The strong point of Busson's play is the quality of his short game. He hits the ball beautifully through the green, but he has an amazing eye for putting. In two recent rounds he had twos at six of the eight short holes.
>
> Merseyside newspaper, c1935

Busson drives off the second tee in a News of the World *Match-Play Championship.*

seemed that his early promise might be fulfilled. He shared the first-round lead in the 1939 Open at St Andrews, played for England's professionals against Scotland and put himself in line for a Ryder Cup place.

But he never quite made the top drawer. His best finish in the Open was 25th, he failed to win tournaments when he had chances to do so and he never made the Ryder Cup team.

And he never equalled his younger brother Jack, who did play in the Ryder Cup, finished equal-fourth in an Open and had a dramatic victory at Walton in the 1934 *News of the World* Match-Play. Good judges rated Harry the better player, but at the crunch Jack had the stronger will. The Merseyside golf writer Leslie Edwards was a fervent admirer of Harry, often prepared to find excuses ('Rain on his spectacles'…'Unlucky to go out when the wind was at its worst'), but even he wrote that 'for some reason he appeared to lack the necessary "devil" to carry him to a winning position.'

Braid's original pro's shop 'modernised' by Busson after he arrived in 1951.
Golf Monthly, *1952*

Busson confided to Macpherson his regrets that he never did himself justice in The Championship (with him it was never 'the Open,' always 'The Championship') and confessed to a recurring dream he had experienced before the event. He was arriving at one of the championship greens… and suddenly that green would be transformed into a sort of springy trampoline, then begin tilting in different directions… and now his ball was rolling back towards him, down to the lowest part of the green, as though chasing him… and then he would wake in a cold sweat.

In 1951 he seemed a surprising choice to replace a five times Open winner, but according to Max Faulkner, that year's champion, Braid himself had at some stage recommended Busson as his successor. In January the board asked Commander Roe, the PGA secretary, to see the Formby man and report back. Within a month chairman William Carr had given Harry the job.

No doubt Busson had brought to his interview the fading testimonial written more than two decades earlier by McEwan:

> He was for two years my chief assistant clubmaker and had extensive experience in the making and repairing of clubs, both hickory and steel. I found him to be a first-class workman and an expert clubmaker. As a teacher he had considerable experience, particularly in teaching ladies, many of his pupils making substantial progress and all speaking of him in high terms. He was a first-class player and his genial, pleasant manner were beyond approach.

Harry, beginning by throwing out 40 years' worth of accumulated rubbish from the workshop area and vastly enlarging the unattractive showroom, would remain Walton Heath's professional for nearly 27 years.

He was an exceptional teacher. English champion Ronnie White called him the finest in the country; Curtis Cup star Jean Donald wrote thanking him for the 'fantastic difference' in her game.

However, he was a perfectionist and was appreciated most by good players. Poor golfers sometimes benefited less. If he respected you he could be sympathetic and he was sincerely admired by many members, but without that respect he could be caustic. For some, even a few of the better players, he was too honest and too forthright.

'Would these suit my game?' asked a member, studying some clubs in the shop. 'Yes,' replied Harry, 'Ideal for a digger and chopper.' 'Alright,' he sighed, approached for lessons by one high-handicapper, 'Hit a few shots for me to see.' The pupil obeyed. 'Right,' said Harry, 'Now which of those swings do you wish me to cure?'

Busson v Beck

When Harry Busson succeeded Braid as professional, Edgar B. Beck decided to put the new man to the test. A game was duly arranged. Busson emerged from the shop to play wearing his customary white shoes. 'We're not playing cricket,' exclaimed Beck, 'Go and get properly dressed!' Several minutes later, wearing black shoes, Busson found Beck walking off the first green. 'Are these shoes alright?' enquired Busson. 'Yes, those are better,' said Beck, 'You're one down.'

He could not stand bad manners, arrogance, aggression, rudeness, dirty shoes or grubby finger-nails. He was a dapper dresser, his footwear immaculately polished, his golf shoes whitened as the first duty of every day even when he no longer played.

He stood on his dignity. 'Is Busson in?' a member might ask. 'It's Mister Busson if you don't mind,' was the response that would come booming back from within the shop. Macpherson says that in all the years he knew him, and although they became family friends, he never called him anything but 'Mr Busson.'

Here was a man kind to those he liked. If he did not like you he would cut himself off. He would generously give clubs to young assistants but chastise them if they failed to look after them. Ask him for an opinion and you got one.

Busson's first two decades as Walton's professional were in the Carr era, but they form only part of his story and we should properly step beyond that period to consider the rest of it...

In 1976 he was feted at a dinner to mark his silver jubilee at the club. There had been a call to elect him an honorary life member, but, although the honour had been conferred on Braid, the committee felt bound by articles of association that restricted it to members. Within weeks an extraordinary general meeting was held at which two resolutions were passed, the first changing the phraseology from 'member' to 'person' and the second granting Busson his life membership.

By 1977 Walton for a second time had a 70-year-old professional and that year Busson retired – well, retired as the club's pro, that is. The committee agreed that he could continue as a clubmaker under his own banner in the workshop converted from Braid's old office overlooking the putting green. There, with its walls adorned by old photos of Hogan and Jones, a map of Braid's Gleneagles and an out-of-date calendar page featuring an anonymous underclad lady, he began work that would extend for another 16 years.

Daily at 4pm sharp the kettle would be put on. Then he would drag Macpherson out to the edge of the putting green for a cup of tea and the sight of Concorde. At 4.07pm they would see it – and, perhaps recalling his young days in Gloucester when Frank Whittle was developing the jet engine, he would watch the supersonic bird from the second it appeared until it vanished, as though, in his thirst for knowledge, it were something he could not quite comprehend.

'The most rewarding years of his working life.'   Phil Sheldon

Macpherson: 'Almost like a third son to him.'

Discussing clubs with Hale Irwin during the 1981 Ryder Cup.

about a liverish secretary at Formby. Every morning this chap would give Harry a vitriolic dressing-down about something, but by the day's end he was invariably legless and Harry would nightly take him by the hand to Freshfields station and pour him safely on to his train home. Next morning it would again be 'Busson, come into my office immediately!' – the usual roasting in store and the previous night's compassionate deeds forgotten!

Later, driven home, Harry would apologise: 'Oh, that was ridiculous. All those stories. How boring I must have been!'

His teaching days were over, but he viewed Macpherson as a special case. Overlooking the demands on the young professional's time, he always wanted Ken to play and practise more. 'Will you be going out to practise today?' he'd ask casually. 'Yes? Well, it's a lovely day, I might be out there myself.' Of course he *would* be there, and at first he was complimentary: 'By Jove, aren't you striking beautifully today!... Good heavens, for a little fellow you're hitting it miles!'

Ken might then produce a quick hook and the mentor's tone would gradually change as the remaining shots were hit: 'Ah, now, does that *trouble* you?... Well of course if you stand closed you'll *get* a few like that... Yes, I've never been very happy with *that* aspect of your grip... Have you *always* stood that distance away?... If it were me I'd think

A firm bond had embraced the two men. 'He was like a second father to me,' says Macpherson, 'and I was almost like a third son to him, perhaps because neither of his own boys to whom he was so attached became absorbed by golf'.

> He came from a fairly ordinary background, yet you could put him into any company and he could discuss any subject. He was a beautiful writer, an expert photographer, particularly of birds, a fine pianist with an exceptional appreciation of classical music, a countryman with a profound knowledge of nature and wild life. He could forecast the weather: 'Oh, you won't need all that clothing today,' he would say, and one would confidently peel off one's waterproofs.
>
> And he could have you in stitches! He never laughed at his own jokes; he would deliver his lines poker-faced, then immediately walk away.

Dinner parties at the Macphersons' were special occasions with Harry present. Called on to retail his memories to the assembled young professionals, he would at first decline ('Oh no, I've told you all those before'), but eventually, after more encouragement and a brace of gin and tonics, he would embark...

There were stories of America, about champions like Hagen and Jones, and tales from nearer home, like the one

'An expert photographer, particularly of birds.'

Critic and Mimic

*P*ersuaded by Bryan Patterson, then professional at Burhill, to walk some holes with him and advise him on his game, the ageing Busson showed that his idiosyncratic style was alive and well.

Shot after shot was played without a single comment; at hole after hole Patterson looked at him, eyebrows raised in anticipation of technical advice... yet still there was silence. Ultimately Bryan felt he positively had to ask for comments. 'Well, what do you think, Harry?' he ventured, and awaited some expert analysis of grip or swing. 'Well frankly, Bryan,' said Harry gravely, 'I don't like the way you take the club out of the bag.'

The story really should end there. However there is a continuation. 'Could you elaborate on that, Harry?' asked the nonplussed Patterson. The response was a series of life-like impersonations, with accompanying commentary, of great champions taking their clubs: Watson, relaxed but decisive... Palmer snorting, tugging at his trousers, stretching out for his club, then exploding into action... Nicklaus deliberating, then selecting.

'But you,' he concluded, 'You just shuffle to your bag and back again... there's no pattern to your game!' A pause followed, and then: 'But then you're Irish and they always were a breed apart.'

about...' – and then he would list all the things he would alter. Finally: 'If you stick to all these pointers you should win The Championship with no trouble at all!' At this point he would walk away – leaving Ken distraught!

Since his arrival as pro all those years ago, when Bob and Brown, the elderly retainers left over from the Braid regime, were still making clubs, Busson had found little time to pursue the craft himself – a few orders for honoured members and connoisseurs, some repairing and that was about it. The new venture was a resumption of the work he began for McEwan in the era of fading hickory and incoming steel in the late 'twenties. It also heralded the most rewarding years of his working life.

The Press rediscovered him. The mighty 1981 United States Ryder Cup team came to admire his clubs and, as Jack Nicklaus has recalled in his foreword, return home with examples. Japan sent journalists, and as a result of their writings the patter of tiny feet of air stewardesses came tip-toeing through the portals to place orders for the folks back home. Wilson, the American sports-goods firm, hired him as a consultant and used his name on some

> I only watch the big tournaments now. Play is so slow I can't watch most of the stuff.

Busson in 1990

Ballesteros and Busson discuss technicalities.
Above: cryptic notes of the Spaniard's requirements.
Photographer: Ken Macpherson

'The international peerage of golf paraded through the workshop.'
Photographer: Ken Macpherson

clubs. Golfers from Seattle to Sydney phoned orders and collected their clubs personally rather than risk precious cargo. One Japanese tycoon wanted to invest in the Busson business, presumably imagining it as a blossoming corporation. 'I could hardly tell him he was dealing with an 80-year-old buffer producing at best three or four clubs a week,' said Harry.

The international peerage of professional golf paraded through the workshop to have clubs made or copied: Norman, Langer, Faldo, Ballesteros, Marsh, Canizares, Vijay Singh and many others. In 1985 half the victorious European Ryder Cup team were said to be carrying Busson woods. Harry first met Vijay Singh when he was an unknown, hard-up youngster with a motley collection of old clubs and made him his first proper woods.

Just as Braid's skill as a joiner helped him when he came to make clubs, so did Busson's early experience as a pattern-maker, working to precise limits with sharp wood turning and carving tools. He made his own patterns for his clubs. 'Others get a rough persimmon block and alter it this way and that,' he said, 'That's not my idea of club-making.'

His wooden master would be sent to a foundry to have an exact copy cast in metal, and after this had been passed to another firm he would eventually receive back a turned persimmon block precisely to his pattern. His metal masters, each of a different shape, were exclusively his; no heads could be turned from them unless they were for him.

The tough persimmon, for which he always had a

sneaking preference, came from Memphis: 'My whole business hinges on its quality,' he would say. He drilled all the bore-holes which took the shafts himself and believed this was the most critical stage because they determined the lie of the clubhead. His magic wand was a specially made jig that enabled him to drill 100-per-cent accurately and if there were only one single factor why Busson clubs are so admired it would be the way they sit.

Most of his clubs stemmed from the same original mould but he could further define the head according to the golfer. He would make them to a player's specification or his own assessment of the golfer's needs or copy exactly a person's favourite wood. 'Langer inclines to hook so to compensate he gets a slightly open face,' he once explained. 'For Sam Torrance I fix a strong shaft and slightly hooked face because he tends to push.' He would make notes of members' height, build, age and strength, his aim, he said, being to help them play better and thus enhance their enjoyment. In the mid-'eighties his woods were priced at around £150, perhaps twice the cost of the factory variety.

He did not always deride mass-produced equipment and was flattered when someone likened his clubs to the MacGregors of the mid-'fifties, which he thought were a masterpiece, but he was critical of designers who didn't understand their subject and emphatic that many golfers were playing with unsuitable clubs ('It's like buying a suit off the peg. You might be lucky and find one that fits you perfectly, but then again you might not').

Busson's clubs reflect the man; they are the outcome of artistry as well as technical know-how. One day a Japanese journalist visited him, doubtless expecting to find a gnarled old craftsman in scruffy overalls. Having recovered from the sight of his snazzy white polo shirt, beautiful trousers and shining shoes, he engaged him in comparisons between clubmaking and classical music. Technicians could copy but could not understand harmony and musicality, said the visitor, wasn't it the same with making clubs? Was Harry, with his insight and understanding, a golfing parallel to Horowitz, the last pianist who could play Chopin and Beethoven with their original meanings?

Featured in Japan. 'I feel like a man making a violin or cello,' Busson told a Japanese journalist.

This must have been a shock to Busson, used to the usual pedestrian questions, but the visitor knew his man and Harry warmed to the theme: 'Clubmaking is a challenge. I suppose I feel like a man making a violin or cello - stage by stage and completely by hand. Look at this club and play with it. You will enjoy a wonderful feeling, as though you are listening to a masterpiece of classical music.'

A legend? 'Oh no, I am neither legend nor ghost, but it may be true that I'll be the last craftsman in clubmaking.' That possibility was increased by the fact that he was not teaching any successors. 'They're not interested,' he would

say. 'Unless you can see a shape in your mind's eye you won't be any good. I have a sort of flair, a gift.'

Eventually his health deteriorated, his wife Mary had died and he lost confidence in travelling, needing Ken as his 'minder.' Shingles affected his eyesight and diverticulitis and tinnitus were other problems.

In 1992 readers of *The Times* were invited to say what they would most wish to take with them when they died. 'All my valuables,' wrote one man predictably; 'My favourite hairbrush,' said a lady. Two readers opted for golfing impedimenta. One wished for his handicap certificate because he was sure there would be courses in heaven or hell. The other chose 'my persimmon driver, beautifully made and exactly as I wanted by Harry Busson, aged 85, at Walton Heath. Left-handed; difficult to get here, perhaps impossible anywhere else.'

The following year, on May 23, 1993, Busson died. It is not recorded what he wished to take with him. Certainly he left the contents of his workshop to his successor. Stuck inside his old locker was his own epitaph. The original composition may or may not have been his, but the handwriting and humour certainly were:

I dreamed I stood at the Pearly Gates,
My head was bent and low,
I meekly asked the man of Fate
Which way I had to go.

'What have you done?' Saint Peter cried,
'To gain admission here?'
'The pro at Walton Heath' I said,
'I was for many a year.'

St Peter opened wide the Gates
And gently tolled the bell,
'Come in and choose your harp', he said,
'You've had your share of hell.'

Left: Douglas Brown with his boss.

Right: Tommy Goodwin, a 'Rookie of the Year,' receives cheque from Henry Cotton.

Jan 22nd 1926.

JAMES BRAID GOLF CLUB MAKE

OPEN CHAMPION. 1901
" " 1905
" " 1906
" " 1907
" " 191

Speciality: DRIVERS and BRAS

ON HEATH GOLF CLUB,
WALTON-ON-THE-HILL,
TADWORTH.

This is to certify that A. marsh was employed at this club about three years prior to 1914 during which time he carried out his work in a very satisfactory and tidy manner. He was an expeditious and tidy workman.

Yours faithfully,
JBraid

Dear Mr Busson,

I am writing appl for the post advertised in the 15th of Fe issue of Golf Illustrated.

I turned professional just over a year ago, I am just over 18 years old and at present I am assistant to my father at Baberton, in Edinburgh. I have not passed my P.G.A. certificate yet, but I have being teach night classes four the less...

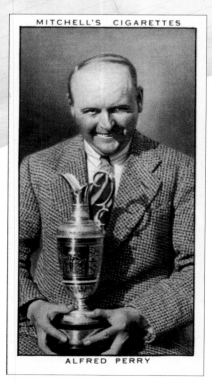

MITCHELL'S CIGARETTES

ALFRED PERRY

Above: Braid's testimonial for Alfred Marsh and job application from Ewen Murray. From far left: Alf Perry, Gus Faulkner and (above) Willie Ritchie.

Chapter Twenty-seven

GRADUATES FROM THE ACADEMY
For assistants, 'Braid' or 'Busson' on a cv was a passport to promotion

ONE OPEN CHAMPIONSHIP, six Ryder Cup places and two *News of the World* Match-Play runners-up spots are among the honours gained by assistants who graduated from learning under the Walton Heath professorships of Braid and Busson. For those ambitious to be full club professionals, the names of such bosses on a cv helped unlock many a door – and the tradition continues under Ken Macpherson[1].

The Braid era

The Open champion was **Alf Perry**, who won at Muirfield in 1935 and was an assistant at Walton as well as at Chipstead and Banstead before beginning his lengthy sojourn at Leatherhead. If he did any teaching it is to be hoped that he did not impress his own style on his pupils, because purists claimed that almost everything about it was wrong. Yes? So how did he win the Open, play in three Ryder Cups and reach a Match-Play final? It worked for *him*!

Through the arts and crafts of clubmaking and professionalism strong family threads run and so it was in Braid's time: indeed, his own nephew, **Philp**, was among his early helpers and went off to Argentina to ply his trade as early as 1909.

Then there were the Browns and the Faulkners. We have already met the longest serving members of Braid's staff: **Bill Brown** and **Bob Horseburgh** – 'Bob and Brown,' the faithful clubmakers whose sojourns stretched into Busson's time. Bill had two sons, **John** and **Douglas Brown**, and they, too, entered Braid's shop. Douglas won the £100 Assistants' Tournament at Stoke Poges in 1928, the third Walton staff man, past or present, to do so by that time.[2]

The Faulkner dynasty, of which Fred survives as a staff member today (and which embraces former Open champion Max) were well represented even before World War I. **Gus Faulkner** was Max's father and Fred's uncle. He went on to Pennard (Swansea) and to win the Welsh professional championship before, for 12 years, serving Bramley,

for whom he won the Surrey Open. **Herbert Faulkner**, another of Fred's uncles, became the first pro appointed by Bull Bay (Anglesey), having been recommended by Fowler who laid out the course. He died from an illness contracted while serving overseas in the Army in the later stages of the war.

The first of Braid's staff to win acclaim as a competitor while still an assistant was Aberdeen-born **Willie Ritchie**. In 1910, not only did he win the assistants' event, then known as the One Hundred Guineas Tournament for Assistants, he finished 16th behind his boss in the Open at St Andrews. The following year he became professional at Worplesdon and after war service went to Addington.

Braid's men moved near and far to jobs as full professionals: between the wars, **Arthur ('Bill') Young** to Sonning, **Albert Luckett** (10 years with Braid) to Chipstead, **Reg James** to Seacroft (Skegness), **Alfred Marsh** to Wells, **Gregor McIntosh** to Nairn…

McIntosh served Nairn for more than a quarter of a century until his retirement in 1980. Trained to make clubs in his Fifeshire birthplace of Leven, he was a boy international and played for Scotland as a professional. The Scottish club's history pays him handsome tribute: 'Beautiful hand-made woods… an outstanding teacher, coaching the best young players in the north of Scotland for many years… one of the club's great personalities.'

This is but fragmentary evidence of what happened to the host of assistants – staffs of up to seven people at a time – whom Braid must have hired during those 46½ years. One wonders what happened to the others and saddens at the thought of how many of those enthusiastic young apprentices may have died in the two wars that punctuated his reign.

The Busson era

Three senior playing assistants stand out from Busson's time:

Ross Whitehead, who lived in the village and apparently had lessons from Braid, was given a £5-a-week contract in 1956. Six years later he told the Press that making a living from golf had proved so tough that he was leaving and taking a job outside the game, though he

---

[1] Chapter 38.
[2] Previous winners were Ritchie and (twice) Perry.

would play in some tournaments as a free-lance – and the club was not best pleased.

Within the year he had won the Assistants' Championship and, at Walton, representing Banstead Downs, reached the final of the Match-Play, losing to Eric Brown at the first extra hole. Subsequently he was made captain of the PGA and, when professional at Moor Park, was Ken Macpherson's boss. He died in 2000.

George Will not only followed Whitehead on the Walton Heath staff but succeeded him as Assistants' champion. He had been British Youths champion in 1957 and twice Army champion before achieving three Ryder Cup appearances (1963-5-7), playing three times for Scotland in the World Cup, working as a professional in Europe and writing a book, *Golf, The Modern Way*.

Tommy O'Mahoney arrived from Ireland in 1963 and stayed until 1971. He enjoyed a somewhat bibulous lifestyle, but when he completely discarded it his career took off. He went to Noordwijk (Holland), where he became head pro and has remained for more than 25 years. He is now the Dutch Federation's national coach.

Ewen Murray, now a Sky TV commentator, with his encyclopaedic knowledge, Scottish burr and the shortest vowels in the business, came to Walton 'as a raw 18-year-old' (his phrase) in 1973 and would stay 14 years, first as an assistant, then as playing professional.

As an amateur he had won Scottish Boys' championships and, when 15, reached the British final. Invited to the States for a World Junior Championship he finished sixth in a field of 580 and won the leading-non-American trophy. Since turning pro on his 17th birthday he had been helping his father Jimmy, the long-serving pro at Baberton (Edinburgh).

'He has the potential for world-class golf,' his manager Derick Pillage told Busson, supporting Murray senior's lauding of his son's merits. 'He is a charming lad, but needs

George Will – played in three Ryder Cup matches.

someone like you to give him a pulling-down now and then.' In two years, reputedly, he had grown from 5ft 2in to 5ft 10½!

In 1973, the year he joined Walton Heath, he finished equal-31st in the Open. The club established a fund to send him on a new European tour for young pro's, his first £1,900 in winnings to go to the subscribers and the player to receive 50-per-cent of anything above that figure. Having been retained as tournament pro in 1977, he was so well established on the circuit three years later that he could no longer benefit from the fund and in 1984 he topped the PGA money list.

He left Walton in 1987 and his fulsome farewell letter to captain Tom Corrigan referred to his 'beloved courses' and the 'treasured friends' he had met. He was a hugely talented player who never quite attained the heights of which he seemed capable.

Another of whom that might be said was **Tommy Goodwin**, who knocked out Dai Rees and Charlie Ward on his way to a Match-play Championship quarter-final at Turnberry in 1963 and won a 'Rookie of the Year' prize.

He became an assistant at places as far apart as Moor Park, Barbados and New York, among others, finally got a full pro's job at Bedlington in 1972 and died when he was 50. His failure to fulfil his promise competitively was due, says his widow, Joan, to his independent personality, family responsibilities and the lack of enough money or sponsorship to enable him to continue playing regularly in tournaments.

Above: Ross Whitehead.

Right: Ewen Murray.

Chapter Twenty-eight

END OF THE MATCH-PLAY

Winds of change – in golf and at the *News of the World*

As THE 1949 *News of the World* Match-Play Championship drew near there was unprecedented interest. An international entry had been achieved. Prize-money had increased to over £2,500, a thousand pounds more than for the Open. By now 64 professionals, not 32, were qualifying for the final stages wherever the event was held.

Moreover, the newspaper's baby, now grown into a lusty adult of more than 40 years, had been declared entirely legitimate by authority. Previously, Pressmen had felt the need to pussyfoot around by calling it, for example, 'the *News of the World* professional golf tournament known as the match-play championship.' Now it was recognised as the official PGA match-play championship.

The event was alive, kicking and growing. In 20 years it would be dead.

First, though, the good news. Everyone concerned was determined that the championship would recapture its pre-war glories, which, so far as Walton was concerned, had ended with the victories of Harry Busson's brother Jack[1] in **1934** and the little Welshman Dai Rees in **1938**.

Busson had beaten Charles Whitcombe despite some erratic drives, one of which hit a lady full on the forehead. The decisive hole was the 35th[2]. One up, he hooked his drive, then rashly took a wood and hit deeper into waist-high bracken. From there he struck what Whitcombe called one of the greatest shots he had seen, powering it to within six feet and holing for a half. A win at the last

Dai Rees (left) and Ernest ('Eddie') Whitcombe, the smallest players to contest a Match-Play final, contrast with referee Braid, still a formidable figure at 68.

earned him the championship by two holes.

For Rees, victory over Charles Whitcombe's nephew Eddie brought him his second championship in three years and was riddled with coincidences. The finalists were born on the same day; both were sons of professionals; Dai had beaten Eddie's father for his first title (at Oxhey, 1936); and at 5ft 6in or under they were the smallest pair to have contested the final.

The first post-war championship, held at Walton in **1945** only two-and-a-half months after Germany's surrender and surprisingly won by Reg Horne, then at a nine-hole course in Hampshire, was a brave effort but not much more. Many professionals were still overseas, there were only 149 entries and no regional qualifying rounds and the matches, all 18 holes, were held over five days on the New course as well as the Old.

But how different everything was in **1949**, when the championship next came to the heath. A frenetic sports boom had mushroomed within the wider post-war euphoria. To me those late 'forties meant queueing outside Highbury Stadium in mid-morning to see Arsenal in the afternoon and rushing from Fleet Street to Lord's to watch Compton, Miller and Bradman in the evening; but that September of 1949, if you were a youngster hooked on golf, you would surely have dashed to Walton Heath. The Yanks were coming! Members of the Ryder Cup team who had just beaten us at Ganton were among the challengers – and to teenagers like Colin Kennard, whose salad-day recollections (page 170) Bob Coombes (1990 captain) has passed to me, these men were invincible gods.

Overleaf: Jack Busson plays from the rough on his way to winning the 1934 News of the World *Match-Play Championship.*

---

[1] Jack Busson became a Walton Heath member after retiring as pro at RAC Woodcote Park. His daughter, Sally Preece, is a member today.
[2] The 17th then is the 16th now.

A TIME FOR HEROES

On arrival I was thrilled to discover Dutch Harrison, Johnny Palmer and Skip Alexander gathered for practice on the first tee with the reigning supremo of American golf, the legendary Sam Snead. Never before having seen players of their calibre, the simplicity of the swings and purity of striking of the first three took my breath away.

Then it was Snead. 'What do I need here, Charlie?' he quietly asked his caddie. 'Er, a four-wood, Mr. Snead,' mumbled Charlie unconvincingly. An upward glance to gauge the wind, a second analytical stare toward the green and Snead's decision was made: 'Gimme a three-iron,' he drawled.

The spine-tingling process of his preparation began. He nonchalantly tossed a ball down... not for him the luxury of a tee peg, nor even a gentle nudge to any minuscule tuft. A quick shuffle prefaced the flawless swing and the ball was swept away, making the cleanest, sweetest noise that had ever befallen my ears

I knew that I had witnessed something very special. I managed to suppress a squeal of excitement, my heart pounded and a form of pins and needles engulfed me as the ball flew on and on, unwaveringly straight. At the entrance to the green, thwarting a bunker, it seemed inevitably to fade in toward the partly hidden flagstick and came to rest 12 inches from the cup. Snead tapped it in one-handed with his iron.

During this whole episode he betrayed no emotion, his manner conveying an air of casual, modest indifference. To him, perhaps, the stroke had been nothing extraordinary, but to my young, impressionable eyes it was sheer genius. The memory is etched indelibly on my mind half-a-century on. I shall take it with me to my grave – and hopefully, beyond.

COLIN KENNARD, 2002

Huge crowds built up. Journalist Tom Scott had to tell his readers that he had been able to see only alternate holes and vented his spleen on certain marshals whose chosen priority, he suspected, was to ensure good views for themselves.

Some of the Americans infused the solemn atmosphere of competition with a fresh, laid-back informality. In a match between Henry Cotton and Lloyd Mangrum, US Open champion three years before, a drive by the British player finished on bare ground on the margin of a path running across the fairway. Was he entitled to drop? 'Do you mind if Mr. Cotton lifts his ball?' the referee asked the American. 'Nope,' said Mangrum, nonchalantly chewing his gum, 'He can stick it on a peg if he likes!'

The American Ryder Cup players confessed that they did not like the Walton Heath layout. In fact, one said to me: 'If this is golf we must play another game.' This is true for them, because American golf is target golf with little variety coming into the game.

These top-grade US players found that such great courses as Walton Heath need learning. One round of casual inspection is not enough.

I had my full share of nasty lies in the rough and heather lining the fairways. This is the greatness of the course. You know that the punishment is severe and it makes straight hitting all the more difficult.

Henry Cotton, *News of the World*, 1949

Mangrum and Cotton, hard pressed by enthusiastic crowds.

The irony of all this is that the Americans failed. Perhaps they were *too* casual, perhaps they had not had *enough* practice on the course. Whatever the reasons, only Mangrum reached the semi-finals, whereupon he was put out by Cotton, and Sam Snead had astonishingly lost to Norman Quigley, the pro at Windermere. Sam, one down at the 18th, looked likely to square the match because Quigley was in the bunker to the left of the green. Norman promptly holed from the sand!

In the final, refereed by a 79-year-old Braid, Cotton faced Rees. Henry had won the title three times, Dai twice. Cotton, recently ill, looked white and drawn, and always near him was his ubiquitous wife 'Toots,' encouraging him

Master stroke! Quigley holes from the sand to beat Snead by two holes.

and once helping the stewards force back the spectators when Henry faced a crucial shot from a bad lie.

Later, Rees disclosed, disappointingly, that before they began and at Cotton's suggestion they had agreed to split the prize-money: 60-per-cent to the winner and 40 to the loser. For all that, the *News of the World,* employing forgiveable hyperbole as sponsor of the tournament and employer of Cotton as golf correspondent, reported it as 'the most dramatic final within living memory.'

Rees, four up after the first round, later recalled that he had dropped to one up as they reached the long 14th in the afternoon but that, while he was just short of the green in two, Cotton had cut his second into bracken among the silver birches…

Henry tried to cut his ball out with his wedge but scythed beneath it: a fresh air shot. He hacked on to the fairway and put his next shot on to the green from where he would hole out. I chipped and got down in five.

Mr. Braid announced, 'A half in five; Rees one up.' He had

made the mistake of thinking Henry's swing in the rough had been a practice shot. I soon put him right and stood two up with four to play.

On the 15th I had a putt from 10 feet for a birdie three to put me in the virtually impregnable position of three up, but bolted it, overran the hole and was left with a 'gimme' of about 10 inches. 'Surely Henry's going to give me this?' I thought, glancing across the green. But Henry turned away.

Instead of concentrating hard I gave the ball a careless push and it spun out from the lip. Now I was back to one instead of being two or three up.[3]

Rees, halving the last three holes, hung on to win – which, he said, caused a sudden change of plan for that night's dinner at the Dorchester. The *News of the World*, he claimed, were so confident that their correspondent would win that Cotton had been placed as guest of honour. Dai's wife was apparently summoned from home and the Welshman transferred to the top seat. 'Make the most of this, Dai, you won't be in the winner's chair again!' Sir William Carr joked. But he was. Next year at Carnoustie he retained his title, thus equalling Braid's record of four victories.

In **1952** came another regular winner: Fred Daly of the jaunty aspect and rolling gait, whistling his Irish tunes and waggling his club like a latter-day Sandy Herd or a circa-2002 Sergio Garcia – anything up to a dozen waggles and sideways glances before each swing. His wood and iron shots, followed by a magician's touch on the greens, convincingly beat Belgium's Flory van Donck for the second time in a *News of the World* final and earned Fred, 41, his third title in six years.

---
[3] *Thirty Years of Championship Golf*, 1968.

One way of seeing over the crowds – the 1952 championship.

In a third-round match Daly and 'Tiger' Poulton had set a professional record for marathons. They played not 18 but 30 holes before the Ulsterman survived – whereupon he went out to play Peter Alliss, who had been waiting two hours, and promptly beat him six and five. It was all part and parcel of a championship that provided standards surpassing anything in the series since the war.

And so, every three years, the match-play championship continued to return to Walton, yielding more winners from our Ryder Cup ranks. In **1955**, with prize money up to £3,000, it was Ken Bousfield, whose outward nine in the first round of a classic, sunlit final against Scotland's Eric Brown was assessed as 32. In **1958** Harry Weetman defeated Bernard Hunt in a final limited to 18 holes.

Two characters: Max Faulkner drives, Peter Alliss watches in 1958.

The match-play championship at Walton Heath has proved a great success again this year.

The winner told our representative that he thought it would be a first class course to hold the Open Championship on and preferably in autumn.

There is no doubt that Walton Heath is a great course which suits the accurate golfer rather than the big hitters, and the suggestion about holding the Open at the end of the season has been made in many quarters and is one well worth consideration.

Golf Illustrated, 1955

Eighteen-hole finals? Yes, things were changing. Concessions were being made to ensure that the top players competed. From 1952 defending titleholders and reigning Open champions had no longer had to qualify from regional competitions; the following year neither had the top 10 in the Order of Merit; in 1956 this was changed to the top seven plus three players nominated by the *News of the World*; later the newspaper would select five.

Then came that tradition-busting edict that even the finals would comprise only 18 holes, not 36. It was part of the trend wherein sundry sports from cricket to bowls have found it necessary to court television money and pander to spectators and players wanting quick fixes rather than protracted dramas.

From **1961**, except for one year, Walton Heath became the championship's permanent home, and the following autumn the regional phase, a traditional part of the championship's format, was abandoned altogether. The qualifying rounds, involving more than 200 players, were to be played on the Old and New at the start of a week-long tournament.

The stars of this Walton Heath decade were Australia's Peter Thomson (five times Open champion like Braid), England's Neil Coles and, in a different way, the Welshman Rees. By **1966**, when Thomson and Coles met in the final, both had won twice. Coles, indeed, had just secured back-to-back victories so was seeking an unprecedented hat-trick.

He had survived a torrid semi-final against Peter Alliss. All-square coming to the last, both drove into the rough, but Coles was able to take a wood and struck a tremendous shot some 20 feet beyond the pin. What should Alliss do? His guardian angel studied his inferior lie and whispered to him to play safe and short with an iron; the devil tempted him to take a wood. The devil was persuasive. Alliss went for the green, finished in the cross-bunker and lost.

In the final against Thomson Coles started woefully. Soon he was three down and despite courageous attempts – notably a wonderful wood to within 18 inches at the 16th which only earned him a half – he never fully

recovered. Thomson won by two and one for his third championship.

This brings us to **1967** and to Rees. He had now won the title four times, but his last was 17 years ago. Yet here he was, at 54, immaculately beating Coles to reach the final. Now he met Thomson, who, when Rees won for the first time, had been seven years old.

Rather like Braid 40 years previously, Dai could not quite roll back the years and toward the end his swing lost some of its rhythm. Thomson beat him four and three, slotting an 18-footer on the 15th oblivious to the wailing of a babe in arms just behind him. He thus became the third player – Braid and Rees being the others – to win four times.

The professionals, or many of them, did not like the sudden-death dangers of match-play and now had a range of bigger-money stroke-play tournaments to enter. The public, though, revelled in it and 7,000 were estimated to have seen Brian Huggett win the 1968 final against Scotland's John Panton.

The crowds, still watching at an unbeatable price, had seen plenty of excitement during the last 10 years at Walton and not only in the finals. In 1958 Alliss and South Africa's Harold Henning had played 13 extra holes before Henning won… In 1962 Robert Halsall, the Royal Birkdale professional, shot a 66 on the New… and the members had basked in reflected glory as Ross Whitehead, their former assistant, unexpectedly reached the final and took Eric Brown to extra time.

Yet, despite all this, the championship was on its death bed. The *News of the World* announced that the **1969** event, the 57th of the series and carrying £5,000, would be its last.

Clockwise from top left: 1965 – Lionel Platts urges in a putt; 1966 – Neil Coles, winner the previous two years, attempts a hat-trick (photo taken by Henry Cotton); 1967 – Thomson and Rees. When Dai won his first Match-Play title Peter was seven years old.

In Longhurst's view the event had become a victim of what he supposed had to be called 'progress' – which he defined as embracing 'jet aeroplanes, television, vast money, professional managers, overseas "circuits" and all the other paraphernalia of modern golf.' No doubt this was true, and certainly at least three British stroke-play tournaments were offering at least £2,000 more than the *News of the World*'s. The salient facts close to home, though, were that the *News of the World* had been taken over by the Australian-born Rupert Murdoch and that Mr. Murdoch was not interested in the Match-Play Championship.

Sadly, certain leading players did not support the last event, for reasons, to quote Pat Ward-Thomas in *Country*

Brian Huggett plays from the rough in 1968.

Golf Illustrated

round in six days, he was beaten by Maurice Bembridge, who at 24 was 32 years his junior.

So ended the '*News of the World*,' golf's oldest sponsored professional series. Other sponsors did arrive to take over this PGA Match-Play Championship and publicise their products: cigarettes and whisky and (in the absence of wild, wild women) insurance. Never again was it played at Walton Heath. On the autumn days previously dominated by the top professionals both courses became once more the exclusive playgrounds of the membership.

This reversion was to the wholehearted satisfaction of some of the dilettante. Let us return for a moment to the championship of 1955 and a match in which Eric Brown was taken to an extra hole by Fred Daly. As Daly prepared for this crucial drive an elderly lady saw fit to play rhythms on the accelerator pedal of her car parked on the nearby road. She was asked to desist. 'Young man,' she declaimed, 'I've been a member here since 1904!'

Life, 'easier to understand than condone' and which probably centred on what they felt was an unfair breakdown of the money below the winner's £1,250. Tony Jacklin, the Open champion, was in the States, others failed to qualify and Thomson went out in an early round.

Appropriately, the indomitable Rees competed, won match after match and, at 56, found himself yet again in the semi-finals. There he met Huggett.

Huggett, three up after 15, slipped to only one up with one to play. Then came one of those shafts of fortune that spell prosperity for one man and ruination to the other.

Rees drove atrociously left. The ball struck a post, rebounded and hit Huggett's bag, which was being looked after by his caddie. The dire penalty prescribed in the rules had to be imposed on poor Huggett: loss of hole.[4] They were now all-square – and at the first extra hole, Rees, after a brilliant recovery from sand, reached his seventh final 33 years after his first.

But there was no story-book ending for him either, only perhaps rough justice. Playing his eighth competitive

'News of the World' finals at Walton Heath

Year	Winner	Result	Runner-up
1905	J. Braid	4 & 3	T. Vardon
1909	T. Ball	7 & 5	A. Herd
1911	J. Braid	1 up	E. Ray
1913	G. Duncan	3 & 2	J. Braid
1919	A. Mitchell	1 up	G. Duncan
1923	R. Wilson	4 & 2	T. Renouf
1927	A. Compston	8 & 7	J. Braid
1934	J. Busson	2 up	C. Whitcombe
1938	D. Rees	4 & 3	E. Whitcombe
1945	R. Horne	4 & 3	Percy Alliss
1949	D. Rees	1 up	H. Cotton
1952	F. Daly	4 & 3	F. van Donck
1955	K. Bousfield	4 & 3	E. Brown
18-hole finals			
1958	H. Weetman	1 up	B. Hunt
1961	P.W. Thomson	3 & 1	R. Moffitt
1962	E.C. Brown	19th	R. Whitehead
1964	N. Coles	3 & 2	P. Butler
1965	N. Coles	19th	L. Platts
1966	P. Thomson	2 & 1	N. Coles
1967	P. Thomson	4 & 3	D. Rees
1968	B. Huggett	1 up	J. Panton
1969	M. Bembridge	6 & 5	D. Rees

NEWS OF THE WORLD

As a steward for the 1958 final I was attached to Harry Weetman. I was told that he could 'explode', so to be careful. He was one up at the 18th, drove miles right and I found his ball under a small bush. He asked me to tell him exactly where the bunker on the left of the green was. He then took a three-wood, the bush went up in the air, the ball landed on the green and went straight into the bunker. "The only way I could stop the ball was in the bunker," he said, "I knew that from there I could get down in two." And he did!

Ken Ohlson to author

---

[4] The rule changed in 1980: no penalty for either player in accidental cases.

Chapter Twenty-nine

FOR SALE – WALTON HEATH GOLF CLUB
Rupert Murdoch ends the Carrs' era

The clubhouse in the 1960s.

IN 1969, YEAR OF THE last Match-Play Championship, the Club was put up for sale. How could this happen? To understand, consider the club's administrative and financial history since the war years.

1941: Sir Emsley Carr died and his 37% holdings in the club company were transferred to the *News of the World* organisation. Thus began the newspaper's role as a share-holder.

1942: Cash problems increased during the war. The *NotW* guaranteed £6,000 of a new £10,000 debenture issue provided it could add two nominees to the club's board.

1947: Mrs. Ridley, Malcolm Bonsor's widow, who had re-married and was now Lady of the Manor, offered to sell the club the manor lands. The directors could not accept in the uncertain financial climate. She put the lands into the hands of trustees.

1955: With big clubhouse improvements necessary, the board welcomed an unsecured loan of £20,000 from the *NotW* via William (later Sir William) Carr, Sir Emsley's youngest son, who by now, like his late father, was chairman both of the newspaper company and the club.

1956: The *NotW*, having acquired more shares from executors and 2,500 from Sir Frederic Hamilton's estate, now held slightly more than 51%. Clubhouse expenditure still loomed and dividends were unlikely, so Sir William proposed that it would be in the general interest if his newspaper bought out all the club's holders at par. Over

the next two years the *NotW* increased its holding to more than 93% and later to 98.3%.

1958: The paper now effectively owned the club but not the manor. Dudley Scholey, a club committee man, nego-tiated privately with the manor trustees, aiming to buy the lands and offer them to the club at cost. He bought and became Lord of the Manor. Carr had agreed that the *NotW* would pay the anticipated £13,000 and set up a holding company (Walton-on-the-Hill Manor Ltd) to acquire and manage the estate. Scholey apparently had considered it preferable to have a company other than the club but financially identical to it.

1963: Walton-on-the-Hill Manor, as a *NotW* subsidiary, acquired the freehold of the courses, clubhouse and grounds. Scholey retained the mere pond, village green, recreation ground and the lordship.

1967: Scholey's properties, shares and title passed to the company – that is to say the *NotW* – and its nominee, Eileen Armstrong,[1] became Lady of the Manor.

Over the years the *NotW* had been the club's supporter, publicist, promoter, benefactor, guarantor, saviour and, finally, owner.

So far so good. The golfers' enjoyment was unaffected; the club ran smoothly; the *NotW* nominees on its board had not interfered. The committee looked after the golf

---

[1] Mrs Armstrong was Clive Carr's mother, who re-married after her husband, Horace Carr, had died during the war.

SIR EMSLEY

Contemporary at Cambridge with Sir Emsley Carr's twin sons, 'Wash' and Horace, I remain one of a generation of undergraduates who have cause to remember him with affection.

He used to entertain us in his home after our matches against Walton – our captain of the day having been duly defeated by Sir Ernest Holderness in the singles – and, though I suppose he was what might be called a 'big shot,' I remember him only as a simple family man presiding at the head of his table, delighting in the company of the young.

We would then be taken to see the giant presses running in Bouverie Street – my own first heady smell of printer's ink – and would finally be deposited on the last train from Liverpool Street, regrettably known then and, as I expect, now as The Fornicator.

HENRY LONGHURST, *The Sunday Times*, September 7, 1969

and kept an eye on the running costs; the directors looked after capital expenditure, investment and major policy.

These recollections by members are shared by Clive Carr, who was increasingly asked by Sir William to deputise for him. His uncle, he feels, ran a board of traditional, old-fashioned quality. His heart was in the club and, according to Clive, he knew that it had become a wholly owned subsidiary of his organisation only when an auditor told him!

But Walton Heath Golf Club was now at the mercy of big business and big businessmen, and in March 1969 it all came home to roost.

Two Walton members were among the *NotW* hierarchy – Sir William, chairman, and Clive, deputy managing director – but the managing director and effectively the controlling shareholder was now Rupert Murdoch. The organisation had just spectacularly increased its pre-tax profits and Murdoch was fervently intent on justifying a forecast of £3.45 million for 1969. Why should he want to keep a minnow like Walton Heath Golf Club?

Unlike the Carrs he had no passion for the game to influence his judgment, although he did come to the heath to play. As we have noted, he stopped the match-play championship. He also decided to get rid of the club.

It was the end of the Carr era, although Clive succeeded his uncle both as chairman and captain of the club during the problematical three years that followed and, indeed, continued for a number of years as a *NotW* director. Thus, as his cousin William junior has pointed out to me, Clive found himself agonisingly in the middle.

Perhaps, as Colin Walpole has suggested to me, the sale would have occurred at some time anyway, even under the Carr oligarchy. More and more money would have been needed, not merely on the courses and clubhouse but on improved wages and accommodation for staff, and the club did not seem geared to generating such income.

The question posed after Riddell died 35 years ago was now being asked again: what would happen to Walton Heath Golf Club?

Sir William

The fateful year of 1969 marked the end of Sir William Carr's reign.

A Cambridge blue, scratch in his prime, Bill Carr had a distinguished war record as an artillery major before establishing himself as chairman of both News of the World *and golf club. He chaired the club for 20 years – shortish, thick set and strong; affable to play with; a powerful, forceful, often autocratic leader, enthusiastic and forthright, abundantly confident about his own beliefs.*

'He was a dictator,' members of the time have assured me. 'If he wanted something, he got it.' His son William condones the word – provided the word 'benevolent' precedes it.

Sir William presents Match-Play trophy to Harry Weetman in 1958.

He is not an easy person to know, for he has a natural shyness which gets misconstrued as 'uppishness', *wrote a columnist.*[1] He has a terrific sense of humour. His swing can be called natural: he tees up, takes a stance and hits all in one motion, and if you tee up for him you have a job to get your hand away before he connects.

One had to know how to handle Sir William. Greenkeeper Dulake had the knack. He always ensured that when the chairman was playing the holes were cut in positions likely to aid his scoring and brighten his mood!

He moved to farm in Sussex and when Murdoch's blows landed he was ill. He courageously underwent critical operations and defied medical odds for several years until he died in his mid-sixties in 1977.

[1] Anonymous, *Golf Illustrated*, Sept 23, 1954.

THE MEMBERS' CLUB

ALICK RENSHAW – the 1978 painting by Joyce Hubbard, presented to him by the members.
He played the pivotal role in negotiating to save the club and courses. After their purchase he became captain,
then the club's first president in recognition of his outstanding services.

Chapter Thirty

AT LAST, A REAL MEMBERS' CLUB
— after two years of struggle

*W*ALTON HEATH *asks its members, Shall we buy the club?* So read a national newspaper headline in 1969. Should they indeed? Rupert Murdoch of the *News of the World* was willing to grant them first option, but the price might be high and the time for decision-making short.

There were wild rumours of prospective buyers – from construction companies to Arnold Palmer. Murdoch was said to be reckoning on around £300,000 for his total Walton assets.

Throughout 1970 the club's fate tottered on tightropes as tabloid-type headlines topped stories factual or fictitious: 'Secret bidder'... 'Shock bid'... 'Houses plan'... '£275,000 shock for golf club'... 'Dollar drive that members fear'... 'Jumbo jets for Walton Heath.' According to the stories the courses might become public... or the playgrounds of some ritzy hotel and country club... and property developers were eyeing the clubhouse and the freehold of the eight-acre area near it, believing that they could demolish the former and build on the latter.

In the 'sixties interest in golf had boomed as TV and Press expanded and popularised their coverage and champions like Palmer, Nicklaus and Player became international personalities. Club memberships filled; waiting lists closed.

But within five years from 1966 social and financial upheavals had exploded like ammunition boxes in the offices of secretaries and finance committees and by no means only at golf clubs: selective employment tax, social security payments, the breathalyser, inflation.

The drink-drive law hit bar takings; members' habits changed; expansive lunches in clubhouses threatened to become memories, subscriptions would soon soar with inflation and the 200 or so new clubs formed in the 'seventies before the economic recession set in meant increased competition for established ones.

In 1964 the Walton Heath committee had told the board that the courses were becoming so congested at weekends that the membership should be curtailed, perhaps by 20%. By 1966 the directors were convinced it should be increased: more revenue was needed and they decided in principle that 100 more males 'of the right type' might be

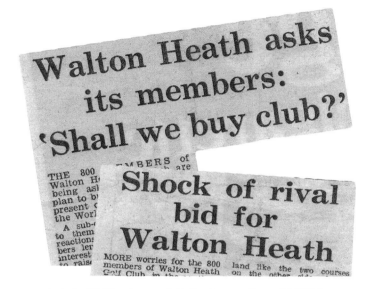

accepted. In 1967, when a deficit of more than £7,000 for the year had been forecast, a sub-committee was appointed to consider the position. Fruit machines, heaven help us, were being considered.

And now the club was to be sold! The 1970 English County Championship finals could not be accepted 'owing to the uncertain future of the club.' Everything was in suspense.

Enter now Alick Renshaw, DSO, MC. As befitted a man who, it is said, had become an acting brigadier at 28, he was an ebullient personality. He rarely spoke of his war record or decorations, got on with his confectionery business, enjoyed his golf and its social periphery and now became the club's chief negotiator and money-raiser as it jockeyed for position to buy itself.

A special negotiating committee was formed. Its first scheme was to find a syndicate of members each willing to make short-term, interest-free loans. These loans would be replaced by debentures and the contributors would pay reduced subscriptions. One notion was a large number of members each advancing up to £1,000, so that control of the club would be broad based and fairly divided.

Colin Walpole, an experienced committee man and one of Renshaw's first negotiating colleagues, recalls a narrower-based scheme along similar lines which stemmed indirectly from an opinion expressed by Dudley

Griggs, one of Murdoch's advisors, that they might well be able to buy what they needed for £125,000, which represented fair market value. This, it was said, should get them all the golfing elements of the *News of the World*'s assets and leave out of the equation the eight acres of freehold land behind the car park that property developers might covet.

Accordingly, says Colin, they set out to raise £150,000. About 14 of the wealthier members were each approached for loans of £5,000, which would total approximately half the target sum, and the bank was on side for the remainder. The approaches apparently succeeded.

At the negotiators' next meeting, Renshaw introduced James Muirie, a chartered accountant with whom he was associated. Muirie opposed offering Murdoch £125,000. 'Play him at his own game,' Colin recalls him saying. 'Never pay the asking price, offer £75,000.' On Renshaw's casting vote Muirie's plan won the day and the three who had opposed it – Walpole, Tudor Davies and Michael Easby – left the committee.

In May 1970 Murdoch informed Renshaw that an American company had made a substantial offer. According to the Press, it was planning to fly charter groups to Britain for golfing holidays and had offered £450,000. Murdoch was still giving the club first option but telling Renshaw that its offer would have to be far beyond any sum talked about so far.

Renshaw notified his members and an incensed Murdoch fired off a telegram to him: 'Astounded by your circular to Walton Heath members in view of my specific request to postpone this. If our current negotiations with prospective purchasers are in any way prejudiced as a result of your actions I must reserve my position – Murdoch.'

The new bidder materialised as Golf Inns International, a company reported to be planning two 24-bedroom blocks and, for sale, 16 detached houses on the eight freehold acres.

Then came a significant development. In July 1970 a planning application made by the *News of the World* on behalf of Golf Inns was rejected by Banstead Urban District Council ('whose chairman, I trust, will figure in the next honours list,' wrote Henry Longhurst in the *Sunday Times*!). The clubhouse, it was pointed out, was of historic and architectural interest, the density of building was considered too intense and any commercial use would be inappropriate in such a residential area.

Renshaw's committee believed that any appeal or revised application would take a long time to resolve and that Murdoch might now be sensing he had a white elephant on his hands. Battle lines were drawn up for a September meeting with Richard O'Shea, the *NotW* property manager.

They would tell O'Shea of their belief that, if competitors

such as Golf Inns were removed from the negotiations, the residents' association, which included many members, might be amenable to an appropriate, strictly residential development. In that case the club would be happy to find a suitable developer with whom they could work out a deal to retain the golf side of things.

At the meeting the club representatives, Renshaw, Guy Newton and Jack Watney, were asked their idea of a price for the courses and clubhouse area. '£100,000,' said Renshaw, '£250,000,' countered O'Shea. Soon afterwards came a letter from Murdoch: 'We will consider any offer you wish to make. However, we are not prepared to continue with our arrangement whereby you had first right of refusal.'

Early in October 1970 Renshaw submitted an offer of £150,000 for the courses, clubhouse, putting green, parking space, Artisans' clubhouse, and the secretary's and greenkeeper's houses. 'I am afraid your offer is insufficient to interest us,' replied Murdoch. 'We are negotiating to dispose of our assets at a figure very substantially in excess of the one you mentioned and as a result are unable to take this matter any further with you.'

Renshaw felt that a proposal would still come the club's way, either from the newspaper or a developer, and that in that case if the members wanted their own private club they would have to stump up their share of the cost. He was right. By the end of the year the stalemate had been broken and money had to be found.

A 'mystery buyer' headlined by the Press turned out to be Donald Betts, chairman of Lawdon, a company specialising in luxury housing. Betts was rumoured to be plan-

deposits – payable by everyone as a condition of membership and ranging up to £500 for those in the full men's category. These would be interest-free loans to the club, repayable only when a member resigned or died.

Second, there would be an issue of £75,000 of unsecured loan stock – irredeemable debentures carrying a five-percent reduction in subscriptions. Any shortfall would be covered by a bank loan.

At a special meeting on December 9, 1970, following further negotiations, the members unanimously approved that the purchase should go ahead on their behalf for £262,000. Thus, while Lawdon took up its option to purchase all the *NotW's* Walton Heath assets, the club agreed to buy all the golf elements from Lawdon. Eventually, on October 4, 1971, the deal was completed.

There were complex arrangements. The legal entity by which the purchase was made was 'Conybury, Ltd,'[1] a company formed by the negotiating committee. Its name would be changed to 'Walton Heath Golf Club Company, Ltd' once the shares of Walton-on-the-Hill Manor, Ltd and Walton Heath Golf Club Company had been acquired. The extraneous companies were then wound up. The final price paid was £260,650 and Renshaw detailed for the members that it had bought:

> Approximately 400 acres of freehold land, which includes the courses (with an automatic watering system to all greens) and land to the north and south of the Dorking Road; the clubhouse, professional's shop, dormy house, other outbuildings and four acres of freehold land on which the clubhouse stands; all fixtures, fittings and greenkeeping equipment; the freehold house in the village occupied by the deputy greenkeeper; and also, believe it or not, the village pond.[2]

The members would be Lords of the Manor. This brought with it responsibilities actual and moral: the care of the entire heath, not just the courses.

The negotiating committee, which had been acting for the club until the purchase was settled, appointed Renshaw captain and soon he would be made Walton Heath's first-ever president, an honour bestowed 'in recognition of his outstanding services' and which he was destined to hold for 10 years until his death in 1983. His popularity was such that any previous understanding that the negotiators would not serve on the committee for a limited time was over-ridden.

Alick had shouldered heavy responsibility during a period of stark uncertainty and he conscientiously drew up new bye-laws and articles of association. Son Peter remembers coming downstairs at home one morning and

ning either a sports centre or a country club replete with pool, sauna and bedrooms. However, it transpired that what he really wanted, subject to planning permission, was to build 16 to 20 £40,000 houses on the development land and that he might be willing to sell off the clubhouse and courses to the club.

Betts secured an option and his bid was said to be £500,000. The sum he demanded from the club was £275,000, and because his option had a time limit he needed a quick decision.

Vast though the asking price was, purchase would mean that the courses and facilities would be saved and moreover be the club's own rather than leased from or shared with others.

Renshaw's committee had hatched a new financial plan, which had two elements. The first involved compulsory

Newspaper report, 1977

[1] Named after the house Renshaw lived in before moving to *Stonecrop*.
[2] The pond was given to the council during the 'seventies as a public amenity. Similarly, the village green opposite the church was given to the council a few years ago.

LORDS of the MANOR of WALTON on the HILL

1878 HENRY PADWICK Purchased manor 4th July 1878

1902 MALCOLM COSMO BONSOR Purchased manor 11th August 1902

1918 SYBIL HENRIETTA BONSOR daughter of Malcolm Cosmo Bonsor

1923 SYBIL HENRIETTA RIDLEY 30th October 1923 (married name of Sybil Henrietta Bonsor)

JULIAN MARTIN SMITH and GERARD MARSHALL ARGLES as Trustees of Sybil Henrietta Ridley

1959 DUDLEY RYBOT SCHOLEY Purchased Manor in July 1959 from the Trustees of Sybil Henrietta Ridley

1967 EILEEN MARY ARMSTRONG

1973 Lordship of the Manor passed to Walton Heath Golf Club Ltd

From the complete roll of Lords of the Manor in St. Peter's Church, Walton-on-the-Hill.

finding him fast asleep amid a mass of papers he had been working on into the night. 'For the first time in the club's history the members have complete control over the club and its future,' Alick announced.

By the end of 1971, with Alec Bryant vice-captain, a new 12-man committee,[3] replete with company directors, solicitors and chartered accountants, was in place, not nominated by directors but elected by the members – that is to say, the *male* members. In effect, said Renshaw, *they* would be the directors of the golf club company. Three sub-committees were set up: finance-and-general purposes, clubhouse-and-grounds and green-and-handicapping.

They faced an arduous task, not helped by the resignation of the secretary, Lt-Col. Pat Badham, who left after seven years of service. To the temporary rescue came two members: Ken Webb, who temporarily took over as honorary secretary, and Peter Souster, recently appointed secretary of Conybury. In 1972 the cavalry arrived in the forthright form of the new secretary Bill McCrea – although 'cavalry' is a misnomer for his background was the RAF.

---

[3] C.W. Allpass, K. Birdseye, L. Joseph, H.M. Knowland, J.R. Muirie, J.E.B. Rae, L.R. St. John Scott, P.J.R. Souster, J. Thornhill, W.R. Tomkinson, K.E.R. Webb, N.P. Woodroffe.

All concerned considered the problems confronting them…

In two years the membership had dropped from 800 to 698 and the finance committee hesitated to recommend higher subscriptions for 1972/3. Up to 75 more full members were needed and applications for other categories were made welcome. Members were asked to propose and second suitable candidates as soon as possible if they wanted to put their club on a firm financial basis.

So far as the negotiating committee's plan was concerned, the members had so far contributed £243,290, but £300,000 was required initially for working capital. A further £10,000 in compulsory deposits was expected, but in difficult times some members were not finding it easy to afford their £500 (the equivalent of £3,600 today). The committee sent an ultimatum: pay your deposits within a month or cease to be members. Ten thousand pounds of the loan stock had not yet been taken up, though soon it would be fully subscribed.

Threatening to undermine the committee's plans and ambitions was the need to dance to the rhythm of inflation, which was beating ever faster. The value of a pound in 1970 would be cut by more than a quarter by the end of the decade. The five-guinea subscriptions paid by Walton

Bill McCrea – became secretary in 1972 and would hold office for 16 years.

GOOD WHILE IT LASTED

When I joined the club as a Cambridge undergrad-
uate in 1938 I was asked to pay an annual subscription of £15 and was assured that this would be 'for
ever'. This proved true until the members' club came
into being in 1971 – when my sub was increased to
the going rate!

Bob Moy, to the author

Heath members in 1903 had risen only to 30 guineas in 60
years, a 25-guinea increase; in the 10 years from 1970 they
rocketed by over £140, from £54 to £198.

Through the 'seventies and into the 'eighties the minute
books describe the roller-coaster ride of the club's fortunes
before the membership got back to 800:

1971 – Membership low and the committee are
concerned.

1973 – Membership up and the golfers complain.

1974 – Limits imposed and reintroduction of entrance
fees (additional to deposits) envisaged.

1975 – Membership shortfall 'disturbing in view of
coming subscription increases;' the deposits seen as a
deterrent to newcomers.

To that inflationary rhythm some committees tread
cautiously; others with abandon. Along the way a captain
warns that there is no hiding place in a national recession;

*The 14th of the Old. The club now owned the courses – and a report on
them by professional Busson and greenkeeper Dulake awaited the new
committee's urgent consideration.*

Alec Bryant, noting a significant cumulative deficit estimate and imminent deposit repayments, criticises what he
considers an inability to control expenditure and predicts
'inevitable financial difficulties'; in 1976 McCrea judges
the cash reserves insufficient and the see-saw continues:

1976 – Subscription increase of 33% after a three-year
standstill triggers resignations and transfers to cheaper
categories.

1979 – 'Sound financial position.'

1980 – Membership back to 800.

Meantime, in 1972, the clubhouse was due for further
reconstruction, the car park had to be extended, the
dormy house was falling apart, a new pro's shop was
needed and the bar and catering arrangements needed
examining.

Then there was golf – one had almost tended to forget
the game amid the worry and financial wrangling! The
members had been short of competitions and wanted
more. A detailed survey of the courses prepared by professional Busson and greenkeeper Dulake awaited urgent
consideration.

Yes, a members' club at last – but with all the problems
of that genre!

LADY CAY

BLUSH
RAMBLER

LADY CAY

UNA

WISTARIA

HIAWATHA

PARADISE

FRANCOIS
FOUCARD

VINE

CLEMATIS
MONTANA

PARADISE

ROSES

BLUSH RAMBLER

AUGUSTE
BARBIER

UNA

FRANCOIS
GUILLOT

LADY CAY

TRELLIS

PERGOLA

10 5

LAWN

TENNIS

POPLAR

The common room

Heyday – the Jekyll garden

The gate to the clubhouse

1907 –
room and bath
five shillings

DORMY HOUSE.

A DORMY House, with 16 bed and 4 bathrooms, has been erected in close proximity to the Club House, for the use of Members and their friends.

A Club has been formed, with an Annual Sub-scription of One Guinea, and all Members of the Walton Heath Golf Club can become Members on application to the Managing Director.

Members can introduce Ladies to the Dormy House on the following conditions :—

Extract from the Rules and Bye-Laws of the Dormy House Club.

BYE-LAW IV.—SUB-SECTION (h) :—

" Until further notice, a Member may introduce as a " Temporary Member his mother, wife, sister or daughter " and having done so, may also introduce one lady friend " of such relative.

" A Member introducing ladies under this Bye-Law " must personally accompany them, and he shall not " introduce more than two at the same time.

" No child under the age of 14 years shall be introduced.

" The Member introducing ladies is liable to all charges " payable by Temporary Members under this Bye-Law."

TARIFF.

					£	s.	d.
Bedroom, with Bath	...	...	...	per night	0	5	0
Tea in Bedroom	...	...	...	,, month	6	0	0
Fires ...	...	...	...		0	0	6
Inclusive Board per Day	...	...		0	12	6
,, ,, Week	...	...		3	10	0

*'Damp, damaged and dilapidated... in deplorable condition' –
a candidate for demolition*

Dormy House

"6" Rooms te	12.6	
to April 7 Bedroom Fires	14.6	
to May 8 Maid Room	4. 0.0	
" Maids Fires	2. 8.0	
Bena Pere Teas	1. 5.0	
9 to may 6 Miss Phyllis	6. 5.0	
15 Mr & Mrs Lawson	10. -	
	15. 15. 0	

*Common room, gate and (opposite page) house – Houses and Gardens
by E.L. Lutyens, Lawrence Weaver. Dilapidated house ©Crown copyright
NMR. Background: Gardens for Small Country Houses, Gertrude Jekyll
and Weaver (Country Life), 1913.*

HERBACEOUS BORDER

Chapter Thirty-one

HOME SWEET HOME
Rise and fall of the Dormy House

LUTYENS' *Dormy House* was home from home for Walton Heath golfers until progress and a changing way of life overtook it. The car turned it into an anachronism, an increase in the number of local members helped erase its *raison d'etre* and abuse of its structure by wartime residents played a shameful role. In the end, Lutyens' creation, which originally had a pantiled roof, big chimneys, white walls, green shutters and red brick quoins, became one huge millstone the Club could not support.

In its prime it boasted a Gertrude Jekyll garden, all rambling roses, foxgloves and summer fragrance, with a gate to the clubhouse. There were 16 bedrooms, a common room, three sitting rooms, four bathrooms and a kitchenette, plus quarters for a house steward – for many years, until he retired in 1937, Twigg, who at other times was Lord Riddell's personal valet. When it opened in 1906 members could pay a guinea to join a 'Dormy House Club' and could have a room and bath for five shillings a night.

Ladies? Absolutely not! Well, not at first. Within a year the doors to the male bastion were broken down:

> A member may introduce as a temporary member his mother, wife, sister or daughter and, having done so, may also introduce one lady friend of such relative...

By 1913 the members could *'also introduce one lady friend.'* What, she didn't even have to be a friend of a relative? Could the directors really mean this? Scandalous! But it was good for gossip and opportunists!

The building as one sees it now was used as a dormy house for not much more than a quarter of its 97-year history. After 1927 it became Riddell's private *Walton Heath House*, and although, following his death, the club bought the freehold and re-opened it for business in 1936, the writing was now clearly on Lutyens' elegant walls. By 1939 the roof had needed re-tiling, income was low and the room rate, which had risen to 10 shillings, was discounted to 7s 6d. By the end of that season the directors had had enough: the place was a liability and would have to be sold.

But the day that decision was made World War II began. The house was requisitioned, first for wartime use and

The Dormy House – by Lutyens.

afterwards by Banstead Council for urgently needed housing accommodation. Not until 1958 was it released, damp, damaged and dilapidated.

There were plans to make it into flats and maisonettes – or for demolishing it. Indeed, applications for demolition were made – and as the house was a listed building, the idea met with predictable horror from Lutyens lovers and Edwardian conservationists.

In 1972, Mike Holloway reported that it was in 'deplorable' condition. 'Any building can be restored,' he told the board, 'but what will it cost and can we get our money back?' Soon the answers came: renovation might cost £109,500 or more, while receipts from selling 99-year leases for six flats could reach £115,000. The equation was too close for comfort; plans for renovation were abandoned and the possibility of demolition returned.

The last rites were performed in 1974, when Michael Page Developments of Banstead finalised purchase of the freehold for £51,000, plus a further percentage of any selling proceeds above £165,000. Thus, the club effectively recouped 20-per-cent of what it had cost to buy the courses and clubhouse. But for nostalgists – not to mention those seeking refuge from the breathalyser – it was all rather sad. If, when next you pass *Dormy House* at night, you hear golfers carousing, rounds being re-played verbally or thirsty throats calling 'Twigg!,' it is only the ghosts.

9

8

Chapter Thirty-two

MOTORWAY INVASION
New holes for Old... and a u-turn on others

THE BRAVE BIRTH of the members' club synchronised with the sad saga of the motorway. The prospect of incursion had been simmering for years and now it had come to a head. Action on new holes had taken shape in the *News of the World* era, with secretary Badham to the fore; responsibility then passed to the new regime.

The villain threatening to invade was the M25, carving its roaring way in a vast circle between the Dartford Tunnel and Heathrow Airport. Various routes were proposed, argued against, inquired into, re-considered, revised or regurgitated. All would revolutionise the local environment; two threatened to slice the courses in half.

The club voiced its opposition. Henry Longhurst, pink gin no doubt at his elbow, wrote a blistering attack against authority – a piece characteristic in phraseology but extreme in its force.

Thankfully, the route finally decided was the least intrusive. The New course escaped unscathed but gruesome deeds were done on the Old: the ninth hole was destroyed and the eighth lost its green. The M25 section was not completed until the 'eighties, but the replacement holes were pronounced fit for play in the summer of 1973.

In the editor's view, here is a case for really camping on the Minister's doorstep. A Luddite at heart when it comes to that most lethal of weapons called a car, he will never, God willing, see the case for raping the countryside with a concrete ribbon of death, particularly when to do so means taking a yard of the land that the Almighty, with a little temporal help from Fred Dulake, so thoughtfully provided for His other golfing creatures.

Peter Ellis, *The Artisan Golfer*, 1968

The new eighth green had to be brought back 100 yards; accordingly, to sustain the hole as a par five, so had the tee. Ten years later, moving, lifting, re-surfacing and installing proper drainage were carried out entirely by the club's own staff. Today the hole still has critics, although others think its green the best on the course. Most of the greens are underpinned by only a shallow layer of earth over the clay; the eighth, says Bill McCrea, closely involved at the time, was given a 'stone carpet' and remains the only complete green built to modern specifications.

US AGAINST THEM

It is the old story of 'Us against Them' again, with 'Them' a certain winner in the end. The irony of it is that what has opened up the fun of golf to hundreds of thousands who never had it before may in the end become one of its principal enemies, namely the motor car.

The car, however, is the sacred cow of British industry and everything appears to be geared to producing as many cars as possible... more and more motors, more and more roads radiating out of bigger 'conurbations' to let the trapped citizens escape to no longer existent countryside or go and listen to their transistors on the oil-fouled beaches.

The roads are bound to drive through more and more golf courses, which are vulnerable to the argument, in the planner's jargon, of 'under-utilisation.' Such is the mentality which we have to put up with. Now on the list is Walton Heath. No doubt an inquiry will be

politely held and the 'Inspector' will duly report. Whatever he recommends, however, it will later be announced that 'the Minister' has decided to go ahead with the scheme. The fact that he, or she, has never been there and knows nothing whatever about it and is merely signing a paper placed before him or her originating from the original planners in the Ministry will be neither disclosed nor admitted.

The two great charms of Walton are the fact that the turf is as nearly seaside as you are likely to find inland and the sense of remoteness and 'away from it all' that you get when playing there, so near to London. The first will remain; the second, when the 'wind on the heath, brother' brings on its wings the roar of the motorway and the stench of diesel, will be destroyed. Who cares? More and more people will get nowhere faster and faster.

HENRY LONGHURST

M25 skirting the course, having necessitated the new eighth and holes. Inset: It could have been worse. Alternative routes might cut the courses area in two.

As for the new ninth, it was built well to the right of its 440-yard predecessor and measured a few yards shorter. At the start it was considered sub-standard. When its green was re-orientated and extended, many, like McCrea, came to regard it as an acceptable short par four. For the traditionalists nothing has compensated for losing the original hole.

So much for the ravages of the M25. What of the rest of the Old course?

One of Alick Renshaw's first acts when the members' club became a reality in 1971 had been to order a report from Harry Busson, and the professional, having consulted greenkeeper Dulake, urged sundry changes, largely concerning bunkers, which he considered 'most necessary to keep in line with present-day design.' Various alterations were promptly made, including the decommissioning of bunkers to save maintenance and the building of new ones – not all in the traditional Walton Heath style.

Two of Busson's proposals raised members' eyebrows. First, having stressed that both courses needed rest, he persuaded Renshaw's committee to close the Old on weekdays throughout the 1971/2 winter. Second, he ignited a controversy which lingers to this day: *'The first hole should be played from in front of the road as a par three.'*

The first had traditionally been played as a short par four, requiring a tee-shot over Deans Lane. Some thought it dangerous because, apart from any risk to people using the lane, a bad slice with a driver could reach the increasingly busy Dorking Road which isolated it from the other holes on the heath. Not that Walton Heath members sliced like that, they hastened to add, but what about those society chaps? Busson's par-three idea was not immediately accepted, but it would come home to roost in the dim and distant future – almost two decades later, in fact.

Meanwhile the first was part of another problem. As a four the first measured about 300 yards, the third was also a short par four, while the second and fourth were longer fours but of similar length to each other. Boards and committees over the years had sought ways and means of varying and improving this sequence.

In 1979, captain John Woods and Bill McCrea pushed for reconsideration of one of those ideas: building a new third green to give a short hole of about 150-165 yards, permit extension of the fourth to 520 and bring various other advantages.

The proposal went to the agm and was carried by 43 votes to 36 – but hardly had the ink dried on the minutes than an omission from the published bye-laws and a discrepancy between them and the articles of association were uncovered. The bye-laws required any resolution calling for material course alterations to obtain 'yes' votes

from at least 75-per-cent of members at a general meeting, but through a printing error in the latest edition this had been left out. The club's solicitor advised the committee that in these circumstances they could not proceed.

Within months of that setback, in 1980, McCrea was urging the need for an architect to study the course and recommend improvements. Meanwhile, he was personally targeting the par-four 15th. It was, he thought, insufficiently challenging to top players; the cross-bunker in front of the green was ineffective and the green featureless.

Architect Donald Steel surveyed the course and his recommendations for the 15th, approved by the committee, went to the agm, where there were strong objections to, among other things, reducing the width of the cross-bunker and planting trees between the 15th and 16th. The resolution to change the hole was carried by 105-18, but only provided that the changes to which the members objected would not be implemented. The other plans – notably a right-hand bunker 240 yards from the tee alongside the ridge and another at greenside starting immediately in front of the grass mound – were given the go-ahead. The revised hole was ready for play during 1981.

Meantime, some compensation for the motorway changes was being received. Recompense for the cost of reconstructing holes and, from the contractors, money for building an amenity bank to shield the course from the sight and noise of the traffic would eventually total nearly £200,000. By 1984 the committee were planning to use the income, or a decent part of it, to improve the courses.

There were other reasons why it seemed timely to propose changes and one was a young man named Clive Osgood. Dulake had died in 1978 and, after a brief spell under Harry Emery, Osgood had been promoted to take over the following year – not without some misgivings because some committee men thought him too young for the job at 28.

As a schoolboy Osgood had caddied for Christy Green in

Clive Osgood became head greenkeeper in 1979, working out of the old sheds in the dip to the left of the 2nd (Old).

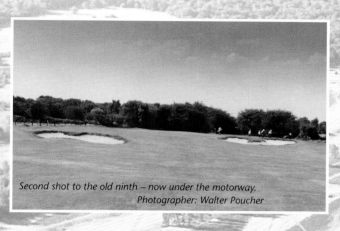

Second shot to the old ninth – now under the motorway.
Photographer: Walter Poucher

The work begins.

Reverse-angle reprise of the 'motorway' end of the course.

Remains of the old ninth and its replacement both visible in the 'seventies before the motorway finally drove in.

Replacement 9th

Original 9th

Altered 8th

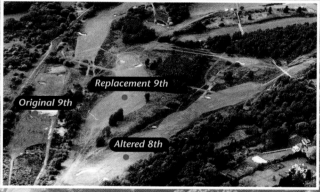

Playing to the new eighth green, but again before the M25 arrived.
Photographer: Walter Poucher

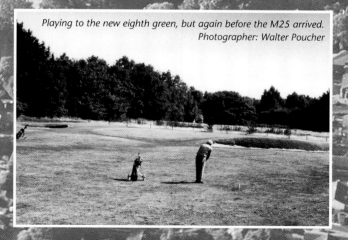

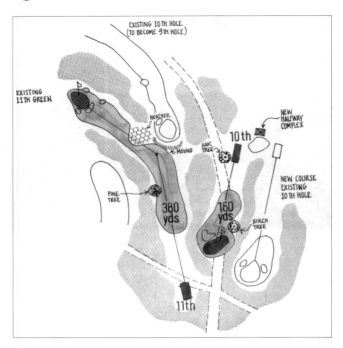

The proposal was to abandon the hole and have the entire course the southern side of the Dorking Road, where it was whispered that a new clubhouse might be built. The second hole would become the first; a new short hole, a reincarnation of Fowler's 'Port Arthur,' would be built after the present 10th; the existing 11th would be converted from par three to par four.

At a general meeting on September 15, 1984, the scrapping of the first hole was agreed by 248 votes to 64, a majority of nearly 80%. Work then proceeded on the new 10th and 11th.

Meanwhile a hush fell on any dialogue about further upheavals, at least to the Old. The club had other things to worry about locally[1] and anyway, at least in the view of captain Keith Way in 1990, the quality of the courses had been put at risk in some years by the green staff having to spend too much time constructing new holes.

Osgood and his men had assuredly had their own problems, from the eradication of a 15-year build-up of thatch, through two years of drought in the mid-seventies and another drought in 1982 to the hurricane of 1987, when more than 2,000 trees on the manor lands were blown down and others damaged.

Less than 100 of the trees were within or near the playing areas, but the staff spent much of the winter helping to remove the debris. A paper company came along offering to take it all away and to pay the club £2 per tonne – 'a windfall,' said outgoing captain Tom Corrigan!

In 1988 bracken, silver birch saplings and alien grasses were gaining ground and threatening to choke the heather... The following summer heat scorched the greens... Gales caused more damage...

In 1990 both courses were closed for two weeks due to snow and a slow thaw, the rabbits of Banstead Heath were damaging holes to the east, horses had scarred the eighth green and protected areas of woodland were again encroaching to the detriment of heath and heather. In June there was a drought; at the end of July rain flooded the greens...

In the early 1990s came successive acts of vandalism: burnt-out stolen cars dumped, equipment stolen and sheds broken into. The staff had other responsibilities, too, not least the preparation of a practice ground on Beechams Field and the establishing of a turf nursery. Nonetheless, in 1990, not for the first or last time, Osgood was being highly complimented on the condition of both courses.

That year came crucial happenings. Early on, shortly after the agm, work suddenly began on destroying and replacing an original Fowler drive bunker to the left of the 10th fairway. Traditionalists were incensed. They felt the

a Match-Play semi-final, came on the staff in 1966 when he was 15, joined the Artisans as a junior and got down to four. He represented Surrey as a colt, played artisan golf at national level, fancied himself as a future Open champion but transferred his ambitions to greenkeeping before disillusionment could set in.

'Things were primitive at Walton in my young days,' Clive recalls. 'We worked out of the old stable block. Now I sit here in our modern greenkeeping compound with computers, security cameras and so forth and I often think back to Fred Dulake and wonder where he would have parked his bike on which he toured the course!'

Clive and his wife Sue, who used to work in the clubhouse, have three children and his son won the club juniors' Ken Macpherson Trophy when he was 14.

He learned his craft under Dulake and had no formal qualifications, yet now respect for his experience and skill as Walton Heath's course manager is such that he was made chairman of the British and International Greenkeepers' Association recently and frequently speaks at conferences and seminars. He has given talks in the States, Canada, Germany, Portugal and Scandinavia.

Back in the 'eighties his and McCrea's work on the eighth green of the Old and the 18th of the New had convinced the committee that the club could handle the planned alterations in-house. If this proved correct it would considerably reduce the estimated cost of £80,000 spread over seven years.

Bernard Holloway, the 1984 captain, felt that the new plans formed 'the most important matter considered by any committee since the members' club's formation.' He and his colleagues explained their main targets:

The weakest hole must be the first, surrounded by roads and houses and where all the golf traffic of both courses, as well as the road traffic using Deans Lane, passes continually between tee and green.

---

[1] Chapter 36.

replacement, 20 or 30 yards nearer the green, was totally alien to the Walton Heath style: laterally aligned and no test at all compared with those presented by a 'Fowler grave.'

Moreover, they said, this was a material alteration and no resolution proposing it had ever been put to the members – when it would have needed 75% support.

Next, in early summer, the new layout opened for play and was doomed to failure. Quite apart from the bunker fracas many members did not like the new holes; they wanted to return to the old order of things!

At the 1991 agm a committee resolution seeking retrospective approval of the bunker change failed and a year later, in February 1992, retiring captain David Barber put forward a special resolution:

> That use of the present 10th hole on the Old course be suspended; that the present 11th hole be reinstalled as a par three of approximately 189 yards and additional teeing ground be constructed; and that the hole east of Deans Lane and north of the Dorking Road be reinstated – as a par three, numbered one, and additional teeing ground be constructed.

After occasionally heated discussion the resolution, seconded by incoming captain Patrick Webb, was carried by 127 votes to 24 with one abstention. Thus, the ambitious and costly plans for a complete course south of the road rapidly came to naught.

So the course officially reverted to its previous form. The old bunker had been recreated and to this day is known by the cognoscenti in bar and lounge as 'Coombes' Tomb' – after Bob, in whose year of captaincy the deed was done!

The ill-fated, short-lived bunker under construction to the left of the 10th (Old).

Since the inception of the members' club tens of thousands of words had been spoken and many more written about plans for changes to Fowler's original course. Yet in the early 'nineties Michael Holloway, charged with compiling a file of past major policy decisions on all subjects, concluded that so far as the Old course was concerned – and omitting the 'motorway' holes which were forced on the club – the only major changes made in the last 20 years had been the bunkering of the 15th and the reduction in length of the first to a par three.

Everything else had been dismissed, outvoted or rescinded. Much ado about nothing!

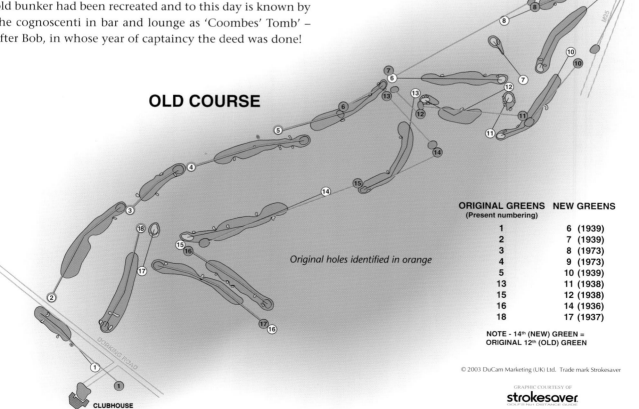

OLD COURSE

Original holes identified in orange

ORIGINAL GREENS (Present numbering)	NEW GREENS
1	6 (1939)
2	7 (1939)
3	8 (1973)
4	9 (1973)
5	10 (1939)
13	11 (1938)
15	12 (1938)
16	14 (1936)
18	17 (1937)

NOTE - 14th (NEW) GREEN = ORIGINAL 12th (OLD) GREEN

© 2003 DuCam Marketing (UK) Ltd. Trade mark Strokesaver

GRAPHIC COURTESY OF
strokesaver
GOLF'S No1 DISTANCE GUIDE

CLUBHOUSE

DORKING ROAD

M25

Chapter Thirty-three

RETURN OF THE PROFESSIONALS
The European Open arrives and the customers pay at last

IN OCTOBER 1978, after nine years of abstinence, Walton Heath again began to drink its fill of professional golf. The first taste of it was the initial European Open, and £16,000 was negotiated for staging it: small beer by today's standards but at the time, it was claimed, a national record.

To lapse into the modern vernacular, it looked a 'nice little earner' for the Club at the right time. 'A major sponsored tournament would hopefully help stem the remorseless rise in subscriptions in this age of inflation,' captain Sir Patrick Macrory had stated 18 months previously.

Behind the championship was Sven Tumba, a 46-year-old Swede who had helped his country to three world ice-hockey titles, represented it at soccer and played golf internationally both as an amateur and a professional. Tumba was 'championship president' and Jack Nicklaus's name was bandied about as 'chairman of the advisory board.'

Tumba planned a 72-hole championship that he hoped would become the world's fifth 'major.' It would be multi-sponsored and £105,000 prize money would make it Europe's richest stroke-play tournament except for the Open. Qualifying rounds would be played locally, but sundry exemptions were in place to ensure entry by the world's top players.

The course was to be a composite, embracing 15 holes from the Old and three from the New. It began with the Old's second and fourth, the latter being played as a 520-yard par-five; then came the holes normally numbered five to 13. From there the 12th and 13th of the New were taken in; then back to the Old until a final switch to the New's 18th.

'The famous Walton Heath finish has lost nothing by using the last hole of the New to minimise traffic distractions behind the green,' claimed captain Cyril Hewertson.

Photographer Poucher captures American Al Geiberger hitting his second shot to the eighth hole of the composite course (the 10th of the Old) in 1978.

...cked grandstands and paying crowds... what a contrast with the old ...e shows of challenge matches and match-play championships! Andrew ...rray holing out to win the 1989 European Open.
Photographer: PHIL SHELDON

Most commentators felt that the first European Open was a worthwhile enterprise. Maybe this feeling comes partly, more than we may realise, from the something extra which playing over the admirable golfing ground of Walton Heath gave it ... or maybe it comes more from the concept itself, with its own healthy internationalism of scope? Perhaps a beginning of a new kind of inter-European identity, some kind of vaguely sensed European nationalism?

John Stobbs, for *Par Golf*, 1979

Various tees were built or changed and it all added up to 7,130 yards, par 73, Walton's longest course so far. 'Fantastic,' said America's Tom Weiskopf, a budding designer himself.

The old place looked as never before: spectator stands, TV towers, scoreboards, a Press centre, hospitality tents, a trade exhibition, car parking on the first of the Old and refreshment tents on the first of the New.

Most significantly, Ministerial authority had been obtained to erect temporary fencing on the heath and to rope off the playing area. Thus, for the first time, admission could be controlled, charges made and undesirables and dogs sent packing. Moreover, secretary McCrea explained, the club was now authorised to enclose the area of the courses for one seven-day period each year. It was all

a vivid contrast from the days of the old matches when hordes surged over the fairways for a free show.

Twenty-five US tour players, including USPGA champion John Mahaffey, Tom Kite and Gil Morgan, third on the world money list that year, competed, and Ballesteros and Faldo, fierce rivals at the time, were among 75 Europeans.

Ballesteros lost his clubs, borrowed some and missed the cut. Faldo set off as though on auto-pilot with a 68 and 70 to lead Weiskopf by a stroke, then turned into a helpless roller-coaster passenger in the third round before holing the 191-yard 17th in one with a six-iron All this left him with a 75 for an aggregate of 213 and a three-stroke deficit behind the new leader, Australia's Greg Norman.

On a glorious fourth day two strokes covered the top 12 as the leaders reached the turn. The unlikely pace-setter was another American, Bobby Wadkins, a young man deep in the shadow of his elder brother Lanny and averaging about $25,000 a year on a US tour when Tom Watson was winning over $360,000. Out in 33, he finished in 68, nine under par for the championship.

Who could catch or beat him? Not Malcolm Gregson... nor Faldo... nor Mac McLendon. All three had had chances to tie. Gil Morgan? He came to the final hole needing a birdie to draw level and got it.

In the last group Norman and the Scot Bernard Gallacher also had chances. Gallacher needed a par to tie

The 1978 play-off. Bobby Wadkins plays his second shot to the 16th. Bernard Gallacher and Gil Morgan look on. A painting by John Young.

Exit Parliament, enter Gold Vase

In 1972 the new committee received a sad farewell note and an invitation too good to refuse.

The farewell message came from the Parliamentary Golfing Society. After 37 successive visits and following the 1973 event it was taking the prized Parliamentary Handicap away from Walton Heath. The society's history states intriguingly that the move was made 'following the purchase of the club by its members from Rupert Murdoch's News of the World.'

The invitation came from the editor of Golf Illustrated. Would Walton Heath be interested, he wondered, in becoming the stage for Britain's most important 36-hole amateur competition apart from the championships? If so, and if it could hold the 1973 event,

there was £150 in it for the club – yes, as much as that.

The competition was the Golf Illustrated Gold Vase, a stroke-play event over 60 years old and won by champions like Bobby Jones, Harold Hilton, Cyril Tolley and Roger Wethered. For the last 21 years it had been held at Sunningdale and before that at various courses, including, on three occasions, Walton Heath.

In 1913 the winner was Abe Mitchell, soon to give up his amateur status, become personal pro to Samuel Ryder and model for the figure on top of the Cup; in 1929, Douglas Grant, a stone-deaf Californian who helped design Pebble Beach; in 1934, Lister Hartley, more often associated with Chislehurst but this time entered as Walton Heath.

Now, nearly 40 years later, came this nicely timed invitation. The Gold Vase would, in effect, replace the Handicap – not in political relationships but, hopefully, in golfing excellence. Walton became its permanent home for 16 years.

Altogether, as I write, the club has staged 26 Gold Vase tournaments. A less impressive statistic is that, although Iain Carslaw and Stephen Keppler won in the 'eighties (in successive years) and Mark James (no relation to the former Ryder Cup man) in the 'nineties, Walton Heath entrants have captured the Vase only four times[1] in the event's 90 – odd years – and never away from home!

[1] Bernard Darwin (1919) also won but entered as Woking.

but hit a woeful drive that barely reached the fairway; Norman, needing a birdie, struck a beauty. The ultimate scenario was that Norman missed the putt he needed and Gallacher, requiring a chip and a putt, succeeded. For the second time, following the long-ago *Daily Mail* event, a professional tournament at Walton had yielded a three-way tie.

By the time Wadkins, Morgan and Gallacher reached the green on the 16th, the first play-off hole, Morgan was out of it. Wadkins had struck a three-iron to a yard or so while Gallacher was within about six feet. Gallacher missed, Wadkins holed. It was the American's first tournament win and he pocketed £18,000 – riches beyond belief!

The course, claimed Hewertson, had emerged 'undefeated by the greatest golfers of the day in a championship that will bear comparison with anything anywhere. That the leaders after four rounds without any Walton Heath wind were not lower than 283 indicates that the modern experts found it, in their way, just as challenging as Vardon, Braid and Taylor had 75 years before.'

Hewertson's eulogy was not unanimously shared by neutrals. The greatest golfers had not competed; and although the course was handsomely praised, a few critics saw in the play-off trio's nine under par a hint that things might profitably be slightly toughened.

Whatever the rights and wrongs, competitors returning for the 1980 championship (it had been held at Turnberry in 1979) found the course subtly tighter and par 72. In the pro-am early in the week America's Keith Fergus promptly

hit a driver and five-iron pin-high from the new tee at the 521-yard 11th and went through the green at the 554-yard 14th with a drive and a seven-iron. He was rewarded for his insolence by failure to make the cut in the championship.

The event was nearly not played. The 1978 organisers had accepted the club's criticisms of their publicity and financial controls, but more problems arose.

Tom Kite – 1980 champion.

dropped and the rain returned, the course completely changed. Tom Kite, out in 31 (five under par), had been forced to take refuge from the storm for half-an-hour and over the finishing holes the howling wind swept rain on to his spectacles. Yesterday he had used a driver and a short iron at the 18th; now he had to hit what he described as one of the three-woods of his life to reach the green and help him to a 67.

On the third day, in a fresh, gusting wind, when Kite (71) got within a stroke of Hinkle, only two players broke 70 and on the fourth only one did so. It was all a reminder that you can never take Walton Heath for granted.

> The heather and bracken can break your heart, not to mention your wrists, and the fairway bunkers are true hazards, *wrote Peter Dobereiner in The Observer*. The possibility of disaster therefore looms on every hole and the sheer length of the course precluded any possibility of playing safely with pawky iron shots off the tees.

Lyle, third overnight, showed himself a man at sixes and sevens on the final day. At Turnberry he had scored six birdies in the first seven; now he dropped seven shots in the first six. Hinkle had a 77 and, having three-putted the last green when two putts would have tied, he did not attend the prize-giving to receive his cheque for the second place he shared with another American, Leonard Thompson.

The winner was Kite, who kept the ball in play and showed a sensitive touch on the greens, but even he was two over par for the round, with not a single birdie, to complete his 284. Like Hinkle, he three-putted the final green, assisted on his second attempt by a three-tone car horn no doubt operated by the ghost of the dear lady who had disturbed Fred Daly a quarter of a century previously.

The tournament's problems continued. Attendances early on had been disappointing and sundry reasons were mooted: apart from publicity concerns and the absence of the top Americans, the British players, to plagiarise Damon Runyan, had collapsed like concertinas. For a second time the club felt the tournament organisation unsatisfactory.

Even *Private Eye* commented on the tournament's debts. Douglas Thomson recalls that at close of play the club had

'Payments of the facility fee were phased over preceding periods and we had difficulty in collecting them punctually,' Douglas Thomson, captain in 1981, recalls. 'By the time of the final payment date we had to give an ultimatum. On the Sunday prior to the event it was "No cheque by midday Monday, no tournament".' The cheque arrived. 'Tumba and his board of management have been forced to underwrite the event in its difficult first two years, but the future now looks assured,' a *Daily Telegraph* correspondent had reported.

Bookmakers made Ballesteros, the Masters champion, favourite, followed by America's Curtis Strange, while the defending champion was Sandy Lyle. First to produce something special, though, was a 15-stone American, Lon Hinkle, who insulted the course with a second-round 65 (32 out, 33 in), eight under par!

The weather, wrote John Hennessey in *The Times*, 'provided a benign morning, a stormy afternoon and a soft, sunny evening when all the leaders except Hinkle were back in the clubhouse looking for drying facilities and cures for frostbite.' Hinkle was delayed 25 minutes by lightning and played 12 holes in wind and rain before the sun came through and the wind dropped. He chipped in for an eagle at the long second and had eight birdies. With a 12-under 134 he led by four strokes.

As the wind swung 180 degrees, the temperature

> I remember thinking in 1980 that the members' club was beginning its second development stage. The early shortage of members and money had eased, the committee system was working quite well and the club was beginning to control its own destiny. Certainly, with the European Open and the imminent Ryder Cup, its reputation as a top championship course had been revived.
>
> Peter Renshaw, 1980 captain, to author.

196

outstanding accounts of between £6,000 and £8,000 and minutes indicate that in August 1981 it was still owed just under £7,000. Douglas finally received payment after attending a meeting of creditors in the West End – but not before he and McCrea had been asked to go for a drink and a sandwich while the cheque was cleared. 'After the 1981 tournament at Hoylake, it all settled down on a more stable basis,' he says.

The committee now felt the club needed a rest from European Opens. Nevertheless, after Sunningdale had held the event five times, Walton Heath made a six-year agreement to stage the event in alternate years.

Accordingly, the championship returned in 1987 (by which time Panasonic had become its sponsor), 1989 and 1991. The champions naturally deserved their wins but did not always have the names or pedigrees for which the organisers and sponsors would have prayed. The first was Paul Way, who had stood 136th on the Order of Merit; then came Andrew Murray, whose future was threatened

Tented village – modest by 2003 standards but a revolution at Walton Heath more than 20 years ago.

Paul Way – winner in 1987.

by spondylitis, a disease of the joints, but who courageously led from start to finish and clinched things with his first sub-70 round of the year.

The 1991 champion came with impressive credentials: the Australian Mike Harwood, runner-up in the most recent Open and winner of the previous year's Volvo PGA and Masters events. On a par-72 course and on a sunny, windless final day, he stormed home with a 65. This gave him an 11-under-par aggregate and earned him £83,330 from a prize fund that had by now reached £500,000.

As for facility fees, the record £16,000 the club had negotiated back in 1978 now looked very small beer. By 1989 it was £70,000 plus a share of the gate and two years later the committee, authorised by the membership to negotiate, were telling Birchgrey, the promoters, that they would be willing to have the event at Walton every third year for £200,000 or a sum equal to the first prize, whichever was greater.

But the tournament did not return. In 1992 Birchgrey told the club that they were sorry but they were leaving Walton. The championship moved first to East Sussex National. Not only was that club not charging a fee, it was paying for the privilege of being the venue. Golf was being transformed commercially just as it had been changing socially.

Overleaf: Storm, sunshine and umbrellas combine to bring their own pictorial drama to the 1981 Ryder cup.
Photographer: PHIL SHELDON

Chapter Thirty-four

GREATEST-EVER AMERICAN TEAM?
Nicklaus, Watson, Trevino, Miller, Irwin...the 1981 Ryder Cup

THE PROFESSIONAL GOLFERS' ASSOCIATION planned to hold the 1981 Ryder Cup match on their own doorstep – on the Brabazon course at their new headquarters at the Belfry Hotel near Birmingham. That set the cat among the pigeons. Critics complained that the course, four years young, would not be ready; players joined in the clamour; Brian Barnes described the Brabazon as not much more than a ploughed field and was fined for his cheek. The PGA, though, saw the light.

So where *should* the match be played? A powerful influence in answering that question was Lord Aldington, chairman of the sponsoring company, Sun Alliance. He was an ardent admirer of Walton Heath – wouldn't you be if you had won the Parliamentary Handicap there four times and incidentally under four different names or titles![1] Two years before the event, an invitation to stage the match arrived at Deans Lane. The committee accepted 'in principle.' 'We then had to sit on the news for six months while the PGA extricated themselves from their commitment,' John Woods, the 1979 captain, recalls.

Eventually the match was accepted unconditionally for September 18-20, 1981. The facility fee, secretary McCrea recalls, was a mere £6,000, plus deals embracing badges for members and a percentage of revenue from tickets sold via the club. Walton Heath, in return, agreed to pay the PGA a similar sum of £6,000 for the exclusive right to sell golf merchandise around the course, the profits to be shared as agreed with professional Ken Macpherson.

The choice of Walton Heath was generally welcomed. 'A course which this country can be proud to introduce to an American team,' commented Peter Ryde in *The Times*. There was even a suggestion that small, unreceptive greens allied with fast-running heathland might negate the Americans' formidable iron play.

The composite course, measuring 7,067 yards, was essentially the same as for the first two European Opens, the one hole toughened being the Old's 15th. The match, with the eyes of the golfing world on it, was a major challenge to the club and not least to greenkeeper Osgood, less than two years in the job.

Britain and Ireland had not once won the Ryder Cup in the last 20 years and, pragmatically disregarding Samuel

The United States team – 36 major titles between them.

Ryder's original decrees, both sides had agreed to move the goalposts – even if that meant mixing metaphors. America's opponents now were not Britain and Ireland but Europe. The only such match so far had been in West Virginia and the States had still won, by 17-11.

To state the obvious, Europe's selectors – non-playing captain John Jacobs, Neil Coles and team-member Bernhard Langer - needed their strongest team. Faced with picking the last two players to supplement the top ten on the European money list, they proceeded to drop Tony Jacklin and Seve Ballesteros – the former presumably because of form and his unease when playing partnership golf, the latter following a wrangle over appearance money for tournaments and his absence from European events for much of the season.

The team lists made a vivid contrast. Europe had Bernhard Langer, Peter Oosterhuis, Mark James, Nick Faldo, Sandy Lyle, Bernard Gallacher, Eamonn Darcy, Des Smyth, Howard Clark, Sam Torrance and two Spaniards, Jose-Maria Canizares and Manuel Pinero. None of them had ever won a major and Faldo and Lyle were still in their early twenties, not the champions they would become.

The United States, with Dave Marr as non-playing captain, fielded Tom Watson (current Masters champion), Bill Rogers (Open champion), Larry Nelson (USPGA champion), Jack Nicklaus, Ray Floyd, Hale Irwin, Lee Trevino, Johnny Miller, Jerry Pate, Ben Crenshaw, Bruce Lietzke and Tom Kite. Only the last three had not won a major (and

---
[1] Brig, A.R.W.Low, MP (1949); A.R.W.Low, MP (1957); Sir Toby Low, MP (1960); Lord Aldington (1973).

was Nicklaus's last Ryder Cup match as a player. He won all his four atches, including three in partnership with Tom Watson.
Photographer: PHIL SHELDON

Left: Canizares drives, Smyth looks on.
Below: Sam Torrance.
Photographer: PHIL SHELDON

Crenshaw and Kite would subsequently do so) and the others had 36 between them. Surely no stronger side had ever been chosen?

European followers found crumbs of comfort in the urbane Mr. Marr's pre-match summing-up, which was good public relations stuff and may even have been sincere: 'We're gonna be in a dog fight for three days – and it's not the size of the dog that counts, it's the size of the *fight* in the dog!'

Osgood's work could scarcely have been worse hindered. At times before or during the three days vandals attacked one of the greens, cloudbursts soaked the course and submerged greens and an estimated 6,000 gallons of water were pumped out of the tented village. Yet everything was completed on schedule.

The first day, attended by 10,500 spectators, was hit by showers and thunderstorms, but the morning foursomes began well for Europe. As the first of the four matches approached the turn the home team were up in three and down in one. By the end, though, Europe and the States were tied with two points each.

Now for the afternoon fourballs. Jacobs had seen his strongest pair, Oosterhuis and Faldo, take a grip on Watson and Nicklaus in the morning, then lose it. The Americans, two down after four holes, had won five in a row from the seventh, including three birdies. Jacobs promptly left out both British players.

In giving a chance to those omitted from the foursomes, he made another controversial decision, pairing an apparently nervous Canizares with Smyth against Rogers and Lietzke. This proved inspired matchmaking, for the Spaniard and the Irishman won by six and five. It had been a bad day for the two Americans but an outstanding one for Smyth, who for the second time had played superbly to win.

Europe's other double winners on the day were Lyle and

James, who beat Pate and Crenshaw three and two. Four times Lyle holed from more than 20 feet, he and his partner had five birdies in seven holes from the seventh and they finished their 16 holes with a better-ball score of eight under par.

This leaves two matches: Torrance and Clark against Kite and Miller and Gallacher and Darcy playing Irwin and Floyd.

Torrance and Clark, clambering back from two down to all-square, had a chance of victory at the last hole where Torrance had a 10-footer for a birdie. The ball hit the cup and stayed out, so their contest, wherein both pairs had better-ball scores of 65, was tied. Europe, then, were assured of a lead at the end of the day.

Gallacher and Darcy also had been two down – in their case with seven to play – but by the time they came to the 15th the match was level, Gallacher having holed a big putt for an eagle at the previous hole. That the entire American team sensed that they were indeed in a dog fight was evident when they appeared *en masse* through the rain to watch and encourage. They were rewarded by seeing Floyd, strong man of his partnership with Irwin, score birdies at both the 16th and 17th (making six for him in all) and gain the States their only win of the afternoon.

So after the first day the Europeans led 4½-3½. That evening Marr acted the all-American boy and, presumably straight-faced, stirred his golfing millionaires with allusions to their country's pioneers and the need now to circle the covered wagons and prepare for the next attack! As for Europe, huge satisfaction, high hopes!

Not for long! The shifts in the weather were matched by the spirits of Europe. After more heavy rain overnight the second day dawned clear and sunny, all blue skies and optimism. Later the clouds darkened, the rains returned and the Europeans struggled in their own gloom, submerged by a storming *tour de force*. Peter Dobereiner,

Left: Faldo – not yet a major champion in 1981.
Below: Nicklaus, Tom and Linda Watson watch anxiously on the first day.
Photographer: PHIL SHELDON

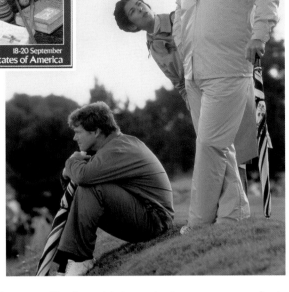

The Observer golf columnist, turned science correspondent:

Just as radio-active molecules popping off at random produce precise and predictable patterns of radiation, so team golf's individual uncertainties add up to a certainty. In the Ryder Cup there is no greater certainty than the American backlash. If you rough them up on day one, then they will hit back hard.

The backlash hurt and was ultimately fatal. The States won the morning fourballs three to one, only Langer and Pinero winning for Europe and the US winning pairs all having better-ball scores of nine under par Ah, well, that put the visitors in front by only 6½-5½, so there was still hope.

Oh, this eternal optimism! In the afternoon foursomes the Americans whitewashed us. That made their tally seven points against one on this damp and dismal day and left the pundits to search retrospectively for the crucial turning-point.

Had it been yesterday, when Floyd fought to win his fourball under the anxious eyes of his mates? There was a feeling that this was the stimulus that unleashed the visitors' team effort.

Had it been before play today, when Trevino beseeched Marr to let him partner Pate in the morning fourballs? 'Jerry's a fantastic player but a poor manager of a course. I'll do the thinking for him, I'll club him, I'll read the putts. It will be his body and my mind.' So spoke the Texan with his own brand of modesty.

Trevino's proposal had been accepted. On the first hole of the leading match Pate fired a symbolic warning to Europe with a four-iron to within inches of the hole. He scored seven birdies and he and Trevino crushed Torrance and Faldo by seven and five.

Had it been two dramatic ripostes in the next fourball? Thanks to a wonderful one-iron approach to within four inches by Lyle at the 475-yard 16th, he and James were all-square with Nelson and Kite, and when Sandy hit a six-iron again to within inches at the short 17th it surely meant the lead... whereupon Nelson coolly holed a 15-footer to halve. At the final hole it was *deja-vu*: another birdie putt from Nelson.

After a tremendous match, in which the two Europeans had struck the ball magnificently and neither pair had ever been more than one ahead, Nelson had negated Lyle's tremendous shots and turned possible defeat into victory. For the first time the visitors led in the overall match, an advantage increased when Nicklaus and Watson defeated Canizares and Smyth.

Had it been Marr's decision, with the players' compliance, to choose Nicklaus and Trevino, both 41, for the afternoon foursomes – two matches for them in the day when the intention had been one?

The Trevino/Pate and Nicklaus/Watson pairings had proceeded to win again – the former over Oosterhuis and Torrance by two and one in the closest contest of the afternoon and the latter by three and two against Langer and Pinero.

Actually, all this searching for the most significant flashpoint was academic. The overall truth was that when it came to crucial moments on greens rendered easy-paced by the rains it was the Americans who holed the putts. In the afternoon they had 'putted out of this world,' said Jacobs, and he was right. If you wanted to see nothing the place to be was the 18th green.

The Europeans, like the former British-and-Irish teams, were beginning to assume the role of gallant losers. 'My boys played their hearts out in terrible conditions,' stressed Jacobs – and again he was right.

The score after two days, then, was Europe 5½, United States 10½. Europe would need nine of the morrow's 12

The Ryder Cup Day by Day

Europe		United States	
DAY 1			
Foursomes			
B Langer/M Pinero	lost to	L Trevino/L Nelson	1 hole
A Lyle/M James	beat	B Rogers/B Lietzke	2 & 1
B Gallacher/D Smyth	beat	H Irwin/R Floyd	3 & 2
P Oosterhuis/N Faldo	lost to	T Watson/J Nicklaus	4 & 3
Fourballs			
S Torrance/H Clark	halved with	T Kite/J Miller	–
A Lyle/M James	beat	B Crenshaw/J Pate	3 & 2
D Smyth/J M Canizares	beat	B Rogers/B Lietzke	6 & 5
B Gallacher/E Darcy	lost to	H Irwin/R Floyd	2 & 1
		Match Score: Europe 4½, US 3½	
DAY 2			
Fourballs			
N Faldo/S Torrance	lost to	L Trevino/J Pate	7 & 5
A Lyle/M James	lost to	L Nelson/T Kite	1 hole
B Langer/M Pinero	beat	R Floyd/H Irwin	2 & 1
J M Canizares/D Smyth	lost to	J Nicklaus/T Watson	3 & 2
Foursomes			
P Oosterhuis/S Torrance	lost to	L Trevino/J Pate	2 & 1
B Langer/M Pinero	lost to	J Nicklaus/T Watson	3 & 2
A Lyle/M James	lost to	B Rogers/R Floyd	3 & 2
D Smyth/B Gallacher	lost to	T Kite/L Nelson	3 & 2
		Match Score: Europe 5½, US 10½	
DAY 3			
Singles			
S Torrance	lost to	L Trevino	5 & 3
A Lyle	lost to	T Kite	3 & 2
B Gallacher	halved with	B Rogers	–
M James	lost to	L Nelson	2 holes
D Smyth	lost to	B Crenshaw	6 & 4
B Langer	halved with	B Lietzke	–
M Pinero	beat	J Pate	4 & 2
J M Canizares	lost to	H Irwin	1 hole
N Faldo	beat	J Miller	2 & 1
H Clark	beat	T Watson	4 & 3
P Oosterhuis	lost to	R Floyd	1 hole
E Darcy	lost to	J Nicklaus	5 & 3
		Match Result: Europe 9½, US 18½	

singles to win, while their opponents required only four. The last rites did not take long. On a course again soaked, the first five matches sufficed.

In the first, Trevino beat Torrance five and three in two hours and ten minutes. In the second, Kite scored 10 birdies in 16 holes to defeat Lyle, who was all-square after 11, six under par to Kite's 10 when beaten and went down with his reputation honourably intact, even enhanced. Gallacher halved with Rogers but Smyth went down six and four to Crenshaw and the *coup de grace* was dealt by Larry Nelson when he beat James on the last green to register his ninth victory in nine matches in his two Ryder Cup appearances.

Any European victories, admirable though they were, were achieved after America's win had been ensured. Nicklaus, beating Darcy in the final contest, joined Trevino and Nelson in winning all his four matches – a fitting farewell to his Ryder Cup playing career.

The final score was Europe 9½, United States 18½ – the widest-ever margin of any Ryder Cup match in Britain and worse than Europe's first combined effort two years previously in West Virginia.

In retrospect the Walton Heath match may perhaps be seen as almost the last of the traditional 'goodwill' meetings as envisaged by Sam Ryder and from a vintage that may have produced partisanship among the 27,000 spectators but not the overt chauvinism and consequent recriminations that would sometimes endanger the event when the battles grew close. Two years later, in 1983, the Europeans would get within a point of the Americans in Florida; two years after that they would win; the knife-edge contests of modern times then began.

Financially, the bad weather having kept down the crowds, the match was something of a disaster for the PGA and Aldington's Sun Alliance did not renew its sponsorship. But none of this was Walton Heath's fault.

The course licked its wounds and the committee judged the club's efforts highly successful. Douglas Thomson, captain that year, felt that the course had been brought to peak condition. The Artisans had been a huge help to McCrea, the American players had been full of praise and Tom Scott, of *Golf Illustrated*, added his own accolade:

> The organisation was magnificent - by far the best ever as far as Britain is concerned. For this the PGA take much credit, as do the Walton Heath secretary Bill McCrea, the professional Ken Macpherson and the entire committee.

That third week of September 1981 provided field days for tradition – a quality the players found amid the heath and heather, in Busson's workshop and in the clubhouse. 'A wonderful place and a great course,' said Ben Crenshaw, high priest of history among America's professionals, 'You could feel the presence of James Braid all week.'

Chapter Thirty-five

CURLY, COURTNEY, PUNCH AND ELI
In praise of the long gone Walton caddies

IT HAPPENED GRADUALLY in the 'seventies and 'eighties, I suppose – a diminution of sight and smell in the precincts near Braid's old workshop. No longer the variegated gaggle of characters, the shows of sartorial ill-elegance, the prattle of prospects for the 2.30 at Epsom, the runs for cover if the Dole man arrived, the acridity of fags and fug in the old hut... the caddies were going or gone.

Today, John Sparks has to rustle up caddies for special occasions. He is the course ranger. Were he exclusively a caddiemaster he might die of loneliness, with no recalcitrant company, no wasters to punish, no job really.

Long ago, hordes of more than a hundred jostled for bags: small, wiry men from the racing stables, schoolboys denying truant, bronzed countrymen walking 10 miles or more from their hamlets, innocents and ne'er-do-wells, smart and scruffy. During the 'thirties Bill Deedes found such scenes at golf clubs 'too close to the slave market'[1] for his tastes. After the war there would still be dozens of hopefuls.

But today the place echoes. The caddies have dissolved through a screen of social progress. We are left in bar and lounge to milk the apocrypha of their oral history and recall their outstanding characters.

And the first of these shall be 'Curly' – Irish son of a trapeze artist, wearing his dirty long overcoat buttoned to

'Curly'

the chin and often with a hat slammed so far down on his head that his unshaven face was half hidden.

His era stretched into the 'eighties, but he was an anachronism, a throwback to the old days of caddie culture. People who say they knew him are using the wrong terminology for nobody really knew Curly. Acquaintances? Often he would avoid or ignore them; on a good day he might swear at you if you greeted him.

He usually conversed only with his players. From such exchanges came his legendary reply to an American player that I have reported already but which, as nearly 200 pages have elapsed since, is good enough to re-quote. 'Gee,' said the visitor, 'they're kinda interesting, these bunkers in the hollows you have here!' 'The 'ollows were Roman stables,' Curly expounded, expressing a disputed view, 'I don't know how they knew how to build them so near the greens.'

The stereotyped picture of Curly is that he was dirty, destitute and disreputable, a shambles of a man sleeping rough on the heath or in the shelter that stood behind the first tee. However, there are always kind people cruel enough to ruin good stories and Fred Faulkner is one of them. Sipping a pint in the Artisans' clubhouse, he will tell you that the legends do Curly an injustice; that he wasn't always scruffy and, deep down, not a bad chap at all.

But Curly's prime defender, indeed his saviour, was Sir John Junor, former editor of the *Sunday Express*. As I have

[1] *Daily Telegraph*, 1997.

FAREWELL TO CURLY

EVERYONE CALLED him Curly, and there
could not have been more than a handful who
knew his real name.

He was a caddie at Walton Heath. A fiercely independent wisp of a man who for many years lived
rough, summer and winter, among the bracken.

Only recently had the luxury been permitted him
of using the caddie hut in which to sleep.

Such a thing as a bed and sheets were unknown to
him. Until he was taken ill. And put in Epsom
General Hospital. I went to see him there last
Monday. He was in a private room and for the
first time in his life he was being treated like
royalty. No one could have had better or more
caring treatment.

Last Friday night Curly died and I mourn his
going.

But I rejoice in the way in which our much
criticised National Health Service can give
dignity in their last days to people such as
Curly, Clarence Langford.

John Junor, Sunday Express, 1981

explained in chapter 22, Curly carried for JJ during some
10 years from the early 'seventies and, in a bizarre and
inexplicable bond of friendship, Junor repaid him with
tenners, booze, slap-up Christmas dinners and constant
company on the course. When Curly died in 1981 the club
paid for his funeral and Junor wrote his obituary in the
Express.

But everyone has to admit to Curly's eccentricities and
contradictory traits – and to the mystery of his past.

Eccentricities? Would *you* turn up at the course in great-
coat and wellies on the hottest of days? Would *you* report
for caddying duties carrying a fishing rod and practise
casting on the tee? If you were thirsty would *you* draw a
glass of water from the pond at the first?

Contradictions? He slept rough yet owned a hugely
expensive motor-bike, his only apparent possession and
his pride and joy. He was, in truth, a skilled and experienced fisherman.

Mystery? His real name, it is said, was Clarence
Langford, or Langdon, and rumours had it that he was
high-born, a drop-out from a wealthy family and still with
money in his pockets. But nobody found out, nobody
knew.

'No-one knew where Curly had come from and no-one
cared,' wrote Penny Junor,[2] Sir John's daughter, and that,
surely, is the truth behind this entire composite subject.
Caddies like Curly lived in shadows and we are no longer
dealing in crystal-clear facts. Time blurs the distinctions

---

[2] *Home Truths – Life Around My Father* (HarperCollins), 2002.

between them and within the apocrypha the legends
become transferable from character to character.

Was it Curly or someone else who said that about the
'ollows? Was it he or Courtney, from a slightly earlier era,
who may have come from the aristocracy? Jo Bryant swore
to me that it was the latter. Between Curly and Courtney
lies much confusion.

Courtney? He was Reg Courtney, apparently, and I say
apparently because here was another mystery man. He did
not fit the mould. He would arrive wearing collar and tie.
He would not be above sleeping in the caddies' shed, but
spoke in educated tones and carried the *Financial Times*.
He was seen in a local pub one night – and in the saloon
bar, not the public – in the uniform of a
Merchant Navy officer. Again, though,
nobody found out, nobody knew.

The procession of caddies, heroic and
tragic, continues to provide fading images
through the mists of time – jumbled in
chronology, legend rivalling truth.

'Sergeant Batchelor' wore highly polished
shoes and threadbare but spotless trousers,
yet would happily sleep rough... 'Punch'
sometimes lived in the shelter and one
night, when working as a night-watchman
in the area, burnt to death having slumped
on to his brazier... Sammy Crutch, known
for wearing outsize trousers, carried for a
week for Henry Cotton for £30... 'Maurice',
smart on the course and an odd-job man for
the club, collapsed and died on the 10th
hole of the Old...

Sammy Crutc

Junor and Curly as seen by Sunday Express *cartoonist Bill Martin. Junor,
Martin, Monty Court, Editor of* Sporting Life, *and Sir Adam Thomson,
chairman of British Caledonian Airways, played regularly on Mondays.*

*The shelter between the 16th and 17th (New) –
among the one-time lodgings of Curly and co.
Photographer: Walter Poucher*

way back, was Peter Weller, a World War I veteran tough on discipline.

During World War II there were inevitable cases of hardship. The members contributed 10-per-cent of sweepstakes to start a caddies' benevolent fund and chairman Sir Frederic Hamilton personally paid £250 to help out. But the market recovered. By 1994 'A-grade' men were getting £18, 'humpers' £9 and trolley-pullers £7. Today at Walton the fee is £30 a round plus a tip – unless inflation-related increases have overtaken me between press-time and publication.

Poucher finds Eli, trilby-hatted and jacketed, caddying on the 10th (Old) in the 'sixties.

Today's regular caddies exist and prosper as a professional elite on the major tours. By 1997, Tom Kite, captain of the American team, was telling his caddies, 'If you want a ride on Concorde go and caddie for the Europeans.'

But gone, virtually, are the regular crowds of workaday caddies at Walton Heath and numerous other clubs. They have been driven off, probably to better things, by the demon trolleys and their electrical offspring. So disintegrates another fragment of the earthy romance of golf.

Some were mere beasts of burden, but others had sound knowledge of golf and sometimes had colourful ways of expressing it. Brian Pope, elected as a 16-year-old in 1927, went out to play with his father Walter under the critical eye of the latter's caddie. Eventually the caddie gave Pope senior his considered technical opinion: 'The young gentleman will do very nicely, sir – but he needs a bigger bottom.'

Lord Castlerosse, another member, told his friend Henry Longhurst how

> When there was an 'orrible murder on the heath and the finger of suspicion pointed to a man who used to bicycle across it every day, the caddies would whistle their fingers to attract his attention and then perform a noose-like motion round their necks, finishing with a hideous upward jerk.

'Wash' Carr, the Cambridge blue, once found his ball deep in a divot mark. 'That would have been a nasty one to get in the medal,' he remarked to his man. 'You'd never 'ave 'ad it in the medal,' the caddie assured him.

Talking of lies, the story is also told of the member who arrived in the heather to find his caddie nudging his ball into a superior spot. The player was outraged. The caddie, struggling for redemption, quickly manufactured false evidence involving the finest sportsman he could think of. 'Well, *Braid* does it,' he announced.

With charges such as these the lot of the caddiemasters was not always a happy one. From the post-war procession Eli Scrace stands out – poor, delightful Eli. He had impediments of speech and movement rumoured to have resulted from being struck by a ball, though again 'nobody knew'. He is fondly remembered – 'always here, part of Walton Heath' as someone told me; a dutiful caddiemaster and a man with an inherent kindness to dogs and other animals.

He caddied himself – for Alick Renshaw among others. At the end of 1979, when he had passed retirement age and given the club nearly a quarter of a century of service, it was announced that he would henceforth work part-time. The club appointed a celebrity – Alfie Fyles, caddy to Gary Player, Tom Watson and other luminaries. Unfortunately his reign was unsuccessful and correspondingly brief. Eli apart, the best-remembered man in the job,

THE CHARM OF A CADDIE

The caddie allotted to me at Walton Heath was advanced in years and had come to know the greens so well that he rarely bothered to consult the line of the putt. 'Three inches left,' he would command, no matter where he happened to be standing. I am not too bad at lining up a long putt and sometimes found his instruction quiet contrary to what my own eye told me. Maddeningly, when I ignored his instructions and took my own course, the putt went wide. When I followed his line, it ran close. Caddies, particularly the older caddies, are like that; it is part of their charm.

W.F. DEEDES, *The Daily Telegraph*, 1997

The short 17th on the Old course. There used to be a gap between bunkers, enabling players to run on, but now sand runs unbroken along the front of the green – a change made in Sir William Carr's reign, when Dudley Scholey (see below) was Lord of the Manor.
                                        Photographer: LIBBY HAGDRUP

WHEN THE LORD OF THE MANOR WAS TOLD TO BUZZ OFF!

It is remarkable and a great tribute to all concerned that over the 50-odd years of the club's existence the rights of the public for air and exercise have not clashed with the rights of the golfers in open and bloody battle.

I remember being somewhat disturbed a few years ago by finding a rather keen game of football in progress on the fairway of the second hole of the Old at the same time as a rather charming tea party – teacloth and all – was taking place on the tee. The tea party I did not mind since there was plenty of room for everybody and they appeared motherly and tolerant-looking souls, obviously prepared to be entertained by our prowess and even more by the lack of it.

The football match was a different matter. The players were mostly youngsters – the Blues and the Reds I think – but there was one man. Walking forward nervously I told him – and he looked large and aggressive enough even to my slightly kümmeled eye – that I intended to hold him personally responsible for any sudden death or injury which might occur as a result of the bullet-like drives of my companions. Both teams took promptly to the heather and the bracken and were seen no more.

I also remember with a strange tinge of sympathy a large and raw-boned teenage girl entertaining her companions, probably her younger sisters, by showing them how to putt the ball into the hole with the aid of a trench-like depression about 8 ft. long which she had made on the first green of the New.

I asked her to stop. She told me to "buzz off"! I told her I would report her (I don't know who to) and she repeated her demand that I should "buzz off." I threatened to fetch a policeman (I can't think where from), but again she told me to "buzz off," and this request was repeated when I asked for her name and address.

As the younger children had started to giggle, I felt somewhat foolish and ultimately decided that the right thing for me to do was, in fact, to "buzz off." I rather admired the girl.

DUDLEY R. SCHOLEY (Lord of the Manor), 1960

Chapter Thirty-six

FALLING OUT WITH THE NEIGHBOURS
In the 1980s the Club receives a cowpat!

NEARLY 20 YEARS AGO the Club fell out with its neighbours... or, rather, the neighbours fell out with the club... or at least some of them did. And not only neighbours. Critics and conservationists, ramblers and riders, politicians and pressure groups, even television, took part in the dispute.

In 1983 the club had bought out the rights-of-common from one of the only two people on the heath who still held them and was threatening High Court action over the other. It was considering moving the clubhouse across the Dorking Road. It was in protracted discussions with the village sports club, whose pitches it wanted to move to make room for a practice ground and car park.

By 1985, intent on improving its courses for big events, it was planning two more holes on the New course between the eighth and the motorway. Indeed, members had approved the scheme by a big majority at a general meeting. Secretary McCrea promptly applied for a public bridleway diversion and went ahead with tree felling and scrub clearance in a 16.8 acre area.

And why not? Why should not the club do *all* these things if it so wished? Was not Walton Heath Golf Club Lord of the Manor and therefore of all it surveyed?

Well, yes and no. To understand the position fully we would need to wrestle lengthily with laws, statutes and agreements replete with references to turbary, estovers,

heriots and inclosure.[1] If we avoid such legal niceties we must at least recognise the following facts:

First, Walton Heath is common land and waste of the manor,[2] subject to normal planning controls. The 1925 Law of Property Act defines such terrain as common land

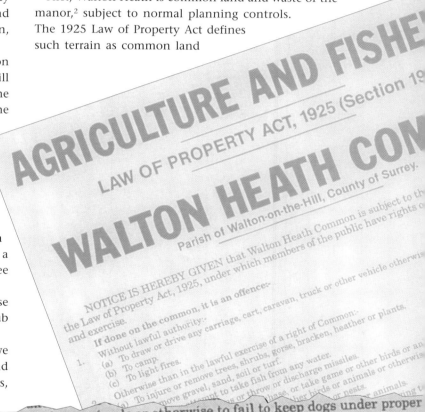

AGRICULTURE AND FISHE

LAW OF PROPERTY ACT, 1925 (Section 19

WALTON HEATH COM

Parish of Walton-on-the-Hill, County of Surrey.

NOTICE IS HEREBY GIVEN that Walton Heath Common is subject to the Law of Property Act, 1925, under which members of the public have rights o and exercise.

If done on the common, it is an offence:-

Without lawful authority:-
1. (a) To draw or drive any carriage, cart, caravan, truck or other vehicle otherwis
(b) To camp.
(c) To light fires.

Otherwise than in the lawful exercise of a right of Common:-
(a) To injure or remove trees, shrubs, gorse, bracken, heather or plants.
(b) To remove gravel, sand, soil or turf.

(f) To permit dogs to chase game or other birds or animals or otherwise to fail to keep dogs under proper
(g) To remove or attempt to remove birds' eggs or nests.
(h) To set traps, nets or snares, or lime trees for birds or animals.
(i) To permit horses, cattle, sheep or other animals (not belonging to a commoner) to graze or stray.
(j) To bathe in any pond or stream.
(k) To post or paint bills, advertisements, placards or notices.
(l) To injure notice boards or seats.
(m) To place or deposit and leave any glass, china, earthenware, tin, carton, paper, lighted matches, lighte cigar ends or other refuse or litter so as to affect or tend to affect injuriously the public amenities.

(o) To hold an
(p) To erect or place
(q) To create any nuisa
annoyance of any person.
(r) Generally to injure or disfigure the Common
exercise.
(s) To play or attempt to play golf on any portion of the to the Order hereinafter referred to which is set out which may at any time hereinafter be set out or u of golf by way of alteration or extension of any ex
(t) To play or attempt to play golf on any greens, tees or bunkers for the or any alteration or extension of the same as afo
(u) To loiter upon the greens, tees or bunkers on the person or persons lawfully playing golf on the

PROVIDED that nothing in this Schedule s
1. Persons authorised by the Walton Heath time being of the Lady of the Manor fr
2. Persons so authorised as aforesaid fro the Common now or hereafter be u sand, soil or turf from the said Comm or bunkers thereon or therein or o newly laid turf or freshly sown grass aining or improving the age of exercise, including hereu

What the public cannot do on Walton Heath.

---

[1] Turbary = Land where peat or turf may be dug; Estovers = Wood, etc, allowed to tenant; Heriots = Payments or return of equipment to lord; Inclosure = Enclosing of common land as private property.

[2] Land not adopted for specific use.

Photographic evidence from the club about the clearance area for the planned new holes. First as it looked in 1965; then, in colour, 1985.

subject to any rights held by others. Such rights might be, for example, to pasture animals. So it always has been and I have already[3] described how Malcolm Bonsor had to satisfy the rights-of-common holders when the club wanted to add the second nine holes of the New course.

Second, the public have rights of access to the heath for 'air and exercise.' But those rights are limited. On the course you may read a notice signed by manor steward Freshfield in 1933 that lists 27 offences, 24 of which concern actions allowable only if they are carried out while exercising a right-of-common. Quite apart from interference with the golf, the offences range from poaching to obscene language.

Third, an order of limitation made in 1933 under the 1925 Act confirmed the boundaries of the courses.

Fourth, by the 'eighties the struggle to keep heaths and commons open to all and sundry had become a powerful campaign and for some people a vocation.

Against that background consider the reactions of local residents already depressed and angered by the effects of the M25 as they read reports and heard rumours of the club's latest activities and ambitions.

What were the golfers up to? The club felt entirely innocent, but some locals imagined a sinister connection between its various plans and activists stirred them into a formidable opposition. It was the tree felling that set fire to the controversy – it was not the first time that council and residents had been angered by such actions – and it remained an emotive issue throughout. But much more was involved and the opposition drew up battle lines based on the following beliefs:

New Holes: They should not be allowed. They would be

outside the agreed boundaries of the courses. Notices objecting were distributed in the villages.

Clubhouse Move: Not possible. It would be on Green Belt common land. When official application was made, Tadworth and Walton Residents' Association were among the objectors and the council's planning officer was recommending rejection.

Rights-of-Common: The club was trying to get rid of the last legitimate rights-of-pasture. Were these the first steps toward de-registering or inclosing the heath, that is to say extinguishing the public's rights?

Tree-Felling: Illegal, said the opposition; disgraceful said conservationists. In March 1985 the Forestry Commission, tipped off about alleged illegal felling, ordered the club to stop and Reigate and Banstead Council prepared to slap preservation orders on all the heath's woodland.

After two months, McCrea, who had been preparing applications to the council and Department of the Environment for use of the additional area for golf, was allowed to resume. This brought further complaints, so he agreed to cease until the club had planning permission for the holes.

McCrea maintained that the felling was within the specified allowances and had been agreed by the council's forestry officer and largely entailed clearance of tangled undergrowth and scrub. 'Scarcely any trees worthy of the name,' observed Brian Calvert, the captain. 'In line with club policy of restoring and maintaining the land's open heathland nature,' said McCrea.

In the latter respect the club took strength from at least two expert witnesses. Don Allom, 83, a veteran member and a local resident almost all his life[4], testified that in the early days there were scarcely any trees except for a few pines, while Jim Arthur, the R&A's agronomist, vehemently agreed. The club could also have quoted the *Golfing Annual* of 1903/4: 'There are hazards in the shape of whins and heather, but no trees.'

Everyone who has any influence should use it to conserve Walton Heath as an open heath, and the fight against continual encroachment by scrub trees must be pursued with energy and enthusiasm. If you do not, then the character of the courses will be altered irreversibly and a status quo would be prohibitively expensive to restore.

Jim Arthur (R&A agronomist) to committee, *c*1984

---

[3] Chapter 10.
[4] Allom was born the day the club received its certificate of incorporation (Aug 5, 1903); was elected an hon life member in 1996; died in 1998.

The riders on the bridleways had generally co-existed happily with the club,
but the 'eighties affair brought them into conflict.

Photographer: PATRICK WEBB

Strong opposition on all fronts continued to come from the residents' association and its 'action group.' Douglas Weir, a Tadworth man whom the club held responsible for calling in the Forestry Commission, had circulated a paper which, in the club committee's judgment, 'contained untruths and distortions and was a further attempt to make things difficult for the club.'

Weir had got one thing right, though: the current clubhouse area was registered not as freehold but common land. The action group threatened to graze animals on the putting green! A few entered the clubhouse; McCrea bought them a drink!

The air was full of rumour and misunderstandings and not only among the residents and pressure groups. Some of the artisans, villagers with feet in both camps, felt ambivalent. 'The sad thing is the support the action group seems to be getting from some members of the club and their families,' commented Colonel Bernard Holloway, who had been captain in 1984. 'One member even had the nerve to bring a petition into the clubhouse and tout for signatories.' At the end of 1985 a brief was prepared to enable the artisans and others to be told the truth as the club saw things:

Tree-Felling: As owners of the freehold the club could cut down trees anywhere on the heath, even outside the course boundaries, subject to Forestry Commission allowances – and in that respect had been found within its rights. Indeed, a letter from the Minister confirmed that he considered the felling within the specified limits and did not require permission.

New Holes: An application to the DoE to adjust the 'limit of courses' had been made. Meantime the two-holes application had been temporarily withdrawn.

New Clubhouse: The council had refused a club request for postponement of the hearing to enable it to clarify and reinforce its case. Therefore this application, too, had been withdrawn and a revised one was being considered. A clubhouse near the starting and finishing holes was an attractive idea and would avoid hazardous crossings of the main road; also the present building needed big money spending on repairs or re-building. A move could therefore be a third option. But it was only an idea. Any actions had been purely exploratory in case re-location were to be thought a good idea in the future.

Existing Clubhouse Land: Rumours that the club did not own the land were untrue. However, in the 'sixties, when common lands and rights had to be registered to establish the precise status of specific areas, the land had been included in error. Rectifying the mistake might take time, but the matter would be relevant only if the club wished to sell the site.

Rights-of-Common: The club could not and never would de-register the common, keep out the public or develop the land not used for golf. The heath had been enjoyed by golfers and public for more than 80 years without trouble until the advent of the 'action group,' which seemed to be driving a wedge between club and village. The club had taken counsel's advice and in the High Court were opposing the transfer of rights from one owner to another, purely to safeguard the courses.

Service Road: Another problem. One was required partly because access to the southern end of the courses had been lost due to the motorway, but the action group had helped influence the council to reject two planning applications. It had now gone to appeal to the DoE and approval was expected.

The service road was indeed granted in April 1986. By now,

though, the opposition's campaign had taken new twists and directions. The first led from the tree-cleared areas to the Channel 4 TV studios in London's Charlotte Street.

The Longest Running Show on Earth programme, involving David Bellamy, a passionate supporter of environmental causes, made an on-screen presentation to Walton Heath Golf Club. Unfortunately it was its 'Cowpat of the Month.' The award, said the producers, was entirely appropriate based on their understanding of the tree-felling and all that went with it.

After the broadcast abusive phone calls were received and two contained threats to burn down the clubhouse. Two young ladies on the catering staff who took the calls, being the only people in the clubhouse, had a frightening night and police were called in for their protection.

The producers explained subsequently that the Open Spaces Society had told them that the club had cut down nearly a thousand trees ('20 acres of mature oak, pine, silver birch and thorn… once the habitat of woodcock, nightjars and shrikes') which lay outside the course boundaries. Philip Truett, the committee member responsible for the courses at that time, protested to all concerned that the programme had been based on untruths and distortions. He emphasised the club's heathland philosophy, but no change was given. McCrea still maintains that the clearance was mainly of scrub and that as far as mature trees were concerned less than 30 were felled – certainly not a thousand.

The second new trail blazed, toward the end of 1985, began among the sacred bridleways and ended in the offices of *Horse and Rider*. As a result committee men and past captains received an unwelcome Christmas present from Janet Miller, Surrey bridleways officer of the British Horse Society: copies of an article which, apart from complaints about the loss of riding country in the area, re-hashed the hoary suspicions and allegations.

Its only valid point, McCrea considered, was that some bridleways had disappeared, been diverted or spoiled following the M25 construction. This was not the club's fault, he emphasised, but he had been urging action by the council, had offered to construct temporary diversions and was willing to restore and maintain all the public bridleways crossing the heath as a gesture to the horse-riders, with whom the club had always had good relations. 'The routes need not involve any felling of trees,' McCrea wearily concluded in a letter to the council, 'but there is such unreasonable opposition in some quarters to anything the club does that I would like your comments before proceeding.'

In April 1986 official notice of the club's application to the DoE to vary the limits of its courses was published. The club was offering the locals two things in return: first, land the far side of the motorway that it had received as part-compensation for its losses to the road; second, from 1992, the area containing the first hole of the Old, which it said it envisaged abandoning for safety reasons.

The immediate reaction was a first batch of 23 letters to the Department, 22 of them objecting to the application and urging a public inquiry. They confirmed that all the club's various actions had become entangled in people's minds. For example:

> One is bound to think that all this is part of a wider scheme involving (i) the service road (already granted on appeal), (ii) a clubhouse and car park south of the Dorking Road, (iii) elimination of the final commoner and (iv) commercialisation of the club.   *A borough councillor.*

Objectors raised even more subjects. Some were convinced that the golfers, in negotiating with the sports club, were pressurising it to move and thus invading common land in pursuit of a practice area, while others were angry about the 'amenity bank' that had been built to screen the courses from the motorway:

> Two-thirds of the playing area lost to the M25 is lying not beneath the motorway but beneath this bank, which was placed… with the agreement of the club and for which the club

LAW OF PROPERTY ACT 1925
COMMON LAND AT WALTON HEATH
PARISH OF WALTON ON THE HILL
COUNTY OF SURREY

WHEREAS:-
(1) By an Order dated the 2nd December 1933 and made by the Minister of Agriculture and Fisheries under section 193(1) (b) of the Law of Property Act 1925 limitations and conditions were imposed on the exercise of rights of public access

(3) Application has been made to the Secretary of State for the Environment by the Walton Heath Golf Club for his consent to alter the portion of the Common set out or used as a Golf Course in accordance with the said Order;

NOW THEREFORE the Secretary of State gives notice that he proposes to give the said consent, the effect of which will be to add to the portion of the common set out or used for golf an area of land of 6.5 hectares or thereabouts situated to the south-west of the 8th Hole on the New Course and to delete from the said portion (i) an area of land of 5.5 hectares or thereabouts, now part of the M25 motorway and amenity bank, and (ii) as from 31 December 1991, an area of land of 4.0 hectares or thereabouts situated to the north-west of the Dorking Road (B2032).

A copy of the application and draft consent, together with a Statement and maps are deposited at the offices of The Reigate and Banstead Borough Council,

April 1986 – publication of the club's application to the DoE to vary the course limits.

was handsomely compensated, allegedly by £50,000. The club have gained financially but without losing any playing capacity in terms of numbers of holes.

Open Spaces Society.

This bank had been built from spoil dug during excavation for the motorway and delivered to the club by contractors, who paid the club a dumping fee. It was sown with a heathland grass mixture, but, like sections of the Gallops, had been churned into mud by riders looking in vain for diverted bridleways – the routes on which McCrea had been urging the council to action. The opposition felt that the bank reduced still further the area of heath available to the public and there was an inference that the club, having received land and money for its M25 losses, was now in effect, in applying to extend the course limits, trying to double up its compensation.

One resident foresaw an apocalyptic scenario on the heath, featuring a clubhouse complex embracing indoor sports and a helicopter terminal. Another alleged that many club members were against an extension of the limits.

The club's offer of lands got a luke-warm reception. The ubiquitous Mr. Weir thought it a bad deal in terms of acreage that would be received and lost and the land over the motorway was considered too distant to be of use to local people.

As to the first-hole area, cynics scoffed at the safety factor. Aware that a new course layout was taking shape entirely south of the Dorking Road,[5] they suspected a revised application for a clubhouse there would follow. 'The club is simply embarrassed at having such an unattractive first hole,' claimed an Open Spaces representative.

The net result of all this was that the DoE ordered a public inquiry. It was held at Burgh Heath in February 1987, lasted three days and involved nearly 20 hours of debate before more than 200 residents. The club was represented by Kenneth Bagnall QC and its witnesses included Tom Corrigan, who had recently succeeded Jack Rae as captain, and McCrea.

All the objections contained in the letters were revived, sometimes colourfully. 'They have turned the best part of the heath into an alien landscape,' said a man from the Ramblers' Association. 'They have created a sad and vulgar imitation of the coast of the Kingdom of Fife with an intricate layout of trees, bunkers and greens.' 'The club resents being branded a vandal,' declared Mr Bagnall, 'You only have to walk over the heath to see that the allegations are a gross abuse of public time.' 'The public must not be deprived of future use of the common just because of the pursuit of first-class golf,' said Charles George for the opposition.

---

[5] Chapter 32.

The Club objects to the proposal to establish a gypsy site at Sturts Lane on the grounds that the close proximity of the site would cause a risk of damage to the courses by vandalism.

We have two of the finest inland courses in the country with an international reputation and on occasions host major tournaments. Maintenance expenses are heavy (£128,000 approx in 1985). To help meet these costs we rely largely on receipts from visitors.

If our courses are vandalised or our visitors' golf balls or other equipment stolen, these receipts could fall dramatically and the reputation of this club and its courses, and our hosting of tournaments, could be put at risk.

Secretary Bill McCrea to Surrey Council, 1986

Bagnall spelt out what he said were the often misunderstood legal positions. The club's rights as freehold owners of the common were absolute, he stressed; subject to any statute and preservation order, the club might remove any trees without permission; it had exclusive golfing rights over the courses and the public, when taking their air and exercise, must accept the common as they find it, any possibility of balls hitting them being one of the hazards to which their rights of access were subject; the club had neither committed an offence nor breached any regulation apart from a minor omission relating to the replacement of public notices.

He contended that, under the 1933 order of limitations issued under section 193 of the Law of Property Act, the Secretary of State for the Environment was required to make any order necessary or desirable to protect the beneficial interest of the freeholder. If the minister judged such an order necessary he must make it. The club submitted that the amendment sought *was* necessary and that no evidence to the contrary had been produced.

The inquiry inspector eventually supported the club's case and reported to the secretary of state. When the minister's decision belatedly arrived it came as a setback. He had decided to defer a decision until planning permission for the proposed new holes was granted by the council.

This dragged the affair back to square one. Had not the club applied for such consent back in May 1985? Had it not sought deferment of that application from the council in July pending a decision on varying the limit of the courses? And had it not so advised the DoE in September? Why had the secretary of state not informed the club *then* that this planning consent was a prerequisite? 'We have become a victim of bureaucratic confusion,' captain Corrigan told his members.

The planning application for the holes was duly restored – and duly rejected by the council.

One compensatory result of the inquiry was that people had a more accurate grasp of the facts: many still think the heath is owned by the state or local authority and that the club is an intruder, but in fact the reverse is the case.

As for the golfers, they now knew better than ever that they needed to foster better relations with their neighbours. The club therefore set up a liaison committee embracing council, residents' association, ramblers, horse-riders, artisans and sports club. Early meetings were difficult, but gradually the atmosphere improved. Soon, club and councillors were playing golf against each other.

Brian Meaby – unearthed vital evidence.

But after all the arguing, much of it costly, what had the club achieved? Not a lot, it would seem. Unless it decided to appeal, the variation-of-limits and new-holes issues were lost causes. A clubhouse move had also been rendered dormant, though it refused to lie down and die.

Late in 1988 captain Findlay Picken's committee confirmed their agreement with club policy announced two-and-a-half years earlier:

> ...It is not practicable (nor in the interests of the club) actively to pursue the matter until it becomes clear that responsible local opinion and the requisite proportion of the members are both satisfied that the project is acceptable, unless other circumstances arise which in the committee's opinion would make it necessary to pursue it further.

In 1992 Peter Renshaw, a former captain, would describe the clubhouse idea as logical and far-seeing but the attempt to implement it 'a political, strategic and tactical disaster.'

All this left alive two issues: the impending High Court action concerning the last remaining right-of-pasture and the problem of de-registering the existing clubhouse land.

The court case, crucial in its own right, was holding up other matters. The club urgently needed a new greenkeeping complex on the common, but felt this could not be progressed until any re-locating of the sports club had been negotiated – and that in turn could not happen until the right-of-pasture case was won. Additionally, Weir was urging that any de-registration of the clubhouse land should not be considered until the High Court action was withdrawn.

Behind the court case lay the club's nightmare scenario of animals grazing on the heath and damaging the greens and other parts of the courses. This, it was claimed, had never really happened, or at least, not in modern times. 'In all my years I have never seen a herd of cattle or sheep grazing on Walton Heath,' Allom said in his affidavit. The club's motive in trying to clear the remaining right was to ensure the nightmare never came true

In 1983, three properties for which grazing rights had been registered still existed: Walton Oaks and the Hermitage, both by then in the possession of Beechams Pharmaceuticals, and Street Farm, whose rights were held by C. Bell (Tadworth) Ltd, a butcher and slaughterhouse operator owned by a Douglas Clay. The golf club then sold Little Heath, south of the motorway, to Beechams and part of the deal was that their rights-of-common would be extinguished. This left Bell the butcher as the last rights holder.

Some years previously, prior to the specific registration of the lands in the 'sixties, Clay's solicitor had told the Commons Commission that the butcher did not wish to pursue registration of his right, attached to Street Farm, to graze 60 cattle. Nonetheless it was registered. The club had lodged objections, but the commissioner dismissed them. The right anyway seemed unlikely to be exercised.

In May 1985 the club approached Clay's firm to enquire whether he would agree to withdraw the right. By then, though, the fracas about the trees and everything else had blown up and, unbeknown to the club, Daniel O'Donnell Ferris, a Banstead Downs conservator, had persuaded Clay to transfer the right to him. The club was objecting to this transfer.

'It meant that the right-of-common could be passed from hand to hand beyond any control of the golf club company,' recalls Brian Meaby, now club chairman but then heavily involved in the affair as the club's solicitor. 'There was obviously danger that it might pass to someone irresponsible enough to graze cattle on the heath and cause damage to the courses.'

A High Court writ against both Clay's butchery firm and Ferris was issued. The club claimed that the letters from Clay's solicitors to the Commons Commissioners estopped the existence or exercise of the right; also that the right had been appendant to Street Farm and that now it had been severed from it the right had become void and unenforceable. Additionally, the right had been abandoned by long non-usage.

SURREY COUNTY COUNCIL
COMMONS REGISTRATION ACT 1965
NOTICE OF APPLICATION FOR AMENDMENT
OF REGISTER
LAND CEASING TO BE COMMON LAND

Application has been made to the Surrey County Council by Walton Heath Golf Club Limited, Tadworth, Surrey, KT20 7TP for the amendment of the Register of Common Land by the removal of the land described below which it is claimed ceased to be common land on the 18th May 1993 in the following circumstances.

By virtue of a Deed of Release dated 18 May 1993 made between Walton Heath Golf Club Limited and the Council of the Borough of Reigate and Banstead, the holder of the Registered Rights of Common in gross, the right of common formerly registered in respect of the whole of Register Unit No. CL355 was released to the applicant in fee simple.

Any person wishing to object to the proposed amendment should, within forty days of the date of this notice, send a written and signed statement of the facts upon which he bases his objection to

County Solicitor (Ref LSCR)
Surrey County Council
County Hall
Kingston-upon-Thames
KT1 2DN
Dated 11 November 1993

Signature
For County Solicitor

DESCRIPTION OF THE LAND referred to above
Land at The Club House, Walton Heath Golf Club, Tadworth, contained within the area of land registered under the Land Registration Acts 1925 and 1936 under Title No SY 232593
Part of Walton Heath – Register Unit CL 355

De-registration of the clubhouse land – almost the end of the problem.

It emerged that the Open Spaces Society had been intending to buy this right but had withdrawn after the writ was issued and that Ferris had now transferred it to Reigate and Banstead Council. A council spokesman was quoted in the Press as saying, 'We now have the right to graze cattle there, which I am sure we will do.'

'Threats were made to graze 400 cattle on the courses, subject only to the greens being fenced,' Brian Meaby recalls. Negotiations with the council took place and the liaison meetings ceased in favour of individuals' efforts, but litigation would continue until 1993.

The breakthrough began in 1992. The council, politically hung, had changed and so had some of the individuals. That was also true at the club. Negotiations were reopened through Richard Bennett, the new council chairman and the local ward councillor, and the door began to creak open.

Eventually an out-of-court settlement was achieved. The club agreed not to contest the council's right and would pay a peppercorn rate of £10 a year to a total of £800. In return the council would not for 80 years exercise the right to graze cattle. 'A hard bargain,' said some at the club; 'a sensible compromise,' thought others.

Delays in finalising the agreement were partly because the club sensed an opportunity, in its new relationship with the council, to resolve the remaining problem – that of the clubhouse and putting-green land having been incorrectly registered as common.

No procedure existed to correct the error under the 1965 Act that had required registration. Nor did subsequent legislation help, because it allowed amendments only to lands embracing a dwelling house and the clubhouse was not regarded as such. The Commons Commission refused one application and the problem appeared insoluble, except perhaps by litigation.

The turning point came when Brian Meaby unearthed evidence that the clubhouse had been bought separately by Cosmo Bonsor in 1903 and that in April 1909 he had paid a tithe redemption: had the land been common a tithe would not have been payable. He also discovered a judgment in an important case that a landowner might obtain cancellation of registration if he could demonstrate that the land had never been waste of the manor – and the clubhouse area obviously hadn't been.

Convinced by this evidence and confirmation of the error by the Registrar of Commons, the council agreed as part of the settlement to release to the club by conveyance the right to graze on this piece of land. This conveyance created unity of ownership and possession with the right-in-common, and when such rights are united the right-of-common becomes extinguished.

The land was duly removed from the register in May 1994 and the club agreed never to de-register any part of the heath apart from the clubhouse area and entrance road. Thus was the value of the land the members thought they had bought unencumbered in 1971 restored to them.

The history of rights-in-common is one of compromise and recognition of custom, *wrote club member Ian Huntington recently in his paper The History of Walton Heath as Common Land*. It produced a very English solution to the needs of landowners and local inhabitants. In the 1990s the club and the council reached a very English solution to their disagreement over Walton Heath.

My year of captaincy (1992) saw the resolution of the problem faced by the club concerning certain grazing rights over the heath. I was interviewed on Mercury Radio and recall the interviewer's final quip that rather than worrying about staff whose livelihood might be threatened or members who might have their enjoyment curtailed we should be concerned for the sheep with nowhere left to graze!

Patrick Webb, to author

7th (New)

2nd (Ol

6th (New)

'IN WINTAH AND SUMMAH...'
Edgar B. Beck's legendary words![1]

Photographs: LIBBY HAGDRUP

1st (Old)

17th (Old)

14th (Old)

[1] Chapter 22

Chapter Thirty-seven

LEADING LADY
Jill Thornhill – Curtis Cup star and British champion

YOU COULD LULL yourself to sleep by counting not sheep but Jill Thornhill's golfing conquests, so numerous and repetitive are they. On the other hand they might open your eyes with astonishment. Sixteen Surrey championships... nine home internationals... four Curtis Cup matches... nine gold medals... and many, many more. The lists would stretch even longer, but for two periods totalling 15 years she virtually disappeared from view.

Her parents, the Woodsides, were Purley Downs members. At eight she was swinging an old hickory shaft and falling victim to the game's inexorable clutches. By the time she was 19 she had met John Thornhill.

In 1962 she joined Walton Heath and won her initial Surrey championship. In 1963 she gathered the first of her gold medals and attracted public notice. England honours were on the way and for the 1964 Curtis Cup she was a non-travelling reserve.

Then, whatever happened to Jill Thornhill? For the next 10 years she was bringing up two children[1] and had only limited opportunities to play.

Returning, she reached the final of the 1974 English Close Amateur Championship at Sunningdale and won the 72-hole Newmark International Tournament at Walton. It seemed that she was about to peak.

Then, again, whatever happened to Jill Thornhill? For nearly five years she disappeared – to Saudi Arabia, where John was working. She made fleeting visits to win more Surrey championships, but her only golf abroad was traditional desert stuff: nine holes for fun, 'browns' to putt on and green mats for approaches.

When the Thornhills returned to Britain thoughts of big championships were gone and her only ambition was to get back into the swing of things in Surrey.

Jill Thornhill – 1984 painting by Tommy Merryweather.

'Go and play in the English', Diane Bailey, the Surrey captain, urged her in 1981, but she didn't. In 1982, though, she did, and reached the last eight. She was restored by England after an eight-year absence and won the decisive match against Scotland by beating Pam Wright at the last.

She now felt she wanted to 'prove' herself. For two hours most days of the week housewifery gave way to practice. She became a perfectionist.

In 1983 she travelled north to play in the British Open Amateur Championship at Silloth-on-Solway. With her was Jill Nicolson, the Scottish international with whom she won the Avia Foursomes. Deep down she lacked confidence; did not like travelling alone and thought of British championships as 'things other people won.' The two Jills made a pact: whoever was knocked out first would stay to keep the other company.

In an early round Mrs T beat Belle Robertson, champion two years previously at 45 and an inspiration for her comeback. After that, her talent, inner strength and pride in performance got her through to the final against the Swiss, Regine Lautens. Some writers found it remarkable that a 40-year-old mother of two could have done so:

> Having read reports describing our heroine as the 'elder stateswoman of English golf,' we were half expecting a weather-beaten old bat in tweeds, so when Mrs Thornhill appeared it was a revelation... she is tall, tanned, slim and an impressive advertisement for the golfing life.[2]

With Jill Nicolson as caddie she went six up with six to play and won the championship by four and two.

Victory brought a fitting coincidence. Silloth was the

---

[1] Daughter Caroline (now Mrs Weeks) plays off 10 at Walton.
[2] Julie Welch in *The Observer*.

ureka! Jill holes at Muirfield's 13th in the 1984 Curtis Cup.
Photographer: PHIL SHELDON

219

HEATHER AND HEAVEN

home club of Cecilia Leitch,[3] winner of the championship a total of four times before and after World War I, and who was made an honorary member of Walton Heath. Now, Jill Thornhill of Walton Heath was elected an honorary member of Silloth. A year later she was made an honorary member at Walton, too.

She was also crowned 'Woman Golfer of the Year' and, like a newly-acclaimed actress, found leading roles opening up to her on stages across the world. Most important of all were the Curtis Cup matches:

1984 at Muirfield: This was transatlantic women's golf before the tide turned. Only twice in 22 matches and never since 1956 had Britain and Ireland beaten the Americans. The most recent defeat, by no means extraordinary, had been 14½ – 3½.

But this time? United States 9½, Britain and Ireland 8½! 'It made us realise, yes, we can do it!' recalls Jill. She won one and halved two of her four matches.

1986 at Prairie Dunes, Kansas: US 5, Britain and Ireland 13! It was our women's first victory for 30 years, their first-ever in the States and the first defeat of any American team at home – Curtis Cup, Walker Cup or Ryder Cup.

Walton Heath basked in reflected glory. With Wentworth it had been the stage for a weekend of practice and preparation; it could, albeit impertinently, point to the outstanding captaincy, for Diane Bailey, of Reigate Heath, had recently joined Walton as well. As for Mrs T, having succeeded in removing a huge divot from the tee with her first practice shot, she had recovered her composure and excelled herself.

She had golfed with the rhythm and élan of an

1983 triumph – the British Amateur Championship trophy.

English champion (recently having won that title at Prince's Sandwich) and in temperatures rising to 110 degrees had helped secure three-and-a-half points. 'Jill Thornhill gave the impression she holed everything she looked at,' Robert Sommers reported ruefully in the USGA's *Golf Journal.*

1988 at Royal St. George's: Our first-ever back-to-back victories. Massive crowds swarmed down the fairways as of old as the home team won 11-7.

[3] Chapter seven.

Mrs Thornhill (standing third from left) with the victorious 1988 Curtis Cup team at Royal St. George's.

The previous year Jill had been runner-up in the British Open Amateur Stroke-Play Championship, confirming that she was still a formidable force at 44. Nonetheless she had decided that this was to be her swan song as a Cup player. Supported by a huge gallery, including her former team-mate Laura Davies, she had helped collect two-and-a-half more points - making eight out of a maximum 12 in the three matches.

Away from Walton Heath the club's leading lady had a competitive career spanning over 30 years, for she emerged from apparent retirement in 1993 to win the Senior Ladies' British Open at Ashburnham, finished second a year later and continued to win Surrey championships until 1997. At Walton in 2001 she won the gold medal a quarter of a century since her most recent one and 38 years after her first, returning 71, the lowest ever recorded. Space does not permit me to detail a myriad of other triumphs for club, county and country.

Recently I gently chided her for being a disappointing interviewee. The lady is so infuriatingly casual and modest about her conquests. Only under pressure will she recall details of her victories, let alone specific shots from her armoury.

She remembers, from nearly 30 years ago, a five iron on to Walton's 17th green in the Newmark ('I can still, to this day, feel it come off the club'). She saw the old champion Enid Wilson nodding appreciation ('It was like a seal of approval'). Needing par over the last three holes to win, she had holed from 30ft for a birdie at the 16th, escaping serious injury when her putter, hurled aloft in triumph, landed on her head.

Then there was her first shot at Prairie Dunes – a six iron on to the green that helped bring an immediate lead to Lillian Behan and herself and a psychological boost to the team.

Her method, she will tell you, was unspectacular: 'I just kept prodding it up the middle.' Add to that accuracy her formidable short game and the ability to scramble and fight and you have the essence of her talent.

A staunch, orthodox traditionalist is our Mrs. Thornhill: a team player, upset by poor behaviour, a graduate from an era when juniors in Surrey were often merely tolerated but when a small clutch of elder stateswomen were powerful influences. Curtis Cup player Molly Gourlay was such a figure – stern but stimulating, formidable but kind.

Jill talks most about those who have helped her. John has been her constant counsel; a formidable foursomes partner, too, for they won at Worplesden and, at the club, took six Heathens Foursomes, four of them in five years. Her early coaches were Jimmy Wallace at Purley Downs and Robin Robson at The Addington. As a rising talent she was lucky to be surrounded by experienced team-mates in Surrey and a nucleus of low handicap players – Shirley Allom, Tess Hurlock and others – at Walton.

Above: Jill Thornhill. Below left: in the 1986 Curtis Cup match in Kansas, our first victory for 30 years.

Photographer: John Kelly (for USGA Golf Journal)

When she got back into the England squad it was largely through Diane Bailey's encouragement, and Vivien Saunders sharpened her confidence and improved her technique. Before the 1984 Curtis Cup match it was Ken Macpherson who took her out to Walton's bunkers and prepared her for the steep monsters waiting for her at Muirfield. She had taken only two lessons from Harry Busson - the chemistry between them wasn't right – but even he played a part in her success because she won her British title with a custom-made Busson driver.

Her international playing career over, she turned to administration and captaincy and succeeded Mrs. Bailey in charge of the Curtis Cup team for the match at Somerset Hills, New Jersey. Preparation and practice proceeded superbly, but her team was (and I use her expression) 'hammered' by 14 points to four.

Her disappointment shows in the passion with which she recalls the event, the frustration of her players and the mystery of why they failed to reproduce their true form. The only obvious factors were the slick greens. She felt even they were an insufficient excuse, but when she chaired the English Ladies' Golf Association the following year she insisted that in fairness to the next wave of players all its events should be played on swift putting surfaces.

Defeat was a cruel closure to a Curtis Cup career without precedent. 'Jill Thornhill,' Laura Davies told me, 'was admirable – as a person and as a player. She was most supportive of me when I was young, as she was with others. Her golf? Oh, so steady – and with a wicked short game!'

Chapter Thirty-eight

MACPHERSON – 26 NOT OUT
The amazing record: three pro's in 100 years

OF THE SPORTS Ken Macpherson played at George Watson's College in Edinburgh golf was the one he found most difficult. Rugby and cricket came easily and at hockey he played for Scottish Schoolboys. But golf? This seemed a highly technical game in which the athleticism and timing natural in moving-ball sports meant nothing. Why, then, did he choose it as a career?

The first of two reasons was emotional. This intricate game fascinated him. As he grew older he became intrigued by all aspects of it: the playing, the equipment, the courses, the literature.

At eight he had begun playing hour after hour with cut-down clubs on Gullane's children's course, that 12-hole phenomenon in the heart of East Lothian's golfing wonder-land where thousands have played their first, kinder-garten rounds. His uncle

Two hard acts to follow.

and aunt ran a local restaurant and there the boy Macpherson would spend holidays, repaying his relations' hospitality by washing the dishes and preparing the straw-berries and ice cream.

At school he utilised metalwork classes for first attempts at clubmaking, producing a usable putter and enjoying the discovery that he had an aptitude for technical work with his hands. His first club membership was as a junior at Ratho Park on the outskirts of Edinburgh. When Arnold Palmer came over and conquered in the 1960s, the youth found a hero and his obsession with the game was complete.

The second reason was more pragmatic. He had failed to gain any academic success at school, which he passion-ately disliked, and had no interest in further education. But he was no dullard. He thought out his future, analysed his strengths and weaknesses and reached a logical conclu-sion: as his only achievements had been on the playing fields his career should be in sport.

That being so, golf surely offered the best prospects? For one thing the game was beginning to boom and for another it afforded more than one strand of opportunity: apart from playing, with its potential rewards of prize-money and public recognition, there was the life of a club professional. Alone among his sports golf offered the prospect of a life-long career.

This was not the future Ken's father had envisaged for the son he had sent to a renowned fee-paying school. Macpherson senior was a natural ball-player himself, in particular a skilful scrum-half, so he realised the attractions of a sporting life, but his own father had been a crofter and he personally had worked his way up in life, winning a bursary to a school of high repute and getting a solid job in insur-ance – perhaps he feared a reversion to the old order of things. On reflection, though, he saw the logic of his son's thinking.

At 16, when he was playing off seven, Ken became a junior member of the Royal Burgess Golfing Society, whose 1735 roots had threaded a nomadic route through Leith, Bruntsfield and Musselburgh and finally fetched up at Edinburgh's Barnton. There the professional, Arthur Davidson, having noted the devotion of the small boy who spent every spare minute on the practice ground, told him that if his assistant moved on he would offer him his post.

As a stopgap Ken took a job as an apprentice clubmaker with the St. Andrew Golf Company at Dunfermline (Fife). The experience has left an indelible mark on Macpherson's memory and conscience: 'Working in a factory is some-thing everyone should be subjected to. The environment was totally alien to the world outside and I have unforget-table recollections of some of the less fortunate men who worked there.'

In 1962, when he was 19, he duly joined Davidson at Barnton. 'The next three-and-a-half years were heavenly. In the workshop I did club repairs. I caddied for Roberto de Vicenzo and Kel Nagle and played with Bob Charles and Dai Rees – three Open champions and a Ryder Cup captain. I went on a one-week PGA course and scored 97-per-cent in the clubmaking exam. Suddenly life had taken on a new meaning.

'Arthur Davidson, immaculate in tweed jacket and plus-fours, was a gentleman. He was treated like royalty by the members and provided them with unsurpassable service. It left a deep impression on me.'

Like most assistants, Ken's early ambition was to be a successful tournament professional, a champion even, but his hopes were never fulfilled.

A defining moment came when, in his early twenties, he played in the East-of-Scotland PGA Championship at Kilspindie, 17 miles east of Edinburgh. On the 5,432-yard old course there, with its sss of 66, he went out in 29 strokes. He then came home in 41.

> It helped to convince me that I was wasting my time. Yes, I was a useful player, but not good enough. I had already played with men more talented than I who had failed on the Tour. I was lucky. I recognised the hard fact as a youngster; others have discovered it after ten years of attempt and failure. I have seen a once highly promising pro in tears as he confided his agonies to Harry Busson.
>
> Looking back, I would have loved to have had the time and opportunity to play more and seen how good I could have become, but the consolation was that I could remain part of golf. After all, there was still clubmaking and, particularly, teaching.

> Given the time, I could practise hitting golf balls all day and never tire of doing so. Late afternoon sometimes provides the opportunity to do this and that is when I am at my happiest.
>
> *Ken Macpherson in club brochure.*

Davidson, with a high opinion of him, advised him that his next step should be a job away from home, so he came south. In October 1965, after a disastrous two months at Shirley Park, he was offered a post at Moor Park (Herts.) under former Walton Heath assistant Ross Whitehead. The job was head assistant, and with Whitehead away playing tournaments he was soon in demand as a teacher.

> The hours were dawn until dusk, but the income compensated. For the first time I had a building society account, quite a status symbol!

Ken had a chance to go to South Africa to work with Sid Brews, winner of eight open championships there and Bobby Locke's partner in the pre-war challenge match against Cotton and Whitcombe at Walton Heath. The thought of leaving his roots dissuaded him and he remained at Moor Park for more than five years.

I have written of Liverpool journalist Leslie Edwards as Busson's publicity guru. In Macpherson's case much the same may be said of Tom Scott, a doyen among post-war writers and editor of *Golf Illustrated*. Scott, who lived in Buckinghamshire, used the Metropolitan Line to get to his

Assistants on the move

*M*acpherson's longest serving assistants – 'the Bob and Brown of the 'eighties,' he calls them for the quality of their work – have been MARTYN LANDSBOROUGH (nine years) and TIM PACKHAM (seven). Both have become full professionals – Martyn at Royal Ashdown Forest and Tim at West Sussex.

KARL HAYLER went to the Welcombe Hotel, Stratford. MARC OSBORNE, (scratch at 16), had to stop playing after a rugby injury and works in golf club management.

The happiest story, though, is of ROBERT DICKMAN. Not only did he win the Surrey Open; after many months of treatment he recovered from cancer and went on to become head professional at Banstead Downs. He now owns and runs Cuckfield Golf Centre in Sussex.

Martyn Landsborough

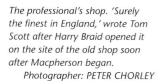

The professional's shop. 'Surely the finest in England,' wrote Tom Scott after Harry Braid opened it on the site of the old shop soon after Macpherson began.
Photographer: PETER CHORLEY

office. So, piling in at stations down the line, did sundry members of Moor Park.

> Smoothly from Harrow, passing Preston Road,
> They saw the last green fields and misty sky.[1]

The members talked golf and not least about their head assistant's teaching. Scott pricked up his ears behind his newspaper and insinuated himself into the conversations.

In January 1971 Macpherson was appointed full professional at Kingswood. Simultaneously, Scott invited him to write an instructional series and also put him on his magazine's front cover. *Golf World* followed up with an article about him and, most beneficial of all in Ken's view, so did *The Director*, with complimentary mentions from Scott.

Early in his six years at Kingswood Ken lodged at the Tadworth Country Club – not quite as luxurious as it sounded but with friendly, hospitable owners. One day a girl named Susan Pearson, due to start work at a nearby company, came to the door also looking for accommodation. She and Ken married in 1974.

His move to Walton Heath? 'I'm a firm believer in fate and the luck of being in the right place at the right time – and fate had decreed that I should come to Walton.'

Fate, though, had arrived in the shape of Harry Busson. Regularly during his time at Kingswood, when Ken visited the Professional Golfers' Cooperative Association's cash-and-carry warehouse at Putney, he would take with him also Busson's own shopping lists of shafts, grips, screws, glue, varnish, pitched thread... all the impedimenta of clubmaking. When he delivered them to Harry's workshop the two men would have a cup of tea and a chat, thus furthering their friendship.

In 1977 Busson confided that he would soon be retiring and expressed trenchant views about the type of man who

should succeed him. He was against any move the club might take to appoint a big-name tournament pro: he didn't think much of some of that breed anyway but was convinced that if one of them got the job he would disappear for long spells and 'leave a *boy* in charge!' 'When the post is advertised, why don't you put in for it?' he suggested.

Ken duly applied and, despite strong competition, got the job. 'He was the unanimous choice,' announced captain Sir Patrick Macrory, 'I am quite sure we have made the right decision.' Unanimous they may have been – but the man who bent the ear of captain and committee was surely Harry Busson.

Macpherson began his duties on August 1, 1977, burdened by the responsibility of succeeding Braid, once the world's greatest golfer, and Busson, perhaps the world's leading wooden-club maker. He was comforted by friends at court. Not only was there Busson, there was Ewen Murray, who had graduated from the role of assistant to that of playing professional. The two had been friends since childhood.

As for Busson, when the club let him stay on as a clubmaker cynics warned Ken that it was bad news ('What? Your predecessor looking over your shoulder all the time? I wouldn't have agreed to that!'). It may well have been to Busson's advantage to have his protégé in place beside him, but what the cynics failed to understand was the camaraderie that had sprung up between the 34-year-old professional and the 70-year-old clubmaker.

The new pro had a hectic and stressful start, both at the club and away from it. Within a year the new shop had been opened by Harry Braid on the site of the old one ('Surely the finest in Britain,' suggested Scott). Also in 1978 the Macphersons' first daughter, Caroline, was born, and a week later came the first European Open. In 1980 the European event again came to Walton; in 1981

[1] *The Metropolitan Line*, from *The Collected Poems of Sir John Betjeman* (John Murray), 1958.

daughter number two, Louise, was born; three months later it was the Ryder Cup match and along the way the Macphersons had moved house.

It has been said that Walton Heath and Macpherson jointly were the first to mount an ambitious selling campaign at a Ryder Cup, producing products bearing a special Cup logo. The weather was wet, umbrellas sold out and piles of short-sleeved shirts remained.

His teaching schedules filled up and eventually overburdened him. Scott recalled peeping at his bookings one day in mid-September and noting that his first vacancy was in late-November. He would return from lessons to find half-a-dozen people waiting to see him, a mass of calls to answer and stock, service and paper work to be dealt with. It had to stop or at least be scaled down. This was rendered a practicality, he says, by hiring the best staff available.

Ken's teaching philosophy is based on fundamental commonsense and logic. His prerequisites, obviously, are the grip and stance, but beyond those fundamentals he derides the mass of technical jargon fed to learners. 'These days pupils expect, indeed *want* to be bombarded with technical information and feel cheated if they don't get it! Similarly, many young teachers tend to want to impress with that sort of stuff.' Ken would never hire a teaching assistant who was over-technical in approach; head assistant Simon Peaford feels much the same about things as his boss.

Behind the easy smile and cheerful chat, Macpherson holds strong views on certain subjects apart from golf. When the idea of his selling cigarettes in the shop was mooted by the committee, as an ardent anti-smoking man he could not, in all conscience, agree. Rather like his mentor, Busson, he is angered by bad manners generally. He derides selfishness, thoughtlessness, lack of courtesy and consideration for others – which in golf ranges from professionals spitting on the course to amateurs entering competitions and not turning up.

The overriding impression one has of him is that of an absurdly young 60-year-old and a man of infectious enthusiasm. In common with developments at other prestigious clubs, his job has changed. Clubmaking has gone, he teaches little; his hands are full serving the members, running the business, masterminding the shop, competing with cut-price stores, contributing his expertise to reviews of course improvements and, not least, playing the part of public relations supremo.

He remembers the responsibility he felt when he got the job. He couldn't play like Braid, nor make clubs like Busson:

> All I could hope to do was provide the best possible service to the members and visitors and ensure that everyone playing golf at Walton Heath gained the maximum pleasure from doing so.

That is what he is still trying to do, and the record of service by Walton Heath's professionals grows more astonishing by the day: only three in a hundred years and Macpherson 26 not out.

Proud moment for Macpherson after 25 years as professional. Surrounded by past captains at the men's dinner in October 2002, he has been made an honorary life member – an honour, ratified in centenary year, which emulates those awarded to his predecessors Braid and Busson.

Photographer: PETER CHORLEY

Chapter Thirty-nine

WANTED: CAPABLE MAN, PATIENT WITH IDIOTS
Thirteen secretaries have tried to live up to Fowler's requirements

HERBERT FOWLER KNEW what a good secretary was. 'What you want,' he told the Abbeydale club in Yorkshire, 'is a man of character who is capable, has good manners and is patient with idiots.'

Of the 13[1] paid secretaries hired by Walton Heath in 100 years, most have been capable, with good manners as well as patience, and the odd one, while not an idiot, proved capable of idiotic acts.

Fowler himself was the club's first secretary until, after eight years, the pressures of being managing director and a course architect grew too heavy. Of those who were to follow him, three stand out.

The first is Captain Herbert Charles Coningsby Tippet, whose stay was brief but his impact considerable. The Newport-born Tippet arrived in 1937 with impressive credentials: the Military Cross, secretarial experience at Ashford Manor in Middlesex, Meadowbrook in the States and latterly Royal Wimbledon, membership of Royal North Devon and a high-class playing pedigree.

He had reached the semi- and quarter-finals of the English Amateur and the last eight of the British, represented the Amateurs against the Professionals and helped win the London Amateur Foursomes for Wimbledon. While in the States he had been runner-up in the Metropolitan Amateur Championship of New York.

Moreover, he had an aptitude for course architecture and this was his most significant contribution to Walton Heath. As you will have read if you have been paying attention, he was responsible for the major alterations to the front nine of the Old immediately before World War II.

He then returned to the Army, leaving the club with a

Captain H.C.C. Tippet, MC. Secretary, player and architect.

problem. Should they appoint Tippet's newly arrived secretary who was currently doing his work? Well, not really. After all she was a woman, Miss Muriel Paul.

Tippet technically remained secretary and attended occasional meetings as late as 1946, but he officially resigned in January 1944. The post was eventually advertised and plenty of candidates replied, but in the unsettled climate of 1947, when food and petrol rationing helped return Britain to wartime austerity, the directors decided it would be 'imprudent' to pay big money to an outsider. Expediently, they appointed Miss Paul.

She was described in the Press, with dubious accuracy, as unique – the only female of the species of the species of golf club secretary! More factually, she did the job, officially or otherwise, for nearly 25 years. At times she also ran the catering and bar and was her own bookkeeper and treasurer. In short the chain-smoking Miss Paul was a winner. Eventually, in 1962, she was made a director.

They had paid her £500 a year at first, but that wasn't important – she had money. She drove fast four-litre Jaguars and their like, rallied in an Austin Healey and travelled far and wide, not least to the Middle East, where she had been born and could converse in Arabic. Off she would go, learning how others lived, to Burma, Formosa, remote parts of India, even Red China – and remember, this was in the 'fifties and 'sixties.

She was, as Tom Scott once wrote, a champion of forlorn causes, helper of the poor, defender of the weak. She died in 2002, aged 97.

Until she retired in 1964, thirsting for more travel and with the gift of a Jaguar from the club, she had the support of assistant secretary Celia Moore. So, indeed, did two subsequent secretaries, because Miss Moore served the club for 16 years until 1977 – a term comfortably beaten by her successor, a Miss Pooley.

---

[1] The number of secretaries traced in my researches. It does not include members who served on an honorary basis during temporary periods, nor any company secretaries who were not also club secretaries.

Muriel Paul with members Dennis Baxter and Michael Easby...

...and with her Austin Healey in the early 'sixties.

In 1978 Miss Pooley, receptionist, became Miss Pooley, assistant secretary. Eight years later this same Miss Pooley became Mrs. Janice Owen. She emulated Miss Paul in both efficiency and a penchant for sporty cars, and in recent times, when secretaries were coming and going every so often, she held things together. When she retired last year she had been 26 years at Walton Heath.

The third outstanding secretary – outstanding, that is for length of service, strength of character and enterprise – was Janice's first boss. This was Bill McCrea, who has already made his mark in these pages: a former wing-commander, a member since 1957 and a golfer good enough to represent Ireland, win Austrian and Dutch championships and finish runner-up to Michael Bonallack in the English Amateur Stroke-Play at the age of 47.

In the 1970 Amateur Championship he played a dramatic match against the American Walker Cup star William Hyndman. Dormy-two down, he forced the American to a 19th hole – whereupon Hyndman chipped in to win.

In the war McCrea won the DFC. Official documents tell of his skill, leadership and bravery on many bombing missions over Berlin, Hamburg and the Ruhr and of his courage and resolution in 1943 when, after a prolonged attack by a fighter, he outmanoeuvred it and nursed his badly damaged Lancaster back to base.

He showed the same forthright, independent attitude in the more comfortable seat of golf club secretary. His 16-year tenure began in 1972 with the task of consolidating the club after its purchase by the members; he helped deal with the motorway incursion; took charge of three European Opens and the Ryder Cup match; involved himself in course alterations through his interest in architecture.

Janice Owen, third from left, at her leaving party in May 2002, with Barbara Guthrie and Charles Harvey, captains of the year, and Bill McCrea, whom she assisted from 1978. McCrea is seen that year with US professional Doug Sanders at the World Junior Match-Play Championship final. Stephen Keppler beat America's Chip Craig by one hole, having been six down with nine to play.

Club Secretaries

1903-11	W.H. Fowler
1911-13	H. Fraser
1913-20	A.J. Sherwood
1920-34	G.J. Hawker
1934-37	J.A. Anderson
1937-44*	Capt. H.C.C. Tippet, MC
1942*-64	Miss M.H. Paul
1964-71	Lt-Col. G.P. Badham
1971-72	K.E.R. Webb (hon.)
1972-88	W/Cdr. W.E. McCrea, DFC
1988-90	A. Heron
1990-92	N.G. Dampney
1992-97	Gp/Capt. G.R. James
1997-2000	N. Lomas
2001-	M. Bawden

Tippet technically remained secretary while serving in World War II, but officially resigned in January, 1944. Miss Paul was officially appointed acting secretary in 1942 and secretary in 1947.

Ken Webb – helped out as hon. secretary when the members' club began.

James Anderson

When the problems with local residents and outside conservation groups came about in the 'eighties he was a central figure. Today, still playing in his early eighties and an honorary life member, even Bill will admit over a gin and tonic that he may occasionally have been slightly guilty of, to use his own phrase, 'pressing home his point of view.'

But of his sincerity, of his love and ambitions for the courses, there can be no doubt. When I asked him whether he could think of something particularly gratifying about his secretarial sojourn or membership his answer was not about any of his successes, on the course or off.

'The *heather's* coming back,' he said. 'That's tremendous, that's *exciting*!'

Oldest Champion

*I*n 1977 at Walton, the English Amateur Championship was won by Terry Shingler (Blackwell, Worcs.), who at 41 years 11 months was reported to be the oldest-ever winner. In a surprise final he beat John Mayell (Copt Heath) four and three, while Walton's James Hopper reached the quarter-finals. In 1983 the club staged its first R&A championship – the British Seniors Open Amateur. A.J. Swann became the first American winner.

GREEN STAFF
Clive Osgood's team

GARDENER
Bill Stanton

HOUSE MANAGER
Neil Day, with Sharon Langton

CLUBHOUSE
Food and drink

OFFICE
Secretary Mike Bawden with, from left, June Watkins (accounts), Caroline Edwards (assistant sec) and Viv Rawlinson (finance manager).

Chapter Forty

CAN ANYONE BEAT BRAID'S 46½ YEARS?
Apparently yes. Is 55 the staff record?

WHO CAN BEAT James Braid's 46½ years at Walton Heath? Who, that is, outside of the pro's workshop, where Bob and Brown, the clubmakers, survived their master whom they had served for half a lifetime.

Clive Osgood, course manager *extraordinaire?* No. Now 52, he may well ultimately exceed James's tenure, but so far he has been at the club a mere 37 years.

Sid Saunders? No. It is said that he helped make the course as a youngster and he retired in 1954, at least 50 years later. But he was not a permanent fixture in the interim. Between boyhood and his 32 years as head greenkeeper he went elsewhere, notably to Cooden Beach (Sussex).

Bill Stanton? Good try, but again no. He joined the green staff in Fred Dulake's day and, approaching 70, still lovingly tends the gardens. But his unbroken service adds up to a meagre 41 years this August!

May I submit the claims of Edith Morgan and a man with no name?

Edith Morgan? She carved the roasts and served in the dining room. It is said that she began work on the club's opening day in May 1904 and I have unearthed evidence that in September 1949 she was planning to retire – no doubt with nostalgic tears for the juicy joints, shepherd's pies and treacle tarts she believed ranked incomparably above golf and golf courses as the peak of Walton Heath's achievements. That would have given her 45 years and four months of service as against Braid's 46 and seven.

But wait. She could not have retired completely, because in July 1954 the board were discussing an impending presentation to Mrs Morgan 'after 50 years of service.' Defeat for Braid? Perhaps that depends on whether our Edie worked full- or part-time in those last few years.

A man with no name? He had one really, of course, but it is unreadable in the board minutes: it looks rather like 'Tach'. I have not found anyone who can remember or identify him. The minute, in 1963, describes him as a

Jim England
Long-serving ranger in 1933

green man no longer fit for work *after 55 years at the club!* Perhaps our winner must remain literally nameless!

Whatever the truths of these minutiae it is clear that longevity of service at Walton Heath has in no way been confined to the pro's shop and that the staff during 100 years have been as interesting as the members.

Consider the stewards (less than 10 of any substance on record)... the course rangers (retired policemen a speciality)... the locker-room attendants ('a good-class Jeeves being sought,' reads an old minute)... the bookkeepers and bartenders, green men and gardeners, waiters and waitresses, cooks and kitchen maids...

For a time, not long ago, almost every waitress seemed Irish – including two close friends, Jean and Bridget. They were almost inseparables. Then, Fred Faulkner tells me, they returned home to Northern Ireland. There, it seems, they never meet – because one is Protestant, the other Catholic.

In the line of stewards begun by Osborn, the Duke of Richmond's old servant, the most legendary figures, present company excepted, remain Ted Foster and Jack Jobson.

Stewards/House Managers

1904-09	J. Osborn
1909-11	T. Bastin
1911-??*	C. Morgan
19??-37*	W.L. Cocker
1937-42	J. Brimley
1942-66	E. Foster
1966-91	J.E. Jobson
1992-	N. Day

* Starting and leaving dates uncertain

231

Greenkeepers/Course Managers

1904-16	J. McNeice
1918-22	S. Ashton
1922-54	S.G. Saunders
1954-78	F.J. Dulake
1978-79	H. Emery
1979-	C. Osgood

Foster, whose son John and two grandsons are among today's artisans, had been chauffeur to Lady Holderness, mother of the champion. He began work at the club during World War II, was for a time the local bobby and helped secretary Muriel Paul ensure the smooth running of the club for more than 20 years.

Ted Foster – 24 years the steward.

'I used to work Saturday mornings, then go to the club at lunchtime,' explains the old rugby international Brian Pope, recalling a typical exchange with the dignified, tactful steward.

'Anyone looking for a game, Foster?'
'Nobody I think *you* would like to play with, sir!'

When Foster retired in 1966 the clubhouse was full for his farewell gold-watch presentation and testimonial and he was apparently the first member of the clubhouse staff to receive a pension. There was a suggestion that he should be made an honorary member. The directors felt it 'not appropriate' but said he should be invited to use the club whenever he wished!

Jack Jobson, who succeeded him, marched in armed with the punctuality and discipline you would expect of a regimental sergeant major in the Coldstream Guards. He imposed high standards. Swearing by visitors (or, God forbid, by members) was stamped out ('*Please* don't use that language, sir') and his opening hours were inflexible to the minute. Entrance at 7.59am was not an option, he would be walking his dog until 8am sharp. After-hours drinks? No chance at all!

He was an admirable ambassador for the club for 25 years until he retired in 1991. The regard in which he was held was reflected in a cheque for £15,000, most of it contributed by individual members.

In 100 years the staffs have inevitably included a few failures and the occasional oddball. Bill McCrea tells of how, as secretary, he once gave his workers a lecture on what to do if the clubhouse ever caught fire. 'Get out immediately,' ordered Bill, 'No heroics. You wouldn't be able to stop the fire anyway once it took hold.'

At one o'clock in the morning his phone rang: there was a fire in the clubhouse that looked deliberate. The culprit turned out to be the assistant chef. 'Well, you reckoned I wouldn't be capable of putting out a fire,' he said, 'So I lit one to find out if you were right.'

A motley procession of servants, their images faded by the years, provides fodder for memories and legends in the artisans' bar and the clubhouse: Twigg in the old dormy house... England the old ranger... George Payne the gardener... Brian Johnston, head chef until he, too, returned to Northern Ireland... Lily Nutley and Winnie Waterlow, described in print as the administrative backbone of the wartime club with Miss Paul until the cavalry arrived in the form of Foster... Edith Boyd... Jessie Watson, behind the bar until 1982... Mesdames Nye and Norah Holley, kitchen maids...

I wonder how many years of service some of *those* could claim? We know that Winnie Waterlow retired at 75 and that Edith Boyd by the end of the war had been tending to members' thirsts for 35 years and was continuing to provide that most essential service. Fred Faulkner, chatting in the artisans' clubhouse, believes that England, who was certainly rangering in the 'thirties, may have begun as long ago as 1906.

My book inevitably is about champions and championships, captains and committee men, the great figures of Walton Heath history. But none of them could have survived without the staff. And (I knew I wouldn't be able to avoid the cliché in the end)... they *also* served!

Jack Jobson – steward for quarter of a century

Chapter Forty-One

THE ARTISANS – 97 YEARS YOUNG
Convivial custodians of village golfing history

WHEN THE ARTISANS are stimulated by questions and a pint or two of Flower's bitter their clubhouse is transformed into a convivial repository of local history. It is a history concerned less with the golf club's eminent members and more with those whose green fingers have nurtured the courses, whose hard hands have been applied in the workshops of Braid, Busson and Macpherson and whose pockets avidly accepted the modest rewards of caddying.

It is an oral, often genealogical history that reaches back and touches hands with the club's distant past. Thus, Tony Saunders' grandfather Syd was an estate manager for Cosmo Bonsor, the club's founder, his father won a prize in the first-ever national artisans tournament and his uncle was Sid Saunders, known for some mysterious reason as 'Soapy,' head greenkeeper for 32 years. Stafford Dulake is the son of Fred, the other long-serving greenkeeper before Clive Osgood, another artisan, came along. As we have observed, Fred Faulkner, locker-room supremo and all-round good egg, represents a dynasty of aspiring professionals who knew Braid's workshop and remembers as a boy continually signing the book in the shop to register his intention to play, as was the village boys' privilege, later in the day.

Fred Faulkner – 'locker room supremo.'

The Walton Artisans are not 100 years old, only 97, and perhaps three years hence they will write their own history. Meanwhile they deserve space in this one, for they have been an important part of the golf club's progress – and by no means merely because of a billion repaired divots.

Their club was founded in 1906, but I have found evidence of earlier existence. In July 1905 the *Surrey Mirror* ran a report, headlined 'Walton-on-the-Hill Artisans Golf,' of an evening sealed-handicap competition played 'among members of the Village Golf Club.'

Possibly this competition was authorised by the golf club or the lord of the manor, but that had not been the norm. In 1904-5 villagers intrigued by the rich man's game and muscling in on it had caused many altercations with the course ranger, reputedly the long-serving Jim England. Manor steward Freshfield took legal advice on the problem.[1]

For all that, irrespective of whether their motive was expediency or genuine goodwill, the reaction of these rich men in 1905 was not repressive but paternalistic. Meetings took place. At the first, with Riddell and Braid representing the club, Fred's father James and others speaking for the

There shall be an Artisans Club known as the Walton Heath Artisans Golf Club ("the Artisans Club"). The number of members shall not exceed 100 and the qualifications for membership are that members should live within the confines of Walton-on-the-Hill village or otherwise as expressly permitted by the Board. The Artisans club will pay ground rent for their clubhouse and such other contributions as from time to time fixed by the Board and will have Rules agreed by the Board.

The starting times for members of the Artisans Club on weekends and weekdays during summer and winter shall be before 8.30 a.m. and after 3 p.m., save that during the months of December, January and February they may also play between 11.30 a.m. and 12.30 p.m.

Walton Heath Golf Club Bye-laws

---
[1] Chapter 4.

233

village golfers and a headmaster and clergyman to ensure temporal and spiritual fair play, Riddell advised the locals to get organised and form a proper club.

At the second meeting, held at the 'Fox and Hounds,' club members promised trophies. Mr Mappin the jeweller said he would provide one each year, Captain Pearson gave a cup that is still competed for today and Riddell gave the two silver teapots, one of which is in the golf club's trophy cabinet, that Fred's father helped win in 1908.

On January 1, 1906, the artisans' club became a fact, and in July 1907 lord of the manor Malcolm Bonsor approved the first notice permitting golf on the heath not only to members of the golf club but to certain locals: members of the Village Club and, early and late in the day, boys under 15 and caddies employed by the golf club.

Much has changed socially in the world since then, when the idea behind the young artisan movement was to offer manual workers free or cheap golf purely in return for maintenance work on courses and buildings, and when:

> Artisans were allowed to play when most members did not want to, although deference and patronage usually came together in an annual competition for which the middle classes provided both the prizes and the refreshments.[2]

Judging from local press reports, the Walton artisans were more competition-minded than the parent club though not necessarily as good: in their first recorded match against the club they were whitewashed eight-nil.

In 1909 they entertained an 11-strong Cantelupe team attached to Royal Ashdown Forest that contained 11 Mitchells, all from the same family. Surely 'A. Mitchell' was Abe, later considered by many to be the greatest professional never to win the Open? The artisans' golf was improving: not only were Cantelupe among the earliest artisan clubs, they were also one of the strongest, but Walton held them to a half.

When the Artisan Golfers' Association was founded in 1921, by now with a principal object 'to extend the game, particularly among the working men of England and Wales,' it owed a debt to Walton Heath Golf Club. It came about largely through J.H.Taylor, Fred Hawtree and Riddell, who became its first president.

The first annual meeting of the association was held in Walton's drill hall and next day the initial Artisan Golfers' Tournament, forerunner of the national championship, was played under handicap over both courses for a challenge cup put up by Riddell's *News of the World*. More than 200 entered and the winner was J.H.Taylor.

No, not *that* J.H.Taylor. We are talking here about Mr. Taylor the village postman. Playing off 21, he did not exactly endear himself to the opposition by returning a net 147 (one report says 146) for the 36 holes to win by

Fred Dudley – bus conductor who had Walker Cup trial.

eight strokes. Bennett, one of the club's green men, won the gold medal for the best scratch score (78+80=158).

Braid's sons, Harry and James, joined and played for the artisans, and Harry, an Old Whitgiftian, became their president, following a lord and three knights.[3] By the 'twenties the heath had become a home for regular matches between representative teams of artisans and members of the R&A, a tradition that was resumed and now continues.

In the 'forties, Fred Dudley, gardener and bus conductor, became a rarity: an artisan offered a Walker Cup trial. It is claimed by artisans that he was beaten only once during the week but was left out of the team. By 1950 a junior section was being set up; indeed an artisan golfers' junior tournament had been held at Walton as long ago as 1938.

In September 1953, l6 artisans flew from Heathrow in an old Dakota for a match against the L'Ancresse club in Guernsey. 'We claim this was the first time an artisans club had flown to a club fixture,' says Fred Faulkner. '2003 is the 50th anniversary and home-and-away fixtures have been planned.'

In the old days artisan headquarters meant the 'Fox and Hounds', where Braid, honorary captain from the start of the club and for the rest of his life, might take the chair and annual meetings traditionally took two nights, but in the early 'fifties the golf club made space available in the old caddiemaster's office and chauffeurs' room. In 1973

[2] *Sport in Britain* (Cambridge University Press), 1989.
[3] Lord Riddell, Sir Emsley Carr, Sir William Carr, Sir Frederic Hamilton.

TWO WORLDS – DIFFERENT BUT THE SAME

Members of artisan clubs and those of private clubs go on living in different worlds – by choice. I could give many instances, but it will suffice to quote that of the Walton Heath artisans, because they share the pleasures of golf on two of our finest inland courses with members of an exclusive and expensive club, and do so in an atmosphere of mutual trust, independence and amity.

Through all the years of social change Walton Heath artisans pursued their own way, acknowledging the great help received from the parent club but enjoying their own kind of independence. They had their own clubhouse, and in 1973 built a new one on an adjacent site made available by the parent club.

In this new home, as in the old, they have their own bar, and on any Sunday from 11am onwards one can see them coming in from the course, having started their rounds when parent club members were sitting down to breakfast or still between the sheets. Soon their clubhouse would be lively with chatter and badinage over pint tankards dispensed by a member taking his turn behind the bar.

If a competition had been played, the cards would be handed in and checked and the result announced with the usual rude remarks about the winner's handicap. In one corner the committee members might be discussing business, and at other tables the playing cards would be out for a few hands of solo whist or rummy before it was time to go home to Sunday dinner.

In its essentials this scene, which can be seen any Sunday morning in nearly 200 artisan clubs up and down the country, is no different from what goes on in the bars and lounges of the parent club a few yards away. The time of day is different, and the circumstances, but both worlds have their place in the universe of golf.

GEOFFREY COUSINS, *Golf in Britain* (Routledge and Kegan Paul), 1975

that accommodation gave way to the present clubhouse. A levy on artisan members was imposed for the building and they did all the internal work.

It would be surprising if the two clubs, being neighbours and relations, had not had differences at some time or other and occasionally there have been disagreements and debates on subjects ranging from starting times to leases and from membership limits to the labour and money required for adequate upkeep of the courses.

Spasmodically there have also been personal actions embarrassing to both clubs, notably when members entered outside events not as Walton Heath Artisans but as Walton Heath. One, long ago, turned out to be a veritable bandit to boot; another, who allegedly made a habit of entering under the senior club's name, was asked to resign. Coincidentally he was being nominated as captain of a county.

For most of the time, though, the relationship has been close. Officers like Bob Armstrong and Briss Lucas have been made honorary members of WHGC. The services to the club have gone far beyond divoting and some until now have remained unrecognised.

They have ranged over the years from patrolling at night in case the Suffragettes attacked to controlling crowds at European Opens and the Ryder Cup. When the motorway threatened to cross the fifth of the Old and the eighth and 14th of the New, an eloquent speech by the artisans' chairman Steve Hayman at a public hearing helped get the plans altered. Also in the 'seventies Eric Armstrong, Bob's brother, was deputy speaker in the House of Commons when the authority to fence off the courses for big events was given by the Minister.

The Artisans' clubhouses – old and new. Stand up the man who owned the Bentley!

The golf club's problems with residents and others in the 'eighties and 'nineties ultimately reminded it that its artisans were a mighty influence in the village and essential allies. 'Great offence was caused when they were not taken into our confidence,' captain Coombes declared in 1990. In a sense, as villagers on the one hand and golfers on the other, they bestride the balance.

Throughout the country clubs have been killing off their artisan sections. In 1996, amid difficult negotiations for a new agreement, the artisans of Walton Heath were formally assured by the board that they were regarded as an integral part of the club's long-term future.

1904: note naïve effort to include some action!

1908

1927

1947: the smoking room, part of which remains as the members' lounge

1942 Building to right was the secretary's office and boardroom. It later became Bussson's pro's shop and was pulled down to make way for Ken Macpherson's shop.

Through the Carr era and the 32 years of the members' club the old clubhouse has undergone much change, extension and modernisation. Any dreams of moving it over the road, nearer the finishing holes, remain unfulfilled: it stays defiantly where it was set down. The surround of the original front door – now at the back – is still there, with 'AD 1903' carved into it. Here is an encapsulation and treasure house of a hundred years.

1953

ZANE SCOTLAND – began his international career in the millennium and won the Spanish and Portuguese Amateur Championships in 2002.
Photographer: PHIL SHELDON

238

Chapter Forty-two

APPROACHING THE CENTURY
A new look as times change

THE 'NINETIES AT Walton Heath were neither nervous nor, so far as I am aware, naughty. They were certainly challenging.

We have already noted some of the happenings: the reversion of the Old course to its former order... the last European Open... the resolution, for better or for worse, of problems involving extra holes, a clubhouse over the road and rights-of-common.

Much more was to happen, but I shall write sparingly of it. For one thing it is history of so recent a vintage that its significance in the overall, century-old scheme of things cannot be foretold. For another the characters concerned are still around. They are not yet history and one cannot write about them objectively in the way one can about, say, Braid, Fowler and Riddell. Who knows? Were I to do so the dreaded night-time knock on the door might come from callers bent on revenge for inaccurate, even libellous reportage.

The world was continuing to alter dramatically: economic recessions and a society as different from that of pre-war as titanium is to hickory. 'We are running a *business*,' stressed a club luminary, trying to convince critical members early in the decade.

In 1990 a group of senior members decided that the club needed re-structuring. Walton Heath was not the only club thinking that way, indeed the R&A had issued a document stressing the need for administrations suitable for modern times. 'At the meeting of past captains[1] in October that year,' Tom Corrigan says, 'Alec Bryant, who would become the club's first president since Alick Renshaw's death in 1983, asked me to prepare outline proposals.'

The club's only governing body was its committee: captain, vice-captain and nine elected members. The reformers argued that the system had weaknesses. There

Congratulations

By kind permission of Stan McMurtry – 'Mac' – of the Daily Mail.

were no trustees; the captains came and went within a year; the elected nine could serve three years at most; no past captains were represented unless they were among the nine elected; net result, no continuity of policy and insufficient long-term planning.

A captain's knowledge and experience were lost as soon as he had acquired them, said those proposing change. The secretary, the only real element of continuity, had almost unchallenged power. Decisions were inclined to be based on whims and be relevant only in the short term.

Eventually, re-drafted articles of association were adopted and a new-look administration came into effect on May 1, 1992.

There would be a *BOARD*, which would look after long-term planning, property, finance and overall policy. It would comprise six elected members plus the captain and vice-captain *ex-officio*. Its chairman, treasurer and green committee chairman would come from the elected six.

A *GENERAL COMMITTEE*, chaired by the captain and comprising his vice-captain and six elected members, would deal with house, golf, membership and related issues.

A *GREEN COMMITTEE* would look after the courses. It was to be chaired by an elected board member and would comprise three elected members and the captain and vice-captain *ex-officio*.[2]

Elected members of the general committee could serve for a maximum of three consecutive years, but those on the board and green committee could remain for nine,

---

[1] The past captains meet annually to nominate a member to be proposed as vice-captain.
[2] From February 2001 the lady captain has sat with a vote on the board and both committees.

DAVID BARBER
SAILOR, GOLFER AND BANKER

PATRICK WEBB
THE CAPTAIN

PHILIP TRUETT
VICE CAPTAIN AND ARCHIVIST

ROBIN ELSDON-DEW
THE CHAIRMAN

a third of them retiring each year but available for re-election.

The first elected directors were Robin Elsdon-Dew (chairman), Tom Corrigan (treasurer), John Woods (green committee chairman), Peter Renshaw, David Barber and Tim Taylor - two chartered accountants, a banker, an insurance broker and a solicitor, suitably chaired by a former GP whose bedside manner remained unsullied as a pharmaceutical physician. All except Taylor were past captains. The current captain was Patrick Webb, who augmented the board, *ex-officio*, with his vice-captain, Philip Truett.

'The structure was designed partly to spread responsibilities,' says Corrigan, who would ultimately succeed Elsdon-Dew as chairman. 'Previously a considerable burden fell on the captain, who was also in effect chairman of the club. The change helped the captains to enjoy their years and the chairman could face any music.'

For the rest of the decade, in the interests of long-term planning, strategy became the 'in' word: strategy groups,

Chairmen

1903-05	The Hon. A. Gathorne-Hardy
1905-28	Sir A.W.B. Kennedy
1928-34	Lord Riddell
1935-35	E. Hudson
1935-41	Sir Emsley Carr
1941-46	Sir Frederic Hamilton
1946-47	J. Carnes
1947-49	Sir John Hay
1949-69	Sir William Carr
1969-71	C.E.B.L. Carr

Those above were the chairmen of the company board. From 1972 the captains were automatically the club chairmen. The organisation was restructured in 1992.

1992-96	Dr. R.W. Elsdon-Dew
1996-2001	T.S. Corrigan, OBE
2001-	B.W. Meaby

strategy papers, strategy reviews. Questionnaires followed liberally. More informal consultations with members took place than ever before.

Long-term? At a 1995 meeting Robin Elsdon-Dew was asking his board how they saw the club in 25 years' time. He pointed to the likely changes in society and club membership and urged them to develop a broad framework to cope with them. A strategic review planned the following year embraced subjects from land issues and future legislation to the club's image, clubhouse, membership... and, inevitably, money.

Finance

The board went on performing the eternal juggling and balancing act involving the inter-related factors of membership numbers, society income, course comfort, subscription rates and major expenditure. In 1990 visitors' fees had been raised by up to 50-per-cent and the subscription was hiked from £408 to £520. At the agm David Barber explained to members surprised by the increase the situation he felt recent committees had inherited:

> By budgeting only for minor surpluses the club has not set aside enough to do more than maintain the status quo, with the resultant state of the clubhouse and course. We have been under-funded for years and paying subscriptions far too low for a club of Walton Heath's standing. As a percentage of turnover our subs average 29-30%. At Sunningdale the figure is 39% and at Royal Mid Surrey 60%.

Nasty shocks had upset plans based on deficit financing and modest subscription increases. Nobody had anticipated interest rates jumping from two to 15-per-cent and remaining high. Then the Health Inspector threw his book at the club about its kitchens. As a result, improvements projected to cost £55,000 required an additional £46,000 in 1990 and similar amounts in the next two years. News about the ageing clubhouse was never good; now work on its roof loomed as a probable and unwanted extra.

But as on the course, so behind the scenes: the luck tends to even out. Following other top clubs, Walton

TIM TAYLOR
THE LEGAL BEAGLE

JOHN WOODS
CHAIRMAN OF THE GREEN

TOM CORRIGAN
THE TREASURER

PETER RENSHAW
CRICKETING GOLFER AND PAST CAPTAIN

Caricatures: P. Stewart Lucus

applied for and, in 1991, received from the R&A an interest-free loan of £50,000, repayable in 10 annual instalments. Three years later, following a European Commission edict exempting subscription income from VAT, the board swept up a windfall of around £235,000 in rebate and interest. Members would no longer pay VAT on their subs, but the refund was retained for the benefit of the club – a policy accepted by most members but inspiring one of them to stand up at the 1995 agm and call treasurer Corrigan a money launderer!

The board was able to afford at least two major items on its wanted list. In 1996 a state-of-the-art greenkeeping facility costing some £350,000 was finally opened south of the Dorking Road, and the following year the 30-year-old irrigation system was replaced for around £250,000 – with dire warnings that its liquor must not ruin the patient's character. By 2002, from what the minutes called 'a strong cash position,' the £41,700 outstanding from the £75,000 unsecured loan stock issued in 1971[3] would be repaid.

Formal or casual?

Ricochets from the bombardment of traditional social customs in the outside world splintered the membership. Youth no longer automatically went to work, let alone play, in jacket, collar and tie; it did not comprehend, and in some cases didn't care about, the accepted standards of dress at golf clubs like Walton, where the rule was jacket and tie everywhere after 11am. The dress code increasingly cropped up at meetings.

In 1991 only 13% of the male members and 7% of the ladies were under 30 and around 20% of both sexes were over 70.[4] A general policy to restrict new members to applicants younger than 50 was adopted.

Young people had to be encouraged. In 1993, when he was captain, Philip Truett embarked on a crusade for them. He had found that the 105 members under 30 rarely used

_____
[3] Chapter 30.
[4] In 2002 the average age of playing men was 50.3 and the ladies 57.9.

the clubhouse. 'We don't know who you are and you don't know your fellows,' he told them. His idea was to group them as under-35s, not under-30s, to engender team spirit under a captain, Sean Horkan (winner of gold medals in 1989 and 1990), and to encourage social get-togethers including mixed matches against clubs.

Some of the not-so-young joined the calls for change and so did societies – for casual dress and a casual bar. In 1995 it was captain Richard Williams' turn to grasp the nettle:

> With the grudging agreement of some of my committee members I introduced, on a three-month trial, casual dress in the members' lounge at all times and in the Renshaw Room at weekends. Members expressed their views either by surpassing their previous sartorial elegance or by sticking their necks out by changing only their shoes and coming into the bar in their golfing clothes. All but the toughest among the latter type were made to feel uncomfortable and, unlike King Canute, Walton Heath members stopped the tide, if only for a few years.

Five-way play-off!

It is 1998. The Gold Vase, revived by Golf Weekly *and held this year at Walton, is being decided on the Old's final green. Four players have tied on 147 (three over par) after rounds on both courses this blustery, rainy September day and darkness is fast shrouding the green as the last contestants arrive. Steve Barwick, from East Berkshire, has a great chance of a 74 for 146 and victory over the waiting four: Mark Side (Shirley Park), Mike Reynard (Moseley), Rupert Rea (Royal Mid-Surrey) and Adam Gee (Leatherhead). He three-putts – it is a five-way tie.*

But what is to be done? Continue? It is too dark. Tomorrow? Impossible. Later? No mutually convenient date for weeks. A countback? Not appropriate.

Eventually an 18-hole play-off over the Old is fixed for November, two months hence. Rea, a 20-year-old economics student at Bath University, wins in a canter with a superb two-under-par 70.

Patrick Webb, 1992 captain, turns coach before the annual match against the Mayor's side.

Further trials have taken place. Calls for a spike bar remained unanswered because of space problems and, while casual dress in the Renshaw Room all week attracted more people, relaxation in the dining room caused a division so that a compromise of jackets-over-casual was implemented. Oh, and, good heavens, younger members and visitors had been wearing caps in the clubhouse! The board, under Brian Meaby (now chairman), decided that the whole subject should be dealt with under the strategy review which would continue to examine all aspects of the club – a decision that promptly resulted in another questionnaire and nearly 600 responses.

Golf

The 1991 European Open was soon seen as Walton Heath's farewell to big professional championships. Thoughts of a Seniors event came to naught and were re-directed:

> The board wants to attract more top amateur golf to our courses as the prospect of top professional events returning dwindles with the advent of so many rich corporate golf centres willing to bid large sums to host events. *So wrote James Hopper, captain in 1999.*

> Walton Heath will not pay fees to attract particular events, *added his successor, Reg Hutchison.* However, while we must be aware of their frequency as they affect our cash flow, the club welcomes the opportunity to host suitable amateur and professional events provided they are in keeping with our aims, history and traditions.

Hutchison was writing soon after two ladies' national amateur championships, the 1998 English Close and 2000 British,[5] had been held. For the men, an amateur England-v-Spain match, the 1999 British Mid-Amateur and 2002 English Amateur followed and the Gold Vase was a recurring theme.

The Mid-Amateur, for over 25s, was won by John Kemp

(John O'Gaunt, Biggleswade). He beat Stephen East (Moortown) by 5 and 4 in the final, but the flashpoint of the championship was his third-round defeat of Gary Wolstenholme, winner of three Mid-Amateurs and never previously beaten in the event.

Last year's English Amateur was a triumph for Richard Finch, from Hull. His final against Giles Legg (Dudsbury, Dorset) had been a comparatively pedestrian affair, but Finch suddenly transformed it with a breathtaking spell of two eagles and a birdie.

At the third, the 21st hole of the two-round final, Finch's ball sat nastily on a pathway left of the green and he was not allowed to lift it from what was deemed an integral part of the course… He proceeded to hole the chip for the first of his two eagles. That put him two up and he bulldozed his way on to win by six and five.

All these events were successfully staged. The 2003 Walker Cup match was hoped for as a fitting celebration in centenary year but the R&A took it to Ganton. It is 20 years since the club staged its first R&A event – the 1983 Senior Open Amateur Championship.

Beneath these heady levels the club's competitions threw up their own highlights and much to declaim about in the bar. Not least there has been the strength in depth at the top. I am told that Walton can field a team of 10 whose combined aggregate handicap totals plus two.

In 1993 the club championship, the Alick Renshaw Salver, much changed over the years, became a 36-hole medal embracing both courses… the previous year Robin Clark had won his tenth gold medal in 11 years and in 1998 would win the Salver for a record seventh time. In a seniors' stableford in 1990, Ken Ohlson, on replacement hips, accrued an obscene 51 points (scores of 77 gross, 58 net), possibly a record also… On the New, Alastair Wells and Richard Hall both equalled the course best of 67…

At home, Mark James won the 1997 Gold Vase and in 2001 Walton Heath boosted its tally of post-war Surrey club championships to nine. Away, Jonathan Collier and James won the London Amateur Foursomes at The Berkshire… Cliff Weight and Chris Dale took President's Putters at Rye… and, more famously, Zane Scotland, from Woodcote Park, joining Walton Heath in his quest for experience on testing courses, began his international career in the millennium.

The most dramatic finish? Anyone would be hard pushed to beat the Gold Vase climax described on page 241, but strong challengers would be the club's team in the 1994 *Mail on Sunday* tournament…

The team (Brian Ling, Richard Williams, Brian Ebbs, John Jessop, Bob Green and his last-round substitute Reg Hutchison) have won through seven rounds to reach the last eight at the Belfry. Victory there will mean going to Deauville for the semi-finals...

With their match against Diss standing at 2-2, John Jessop, winner of his previous eight matches, finds himself in his third sudden–death play-off in the series. He loses – at the fifth extra hole.

The courses

Early in the 'nineties the yob culture endemic in modern society inflicted a spate of vandalism, cars careering across greens. Over the years, considering the circumstances of common land, such incursions have been mercifully rare, but they were a frustration to a green staff and committee wanting to concentrate on the courses' future development. As the R&A was preaching, even the best courses could be made better.

The first hole remained a problem child and its guardians continued to concern themselves with it. Adjustments of tee, green and left-hand bunker were made to encourage play away from the road.

But one question inevitably returned: should it become a par four again? In 1995, as an experiment, the medal tee was moved to a par-four position at weekends and proved popular. The following year a board resolution to make it permanent was put to the agm.

It would be a weak and dangerous four, said the opposition; the shorter version was a safer and testing three and an excellent 19th. No, said those behind the resolution, the par three was the more dangerous option through the prox-

Robin Clark – won 10 of his gold medals in 11 years

imity of the road. Anyway, Fowler had designed it as a subtle four and would never have condoned a long, difficult opening par three that slowed play.

The par-four resolution won the vote but lost the day. It attracted 51 supporters against 32, not the 75% majority needed.

It seems that play at the first, never mind the par, had not caused an insurance claim in 92 years. I know of one case where a ball struck a lady's car, but members who never hit bad shots will not need my confirmation that it was propelled by a society golfer. Perhaps, someone suggested, the hole could be a four for members and a three for visitors!

Advance of the Juniors

The Juniors were seen and heard of more in the 'nineties than in any previous era. It was the modern chapter of a story that began 100 years ago. The first rules stated that on weekdays schoolboys under 18 (no mention of girls until some years later) who were sons of members

may be permitted to use the green, the consent of the committee having been asked and given, at a nominal fee of 10 shillings per annum.

There was no section as such. Veterans who were youngsters before World War II were not aware of one even then. Club elders or their own fathers would give them the nod and the boys and girls went out to play. 'Possibility of a junior section to be considered,' then appeared in the minute books – but that was in 1972, when the club was 69 years old! Over the years the section rode peaks and troughs. John Jessop recalls 1996, his year of captaincy:

Entry was open almost exclusively to close relatives of members or artisan members; enthusiasm was low; organisation was by a few dedicated members, mainly ladies. That year, a junior, Robert Hynson, won the autumn gold medal, but could not receive it because he was under 18 and not a full member.

The rules were later changed. Now, 24 of the hundred juniors are not related to members. The quality of golf has improved enormously. Respected members have helped. Juniors can win competitions. In 2002 Lewis Parker (handicap 4) equalled the New course record of 67 from the white tees. In short, the section flourishes and boosts the club. Only one pity. Where are the girls?

In March 1998, following a report by architect Donald Steel, an egm was called to approve 22 changes on the two courses on a single vote. However, some members believed that material alterations deserving individual resolutions were involved and the meeting was cancelled.

That July, after members had answered a questionnaire, and studied papers prepared by John Jessop outlining a proposed long-term courses policy, another egm was held and the 75% majority was achieved for a batch of separate proposals. The changes to the Old included construction of two fairway bunkers (left of the sixth and right of the 13th) and the retirement or re-shaping of others.

Ambitions for both courses are high. The determination is to have them of equally high championship standard and, in an era when impressive courses are appearing in various parts of the world, to maintain and improve the Old's position within the top 100 in the unofficial rankings.

The Old, having slipped down the list with other courses like Wentworth, Ganton and Woodhall Spa, improved by 16 places to 76th in *Golf Magazine's* world lists in 1999 and 2001 and in 2002 *Golf World* raised it to 18th in the UK overall and sixth inland. The New, to the chagrin of those who regard it as Fowler's untouched masterpiece, has not

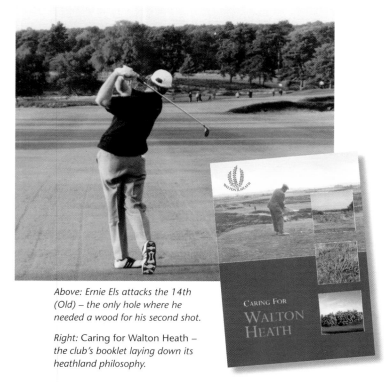

Above: Ernie Els attacks the 14th (Old) – the only hole where he needed a wood for his second shot.

Right: Caring for Walton Heath – the club's booklet laying down its heathland philosophy.

yet made the world's top 100, nor achieved British ranking, and a need to heighten its profile has risen. Such rankings, arbitrary and sometimes infuriating, nevertheless represent significant publicity, perhaps influencing choices for championships and certainly the minds of American visitors.

In 1999 came a salutary sight and a defining moment. Ernie Els played the Old from the then championship tees and hit nothing more than a seven iron for any second shot except at the 14th, where he needed a three wood and holed for an eagle three!

New back tees have been built on both courses, each of which now measures over 7,000 yards (how many clubs can claim the same?), and bunkering and other changes aim to counter modern equipment, strength and expertise. Acres of scrub birch and oak have been cleared, resurrecting long-forgotten vistas and the open heathland Fowler inherited a century ago.

A driving force behind research and planning these past few years has been Jessop, green-committee chairman from 1998 until succeeded by Findlay Picken. The papers he wrote in 1998, year of the proposals mentioned above, aimed at looking comprehensively at the future overall development of the courses. The resultant findings have been implemented in degrees and are still on the table while priorities, not least course presentation, are acted on. They reflect the perennial struggle to provide courses tough enough for champions yet fair and enjoyable for the rank and file of both sexes. The vision is one of courses changed and updated in the way Fowler would have transformed them and around which a 'sea of heather' will survive and regenerate in all its glory.

That heathery vision is central to the club's policy – as

lords of the manor and with the responsibilities of stewardship that go with it – of gradual restoration of the heath. In 2001 the club published a booklet, *Caring for Walton Heath*, and therein laid down its philosophy:

> The club's policy is to restore and conserve the heathland of Walton Heath, thus fostering the flora and fauna that depend on the unique habitat. It will continue to be advised by the best available expertise and will consult with all other parties that benefit from the heath and have an interest in its conservation; in particular it will consult with the local community through the Tadworth and Walton Residents' Association and the Reigate and Banstead Council... Supporting the wider ecological imperative to restore and conserve lowland heathland is not only most rewarding in its own right but is in the best interests of the club and all others who use and enjoy the heath.

Any other business?

Yes, indeed! To begin with, in 1990 a resolution was passed to ensure that the club could not be sold without the approval of the members. In 1994, with membership generally replete, the waiting list, which had opened and closed by turns, was replaced by a 'candidates book,' in which entries would not imply any order of acceptance but would enable the committee to choose from the widest possible field of applicants.

Costly work on the old clubhouse was on just about every agenda. Some members still liked the idea of a new HQ across the road; others dismissed the vision as unrealistic and swore undying love for the existing building with its tradition and cosy, peaceful, tucked-away location. 'A planned programme of maintenance and replacement is the most financially advantageous option,' the board declared in the mid-nineties, 'and one that should enable the property to be preserved to a high standard for at least 50 years.'

More matches were planned, more social events: dinners and dances, bridge and barbeques. Walton Heath used to be essentially a golf club. In the modern age those in charge believed it had to be something more and as a result believe it is a better place to be than ever. The trouble is, a lot of the members have been hard to convince about the social side. Ninety-six per-cent of those who answered the latest questionnaire this year agreed that Walton Heath is and should remain primarily a *golfer's* club!

My wife after a series of lessons from Ken Macpherson, has announced that she has the secret of golf. "It is all terribly easy. You point the clubhead at the target, then place your feet, hips and shoulders parallel to the target, give the club a waggle and then, just before striking the ball, you SMILE." Now that's what I get wrong!

James Hopper, captain's letter to members, 1999

Chapter Forty-three

EQUALS AT LAST!
Ladies get the vote, club gets its licence

THE LADIES MAY NOT have had any rules in the past, but once the members' club was formed in 1971 they knew precisely where and how they stood. Bye-laws were published binding them to the rules of the overall club and company; their captain was to be elected annually by a committee of past holders of that office; their committee was a sub-committee of the club's; election of members was within its 'discretion' but subject to final approval by the main committee.

Restrictions on weekend play were made clear. Between 9.30 and 10.30am and 1 and 2pm during November to February, with a fractional difference on March afternoons, the ladies could not start on the course on which two-balls were being played and they were allowed to start on the three- and four-ball course only if each lady was playing with a gentleman. They could not play on a course where a men's medal or competition was being held – normally on the first Saturday of each month.

Hilary Lydall, the captain, felt the rules 'generally accorded with our original wishes,' but not everyone was satisfied. Lady Costain felt that as they had 'put up at least £30,000' for the new club they should be entitled to full representation on its committee. And why should they not have a vote when attending annual general meetings? 'If we pressed a claim a number of male members would withdraw their support from the club,' said Mrs Lydall.

Nevertheless, the men performed a few acts of chivalry. Traditionally, the committee had paid an annual sum to the ladies to cover expenditure. In 1972, confronted with a request for £180, they gave them £250, plus additional sums for specifics. This, wrote Ken Webb, then finishing his stint as hon secretary, was 'in appreciation of all the work you do for the club and to relieve you from the necessity of running your affairs on a shoestring.'

At that years' agm thanks were conveyed to chairman Alick Renshaw 'for all he had done to make the ladies'

The victorious 2001 Hicks Trophy team. From left, standing: Alison Taylor, Jenny Pain, Savi Boex; seated: Chris Griffith, Alison Barratt (captain), Jill Thornhill, Kathy Daly.

The supporting cast

Competitively, so far as the ladies are concerned, the members' club years have been dominated by Jill Thornhill,[1] but a supporting cast has contributed sundry highlights:

1971: *Club team win Pearson Trophy, beating Royal Cinque Ports and Muswell Hill in final stages at Brookmans Park.*

1973: *Walton Heath win Hicks Trophy – and will repeat the achievement six more times. Three of four Surrey championship semi-finalists are from Walton: Jill Thornhill (winner), Mrs Harvie (runner-up) and Miss Buxton.*

1974: *Hillary Kaye sets first sub-70 Old course record with 68.*

1975: *Diane Strickland wins Surrey championship, only Walton Heath player apart from Mrs Thornhill to do so since the war.*

1976: *Mrs Strickland and Margaret Nunn win London Foursomes at Langley Park.*

1978: *Mrs Strickland takes Jill Thornhill to 19th hole in Surrey championship final.*

1979: *Mrs Piper, who had helped Jill T. win London Foursomes in 1970, involved in dramatic finish to this year's event. She and Margaret Nunn lose final by one hole, last putt deciding, in day of wind and storm.*

1982: *Pru Riddiford wins Senior Ladies' Open Amateur Stroke-Play Championship.*

1985: *Surrey, led by Mrs Thornhill, take fourth consecutive county championship – Walton players assisting.*

1986: *Mrs Riddiford again wins Senior Ladies' Open Amateur Stroke-Play – from record entry of 76 at Longniddry.*

1989: *Diana Walpole helps Jill T. to win London Foursomes at Royal Ashdown Forest.*

1998: *First-ever Oxford-Cambridge university match for ladies played at Walton. Club's Emma Truett, the instigator, captains Oxford to 7-2 victory.*

2000: *Club win Druce Trophy, Hicks Trophy and Pearson Trophy Surrey Cup.*

2001: *Walton Heath retain Hicks Trophy; become first winners of SLCGA Centenary Bowl.*

2002: *Club again win Centenary Bowl.*

[1] Chapter 37.

section feel an important unit of the club;' the section 'had acquired a glow of happy contentment through the consideration shown to us.'

Meanwhile the social campaign for equal opportunities and rights in all walks of life was growing in strength and at Walton Heath toes were timorously dipped into muddied waters.

In 1975 Jimmy Irvine Edwards, having contacted the committee, was informed that the term 'men's bar' would no longer be used: 'The room will in future be known as 'the bar' and, although ladies will not be encouraged to use it, neither will they be prevented from doing so.'

Playing restrictions were tinkered with, to the slight advantage of the ladies, and, while subscriptions rose to 70% of the men's rate, Bill McCrea, then firmly installed as secretary, claimed that at comparable clubs the average was 79%. The ladies had been very co-operative over the years, he said, had interfered with the men's golf very little and had arranged their competitions so that they did not significantly affect receipts from societies and visitors.

But representation in the club's corridors of power? A vote? Not yet. But gradually there were moves…

In 1986, Denis Waugh told his committee colleagues that the ladies and mid-weekers should both be represented among them – an opinion that, according to the minutes, received 'limited support.' In 1988 'the possibility of equal subs being paid to entitle them to a vote at general meetings' was being considered by the ladies' officers. In 1989 some disappointment was expressed that while the club was lowering the voting age from 25 to 21, women were still precluded.

Similar things were happening in many clubs. At Walton the first chinks in the walls of tradition were being chiselled and a blend of goodwill, understanding, expediency, pragmatism and necessity would eventually knock them down.

At the heart of the matter was the club's registration certificate, its 10-year drinks licence, which was due for renewal after December 31, 2000. Up and down the country golf and other clubs were facing the same examination from the magistrates. In summary it went something like this:

So you wish to renew your licence and to sell drinks on a private-club basis?
Yes, of course.
So does everyone over 21 in your club, men and women, have equal rights in every way?
Well, er, no, not quite.
Then you may not get your licence.

Championships return

*B*eginning in the 'eighties, national championships for women came back to Walton Heath.

1982: The **British Amateur** returned after 14 years and was won by Katrina Douglas.

1998: The **English Close Champion-ship**, last held on the heath in 1928, provided a thrilling end. Liza Walters (Chevin, Derby) stood two up with three to play against future Curtis Cup player Elaine Ratcliffe (Sandiway, Cheshire), but was all-square after Elaine hit a wedge to four feet at the 18th. At the first extra hole, measuring 273 yards, Walters, failing to get up and down from wide of the green, let the championship slip to Ratcliffe, who hit a three wood just short and made par.

2000: Walton's third **British Amateur**. A memorable finish to a semi-final when Emma Duggleby hit her wooden second to five feet at the 448-yard 16th, saw opponent Maria Boden get to eight feet, holed for an eagle to draw all-square, then won the last hole to reach the final.

Rebecca Hudson, Yorkshire Curtis Cup star, winner of the qualifying trophy and playing at somewhere near the speed of light, avenged her English final defeat by beating Duggleby five and four and finished 19 under par for the week. 'The Old course received as many plaudits as the players,' wrote Lewine Mair in The Daily Telegraph.

Left: Rebecca Hudson receives trophy from Reg Hutchison.

If Walton Heath's scenario differed from that in many clubs it was in the ladies' avowed contentment with their present lot.

By 1990 the subject was hotting up. In principle, captain Bob Coombes and his committee, with one dissenter, were in favour of granting the vote if the women wanted it. The ladies awaited specific proposals.

However, a 'serious level of opposition' to a women's vote was anticipated. Perhaps, the men thought, there was an acceptable alternative: the lady captain, possibly plus one of her members, might be invited to meetings to improve communications. At the 1991 agm, indeed, incoming captain David Barber announced that he intended to invite the lady captain to attend his committee meetings with a voice but no vote. Accordingly, Diana Walpole attended her first meeting in February 1991, and her initial, characteristically feminine contribution was a plea for curtains in the locker rooms.

In 1995, Barber urged his colleagues to grasp the nettle once and for all – because of the ever-growing pressures within society to treat everyone alike and the demands being placed on members' clubs by the licensing justices.

By this time a Special Strategy Group had been formed to plan for the future in all sorts of ways. It felt that there was a strong moral argument in favour of enfranchising the ladies and in 1997 emphasised its view that any proposals to do so should be based on the best interests of the club in every sense and not driven primarily by the Licensing Act. It had already recommended that the board

should consider amending the club's articles of association accordingly, but others felt that further discussions should be held. Papers on the subject were prepared, first by the strategy group, then, at the board's request, by secretary Nick Lomas.

In 1998 a strategy meeting attended by club chairman Tom Corrigan, Brian Meaby, John Jessop and Lomas agreed on proposals to be put to the board, but the directors felt the matter should not be progressed until the course-alterations issue[1] then topical had been settled.

In the interim Corrigan and his group raised an interesting point. Did the ladies really *want* equality considering that their subscriptions would have to rise? If not, the whole issue, which they recognised as 'most sensitive and potentially divisive,' might be re-thought.

It was decided to recommend to the board that, as on the last occasion, the ladies' committee should be invited to support the application for the renewal of the licence. If the ladies did not request voting rights the matter need not urgently be pursued; if they did it would be necessary to explain the position to the men before entering into further discussion with the women.

In November 1999, captain Edda Harvey circularised her members, inviting their support for the renewal, analysing the position and asking them to indicate their preferences from two options:

1. *We can continue as we are.* We do not have voting rights but are able to attend and take part in all general meetings and the

---

[1] Chapter 42.

Diana Walpole – first lady to attend a Club committee meeting.

Edda Harvey – first to go to a committee meeting with a vote.

Mary Coakes – first to go to a Board meeting with a vote.

ladies' committee is frequently invited to give its views on various issues. We have access to all the club rooms. We have some restrictions on weekend playing times. Full lady members benefit from a 30-per-cent reduction in entrance fees and subscriptions compared with the men.

2. *We can request that our status within the club be reviewed.* This would include a review of voting rights and restrictions on playing times. Any changes would result in a higher level of subscription.

The ladies replied that they would support the licence application. Seventy-five per-cent of them did not wish to see any change in their status.

Then, on July 7, 2000, those views notwithstanding, the Justices declined to renew the certificate so long as the ladies were not afforded voting rights equal to the men's. The rejection, in Corrigan's word, was 'frosty' and the hearing was adjourned until November.

Board members promptly put suggestions to the ladies and, in the autumn, an informal meeting of all club members was held. The ladies had accepted the suggestions in principle, while expressing a few concerns. Some of the men complained, but most of them attacked 'interference' in the club's affairs by the magistrates as distinct from raising fundamental objections to their wives, female relatives and friends obtaining the vote. Corrigan pointed out that such attitudes cut no ice legally:

> The board has taken counsel's advice on the Licensing Act and other relevant legislation. It seems that irrespective of members' wishes – based in this case on the ladies' majority view – the Law overrides, and the chance of a successful appeal against the Justices' ruling is considered most unlikely.
>
> The board has considered the other available options in an endeavour to accede to the lady members' majority view: applying for a 'full-on' licence (equivalent to a 'pub' licence) or establishing separate ladies' and mens' clubs. Neither of these is considered to be in the members' best interests. The board therefore unanimously proposes that full and country lady

members be granted the same voting rights as currently apply to their male counterparts.

The proposals were that as full voting members the ladies would pay 90% instead of 70% of the men's subscriptions, the increase for existing members to be gradually phased in annually; they could not play before 9.30am at weekends...

Oh, no, we can't agree that, said the women. The objections came particularly from the 'business ladies.' For eight months a year they had not had any restrictions on their playing rights. Now it was being proposed that they could not play before 9.30am and at the same time they were being asked to pay a substantially higher sub. This was not on!

On October 28, 2000, history was made at an egm when revised proposals were unanimously carried:

> Full and country members (75-100-miles category) were granted the same voting rights as their male equivalents and they would pay the same subscription as a man. This increase, for existing members, would be phased in over two years, so that by April 1, 2003, all members' subscriptions would be identical irrespective of gender.
>
> There would be no playing restrictions; full lady members would be eligible for election to the board and to the green and general committees, on which the lady captain would sit *ex-officio*. For continuity purposes, the lady vice-captain would be invited to attend meetings of these bodies but without a vote.
>
> The lady captain and vice-captain would continue to be elected in accordance with the existing ladies' bye-laws; only full and country men members would be eligible to confirm the appointment of the club captain and elect the vice-captain; the ladies' section to continue as before under the bye-laws relating to it.

Thus did the ladies of Walton Heath achieve equal rights. Much the same had happened and would continue to happen in other clubs – and the ladies, while some observed with cynicism the reasons that provoked the change, found a new confidence in their world of golf. Emmeline Pankhurst smiled down!

A hundred years is not an inordinately long life in golf. As we all know, many clubs are considerably older than Walton Heath.

No, what makes Walton Heath's century so special is the RICHNESS of its history. The story is in many ways unique and I can only hope that I may have done it some sort of justice.

To the thousands of tributes that will be bestowed on the club in 2003, may the author please be allowed to add his own.

Congratulations, Walton Heath!

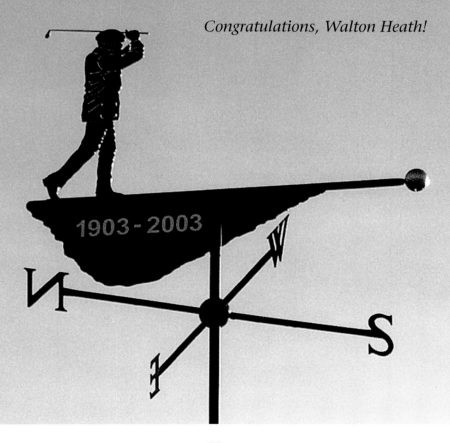

APPENDICES

The Club gold medals for men. Left: the Spring medal depicting the club-house; first played for in 1905. Right: Autumn, dating from 1907, bearing the seal of the Surrey Council, shields representing Guildford, Kingston and The Earls of Surrey, and Vi et Arte ('By strength and skill')

Men's Captains

1935-6	HRH The Prince of Wales, KG	1973	A.C. Bryant	1989	K.E. Way
	HM King Edward VIII	1974	J.R. Thornhill	1990	R.J. Coombes
1937	Sir E.W.E. Holderness, Bart	1975	L.R. St. J. Scott	1991	D.G. Barber
1938	The Rt. Hon. Lord Russell of	1976	M.K. Holloway	1992	P.J.R. Webb
	Killowen	1977	Sir Patrick Macrory	1993	P.A. Truett
1939	The Rt. Hon. Sir John	1978	C. Hewertson, OBE	1994	A.R. Eustace
	Simon, PC., GCSI, GCVO	1979	N.J. Woods	1995	R.H. Williams
1940	The Rt. Hon. Lord	1980	P.J. Renshaw	1996	R.J.B. Jessop
	Ebbisham, GBE	1981	D.B. Thomson	1997	M. Simmonds
1941	Sir Emsley Carr	1982	Dr. R.W. Elsdon-Dew	1998	B.H. Ling
1944-53	Sir Frederic Hamilton	1983	B.W. Meaby	1999	J. Hopper
1953- 55	H.M. Braid	1984	Lt. Col. B.H.J. Holloway	2000	R.H.P. Hutchison
1955-58	Sir John Hay	1985	B.D. Calvert	2001	P.J.R. Souster
1958-69	Sir William Carr	1986	J.E.B. Rae	2002	C.P. Harvey
1969-71	C.E.B.L. Carr	1987	T.S. Corrigan	2003	P.M. Franklin-Adams
1971-72	A.J. Renshaw, DSO, MC	1988	F.F. Picken	*NB. No captains were elected before 1935*	

Ladies' Captains

1912	Mrs Allom	1950	Mrs R.L. Cooper	1978	Mrs M. Pattisson
1913	Mrs C.E. Dick	1951	Mrs G. Holder	1979	Mrs N.M. Hockley
1914	Mrs E. Johnstone	1952	Mrs Pelham Foster	1980	Mrs H.M. Murray
1919	Mrs Barry	1953	Mrs R.H.A. Ritchie	1981	Mrs E. Gill
1920	Mrs Allom	1954	Mrs R.H. French	1982	Mrs P. Dring
1921	Lady Holderness	1955	Mrs F.N. Turner	1983	Mrs M. Steele
1922	Lady Holderness	1956	Mrs F.O. Faull	1984	Mrs I.M.J. Nunn
1923	Hon. Mrs Beresford	1957	Mrs D.S. Allom	1985	Mrs P.M. Hooper
1924	Lady Holderness	1958	Mrs M.L. Banks	1986	Mrs P.G. Endacott
1925	Mrs Rutherford	1959	Mrs.C.H. Jameson	1987	Mrs P. Jardine
1926	Lady Holderness	1960	Mrs J.G.H. McNabb	1988	Mrs J. Riddell
1927	Mrs Heriot Glen	1961	Lady Costain	1989	Mrs B. Hodges
1928	Mrs E. Hill	1962	Mrs H.J. Nash	1990	Mrs P. Freeman
1929	Miss J. Spurling	1963	Mrs G.B. Dove	1991	Mrs C.L.A. Walpole
1930	Mrs Kirkpatrick	1964	Mrs D.W. Piper	1992	Mrs M. Bransby-Zachary
1931	Mrs E. Hill	1965	Mrs G.B. Dove	1993	Mrs G. Williams
1932	Mrs A.S. Matthews	1966	Mrs C. Hurlock	1994	Mrs A. Skehens
1933	Mrs Knight	1967	Mrs A.C. Bryant	1995	Mrs E.C. Hagdrup
1934	Miss J. Hughes	1968	Mrs N.P. Woodroffe	1996	Mrs A. Marjoribanks
1935	Miss N. Halsted	1969	Mrs J.F. Prickett	1997	Mrs V. Lunt
1936	Miss J. Spurling	1970	Mrs G. Lewis	1998	Lady Woodward
1937	Mrs G.S. Joannides	1971	Mrs E.H. Lydall	1999	Mrs J. Eustace
1938	Miss Joan Taylor	1972	Mrs C. Falconer	2000	Mrs E. Harvey
1939	Mrs H. Morison	1973	Mrs M.K. Holloway	2001	Mrs M. Coakes
1946	Mrs H. Morison	1974	Mrs J.R. Thornhill	2002	Mrs B. Guthrie
1947	Mrs C. Wilson	1975	Mrs P.J. Baxter	2003	Mrs A. Barratt
1948	Mrs T.E. Morel	1976	Mrs C.M. Cronk		
1949	Mrs E. Hill	1977	Mrs P.J. Geen		

Winners at Walton

Year	Event	Winner
1904	Inaugural Triangular Match	
	J. Braid v. J.H. Taylor v. H. Vardon	H. Vardon
1904	Open Professional Tournament	R. Jones
1905	News of the World Match-play	J. Braid
1906	Challenge Match	
	G. Duncan/C. Mayo v.	Braid/Vardon
	J. Braid/H. Vardon	
(1st 36 holes at Walton; 2nd 36 at Timperley)		
1909	Challenge Match	
	G. Duncan/C.Mayo v.	Braid/Taylor
	J. Braid/J.H. Taylor	
(1st 36 holes at Burhill; 2nd 36 at Walton)		
1909	News of the World Match-play	T. Ball
1910	Man v. Woman Challenge	
	H. Hilton v Miss C. Leitch	Miss C. Leitch
(1st 36 holes at Walton; 2nd 36 at Sunningdale)		*(rec'd 9 strokes per round)*
1911	News of the World Match-play	J. Braid
1911	Challenge Match	
	A. Kirkaldy v. B. Sayers	B. Sayers
(1st 36 holes at Sunningdale; 2nd 36 at Walton)		
1911	The Sphere and Tatler Foursome	A. Herd/ S. Bradbeer
1913	Challenge Match	
	G. Duncan v. E. Ray	Match halved
1913	County Golf Unions Tournament	R.W. May
1913	News of the World Match-play	G. Duncan
1913	Golf Illustrated Gold Vase	A. Mitchell
1914	English Ladies' Championship	Miss C. Leitch
1919	PGA Victory Tournament	J. Braid
1919	News of the World Match-play	A. Mitchell
1923	News of the World Match-play	R.G. Wilson
1926	English Amateur	T.F. Ellison
1927	News of the World Match-play	A. Compston
1928	England and Wales Ladies' County Finals Cheshire	
1928	English Ladies' Championship	Miss E. Wilson
1929	Golf Illustrated Gold Vase	D. Grant
1934	News of the World Match-play	J.J. Busson
1934	Golf Illustrated Gold Vase	W.L. Hartley
1934	Dunlop Metropolitan Tournament	E.R. Whitcombe
1936	Metropolitan Shield	S. Anderson
1937	Challenge Match	
	D. Shute v. H. Cotton	H. Cotton
1937	Metropolitan Shield	S. Anderson
1938	News of the World Match-play	D. Rees
1938	Challenge Match	
	S. Brews/B. Locke v.	
	H. Cotton/R. Whitcombe	Cotton/ Whitcombe
1938	Metropolitan Shield	R.R. Costain
1939	Metropolitan Shield	D.B. Anderson
1945	News of the World Match-play	R. Horne
1949	News of the World Match-play	D. Rees
1950	Daily Mail Tournament	C.H. Ward
1952	Challenge Match	
	B. Locke/E. Brown v.	
	H. Cotton/F. Daly	Cotton/Daly
1952	News of the World Match-play	F. Daly
1954	Spalding Women's Tournament	Miss J. Donald
1955	News of the World Match-play	K. Bousfield
1955	Spalding Women's Tournament	Miss E. Price
1958	News of the World Match-play	H. Weetman
1958	English Amateur	D.N. Sewell
1961	News of the World Match-play	P. Thomson
1962	News of the World Match-play	E. Brown
1964	News of the World Match-play	N. Coles
1964	Hovis Women's Tournament	Miss M. Nichol
1964	Smart-Weston Tournament	G. Will
1965	News of the World Match-play	N. Coles
1965	Hovis Women's Tournament	Mrs. M. Spearman
1965	Smart-Weston Tournament	B. Huggett
1966	News of the World Match-play	P. Thomson
1967	News of the World Match-play	P. Thomson
1968	News of the World Match-play	B. Huggett
1968	English Open Amateur Stroke-play	M.F. Bonallack
1968	Ladies' British Amateur	Mlle B. Varangot
1969	News of the World Match-play	M. Bembridge
1973	Golf Illustrated Gold Vase	J. Davies
1974	Golf Illustrated Gold Vase	P. Hedges
1974	Newmark International	Mrs. J. Thornhill
1974	English County Championship	Lincolnshire
1975	Golf Illustrated Gold Vase	M.F. Bonallack
1976	Golf Illustrated Gold Vase	A. Brodie
1977	Golf Illustrated Gold Vase	J. Davies
1977	English Amateur	T.R. Shingler
1978	Golf Illustrated Gold Vase	K.J. Miller
1978	European Open Championship	B. Wadkins
1979	Golf Illustrated Gold Vase	K.J. Miller
1980	Golf Illustrated Gold Vase	G. Brand Jr
1980	European Open Championship	T. Kite
1981	Ryder Cup	Europe 9½, USA 18½
1981	Golf Illustrated Gold Vase	P.F. Garner
1982	Golf Illustrated Gold Vase	I. Carslaw
1982	Ladies' British Amateur	Miss K. Douglas
1983	British Seniors' Open Amateur	A.J. Swann
1983	Golf Illustrated Gold Vase	S.D. Keppler
1984	Golf Illustrated Gold Vase	J.V.T. Marks
1985	Golf Illustrated Gold Vase	M. Davies
1985	England and Wales Ladies County Finals Surrey	
1986	Golf Illustrated Gold Vase	R. Eggo
1987	Golf Illustrated Gold Vase	D.G. Lane
1987	European Open Championship	P. Way
1988	Golf Illustrated Gold Vase	M. Turner
1989	European Open Championship	A. Murray
1990	Golf Illustrated Gold Vase	A. Rodgers
1991	European Open Championship	M. Harwood
1992	Golf Illustrated Gold Vase	P. Page
1994	Golf Illustrated Gold Vase	S. Burnell
1997	Golf Illustrated Gold Vase	M. James
1998	English Ladies' Close Amateur	Miss E. Ratcliffe
1998	Golf Illustrated Gold Vase	R. Rea
1999	England v. Spain (amateurs)	Eng. 16, Spain 8
1999	British Mid-Amateur	J. Kemp
1999	Golf Illustrated Gold Vase	M. Side
2000	Ladies British Amateur	Miss R. Hudson
2000	Golf Illustrated Gold Vase	J. Kemp
2001	PGA Centenary Tournament (South)	G. Lingard
2002	English Amateur	R. Finch

Gold Medals – Men

Year	SPRING		AUTUMN		Year	SPRING		AUTUMN	
1905	J. Oswald	83			1959	M.T.W. Easby	75	M.T.W. Easby	73
1906	W.C. Michie	83			1960	H.M. Braid	75	W.E. McCrea	76
1907	C.E. Dick	84	C.E. Dick	85	1961	W.E. McCrea	75	J.R. Thornhill	72
1908	C.E. Dick	84	C. Micklem	80	1962	M.T.W. Easby	78	C. Walpole	71
1909	W.C. Michie	82	C.E. Dick	84	1963	R.E.B. Craven	75	W.E. McCrea	71
1910	C.E. Dick	80	C. Micklem	80	1964	J.R. Thornhill	77	W.A. Slark	70
1911	C.E. Dick	81	C.E. Dick	81	1965	C. Walpole	74	J.R. Thornhill	76
1912	W.H. Fowler	82	C.E. Dick	83	1966	D.E. Pearce	77	J.R. Neller	75
1913	P. S. May	80	A. Hambro	78	1967	W.E. McCrea	74	P.J. Easby	73
1914	W.W. Bruce	80			1968	J.R. Thornhill	73	W.E. McCrea	72
1919	E.N. Layton	81	P. Quilter	78	1969	D.W. Piper	73	D.L. Baxter	76
1920	A.H. Read	80	E.N. Layton	80	1970	D.L. Baxter	76	R.P. Beames	72
1921	E. Legge	81	E.W.E. Holderness	74	1971	R.J. Coombes	77	W.E. McCrea	72
1922	E.W.E. Holderness	76	H. Braid	74	1972	D.L. Baxter	75	P.J.R. Souster	77
1923	E.W.E. Holderness	72	H.C. Pearson	76	1973	C. Travers	73	R.J. Coombes	74
1924	E.W.E. Holderness	76	Sir E.W.E. Holderness Bt	75	1974	R.J. Gray	71	R.J. Coombes	72
1925	E.N. Layton	81	Sir E.W.E. Holderness Bt	73	1975	D.L. Baxter	75	J. Hopper	73
1926	H. E.Le Bas	77	R. Straker	77	1976	S.F. Robson	77	N.S. Kelly	75
1927	H. Braid	79	E.N. Layton	75	1977	J. Hopper	74	J. Hopper	75
1928	Sir E.W.E. Holderness Bt	76	E. Legge	77	1978	R.J. Coombes	73	J. Hopper	72
1929	Sir E.W.E. Holderness Bt	79	J.C. Wood	80	1979	A.L.V. Godfrey	77	J.G. Bennett	73
1930	Sir E.W.E. Holderness Bt	76	E.N. Layton	72	1980	J. Hopper	76	R.J. Gray	74
1931	Sir E.W.E. Holderness Bt	72	Sir E.W.E. Holderness Bt	75	1981	J. Reynolds	78	C.J. Weight	76
1932	R.R. Costain	77	E.N. Layton	73	1982	R.H.A. Clark	75	P.J. Benka	73
1933	E.B. Tipping	74	Sir E.W.E. Holderness Bt	73	1983	M.S.R. Lunt	74	P.J. Benka	73
1934	H. Braid	75	Sir E.W.E. Holderness Bt	77	1984	R.H.A. Clark	76	S.F. Robson	74
1935	H. Braid	74	H. Braid	67	1985	K.W. Dent	73	T.J.K. Leonard	76
1936	R.R. Costain	76	E.B. Tipping	76	1986	R.H.A. Clark	71	P.J. Benka	74
1937	Sir E.W.E. Holderness Bt	75	D.A. Drayson	75	1987	R.H.A. Clark	78	R.H.A. Clark	76
1938	L.C. Nunneley	73	F.M.M. Forster	74	1988	R.H.A. Clark	74	R.H.A. Clark	71
1939	L.C. Nunneley	73			1989	S. Horkan	77	R.H.A. Clark	74
1946	Sir E.W.E. Holderness Bt	79	Sir E.W.E. Holderness Bt	75	1990	S. Horkan	71	C.W. de Haan	80
1947	W. A. Slark	79	Sir E.W.E. Holderness Bt	75	1991	R.H.A. Clark	75	P.A.F. Stanford	76
1948	J.R. Thornhill	78	M.T.W. Easby	79	1992	J.C.A. Collier	71	R.H.A. Clark	70
1949	R.R. Costain	77	Sir E.W.E. Holderness Bt	72	1993	J.C.A. Collier	70	J.M. Allen	73
1950	I. Caldwell	72	I. Caldwell	73	1994	R.D.H. Hall	74	R.D.H. Hall	73
1951	A. U. Clark	78	I. Caldwell	77	1995	P.A.F. Stanford	72	S. Horkan	75
1952	J.R. Thornhill	77	W.A. Slark	76	1996	M.W. James	71	M.W. James	75
1953	J.R. Thornhill	80	W.A. Slark	74	1997	M.T.C. Waugh	79	Z. Scotland	71
1954	W.A. Slark	76	I. Caldwell	75	1998	R.J. Gray	74	R.M.G. Hynson	69
1955	J.R. Thornhill	75	J.R. Thornhill	74	1999	R.M.G. Hynson	70	M.S.P. Benka	71
1956	Sir Richard Costain	74	J.R. Thornhill	76	2000	J.C.A. Collier	70	M.S.P. Benka	71
1957	W.A. Slark	68	J.R. Thornhill	75	2001	R.H.A. Clark	74	J.C.A. Collier	69
1958	W.A. Slark	72	W.A. Slark	76	2002	S. Horkan	72	R.H.A. Clark	70

Gold Medals – Ladies

Year	SPRING		AUTUMN		Year	AUTUMN		Year	AUTUMN	
1906	Mrs W.H. Fowler	104			1933	Mrs I.B. Knight	84	1972	Mrs J.R. Thornhill	77
1907	Mrs Hughes	105	Miss N. Bovill	108	1934	Mrs J.D. Crosthwaite	84	1973	Mrs J.R. Thornhill	74
1908	Miss D. Barker	101	Miss Cotton	99	1935	Miss N.E. Halsted	83	1974	Mrs J.R. Thornhill	72
1909	Mrs Hughes	93	Miss D. Barker	98	1936	Miss N.E. Halsted	85	1975	Mrs J.R. Thornhill	77
1910	Miss D. Barker	95	Miss D. Barker	90	1937	Miss M. Cohen	82	1976	Mrs J.R. Thornhill	76
1911	Miss D. Barker	96	Mrs E. Johnstone	96	1938	Mrs G. Holder	88	1977	Mrs P. Harvie	80
1912	Miss P. Fowler	95	Mrs E. Johnstone	92	1946	Mrs Sellick	85	1978	Mrs J. Piper	75
1913	Miss C. Leitch	86	Miss C. Leitch	91	1947	Mrs Ritchie	84	1979	Miss D. McCurrach	76
1914	Miss A.W. Taylor	93			1948	Mrs Crosthwaite	83	1980	Mrs P. Harvie	80
1919			Miss N. Paull	93	1949	Miss E. Halsted	77	1981	Mrs P. Millar	78
1920	Mrs A. Patey	88	Mrs E. Hill	92	1950	Miss B. Waugh	79	1982	Mrs D. Monasterio	82
1921	Mrs Cruise	85	Mrs Hetherington	88	1951	Mrs Holder	82	1983	Mrs D. Monasterio	82
1922	Mrs Hetherington	85	Mrs I.B. Knight	88	1952	Mrs S. Allom	84	1984	Mrs P. Riddiford	85
1923	Mrs Hetherington	90	Mrs I.B. Knight	88	1953	Mrs De Pinna Weal	82	1985	Miss D. McCurrach	84
1924	Mrs A. Patey	89	Mrs I.B. Knight	82	1954	Mrs D.S. Allom	87	1986	Mrs P. Harvie	80
1925	Miss J. Spurling	93	Mrs D. Heriot Glen	89	1955	Mrs King	83	1987	Mrs P. Riddiford	73
1926	Miss P.M. Pearce	94	Mrs A. Patey	90	1956	Mrs D.S. Allom	84	1988	Mrs R. Ticehurst	81
1927	Mrs D. Heriot Glen	87	Miss J. Spurling	90	1957	Mrs G. Holder	82	1989	Mrs P. Benka	76
1928	Mrs E. Hill	84	Mrs I.B. Knight	87	1958	Mrs D.S. Allom	80	1990	Miss K. Pudner	78
1929	Miss V. Benson	97	Lady Alness	85	1959	Mrs D.S. Allom	77	1991	Miss K. Pudner	78
1930	Mrs A.S. Matthews	86	Mrs I.B. Knight	86	1960	Mrs M. Kaye	73	1992	Miss K. Pudner	84
1931	Mrs R.N. Ramsey	89	Mrs R.M. Ramsey	84	1961	Miss W. Clark	81	1993	Mrs D. Bailey	81
1932	Mrs A.S. Matthews	88	Mrs I.B. Knight	84	1962	Mrs D.W. Piper	80	1994	Mrs J. Burrage	87
					1963	Mrs J.R. Thornhill	77	1995	Mrs A. Barratt	84
					1964	Mrs D.S. Allom	79	1996	Miss K. Pudner	77
					1965	Mrs C. Falconer	82	1997	Mrs D. Bailey	84
					1966	Mrs C. Hurlock	83	1998	Dr A. Taylor	81
					1967	Mrs J.R. Thornhill	85	1999	Mrs A. Barratt	87
					1968	Mrs D.W. Piper	75	2000	Mrs J. Vaines	83
					1969	Mrs J.R. Thornhill	80	2001	Mrs J.R. Thornhill	71
					1970	Mrs D.W. Piper	75	2002	Mrs C. Griffith	78
					1971	Mrs D.W. Piper	79			

Course Records – Men*

Old

Amateur			Professional		
1906	R. Maxwell	75	1904	J. Hepburn	77
	W.H. Fowler	75	1905	J. Braid	70
				J. Braid	69
1907	J. Osborn	74			
(No explanation found for the 74/81 anomaly)					
1908	A.H. Read	81			
	W.C. Michie	81			
1909	C. Micklem	80			
1911	W.C. Michie	80			
	C.E. Dick	80			
			1913	J. Braid	67
1914	H.D. Gillies	74			
1921	E.W.E. Holderness	74			
1922	H.M. Braid	74			
1923	E.W.E. Holderness	72			
1930	E.N. Layton	72			
1931	E.W.E. Holderness	72	*(Golf Illustrated reported that there was no official pro record before 1935)*		
			1935	W. Laidlaw	70
				J. Field	70
(Major course changes in 1935/8)			1937	W. Laidlaw	70
1938	F.M.M. Forster	74			
1939	L.C. Nunneley	73			
(Further changes had taken place immediately before war)					
1946	E.W.E. Holderness	79			
1946	E.W.E. Holderness	75			
1949	E.W.E. Holderness	72			
1950	I. Caldwell	72			
			1951	K. Bousfield	66
1957	W.A. Slark	68	*(Course changes)*		
1976	R. Revell	68	1976	K. Bousfield	68
			1977	T. Horton	67
			1978	D. Vaughan	66
			1980	P. Townsend	65
				(6181 yds)	
			2001	G. Lingard	66
				(7019 yds)	

New

Amateur			Professional		
1910	W.H. Fowler	79			
	(2x9 holes)				
1914	W.H. Fowler	79			
			1920	J. Braid	66
			(Believed to be course changes)		
			1934	E.R. Whitcombe	69
			1934	E.R. Whitcombe	68
			(Whitcombe scored his 69, twice, and 68 in Dunlop-Metropolitan tournament. Some special tees were used to stretch the course).		
1937	R.R. Costain	73			
			1938	J. Braid	64
			(Not reported in any detail, but scorecard exists signed by two members of the Carr family).		
1968	M.C. Bryant	67			
1974	R. Revell	68	1968	C. Clark	64
1975	J.K. Tate	67			
1976	B.J. Winteridge	67			
1992	A.J. Wells	67			
1994	R.D.H. Hall	67			
2002	L. Parker	67			

Championship (Composite)

1978	N. Faldo	68
1978	D. Ingram	67
1978	B. Langer	67
(All three records set in European Open. Course 7130 yards)		
1980	L. Hinkle	65
(European Open. Course 7230 yards)		
1987	I. Woosnam	64
1991	M. Harwood	65
(European Open. Course 7200 yards)		

* Official records can be set only in stroke-play. However, some of the scores above were reported (and apparently regarded by the club) as records although they may have been made in match-play or under other circumstances. No official lists of records exist for either men or women.

Course Records – Ladies

Old

1909	Mrs F. Hughes	93
1912	Miss C. Leitch	88
	Miss I. Dick	
1913	Miss C. Leitch	86
1921	Mrs Cruise	85
1922	Miss J. Wethered	78†
1928	Mrs J.D. Crosthwaite	80†
(Course alterations in '30's)		
1954	Miss J. Donald	76
1955	Miss E. Price	73
	(Twice: on consecutive days)	
1973	Mrs J. Thornhill	72
1974	Miss J. Mark	72
1974	Mrs H. Kaye	68

New

1955	Miss E. Price	73
1955	Mrs G. Keiler	72
1971	Mrs J. Thornhill	71
1983	Mrs J. Thornhill	69

(† Miss Wethered's 78 was reported in Golf Illustrated as being scored in Surrey Open; Mrs Crosthwaite's 80 was reported as the first score to equal the standard score).

INDEX